EASY Machine Quilting

EASY Machine Quilting

12 STEP-BY-STEP LESSONS FROM THE PROS, PLUS A DOZEN PROJECTS TO MACHINE QUILT

JANE TOWNSWICK, EDITOR

Rodale Press, Inc.
Emmaus, Pennsylvania

Originally published as a hardcover edition in 1996

Printed in the United States of America on acid-free ∞, recycled paper ♻

We're always happy to hear from you.

For questions or comments concerning the editorial content of this book, please write to:

Rodale Press, Inc.
Book Readers' Service
33 East Minor Street
Emmaus, PA 18098

Look for other Rodale books wherever books are sold. Or call us at (800) 848-4735.

For more information about Rodale Press and the books and magazines we publish, visit our World Wide Web site:
http://www.rodalepress.com

The Library of Congress has cataloged the hardcover edition as follows:
Townswick, Jane.
Easy machine quilting : 12 step-by-step lessons from the pros plus a dozen projects to machine quilt / Jane Townswick.
p. cm.
Includes index.
ISBN 0-87596-708-6 (hardcover : alk. paper)
1. Machine quilting—Patterns. 2. Patchwork.
3. Quilts.
I. Title.
TT835.T683 1996
746.46—dc20 96-11971

ISBN 0-87596-995-X paperback

Distributed in the book trade by St. Martin's Press

4 6 8 10 9 7 5 3 hardcover
4 6 8 10 9 7 5 paperback

EASY MACHINE QUILTING EDITORIAL AND DESIGN STAFF

EDITOR: Jane Townswick
INTERIOR AND COVER DESIGNER: Diane Ness Shaw
ILLUSTRATORS: Janet Bohn, Sue Gettlin, Maureen Logan, Ian Warpole
INTERIOR PHOTOGRAPHERS: Mitch Mandel, Kurt Wilson
INTERIOR PHOTO STYLISTS: Karen Bolesta, Marianne Laubach, Diane Ness Shaw
COVER PHOTOGRAPHER: Robert Gerheart
TECHNICAL ARTISTS: Chris Rhoads, Richard Snyder
COPY EDITORS: Candace Levy, Nancy N. Bailey
MANUFACTURING COORDINATOR: Melinda B. Rizzo
INDEXER: Nanette Bendyna
EDITORIAL ASSISTANCE: Susan Nickol, Jodi Rehl

RODALE HOME AND GARDEN BOOKS

VICE PRESIDENT AND EDITORIAL DIRECTOR: Margaret J. Lydic
MANAGING EDITOR: Suzanne Nelson
ASSOCIATE ART DIRECTOR: Mary Ellen Fanelli
STUDIO MANAGER: Leslie Keefe
COPY DIRECTOR: Dolores Plikaitis
PRODUCTION MANAGER: Helen Clogston
OFFICE MANAGER: Karen Earl-Braymer

PROJECT DESIGNERS: Anne Colvin, Caryl Bryer Fallert, Jeannette Muir, Sue Nickels, Caroline Reardon, Sharee Dawn Roberts, Sherry Sunday, Debra Wagner, and Hari Walner

THANKS to Pine Tree Farm, Doylestown, Pennsylvania, for providing a location for photos.

ON THE COVER: The cover quilt was inspired by the quilts in this book, designed by Diane Ness Shaw, and stitched by Hari Walner using Cherrywood hand-dyed fabric and Sulky Variegated Rayon thread.

Thank you to the nine wonderfully talented machine-quilting experts who spent so many hours and gave such careful attention to preparing the information and quilt samples for the lessons and projects.

It was a privilege and a pleasure to work with all of you.

J. T.

Contents

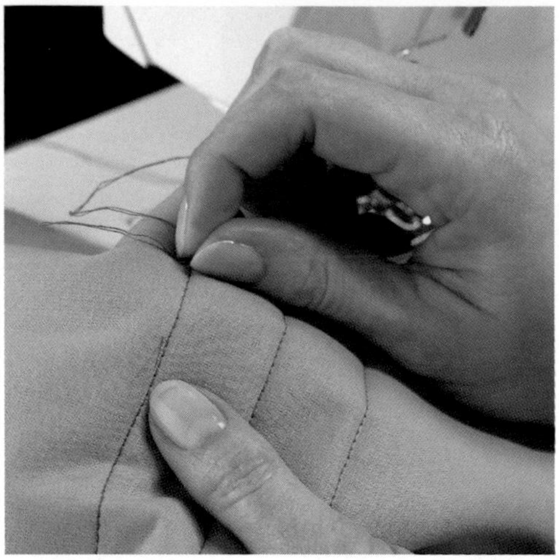

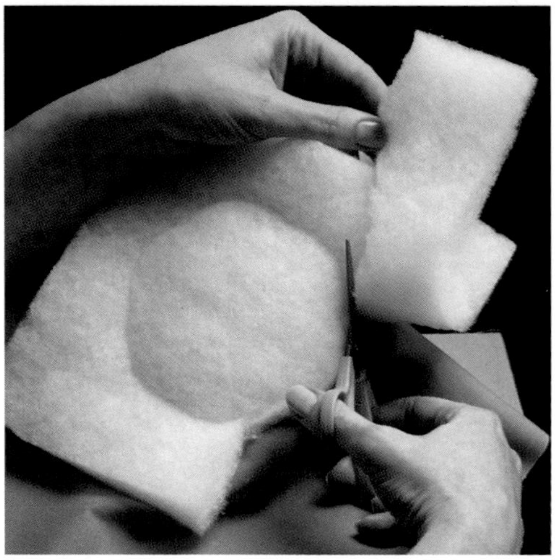

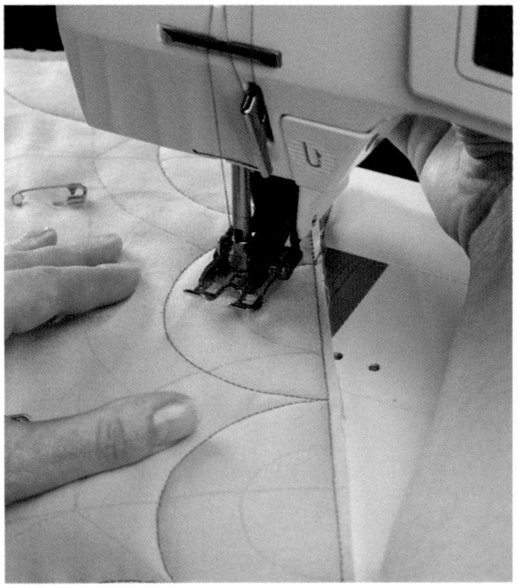

THE PROJECTS

Introduction

As quilt book editors, my colleagues and I attend quilt shows from coast to coast, and over the years, we couldn't help but notice how machine quilting has grown from dubious distinction ("that's not really quilting . . .") to glorious recognition as a beautiful technique in its own right.

There are lots of reasons why machine quilting has been embraced with such enthusiasm by today's quilters. Machine-quilted quilts have all the beauty and heirloom quality of their hand-quilted counterparts. The versatility of machine quilting makes it appropriate for virtually any type of project, running the full range of miniature quilts, wall quilts, bed quilts, and embellished garments. Styles of machine quilting can be tailored to suit both traditional and art quilts. And last (but in no way least), machine quilting allows quiltmakers to complete beautiful quilts faster than ever before.

The ideal way to learn how to machine quilt is to take a class from an expert who can demonstrate techniques at a sewing machine and stand by to offer helpful advice and troubleshooting tips. Recognizing this, we set about to make today's top machine quilting experts available to every quilter in the form of a book. In Easy Machine Quilting, *nine of the most talented machine quilters in the world—Anne Colvin, Caryl Bryer Fallert, Jeannette Muir, Sue Nickels, Caroline Reardon, Sharee Dawn Roberts, Sherry Sunday, Debra Wagner, and Hari Walner—offer you their very best advice. This comes in the form of 12 lessons, featuring step-by-step photos and detailed instructions in all areas of machine quilting. And just like in the best class, you'll discover lots of "insider" tips and tricks to make your machine quilting even more enjoyable.*

The project section of the book offers 12 exciting quilts especially designed by each expert to feature techniques from the lessons. Whether you are a person who has always wanted to quilt by machine but were afraid to try, or if you're already in love with machine quilting and are simply looking for new projects and ways to expand your repertoire of skills, you're sure to enjoy the adventure that awaits you in the pages of Easy Machine Quilting.

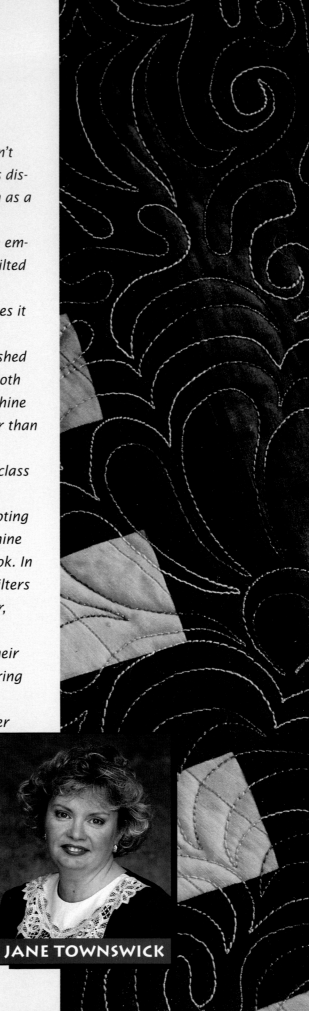

JANE TOWNSWICK

How to Use This Book

To make it easy and enjoyable for you to use this book, we've provided these helpful features.

THE LESSONS

Preparing a Practice Quilt Sandwich: For each lesson, you will need to make one or more practice quilt sandwiches to gain hands-on experience as you follow the step-by-step instructions and photos. You will find information about what size pieces of fabric and batting to cut and how to layer and pin-baste them together. If a patchwork or appliqué block is needed, you will find instructions for making those, too. If desired, make as many practice quilt sandwiches as you like for practicing the techniques in each lesson.

Get Set Boxes: Here you'll find all of the things you need to do to set up your sewing machine correctly for each lesson. In lessons covering several techniques, you'll find more than one Get Set box.

Try This Technique on These Projects: On the opening page of each lesson, you'll find a listing of page numbers for projects featuring the techniques you are learning.

Great Ideas: Watch for these boxes throughout the book. You'll learn tricks and helpful hints, plus you'll find tips on how to avoid common problems in machine quilting.

THE PROJECTS

Skill Level Ratings: The words "Easy," "Intermediate," or "Challenging" at the beginning of each project give you an idea of the skill it will take to complete that quilt or garment.

Techniques You'll Need: On the opening page of each project, you'll find a list of the techniques used for making that project, along with the page numbers of the lessons explaining each technique.

Fabrics and Supplies Lists: Read through the Fabric and Supplies list for each project to find out how much fabric you'll need and what part of the quilt or garment each fabric is used for.

Rotary Cutting Instructions: Wherever possible, rotary cutting instructions are given for the projects. The instructions also state whether or not the measurements include ¼-inch seam allowances.

Quilting Diagrams: These detailed black and white drawings of quilts show where you should place the quilting design.

Quilting Designs: Wherever possible, full-size quilting designs in heavy, solid black lines (to make tracing easier) are given. For some, percentages for enlarging the quilting designs on a photocopier are provided.

THE BASICS

Don't skip the basics! Here's where you'll find ways to transfer quilting designs to fabric, an easy method for binding a quilt or garment, and tips for how to handle a large quilt at the sewing machine.

LESSON
1

Getting Ready

The first step to mastering the basics of machine quilting is becoming familiar with your own sewing machine and how it works to create even, consistent quilting stitches. Learning about the characteristics of fabrics, batting, thread, and needles will help you to develop your own preferences and make informed decisions about the materials you use for your projects. In this lesson, Debra Wagner will get you started with an overview of the parts and features of a sewing machine and how they relate to machine quilting. Then, Sharee Dawn Roberts will introduce you to the ever-changing, fabulous world of threads and needles. Anne Colvin will discuss the many types of batting that are now available and how they can be used to create the appearance you want in a quilt. And last, but by no means least, you'll find a number of helpful tips from Sharee Dawn Roberts for setting up your own quilting studio for maximum ease and efficiency.

Inspiration plus
BERNINA 1630
PATENTED BERNINA LIFTER-SYSTEM
BERNINA
SCHMETZ
STICK-NADEL
EMBROIDERY
NEEDLE
130/705 H-E
No. 100
SILVER METALLIC

LESSON 1

Sewing Machine Savvy

Debra Wagner

PARTS AND FEATURES

Although virtually any sewing machine is capable of doing beautiful machine quilting, several basic features contribute to getting the best possible stitching results. The following descriptions of parts and features apply to most sewing machines. The machine in the photos is a Bernina 1630.

■ **UPPER THREAD TENSION ASSEMBLY:** The tension on the upper thread in your sewing machine is important for producing even stitches, both in machine-guided and free-motion quilting. When the thread is not situated correctly in the upper thread tension assembly, loops of thread can occur on the bobbin side of a quilt.

■ **NEEDLE CLAMP:** Whenever you insert a new needle into your machine, be sure to tighten the screw with a small screwdriver, so that the needle clamp will not work loose during the quilting process and allow the needle to fall out of your machine.

■ **MOTOR SPEED CONTROL (NOT SHOWN):** A slower stitching speed gives better control. If your machine has a dial that allows you to switch from high to low gear, consider stitching at the slower speed while you learn to machine quilt and progress to faster speeds as your skills improve.

■ **FOOT CONTROL (NOT SHOWN):** This pedal controls the motor speed of a sewing machine. Electronic controls offer greater accuracy than thermal controls and won't become hot after long periods of stitching.

■ **NEEDLE PLATE:** A regular zigzag needle plate has a needle hole opening that allows the needle to move both left and right to accommodate the widest zigzag stitch. This is especially helpful for tying a quilt by machine. A straight-stitch plate has a small needle hole opening that will not permit the needle and thread to move from side to side, which produces consistently even, smooth machine-guided quilting stitches. A darning plate snaps over the feed dogs on a regular needle plate for free-motion quilting, so the feed dogs don't get caught on the back of your quilt.

■ **FREE ARM AND EXTENSION TABLE:** The free arm is the lower portion of the sewing machine and contains the needle plate, feed dogs, and bobbin. Its small surface is inappropriate for machine quilting. To make it more suitable, place an extension table around the free arm.

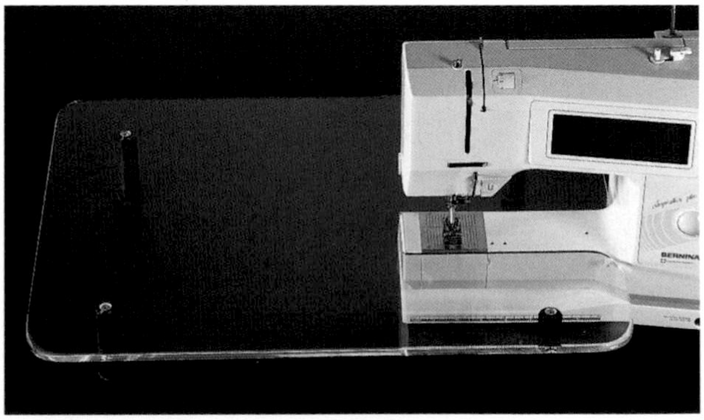

An extension table maximizes space around the free arm of a sewing machine.

■ **STITCH WIDTH CONTROL:** This control knob allows you to adjust the width of zigzag stitches for tying a quilt by machine.

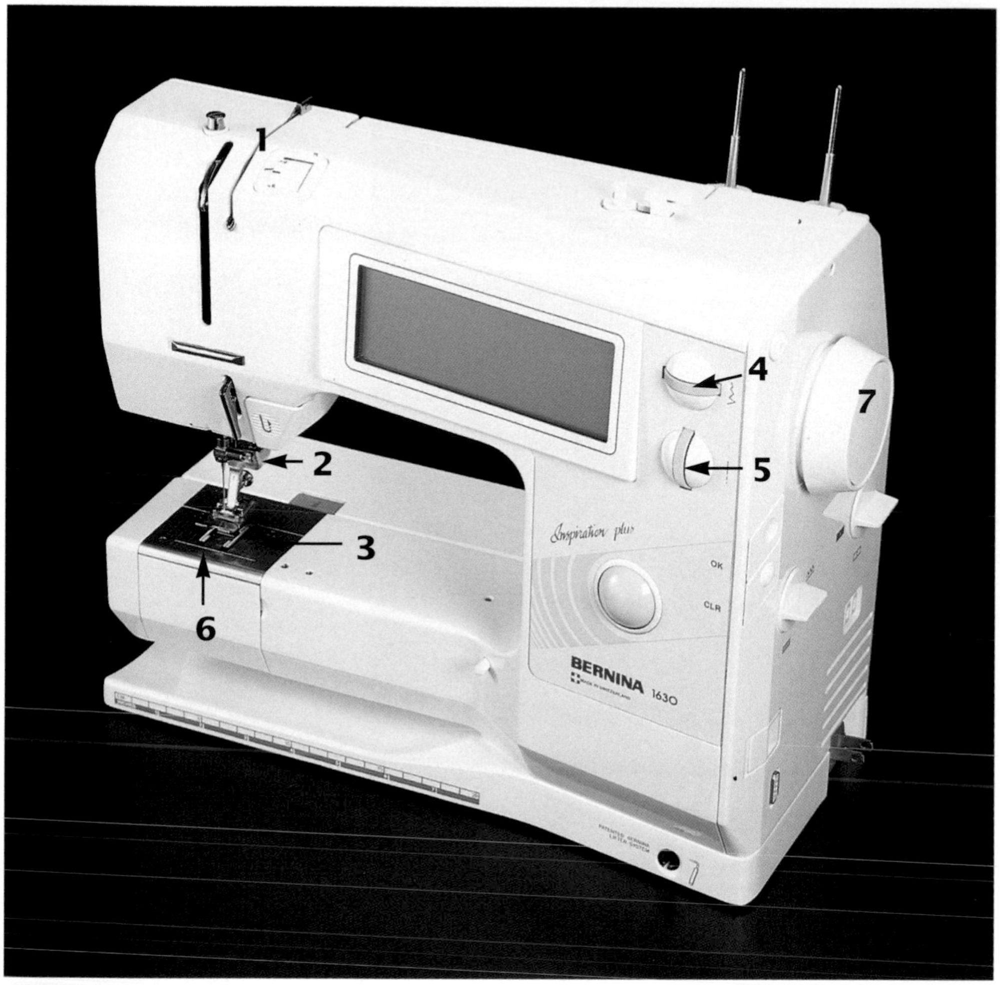

Becoming familiar with the parts and features of your sewing machine will make it easier to learn machine quilting. Learn how to adjust these features to help improve your machine quilting:
1. upper thread tension assembly
2. needle clamp
3. needle plate
4. stitch width control
5. stitch length control
6. feed dogs
7. hand wheel

■ **STITCH LENGTH CONTROL:** This dial adjusts stitch length for machine-guided quilting.

■ **FEED DOGS:** The feed dogs are sharp teeth that grab the fabric and move it under the presser foot. They lie directly under the presser foot. Whenever you adjust the stitch length, you are also adjusting the way the feed dogs move. The feed dogs are raised for machine-guided quilting and lowered or covered for free-motion quilting. When the feed dogs are inoperative, they are situated below the level of the needle plate. On machines that do not have a built-in mechanism for lowering the feed dogs, they can be covered with a special plate.

■ **NEEDLE DOWN (NOT SHOWN):** For free-motion quilting, a machine that has the ability to stop with the needle down is helpful. It will allow you to stop stitching with the needle in the fabric. This provides greater stability, so that you can reposition your hands on the quilt sandwich easily. This ultimately means that your stitching lines can flow smoothly, without jagged breaks.

■ **HAND WHEEL:** The hand wheel on the right side of the machine raises or lowers the needle, which is helpful for bringing up bobbin threads or starting or ending a line of quilting stitches. Be careful to always turn the hand wheel toward yourself because if it is turned in the opposite direction, it can cause skipped stitches or broken threads.

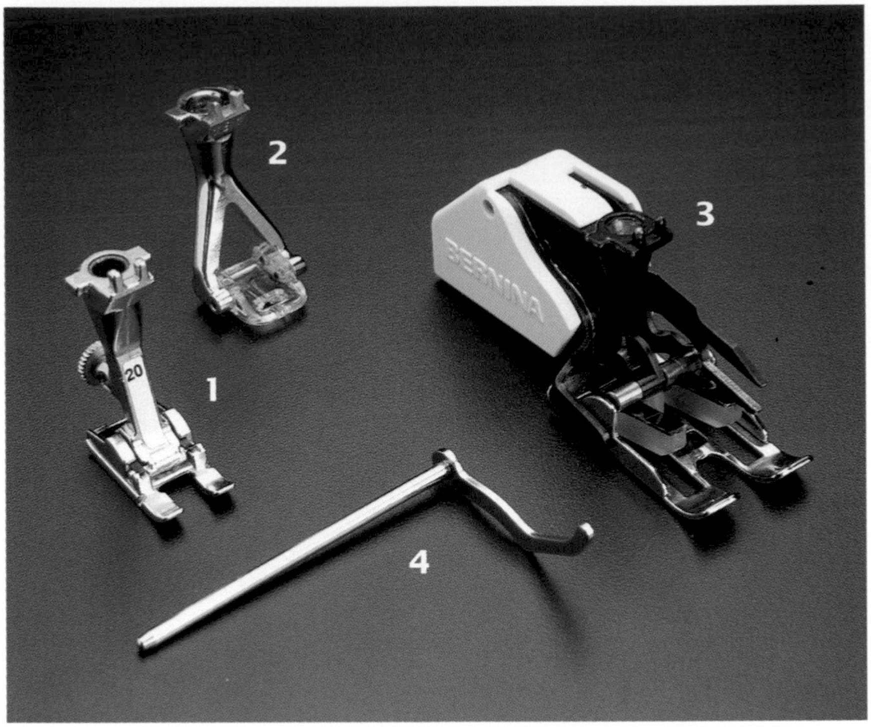

Machine-guided quilting is simple to do with the following accessories:
1. open-toe foot
2. no-bridge foot
3. even feed/walking foot
4. quilting guide

ACCESSORIES FOR MACHINE-GUIDED QUILTING

The following presser feet and accessories for machine-guided quilting will enable you to feed the layers of a quilt sandwich evenly through your sewing machine and stitch across thick seams easily.

■ **OPEN-TOE AND NO-BRIDGE FEET:** Both the open-toe and the no-bridge feet offer a clear view of a stitching line and were originally designed to do machine appliqué. These feet are cut away to permit an unobstructed view of the needle. Both feet are suited to small sections of intricate straight-line machine quilting, where accuracy is important. The disadvantage to these feet is that they can also cause the layers of a quilt to shift, creating pleats in the top or backing fabric.

■ **EVEN FEED/WALKING FOOT:** The even feed, or walking, presser foot provides an upper set of feed dogs to match the lower set of feed dogs. It is larger than a traditional presser foot to accommodate the mechanism that operates the upper feed dogs. Usually, this foot has a lever that hooks over the needle clamp. On some brands of sewing machines, an extra feed dog system is built right into the presser foot ankle and can be engaged by simply snapping it in place. A built-in upper feed system is more compact and easier to engage and disengage than a walking foot. The even feed/walking foot is helpful for large areas of machine-guided quilting because it keeps the fabric layers smooth and unpuckered.

■ **QUILTING GUIDE:** A quilting guide is very useful in combination with presser feet for machine-guided quilting. It is a metal bar that fits into a slot in the back of the presser foot. The bar has an arm that lies on the fabric on either side of the presser foot, and it is used as a guide to make uniformly spaced lines of stitching.

ACCESSORIES FOR FREE-MOTION QUILTING

For free-motion quilting, the presser foot must hold a quilt firmly to the needle plate as each stitch is formed, yet release the fabric between stitches to allow unconstrained movement of the quilt sandwich. With the needle in the highest position, the fabric will move freely under the foot.

■ **OPEN DARNING FOOT:** An open darning foot looks like the capital letter C. Removing the part of the foot in front of the needle allows an unobstructed view of both the needle and the stitching line. The open darning foot also holds the fabric tightly to the needle plate as each stitch is formed. This foot is best for low-loft batting.

■ **DARNING FOOT:** The darning foot has a low clearance that holds the fabric very tightly to the needle plate as the machine stitches. This gives a good-quality stitch without any skipped stitches. It has a small needle hole opening, and it is the most basic foot used for free-motion quilting. A darning foot is very small, which means that the needle hole opening is just ¼ inch in diameter, which can obscure stitching lines. This foot can cause problems with very thick batting because high-loft batts can force the layers of a quilt sandwich to cup around the darning foot. This can completely enclose the foot and make it difficult to guide the fabric easily. A darning foot is most useful for stitching designs on low-loft batting.

■ **LARGE QUILTING FOOT:** A quilting foot is made of plastic or metal, and it has a large round sole about the size of a nickel, with a large needle hole opening. This type of presser foot is perfect for working with thick battings. The larger sole holds more of the quilt to the needle plate, which prevents thicker batting from cupping around the foot. This allows a clearer view of the stitching line. A quilting foot has a higher clearance than a darning foot. That plus a larger needle hole opening in the foot can cause skipped stitches on low-loft batting. A quilting foot is best for medium- to high-loft batts.

■ **THREAD STAND:** A thread stand is used for holding novelty threads and monofilament threads that come on nontraditional, oversized spools. A thread stand will pull the thread off the top of the spool easily, without causing it to spin. Because a thread stand is larger than a spool pin, it will accommodate most commercial-size spools.

These accessories are useful for free-motion quilting:
1. open darning foot
2. darning foot
3. large quilting foot
4. thread stand

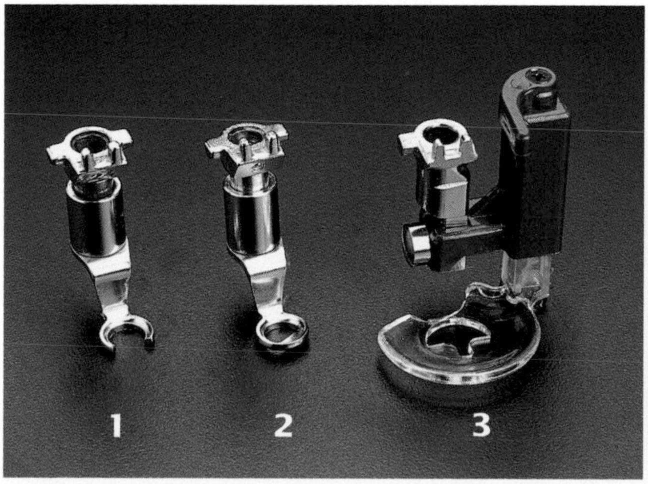

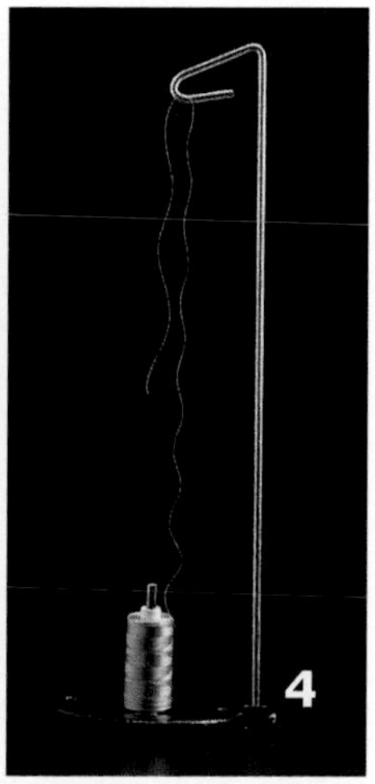

WHAT TO DO WHEN THE MACHINE WON'T WORK

If you encounter problems in your machine quilting, such as threads breaking, the bobbin thread showing on the surface of a quilt top, or stitches that simply do not look the way you want them to, use this checklist to help you identify the cause and correct the situation.

- **IS THE MACHINE THREADED CORRECTLY?** Take out both the top and bobbin threads and rethread your machine.
- **IS THE BOBBIN THREADED IN THE CORRECT DIRECTION?** A sewing machine can sew with the bobbin in backwards, but the results are usually a jammed machine or a line of stitching that looks crooked on the bobbin side of the quilt sandwich.
- **IS THE BOBBIN THE CORRECT BRAND FOR YOUR MACHINE?** Use only bobbins that are made specifically for your sewing machine. Although the difference in size between any two bobbins may not be apparent to the naked eye, there can be minute differences in the diameter of the center holes. This can greatly affect the way a bobbin spins in your sewing machine and, therefore, the quality of your quilting stitch.
- **IS THE PRESSER FOOT RAISED OR LOWERED AT THE APPROPRIATE TIMES?** Make sure the presser foot lever is raised whenever you are threading your sewing machine. When the presser foot is down, it can prevent the thread from sliding into the upper tension disk and cause the machine to stop working. This is an especially common mistake when using a darning foot, which does not cause pressure on the quilt sandwich when it is lowered. Be sure to lower the presser foot before beginning to stitch. When using a darning foot, it can be difficult to tell whether the foot is raised or lowered. When it is raised, there will be no tension on the upper thread. Forgetting to lower the darning foot will cause large loops to form on the bobbin side of a quilt or jam the machine, causing it to stop.
- **IS THE NEEDLE DULL, NICKED, OR BURRED?** Change needles frequently. A bent needle can cause skipped stitches and make your machine run noisily as well.
- **IS THE NEEDLE INSERTED CORRECTLY?** The flat side of the shank should be facing in the correct direction for your machine. Check also to make sure that the needle you are using is the correct type and that it is all the way into the clamp. Tighten the screw with a firm twist, if necessary.
- **IS THE NEEDLE THE CORRECT SIZE?** The most common cause of skipped stitches is using a needle that is too small. See if changing to one size larger will correct the problem. As a rule, the eye of the needle should be twice the size of the thickness of the thread. The thread should never bind or catch in the eye as you thread the needle.
- **IS THE UPPER THREAD TENSION CORRECT?** Most problems can be solved with threading or needles, but occasionally the upper thread tension may need adjusting. Before you begin any tension adjustments, write down your current settings. Then start by making small adjustments to the tension dial, no more than a half number at a time. When the top tension is evenly balanced with the bobbin tension, the knots formed by the interlocking of the stitches will be concealed in the quilt sandwich. The rule to follow is "TNT"—check the Thread first, the Needle second, and the Tension on the upper thread last. If loops of thread are formed on the back of your quilt sandwich, tighten the top tension slightly by turning the dial to a higher number. If there are loops of thread on the top of your quilt sandwich, loosen the top tension slightly by turning the dial to a lower number.

Threads and Needles

Sharee Dawn Roberts

THREADS

The following threads are good choices for learning to machine quilt. It is a good idea to begin with cotton or cotton-coated polyester as you stitch on practice quilt sandwiches for the ten step-by-step technique lessons in this book. Then try using other threads and compare the results and effects you achieve with each of them.

■ **COTTON AND COTTON-COATED POLYESTER:** Both cotton and cotton-coated polyester threads are easy to use and widely available. Cotton-coated polyester threads are very strong, which makes them less appropriate for machine quilting because they tend to stretch and can wear away cotton fabric underneath your quilting stitches.

Cotton is the first choice among many machine quilters because it makes a nice, crisp depression in the surface of a quilt sandwich and it comes in finer weights. It does not stretch, which means that it is usually not necessary to make any drastic adjustments to the top or bobbin tension. Cotton is perfect for the bobbin thread, regardless of which type of thread you use in the top of your machine.

Both cotton and cotton-coated polyester threads are usually labeled with two numbers. The first number refers to the size or "denier" of the thread, meaning the diameter of each individual strand. The second number refers to how many "plies," or strands, are twisted together to create the thread. The fewer the number of plies, the smoother the thread, and yet the higher the number of plies, the stronger the thread. For example, the label 50/3 means that the thread is 50 weight, which is fairly thin, and that three plies were twisted together to create it. This type of thread would be a good choice for most machine quilting tasks. In comparison, a thread that is labeled 80/2 would be a much finer thread, with only two plies spun together. This fine thread would be a good choice for stipple quilting because it would melt into the background and the density of the stipple stitching would help increase its strength. A size 30/2 cotton thread is a heavier thread and a good choice for creating a strong, well-defined line of quilting stitches.

Widely available brands of cotton and cotton-coated polyester include Metrosene cotton, Madeira Tanne and Cotona cottons, Gütermann cotton, and cotton-coated polyesters like J. P. Coats & Clark Dual Duty or Signature cotton/polyester blend.

■ **100 PERCENT SILK:** Silk combines the strength of polyester, the nonstretchability of cotton, and a distinct sheen that cannot be matched by any other type of thread. Silk is manufactured in a wide range of colors, and it comes in a variety of weights—60 and 50 weight are almost hairlike and 30 weight is a heavier, embellishing thread suitable for outline quilting. Silk will withstand almost any treatment, and it is one of the most trouble-free threads to use for machine quilting. Two brands of high-quality silk thread are Kanagawa and Tire.

■ **NYLON:** Commonly called "invisible," or monofilament, nylon thread is popular because it is very forgiving and it flatters less-than-perfect stitches. It is almost invisible, and it does leave a crisp indentation in

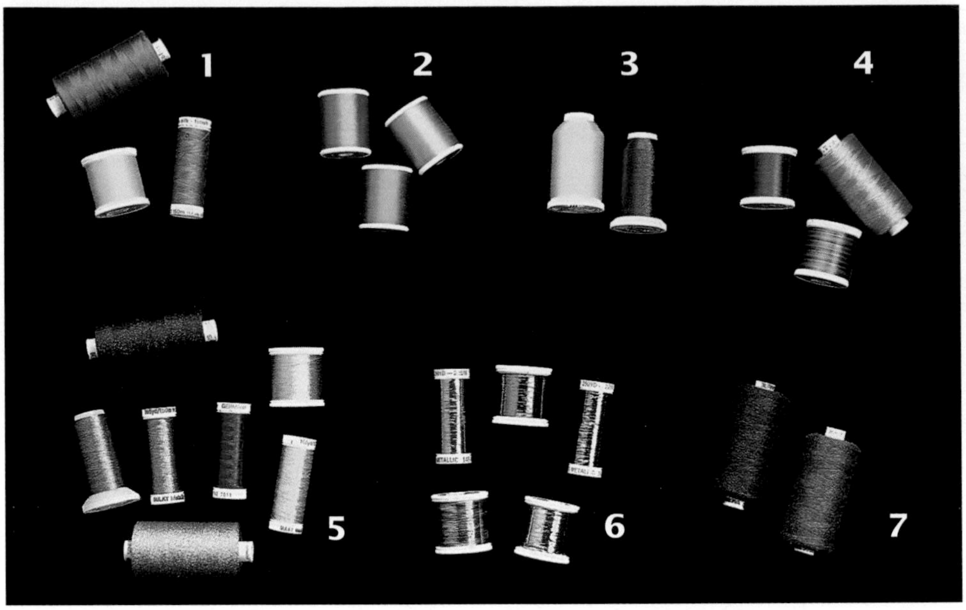

A wide array of beautiful threads are suitable for machine quilting, as follows:
1. cotton and cotton-coated polyester
2. 100 percent silk
3. nylon
4. 100 percent rayon
5. metallics
6. Mylar
7. wool/acrylic

the surface of a quilt sandwich. Purchase a high-quality thread that has a 0.004 weight, in one of two colors: a clear shade for light to medium fabrics and a smoke tone for dark fabrics. Even high-quality nylon thread tends to be stiff, so combine it with cotton thread in the bobbin. It is a synthetic fiber, and it may cut into the weaker fibers of cotton fabric over time. Widely available brands of nylon include Wonder Thread by YLI and Signature.

■ **100 PERCENT RAYON:** Rayon is a perfect choice for machine quilting when a high sheen is desired. Rayon threads are easy to use and come in a variety of weights and spool sizes. The 30-weight rayon thread is heavier than 40-weight thread, so experiment with both to determine the results you prefer. Easy-to-find brands of rayon thread include J. P. Coats & Clark, Madeira, Mez Alcazar, Signature, and Sulky.

■ **METALLICS:** Today's newest metallic threads are trouble-free and quite easy to handle. When you use them, lower the top tension setting on your machine slightly, stitch at a reduced speed, and use either a Metafil or a large-eye topstitching needle and a high-quality lightweight thread in the bobbin.

Metallic threads come in different weights. The strength and durability will depend on the type, weight, and brand as well as how you use them. High-quality brands of metallics include Madeira Dazzle, Madeira FS/Jewel, Madeira Supertwist, Sulky metallic, and YLI 601 fine metallic.

■ **MYLAR:** Mylar aluminized thread is flat, with a highly reflective surface. Because of this, it is easiest to use by pulling it from a vertical spool pin to minimize coiling, which could eventually twist the thread and cause it to snap. High-quality brands of aluminized nylon include Horn of America Stream Lamé, Madeira Prism, and Sulky Sliver.

■ **WOOL/ACRYLIC:** Wool/acrylics are fuzzy, special-effect threads that are great for making wool quilts with an old-fashioned look. They are heavy, so use a large-eye needle, and clean your bobbin case often to avoid accumulating fuzz. The most easily available brand of wool/acrylic thread is Madeira Burmilana.

NEEDLES

The following information will help take the guesswork out of needle choices for machine quilting. This list includes specific brands because these needles will produce excellent results and they're easily available at quilt shops or sewing stores. You will find needles suggested for each thread type in the "Machine Quilter's Thread Guide" on page 12.

- **SCHMETZ UNIVERSAL NEEDLES:** Universal machine needles are suitable for all woven materials. Universal needles are available in packs of single size 60, 65, 70, 75, 80, 90, 100, 110, and 120 needles, and assorted packs that contain sizes 70, 80, and 90.
- **SCHMETZ QUILTING NEEDLES:** These needles are designed to successfully sew over four to six seams, so if you are stitching through multiple layers of cotton fabric or particularly heavy fabrics, these are the needles to choose. There are five needles per card: three 75 and two 90 size needles.
- **SCHMETZ MACHINE EMBROIDERY NEEDLES:** Machine embroidery needles have a scarfed side edge and a large eye to prevent shredding and breakage when sewing with fine metallic thread or other fine machine embroidery threads, such as rayon and silk. This type of needle is identified by its red band between the shank and the shaft. The package includes three 75 and two 90 size needles.
- **LAMMERTZ METAFIL NEEDLES:** The Metafil needle is designed specifically to accommodate metallic threads, especially the heavier 30-weight metallics. Its specialized Teflon-coated eye and scarf virtually eliminate stripping and splitting of metallic threads. It is available in size 80 only.
- **SCHMETZ METALLICA NEEDLES:** The Metallica needle features an extra-large eye, a specially constructed point, and a large groove to allow metallic threads to make stitches with less friction. These features prevent the metallic threads from shredding and breaking. Packed five needles per card, this needle is available in size 80 only.
- **SCHMETZ TOPSTITCHING NEEDLES:** The topstitching needle is extra-sharp and has an extra-large eye and a large groove to accommodate topstitching thread. It is similar to the Metallica needle, so it may be used when a larger or smaller size is required. This needle is available in sizes 70, 80, 90, 100, and 110.

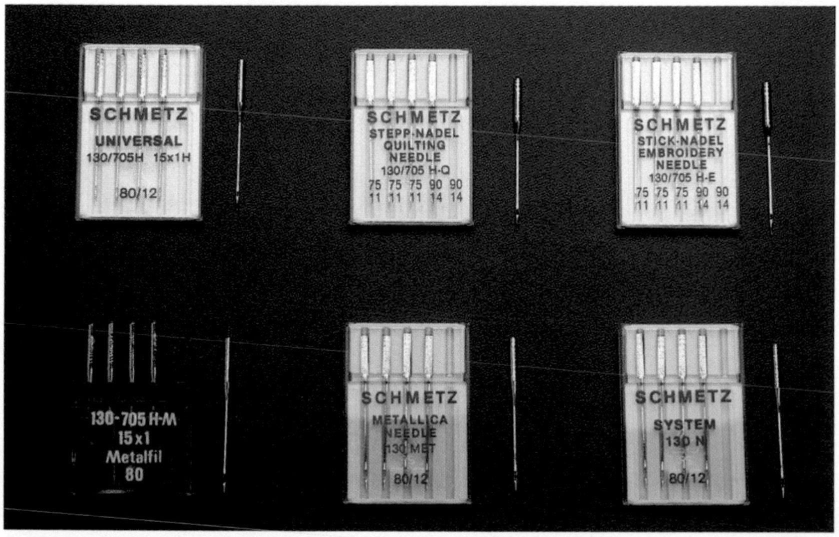

Selecting the right machine quilting needle for your projects will help ensure the best possible stitching results.

Machine Quilter's Thread Guide

THREAD WT.	FAMILIAR BRANDS	YARDAGE	STRENGTH	TOP TENSION SETTING	SUGGESTED NEEDLE	SPECIAL FEATURES	EASE OF USE
COTTON							
30	Madeira Tanne	714	Strong	4–5	Topstitching	Beautiful colors; strong embellishment thread; economical	Easy
30	DMC	328	Strong	4–5	Topstitching	Beautiful colors; strong embellishment thread; economical	Easy
30	Metrosene	219	Strong	4–5	Topstitching	Beautiful colors; strong embellishment thread; economical	Easy
40	Mettler	547	Strong	4–5	Machine embroidery	Silk finish; high quality	Easy
50	DMC	223	Medium	3–4	Machine embroidery	Highly mercerized	Easy
50	Madeira Tanne	1,265	Medium	3–4	Machine embroidery	High-quality, long-staple Egyptian cotton embroidery; wide color range; economical	Easy
50	Mettler	547	Medium	3–4	Machine embroidery	Silk finish; wide color range	Easy
50	Gütermann	110	Medium	3–4	Machine embroidery	High-quality cotton; beautiful colors	Easy
60	Metrosene	219	Weak	3–4	Machine embroidery	Fine machine embroidery weight; wide color range	Easy
80	Cotona	250	Weak	3–4	Machine embroidery	Very fine weight; perfect for stippling	Easy
NYLON							
—	YLI Wonder	1,200	Strong	3–4	Machine embroidery	0.004 finest-weight nylon; lightweight; comes in smoke and clear shades; economical	Easy
—	Signature	250	Strong	3–4	Machine embroidery	Lightweight transparent nylon; comes in clear and smoke shades	Easy
RAYON							
30	Sulky	180 or 700	Medium	3–4	Machine embroidery	Smooth, silky luster	Easy
30	Madeira	165	Medium	3–4	Machine embroidery	Smooth, silky luster	Easy
30	Finishing Touch	720	Medium	3–4	Machine embroidery	Smooth, silky luster with some variegated colors	Easy
30	Scansilk	530	Medium	3–4	Machine embroidery	Smooth, silky luster; wider color range than Finishing Touch	Easy
40	Sulky	250 or 1,050	Weak	3–4	Machine embroidery	Fine silky luster; wide color range	Easy
40	Madeira	220 or 1,050	Weak	3–4	Machine embroidery	Fine silky luster; wide color range in large size only	Easy
40	Scansilk	250 or 1,100	Weak	3–4	Machine embroidery	Fine silky luster	Easy

THREAD WT.	FAMILIAR BRANDS	YARDAGE	STRENGTH	TOP TENSION SETTING	SUGGESTED NEEDLE	SPECIAL FEATURES	EASE OF USE
40	Mez Alcazar	220 or 1,100	Weak	3–4	Machine embroidery	Fine silky luster	Easy
40	J. P. Coats	200	Weak	3–4	Machine embroidery	Readily available; few colors	Easy
40	Signature	200	Weak	3–4	Machine embroidery	Readily available; few colors	Easy
METALLIC							
30	Madeira Supertwist	1,100	Strong	2–4	Metafil topstitching	Very sparkly; beautiful colors, including opalescent shades	Not easy
30	FS Jewel	612	Strong	2–4	Metafil topstiching	Strong textured polyester filament core with a metalized foil wrap; patina-like shine	Not easy
30	Metallic no. 15	330	Strong	2–4	Metafil topstitching	Very heavy plied metallic; soft patina-like luster	Not easy
40	Sulky metallic	165	Medium	2–4	Metafil topstitching	Good-quality metallic; readily available; smooth finish with soft shine	Not easy
40	YLI fine metal	250	Medium	2–4	Metafil topstitching	Good-quality metallic; readily available; smooth finish with soft shine	Not easy
40	Madeira Dazzle	220	Medium	2–4	Metafil topstitching	Readily available in smooth and sparkling textures	Not easy
40	Gütermann	55	Medium	2–4	Metafil topstitching	Special metallic effect thread; heavy texture; tends to shred	Not easy
40	Sulky Sliver	250	Medium	2–5	Metafil topstitching	Thin, flat, ribbon-like thread; highly reflective; use vertical spool pin	Not easy
40	J. P. Coats	200	Weak	2–4	Metafil topstitching	Readily available; few colors	Not easy
40	Signature	125	Weak	2–4	Metafil topstitching	Readily available; few colors	Not easy
SILK							
30	Silk Stitch	55	Strong	2–4	Topstitching	Luxurious and heavy; perfect for outlining; brilliant colors; expensive	Easy
50	Kanagawa	109	Strong	3–5	Embroidery	Beautiful, smooth sheen; ties knots easily; brilliant colors; expensive	Easy
50	Tire	109	Strong	3–5	Embroidery	Beautiful, smooth sheen; ties knots easily; brilliant colors; expensive	Easy
WOOL/ACRYLIC							
30	Burmilana	400	Strong	2–4	Topstitching	Very fuzzy, so clean bobbin case often; woolly look; works best with 50-weight cotton in bobbin	Not easy
30	Renais-sance	400	Strong	2–4	Topstitching	Very fuzzy, so clean bobbin case often; woolly look; works best with 50-weight cotton in bobbin	Not easy

WHAT KIND OF LOOK DO YOU LIKE?

The following photos show the same motif stitched in four different types of threads. The fabrics and the batting are all the same. Note the differences in each sample and think about which ones appeal to you most. Use the information in the "Machine Quilter's Thread Guide" on page 12 to help you select the right threads for achieving the results you desire in your machine quilting projects.

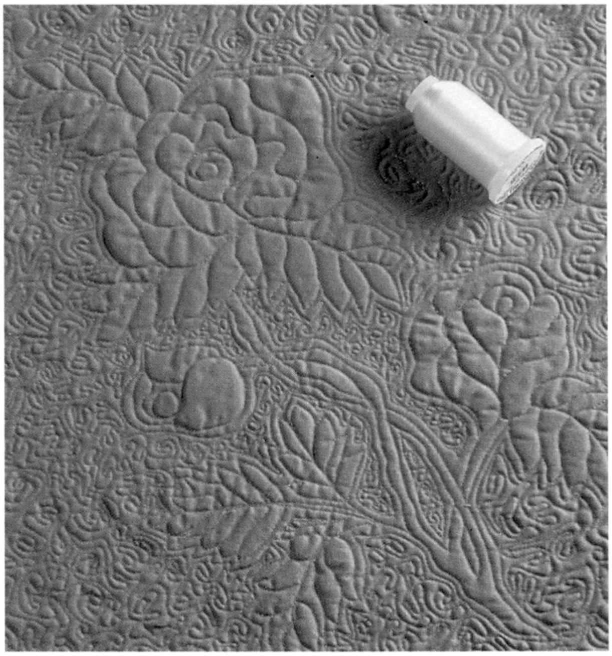

■ The combination of YLI Wonder Thread monofilament nylon as the top thread with Madeira Tanne 50-weight cotton in the bobbin makes the quilting stitches in this design look almost invisible, while it emphasizes the stippled surface texture and defines the rose itself.

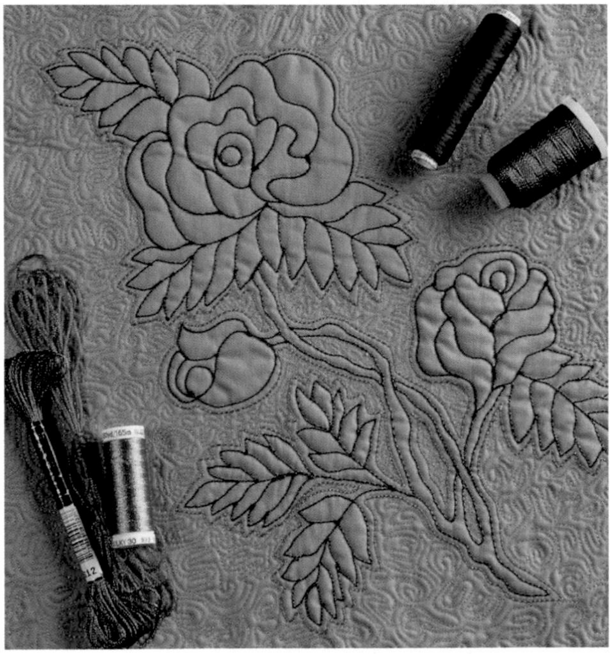

■ Bobbin drawing allowed me to use heavy threads to accentuate the motifs in all three of the following quilts. For this example, I chose a deep green YLI Pearl Crown rayon to create a pebblelike texture around the edges of the leaves. I used a raspberry shade of Madeira Decor 6 for the blossoms because the smoothness of this thread echoes the satiny surface of a rose petal. The high sheen of the coral Anchor Marlitt thread defines and enhances the outline stitching around the roses, and the background texture is softened by stipple quilting in a matching shade of Sulky 40-weight rayon.

■ I used a hand-dyed, variegated shade of Caron Wildflowers thread here to emphasize the outline of the roses, along with a different weight of variegated green Caron Watercolors thread for the leaves. The outline stitching around the roses is done in a soft, clear coral shade of 30-weight Madeira Tanne cotton. This matches the background fabric well, yet it is heavier than the stippled background, which was done in a dusty coral shade of 80-weight Madeira Cotona thread.

■ A variegated shade of Kreinik 1⁄16-inch ribbon combines shades of wine, red, and a hint of blue to create a rich, Victorian look for the roses in this quilt. The clear, bright green of the YLI Candlelight thread creates a high level of contrast in the leaves; and the smooth, shiny Madeira no. 6 metallic gold thread in the outline stitching is a perfect complement to the texture of the roses and leaves. A soft rusty coral, variegated, 30-weight Madeira Supertwist thread matches the background fabric and gives it an understated sparkle.

Best Bets in Batting

Anne Colvin

CONTENT AND CHARACTERISTICS

Use the following information about the general characteristics of cotton and cotton/polyester blends, polyester, and wool battings to help you determine the fibers you will enjoy most for machine quilting. The "Machine Quilter's Batting Guide" on page 18 will give you helpful information about specific brands of each type of batting.

COTTON AND COTTON/POLYESTER BLENDS

■ **PREPARATION:** Some cotton and cotton/polyester blended batts can be washed before using them in a quilt, but this is always a personal choice. In general, for any quilt you plan to launder, I recommend washing everything, from the batting to the fabrics, before you layer the quilt. Check the package for manufacturer's instructions, but in most cases, a soak in clear water in the washing machine without agitation will preshrink the batting. Then you can spin it to remove excess water and let it tumble dry in the dryer. If you decide against washing your batting, it is a good idea to put it into the dryer on air fluff to help take out the wrinkles and folds.

■ **SHRINKAGE:** Shrinkage applies only to battings that have natural fibers; polyester batts do not shrink. Shrinkage helps quilting stitches sink into a batt, and it can add to the drapability of a quilt. It will produce a cuddly quilt with the puckered, flat look of an antique, and it can sometimes change the size of a quilt dramatically. Because of this, I recommend washing all of the materials for any quilt that will be laundered. Make sure you follow the manufacturer's instructions for washing any batt.

■ **SCRIM:** Several cotton battings have a scrim, which is a thin polyester sheet that looks like interfacing. The cotton fibers are bonded to one side of the scrim, which produces a batting that is very flat and extremely durable. These batts can be quilted at intervals up to 8 inches apart, but usually it is best to quilt more closely, so that the quilt does not sag between the quilting lines. Cotton battings with a scrim are best for projects that need to be flat, durable, and quilted at 3- to 4-inch intervals. Cotton battings without a scrim will produce a softer and more drapable quilt that will need to be quilted at approximately 2-inch intervals.

■ **BEARDING:** Bearding, or fiber migration, happens when batting fibers work through the top and/or backing fabric. To some extent, all battings beard. Cotton fibers break off easily, and the bearding may resemble a powder. Long polyester fibers are more noticeable, and you may be tempted to pull on the fibers. Batting companies have tried to solve the bearding problem with improved bonding methods to keep the fibers together.

There are other factors that affect bearding. Fabrics used in the top and backing of a quilt will influence bearding, so it is best to use only high-quality, tightly woven fabrics for making any quilt.

■ **WARMTH AND DURABILITY:** Any batting that has cotton in it will be lightweight, durable, and comfortable to sleep under, even in summer, because cotton is a natural fiber that breathes.

■ **LOFT AND DRAPE:** Cotton battings and blends have less loft, or puffiness, than do polyester batts. They are very soft and drapable, without being stiff. Whether they are prewashed or not, cotton battings and blends will enable you to re-create the flat look of an antique quilt.

■ **EASE OF HANDLING:** Fabric naturally sticks to both cotton battings and blends, which means that safety pins can be placed at wider intervals on a quilt that has cotton batting in it. This will cause less shifting or puckering while you quilt. A large quilt is more compact with cotton or cotton/polyester blend batting, which means it will be easier to manipulate the quilt through a sewing machine.

Many cotton batts require quilting at closer intervals than do polyester batts, some as close as 1 or 2 inches apart. Cotton will compress wherever it is quilted, and the stitches will sink down into it. This means that the stitching lines are more noticeable than the individual stitches, creating hills and valleys that catch the light and produce a sculpted look.

■ **COST:** Cotton battings and blends fall into a medium price range.

POLYESTER

■ **PREPARATION:** It is not necessary to prewash polyester batts, although it is a good idea to put them into the dryer on air fluff to allow the folds and wrinkles to relax.

■ **BEARDING:** 100 percent polyester batts are more likely to beard than cotton, cotton/polyester, or wool.

■ **WARMTH AND DURABILITY:** Polyester is a synthetic fiber that traps body heat, so it will produce a quilt that is very warm. Polyester is durable enough to hold up well with repeated washings.

■ **LOFT AND DRAPE:** Polyester battings have a relatively high loft, which creates a puffier look in a finished quilt. They can be quilted at greater intervals than cotton or wool, and they will hold up well through repeated launderings.

■ **EASE OF HANDLING:** Polyester batts can be quilted farther apart than other types of batting, which makes the quilting process go more quickly and easily.

■ **COST:** Polyester battings are generally less expensive than natural fibers like wool or cotton.

WOOL

■ **PREPARATION:** Wool is a natural fiber that can be preshrunk if you like. This is not always necessary; it is a good idea check the manufacturer's instructions on each package you buy. If you wash it, remember that wool needs to be laundered in cold water, because it may "felt," or become compressed in hot water.

■ **SHRINKAGE:** Because wool battings will shrink when they are prewashed, it may be helpful to test them for shrinkage before use. Cut two pieces of batting the same size and preshrink one of them. Then compare the differences in size; this will help you determine whether you want to preshrink the batt for the quilt. Quilters sometimes blame shrinkage on the batting, when, in fact, it could be due to other factors, such as tight tension on the top and/or bobbin threads, which can cause the threads to gather the fabric slightly. Over a whole quilt, this type of gathering can cause puckers and distortions in size.

■ **SCRIM:** There are wool battings available with a scrim, which is a thin layer of polyester that gives strength and durability. Batting that has a scrim cannot be split. Wool battings without a scrim can be split, or separated by pulling them apart gently to create two equal pieces. This will give

Machine Quilter's Batting Guide

BATTING	CONTENT	CHARACTERISTICS	MAXIMUM QUILTING INTERVALS	SHRINKAGE*	SIZES	COST
Hobbs Heirloom Cotton	80% cotton, 20% polyester	Low loft, soft, medium weight	3½"	5%, if not preshrunk	45" × 60", 90" × 108", 120" × 120"	$$
Hobbs Heirloom 100% Organic Cotton	100% cotton; no scrim	Flat, compact, thin, unbleached, chemical-free, lightweight to medium weight	2"	5%, if not preshrunk	90" × 108"; by the yard, 96" wide	$$
Hobbs Heirloom Organic Cotton	100% cotton; polyester scrim	Flat, compact, unbleached, chemical-free, medium to heavy-weight	6"–8"	5%, if not preshrunk	36" × 45"; 90" × 108"; by the yard, 96" wide	$$
Fairfield Polyfil Cotton Classic	80% cotton, 20% polyester	Thin, soft, nice drape, antique look, can be split, light-weight	2"–3"	2%–3%, if not preshrunk	36" × 45", 81" × 96"	$$
Mountain Mist Blue Ribbon	100% cotton; no scrim	Flat, soft, nice drape, antique look, lightweight	1"–2"	Cannot be preshrunk; 5% after washing quilt	45" × 60", 90" × 108"	$$
Warm Products Warm & Natural	100% cotton; polyester scrim	Flat, compact, contains cotton seed particles, stiff when closely quilted, heavyweight	6"–8"	Slight	34" × 45"; 90" × 108"; by the yard, 90" wide	$$
Mountain Mist Cotton Choice	90% cotton, 10% polyester; scrim	Flat, thin, compact, seedless, bleached white, lightweight to medium weight	6"–8"	Slight	By the yard, 90" wide	$$$
Fairfield Soft Touch Cotton	100% cotton; no scrim	Flat, thin, compact, seedless, bleached white, lightweight to medium weight	2"	Minimal	45" × 60", 90" × 108"	$$
Hobbs Heirloom Wool	100% wool	Low loft, soft, nice drape, can be split, medium weight	3"	5%, if not preshrunk	90" × 108"	$$$
Warm Products Wool Naturally	100% wool; polyester scrim	Flat, compact, warm, nice drape, medium weight	6"–8"	3%, if not preshrunk	27" × 34"; 34" × 45"; 90" × 108"; by the yard, 90" wide	$$$$
Mountain Mist Quilt Light	100% polyester	Puffy, fibers shift, stretches, medium weight	3"	None	45" × 60", 81" × 96", 90" × 108"	$
Fairfield Polyfil Low Loft	100% polyester	Puffy, fibers shift, stretches, medium weight	3"	None	45" × 60", 81" × 96", 90" × 108", 120" × 120"	$
Fairfield Polyfil Traditional	100% polyester	Blanketlike, low loft, stiff, stretches, medium weight	3"–4"	None	36" × 45", 45" × 60", 72" × 90", 81" × 96", 90" × 108", 120" × 120"	$
Hobbs Thermore	100% polyester	Flat, thin, stretches, lightweight to medium weight	3"–4"	None	45" × 54", 90" × 108"	$$

*Shrinkage refers to the process of laundering the quilt.

you two paper-thin pieces of batting, which can be excellent for small projects, garments, or miniature quilts. Consider that you will lose one side of the bonding when you split a batt, which means that the unbonded side may produce a greater amount of bearding, or fiber migration, through the quilt top or back.

- **BEARDING:** Bearding is less of a factor with wool batts than with polyester batts, with the exception of those that have a scrim, as described above.
- **WARMTH AND DURABILITY:** In general, wool has the same type of durability and breathability as cotton, and wool will allow you to create a quilt that has a great deal of warmth.
- **LOFT AND DRAPE:** Wool batts vary from a very flat to a medium loft and make quilts are soft and drapable. Quilting stitches will sink down into wool batting, giving the quilt a richly sculpted look. The lines of quilting are more visually prominent than individual stitches.
- **EASE OF HANDLING:** Bearding is not a terrible problem with wool batts, and wool sticks to fabric naturally, which makes it easy to handle.
- **COST:** Wool is much more expensive than cotton and polyester batts, but its properties may make up for the increased cost.

LAYERING AND BASTING

To learn the basics of machine quilting and practice the techniques in each of the lessons in this book, you will need to layer and baste a series of practice quilt sandwiches. You may find it helpful to read through the information in the "Machine Quilter's Batting Guide" on the opposite page, and select at least three different types of batting. That way, you can compare the results you get from using each batting and develop your own likes and dislikes as you practice.

You'll also find helpful information in this section about layering and basting wall quilts and bed quilts.

PREPARING PRACTICE QUILT SANDWICHES

STEP 1. Cut a 14-inch square *each* of batting, a light to medium solid-colored top fabric, and a muslin backing fabric.

STEP 2. Layer the muslin fabric wrong side up with the batting and the top fabric on top of it. Place safety pins through all three layers at 3- or 4-inch intervals.

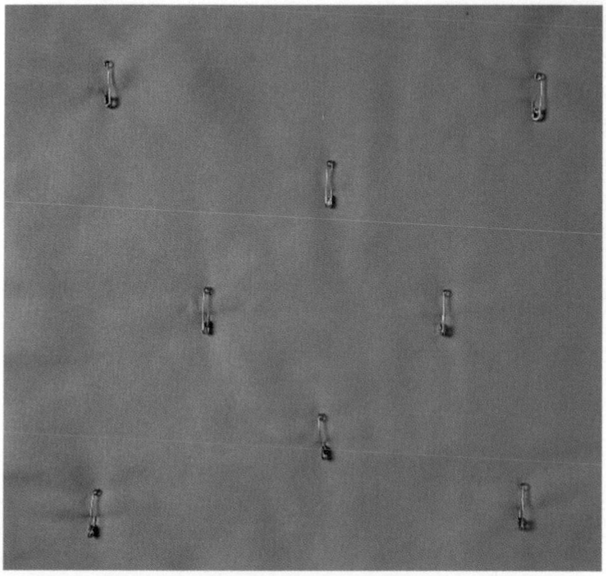

LAYERING AND BASTING A LARGE QUILT

STEP 1. Cut the backing fabric of a large quilt 8 inches longer and 8 inches wider than the quilt top. This margin will allow at least 3 to 5 inches of backing fabric to extend beyond the quilt top on all sides.

STEP 2. If you must piece the backing fabric for a large quilt, remove all selvage edges before stitching the pieces together and make sure that the seams will lie parallel to the lengthwise or crosswise grain of the fabric. Press the seam allowances to one side for greater strength, so the stitches don't show.

STEP 3. Find the grain line of the batting you are going to use by pulling on it gently in both directions. The direction that has less stretch is comparable to the lengthwise grain of the fabric. Running the grain lines of both batting and fabric in the same direction will give a quilt the greatest amount of strength.

STEP 4. Cut the batting the same size as the backing fabric.

STEP 5. Lay the backing fabric wrong side up on a clean surface. Smooth out any wrinkles or folds.

STEP 6. Place the batting over the backing fabric, smoothing out wrinkles or folds without stretching it.

STEP 7. Lay the quilt top over the batting, centering it right side up on the batting. Smooth the quilt top gently.

STEP 8. With size #1 rust-proof safety pins, pin the three layers of the quilt together, working from the center toward the edges in rows. Wait to close the pins until all of them are in place. If the batting is cotton, it will stick to the fabric easily, so pins can be placed at 3- to 4-inch intervals. For polyester batts, place the pins at 3-inch intervals. For cotton or wool batts, 4-inch intervals will work well. Place pins near rather than directly on the lines of your quilting designs.

Great Idea!

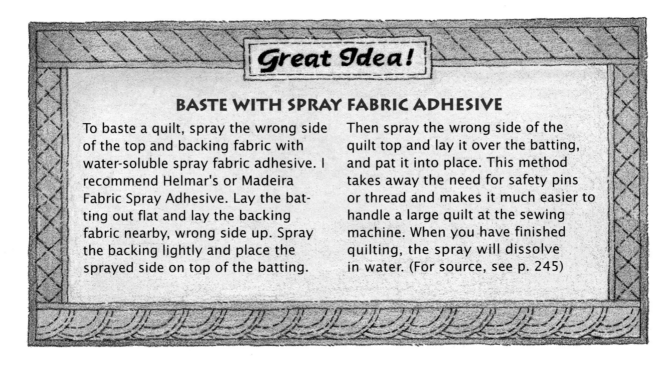

BASTE WITH SPRAY FABRIC ADHESIVE

To baste a quilt, spray the wrong side of the top and backing fabric with water-soluble spray fabric adhesive. I recommend Helmar's or Madeira Fabric Spray Adhesive. Lay the batting out flat and lay the backing fabric nearby, wrong side up. Spray the backing lightly and place the sprayed side on top of the batting. Then spray the wrong side of the quilt top and lay it over the batting, and pat it into place. This method takes away the need for safety pins or thread and makes it much easier to handle a large quilt at the sewing machine. When you have finished quilting, the spray will dissolve in water. (For source, see p. 245)

Organizing a Quilting Space

Sharee Dawn Roberts

A good quilting space should be comfortable and flexible enough to be organized the way you want it, and it should allow you to rearrange or add things as your quilting skills change and grow. Whether you have a little or a lot of space, the following ideas will help you create a work area that is perfectly suited to your own needs.

FURNITURE AND LIGHTING OPTIONS

TABLES: Placing your sewing machine on a large table is helpful because it will support the bulk of a quilt while you are stitching. It is also good to orient your machine so that you will face the inside of the room while you quilt. This will give you maximum freedom of movement and permit you to adjust the angle of your machine whenever necessary. If you have the space, placing another table to the left of your sewing machine is ideal for allowing a quilt to spread out while you stitch.

INDIRECT LIGHTING: A source of indirect lighting is important for illuminating your overall stitching area. Fluorescent lights provide more light and use less energy than incandescent bulbs, and they do not give off heat.

DIRECT LIGHTING: Use direct lighting to eliminate shadows within your work area. Mount incandescent lights on a wall or place them close to your sewing station. Combining both fluorescent and incandescent lighting in your quilting studio will help to prevent eyestrain.

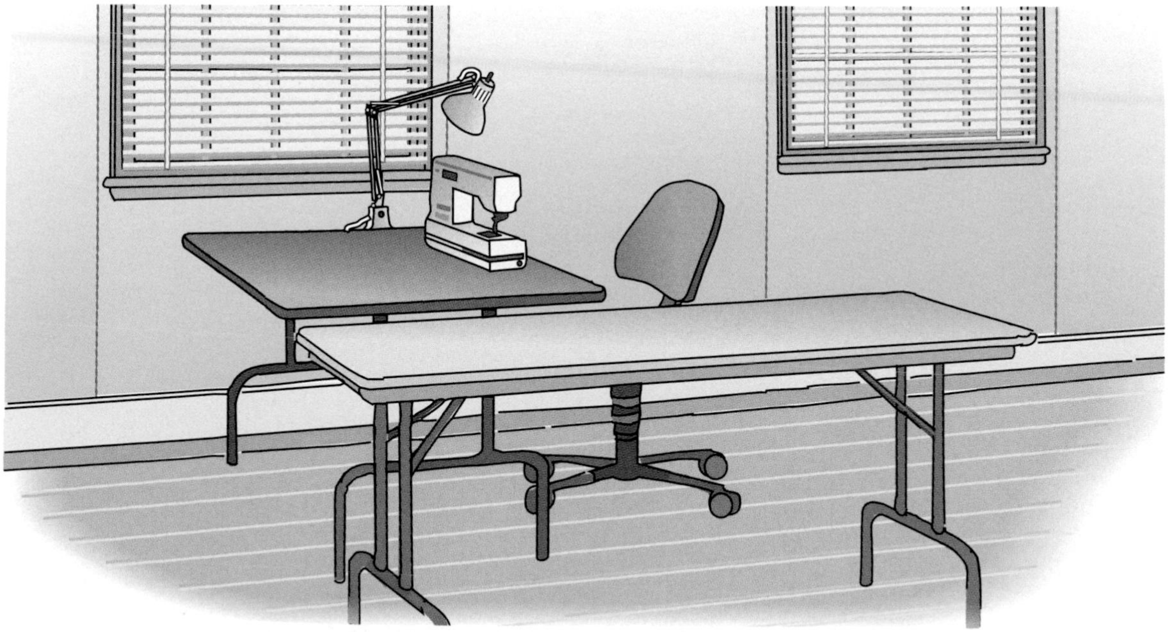

A sewing machine is the heart of a well-organized quilting space, and it should be placed where you can use it most easily.

A COMFORTABLE CHAIR: It is important to consider the way your body will be positioned while you are quilting. When you sit at your sewing machine, your knees should not be higher than your hips, and your arms should be able to rest comfortably on the table without having to raise your elbows. It should not be necessary to bend your neck at a sharp angle, and you should be able to see what you are working on easily, without causing any stress in your neck, arms, or back. An office chair that can be adjusted to different heights will allow you to experiment until you find the position that makes you feel comfortable. A chair with casters is especially nice because it will enable you to roll from one place to another, which can be a real time- and energy-saver.

Perforated hardboard is inexpensive and perfect for storing many things, either directly on hooks or in Ziplock bags. It is easy to install on walls and over doors and windows for holding thread trees, racks, spool caddies, and other quilting supplies.

Wire shelving can be mounted easily on perforated hardboard and used to store items you want to keep within easy reach of your sewing machine, such as fabrics, books, oversized spools, and plastic bins.

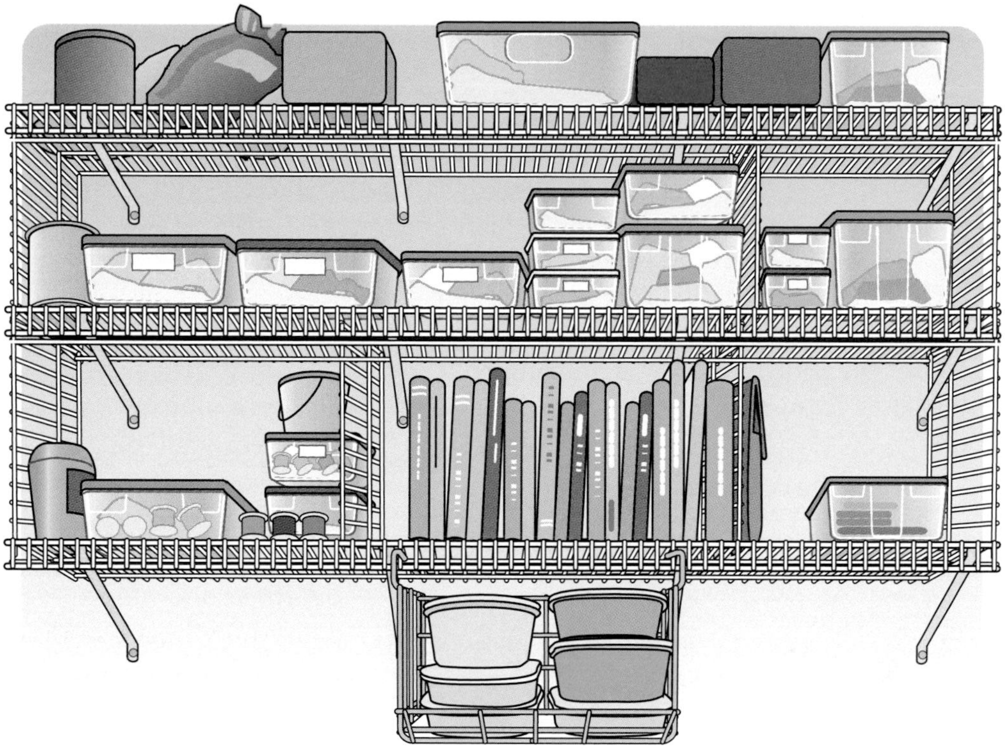

CREATIVE STORAGE IDEAS

Evaluate your available space to decide what types of storage you can use and try some of these ideas to customize your quilting area for maximum efficiency.

- **PLASTIC BINS:** Plastic bins are durable, lightweight, and see-through, stack together neatly, and come in a multitude of shapes and sizes. Use a self-adhesive label on each bin to describe the contents, or buy plastic bins with different colored lids to help separate the things you store in them.
- **WIRE BASKET SYSTEMS:** Vinyl-covered wire basket systems are sturdy, have open trays that make it easy to organize fabric collections, and can be customized to fit any size space you have.

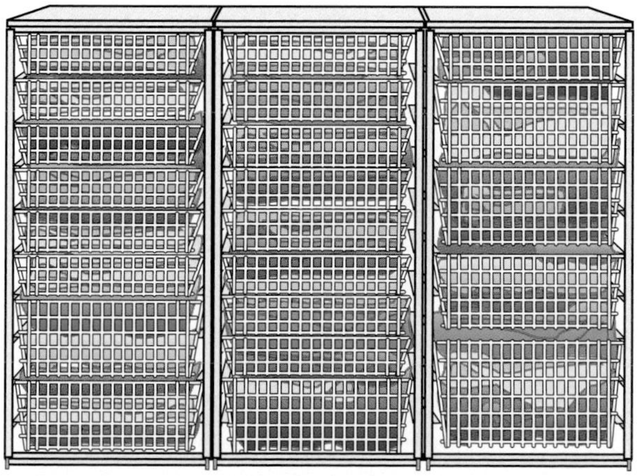

Storing tools, notions, and fabrics in plastic bins and wire shelving systems keeps them easy to find at a moment's notice.

TOTE BAGS: Tote bags are durable and practical for storing just about any size or type of supplies you need for quilt classes, workshops, guild meetings, and more. You can also use them for keeping instructional handouts, quilt samples, projects in progress, and anything that will not stack neatly on shelves or fit in drawers. Hang them on hooks on perforated hardboard for a colorful addition to your quilting studio, and they'll be ready to take anywhere at a moment's notice.

A colorful collection of tote bags keeps projects and irregularly shaped tools and notions within easy reach.

CLOSET POLES: Many newspapers are happy to give away rolls of newsprint that remain after printing a daily newspaper run, and there are usually many yards of newsprint

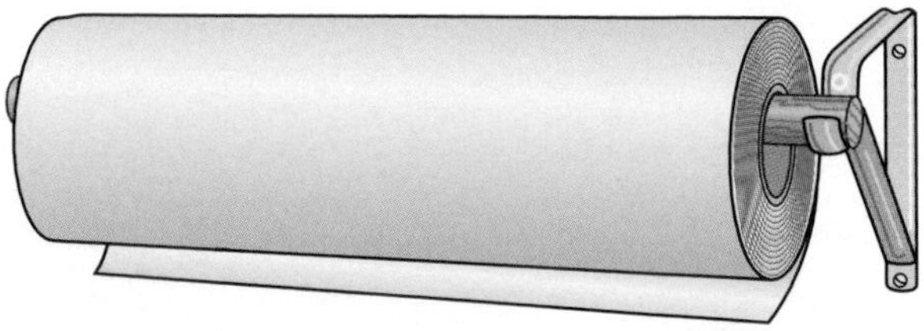

Newsprint can be useful for sketching quilting designs, especially for long expanses of border space.

left on them. This type of paper is very useful for designing quilts and sketching out ideas for quilting designs. If you have enough free wall space in your quilting area, purchase two closet braces and mount them on a wall with a wooden pole between them to form a giant reel. This will make it easy to pull out the paper and cut or tear off as much or as little as you need.

MAKING YOUR OWN LIGHT TABLE

As your machine quilting skills improve, you will discover that a light box can be very helpful for transferring quilting designs to a quilt top. I have a free-standing light table that enables me to stand for long periods of time without causing back strain. The bottom and the sides of my light table have extra storage space for bulky items, such as paper tablets, a bolt of fusible webbing, a square, and various file boxes.

It's easy to make a custom light table for your own quilting space with a few inexpensive items: a piece of glass or plexiglass, a light source, and something to suspend the glass over the light source. If you are handy with tools or know someone who is, you can use 2 X 4s and plywood to build a table in any size you like. Just place a piece of glass on top and add a small shelf to support a light source underneath the glass.

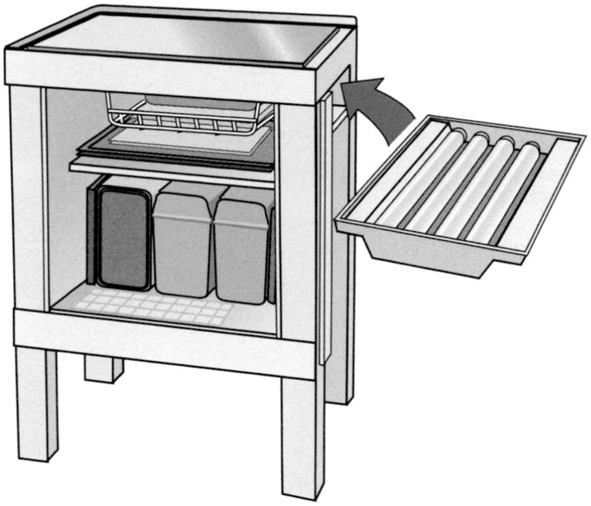

An undercounter light source like the one shown at left is approximately 2 inches deep. This type of light and others are widely available at hardware stores or building supply centers.

Great Ideas!

EIGHT WAYS TO MAKE MACHINE QUILTING FASTER AND MORE FUN

1. Put on a cassette tape of your favorite music to soothe your mind while you stitch.
2. Use a nonskid carpet pad for keeping the foot pedal in the proper position at all times.
3. Keep a thread clipper handy for cutting threads close to the surface of a quilt.
4. Use a Kwik Klip tool for inserting and removing safety pins swiftly. (See "Quilting Supplies by Mail" on page 245.)
5. Set a kitchen timer to remind yourself to take frequent stretch breaks.
6. For free-motion quilting, coat your fingertips with a thin layer of rubber cement and allow it to dry before beginning to quilt. The dried glue will grip the quilt sandwich and make it easy to guide through the machine.
7. Keep canned air handy for cleaning out the lint, dust, and debris that can accumulate in the bobbin case or feed dogs after long periods of machine quilting.
8. Purchase two (or more) of any tools or notions you use repeatedly, like marking tools, a container of safety pins, a quilter's ruler, or a tape measure, so that they are within easy reach at all times.

LESSON 2

Planning and Interpreting Quilting Designs

The fun in quiltmaking is in watching colors and fabrics come together into a beautiful whole. The quilting process itself sometimes gets shortchanged because we tend to spend less time thinking about it. Quilting is the final step in any quilt, and it helps to make a quilt distinctive and unlike any other. Because of this, thinking about how you want to quilt any project should be as creative and just as much fun as every other part of the quiltmaking process. If you think about quilting from the very beginning, it can be a factor in deciding what kind of quilt you want to make as well as in selecting fabrics and batting. For example, if you wish to include feathered quilting designs, you may decide to make a quilt that has large expanses of solid space for showcasing the feathers' intricate curves. And if you are making your first project, crosshatched grids or quilted channels may be just right because they are done with machine-guided rather than free-motion techniques.

In my lesson, we will look at several examples of quilt styles; talk about primary, secondary, and continuous-line designs; and learn where to place them to the greatest advantage in various areas of a quilt.

SUE NICKELS

DMC
Quilt
Sharpie

LESSON 2

Planning and Interpreting Quilting Designs

QUILT STYLES

Quilting is often an important factor in why we are drawn to any quilt. So, for inspiration, it is helpful to look at designs that have been popular for quilts made in the past. Most quilts fall into certain style categories, such as Amish quilts, traditional nineteenth- or early-twentieth-century quilts, and contemporary quilts. As you look through this selection of popular quilting designs in four different styles, think about where you could incorporate these or similar designs into your own quilts.

A good way to gather ideas for quilting designs is to go to quilt shows and make notes about the quilts you like. Take a notebook with you and do quick drawings of quilting designs you like. Note how they are used in quilts and whether they are primary or secondary designs. Keep your notes to use as references for choosing or adapting quilting designs for your future quilts.

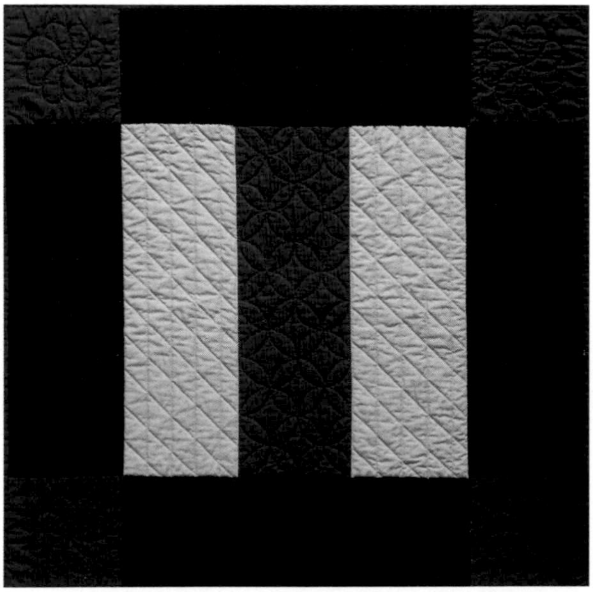

■ **AMISH QUILTS:** Quilts that have large expanses of solid color, like this classic Amish Bar quilt, allow plenty of room for intricate and curved quilting designs, such as the feathers in the two side borders and the pumpkin seed design in the center bar. Diagonal grids, flowing cables, and single floral motifs are also used frequently in Amish quilts.

■ **NINETEENTH-CENTURY QUILTS:** Antique quilts yield an endless variety of quilting designs. These are a few of the many feathered and stipple quilting designs featured in nineteenth-century quilts. Feathered designs that have fluid, undulating curves will give a quilt an appealing old-fashioned look, while both echo and random stipple quilting create an interesting visual texture behind appliqué shapes.

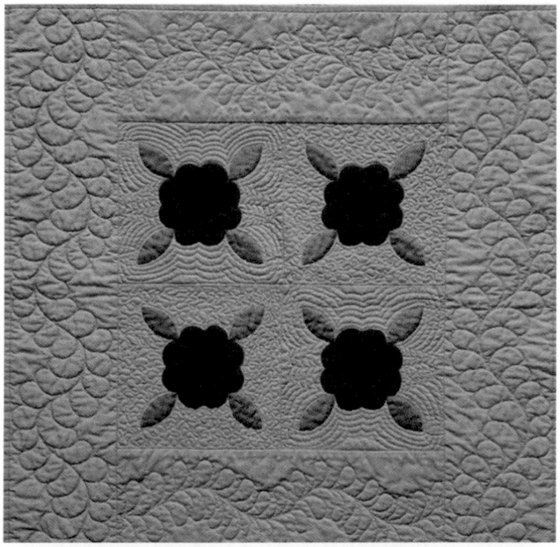

■ **TRADITIONAL EARLY-TWENTIETH-CENTURY QUILTS:** This quilt highlights some of the quilting designs that were popular during the early part of this century, when floral quilts and appliqué designs were in vogue. Designs like diagonal crosshatching were very easy to do and created effective backgrounds for curved shapes in appliqué quilts. Designs like fans, flowers, leaves, feathers, and snowflakes were complimentary to large expanses of solid space, such as individual blocks or borders.

■ **CONTEMPORARY QUILTS:** The main focus in a contemporary quilt is usually the interplay of color and line in the quilt top itself, rather than the quilting. Because of this, patterns of winding lines, straight lines, and all-over curved patterns such as this clamshell are popular. These quilting styles allow the focus to remain on the design of the quilt top.

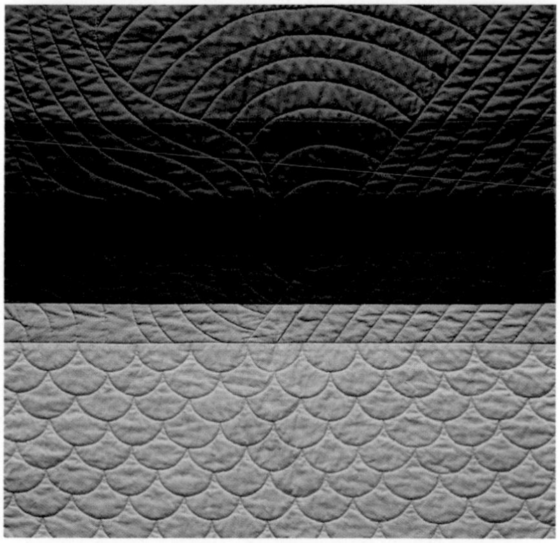

PRIMARY AND SECONDARY DESIGNS

Planning quilting designs for any quilt depends on the style of the quilt you want to make, where you want the quilting to figure prominently, and how to balance the quilting designs so that they are spread evenly throughout the quilt. When quilting designs figure prominently in a quilt, they are called primary. When quilting designs are not as visually important as other elements, like piecing or appliqué, they are called secondary. The following photos show examples of both primary and secondary designs in various areas of a quilt, such as blocks, sashing strips, squares, and borders.

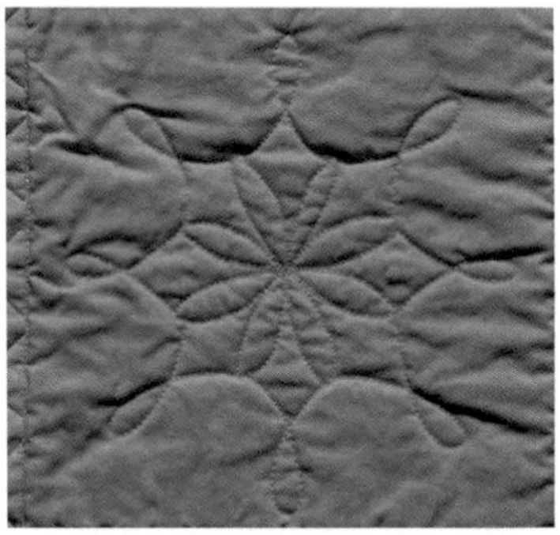

■ **INDIVIDUAL MOTIFS:** Isolated motifs tend to be primary, or of more visual importance, than functional, straight-line quilting such as crosshatching. Solid alternating blocks or large, open spaces behind appliqué shapes are perfect for featuring individual quilting designs like this snowflake.

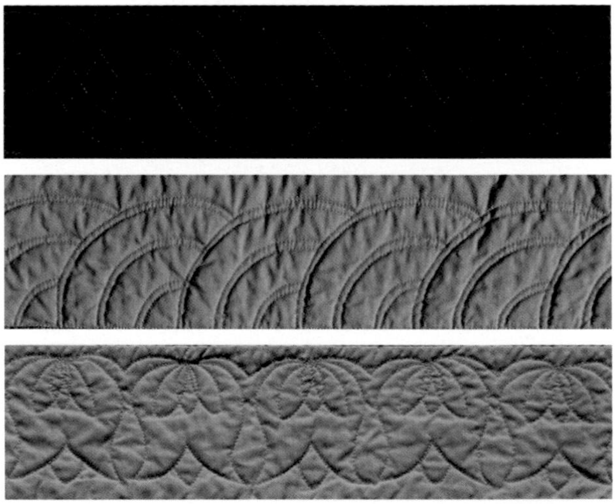

■ **REPEATING DESIGNS:** Cables, fans, and floral patterns that can be connected and repeated as many times as needed are good choices for filling long expanses of space in sashing strips or borders. These would be considered primary quilting designs because of their decorative, rather than functional, quality.

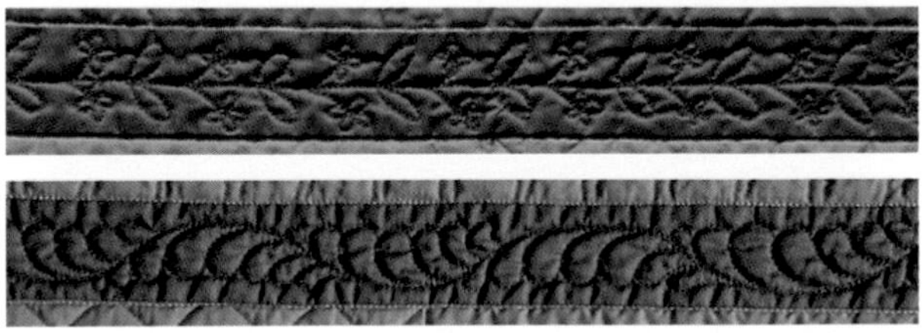

■ **NARROW DESIGNS:** Quilting designs that are narrow and have a short repeat, like this alternating feather and the flower and leaf, are wonderful for filling long, narrow spaces in a quilt, such as sashing strips. These are examples of primary designs because the viewer's focus is drawn to the quilting itself.

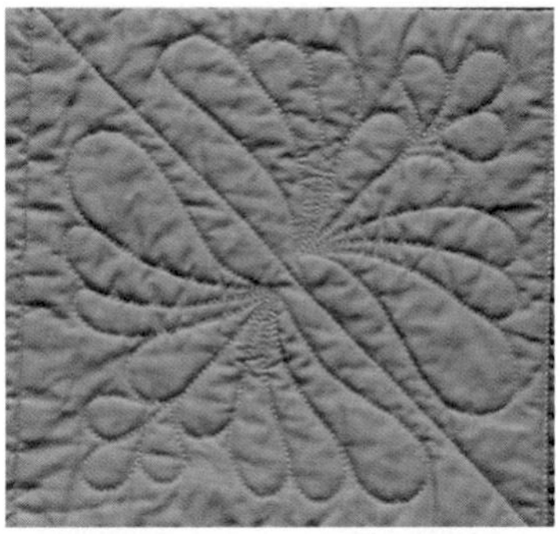

■ **TRIANGULAR DESIGNS:** Quilting designs that have a triangular shape can be mirrored or reflected, as shown here, to create quilting designs for square spaces. They can also be used in various other configurations to fill spaces like hexagons, trapezoids, or parallelograms. These are examples of primary quilting designs.

■ **STIPPLE AND MEANDER QUILTING:** Echo, random stipple, and meander quilting create puckered textures that are suitable for filling in background areas around appliqué shapes or primary quilted motifs. Stipple and meander quilting qualify as secondary designs because they are less prominent visually than appliqué shapes or individual quilted motifs.

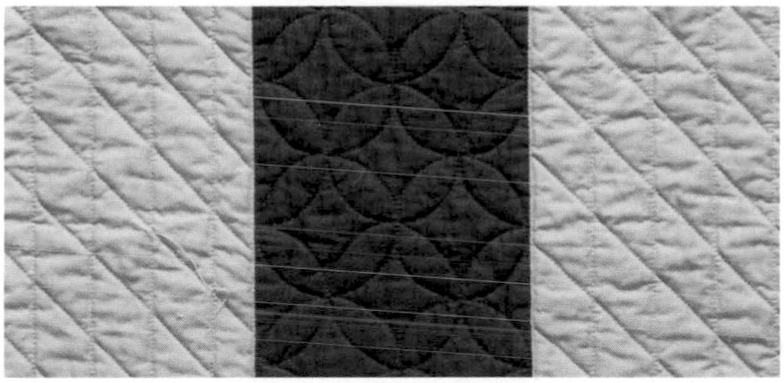

■ **STRAIGHT-LINE DESIGNS:** Crosshatched grids or 60-degree hanging diamonds serve the functional purpose of holding the three layers of a quilt together, which makes them secondary designs. They are suitable for filling in areas around appliqué shapes and individual quilted motifs or for doing all-over designs on a busy quilt.

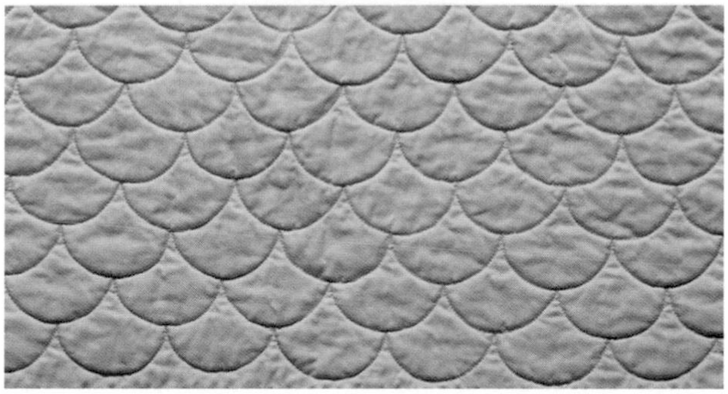

■ **ALL-OVER CURVES:** This all-over clamshell pattern works well to cover large expanses of space with an interesting visual texture. It is a secondary type of quilting design because it is less prominent than individual quilted motifs. This type of free-motion quilting design is quick and easy to do, and it is a wonderful choice for heavily pieced quilts because it allows you to avoid quilting through many seam allowances.

CONTINUOUS-LINE DESIGNS

Free-motion continuous-line designs can be stitched in a single, unbroken line, and they are good choices to include in almost any area of a quilt. The first two examples will show you the difference between designs that can be stitched continuously and those that cannot. Use this same type of comparison whenever you are looking for continuous-line quilting designs.

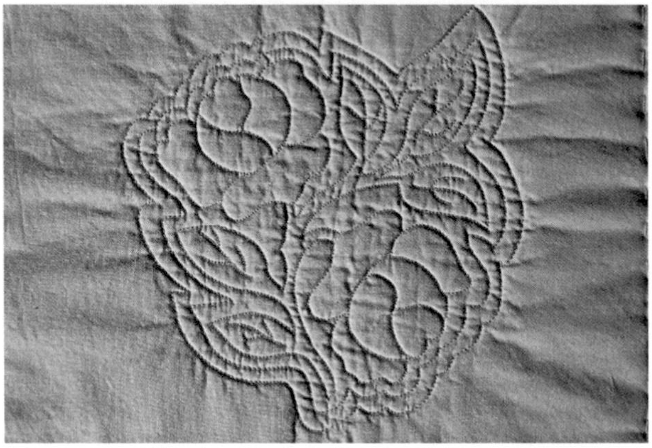

■ **UNCONNECTED MOTIFS:** This design consists of individual roses and leaves that cannot be connected by stitches. It is impossible to stitch from one element to the next in an unbroken line. There are many stops and starts required to stitch this type of design, which means that it would probably be more suitable for hand quilting than for machine quilting.

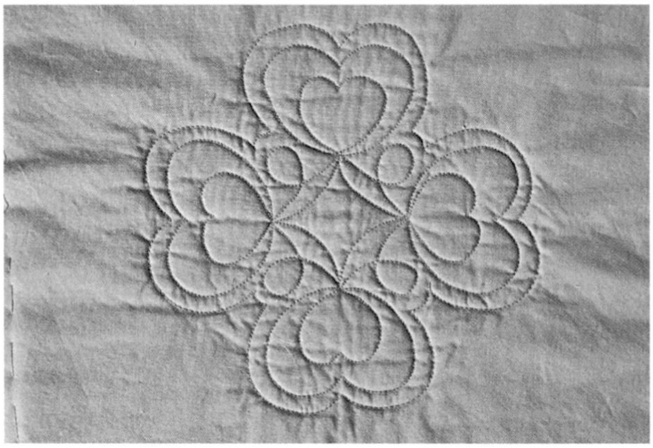

■ **CONTINUOUS-LINE DESIGNS:** This entire heart design can be stitched in a single line, without stopping until the design is completed. Designs like this are called continuous-line designs, and they are good choices for machine quilting.

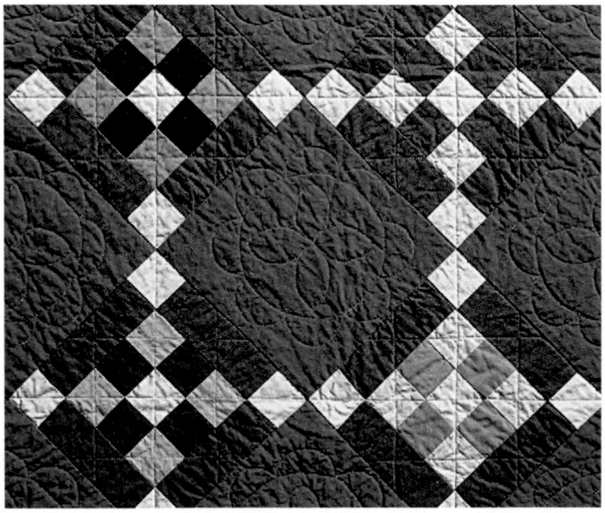

■ **CONTINUOUS-LINE BLOCK DESIGNS:** This Nine-Patch quilt incorporates continuous-line designs that are in keeping with an Amish style. The alternating plain blocks have a circular design with scallops around it, which was inspired by an antique Amish quilt.

■ **ALL-OVER CONTINUOUS-LINE DESIGNS:** Although fans cannot always be stitched in a continuous-line, this design was adapted from a traditional hand quilting pattern, and it can be stitched in an unbroken line. It takes on a secondary role because of the heavy piecing in this quilt, titled "A Simple Quilt. . . Really," made by Pat Holly.

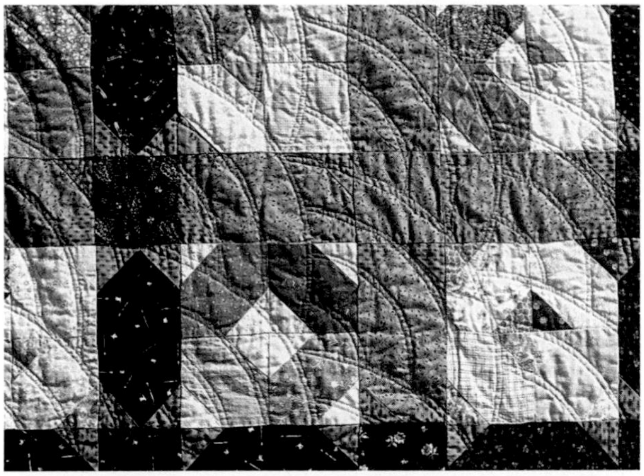

■ **CONTINUOUS-LINE BORDER DESIGNS:** A continuous-line design of curving vines and leaves is perfect for a solid border, where it can be highlighted by contrasting thread. Use your finger to follow the lines of the vine, tracing around each leaf as you go from one side to the other.

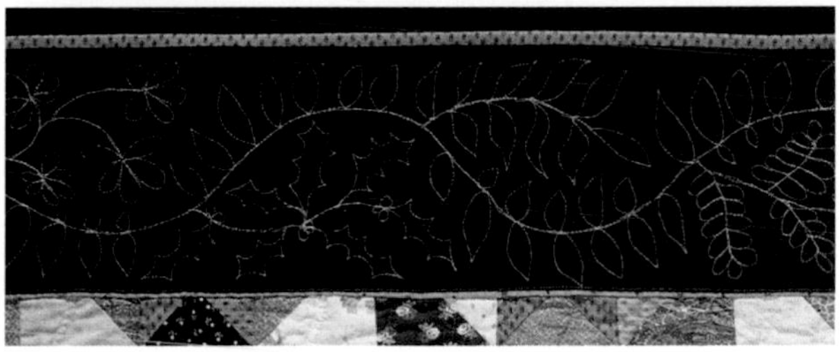

Great Idea!

SKETCH YOUR QUILT ON GRAPH PAPER

When you have decided what kinds of quilting designs you want to use in a quilt, use colored pencils to draw your quilt on a piece of graph paper. Then lay a piece of tracing paper over your drawing and sketch in your quilting ideas. This will allow you to evaluate each quilting design before you actually mark your quilt top. Another helpful idea is to draw the quilting designs you have selected full-size on pieces of tracing paper, cut them out, and lay the paper cutouts on your completed quilt top. This will tell you whether each design is right for its specific area of your quilt.

LESSON 3

Starting and Stopping

Anchoring the threads at the beginning and end of a stitching line is essential for successful machine quilting because if these stitches are not properly secured, even the most beautifully quilted designs can become unraveled.

There are several easy ways to start and stop a line of stitches including knots, backstitches, very short stitches, or securing all of the threads by hand after you have finished quilting. I think it's helpful to try out these techniques on a practice quilt sandwich to determine which ones you like best.

Some methods of stopping and starting work better for some quilting techniques than others. Depending on the kinds of quilting designs you choose, you may decide to vary your approach from project to project. In the lessons that follow, specific methods for starting and stopping will be given wherever they are called for. If no particular method is mentioned, feel free to use whichever one you prefer.

To practice these techniques, gather up your fabrics, batting, and basic supplies and assemble a practice quilt sandwich; let's start at the very beginning.

SHERRY SUNDAY

TRY STARTING AND STOPPING TECHNIQUES ON:
All of the projects in the book

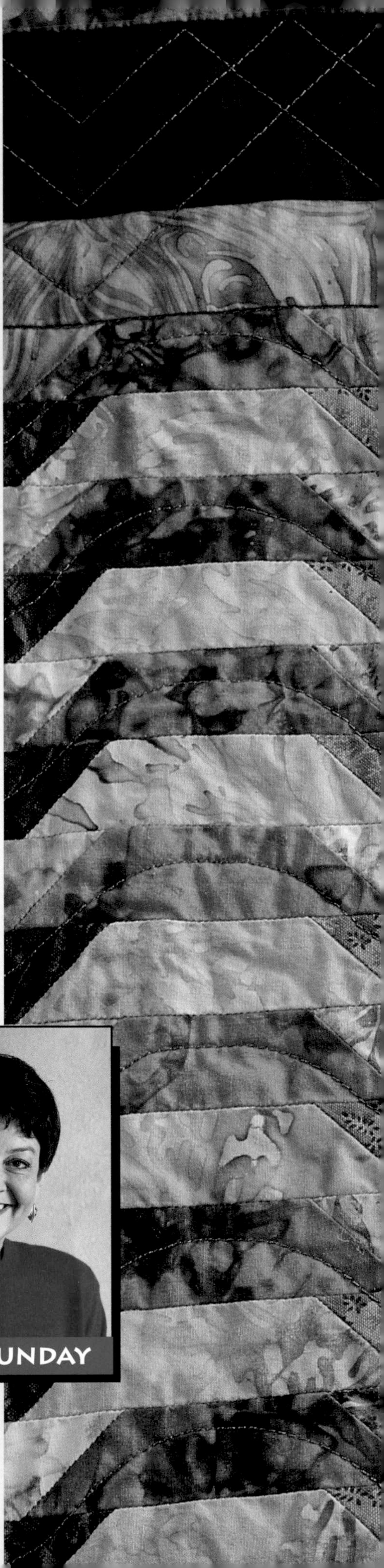

No. 100

LESSON 3

Starting and Stopping

PREPARING A PRACTICE QUILT SANDWICH

To prepare a practice quilt sandwich, cut a 14-inch square of light or medium solid fabric for the top. Cut a 14-inch square of batting and another 14-inch square of backing fabric. Place the backing fabric wrong side up on a flat surface and lay the square of batting on top of it. Add the top fabric right side up over the batting. Pin-baste the three layers together by placing rust-proof quilter's safety pins at 3- to 4-inch intervals over the surface of the practice quilt sandwich, as shown in the photos on page 19. Make as few or as many practice quilt sandwiches as you like for practicing the techniques in this lesson. If you make more than one, consider using different types of batting in them, so you can begin to develop your own likes and dislikes while you stitch.

Get Set

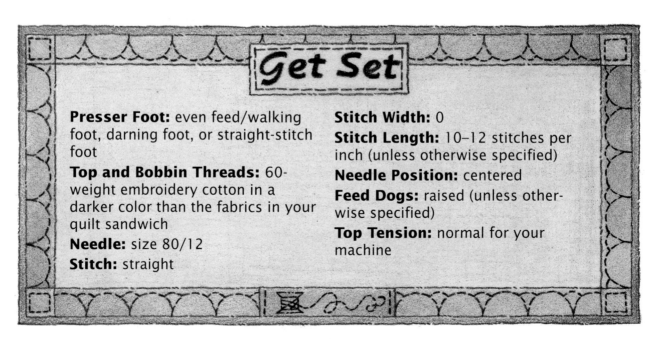

Presser Foot: even feed/walking foot, darning foot, or straight-stitch foot

Top and Bobbin Threads: 60-weight embroidery cotton in a darker color than the fabrics in your quilt sandwich

Needle: size 80/12

Stitch: straight

Stitch Width: 0

Stitch Length: 10–12 stitches per inch (unless otherwise specified)

Needle Position: centered

Feed Dogs: raised (unless otherwise specified)

Top Tension: normal for your machine

KNOTS

This method can be used for either machine-guided or free-motion quilting techniques because the knot is formed by stitching in a stationary position. It is a good choice whenever you use a printed fabric for the backing in a quilt because the knots will not be noticeable. And it is especially useful for channel quilting, stipple quilting, meander quilting, or whenever you can place the knots at the edge of a quilt because they will be hidden inside the binding.

STARTING

1 Place the practice quilt sandwich under the presser foot of the sewing machine, approximately 3 inches in from the right side of the fabric. Keep the presser foot raised, move the hand wheel slowly, take one stitch, and pull a loop of bobbin thread to the top of the fabric. **Note:** This step is necessary for all methods of starting a line of stitches.

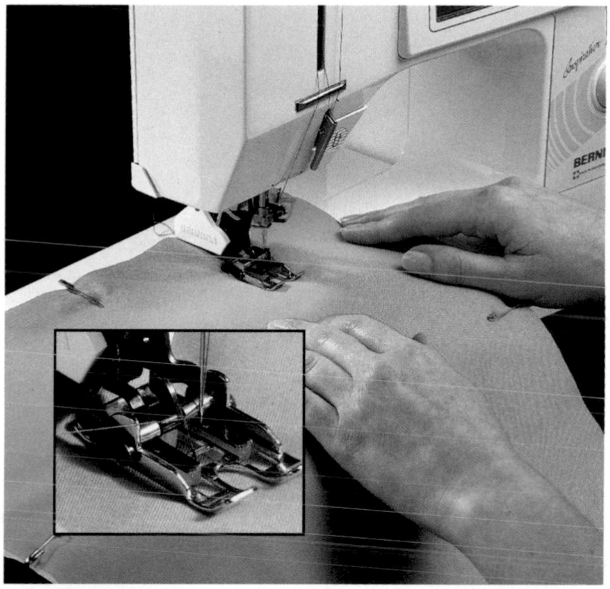

2 Lower the feed dogs and pull the top and bobbin threads out to the left of the presser foot. Lower the presser foot and adjust the stitch length to 0. Insert the needle back into the fabric at the point where the bobbin thread came up. Take a few stitches in a stationary position to anchor them securely. A small knot will be formed on the back side of the quilt sandwich, as shown.

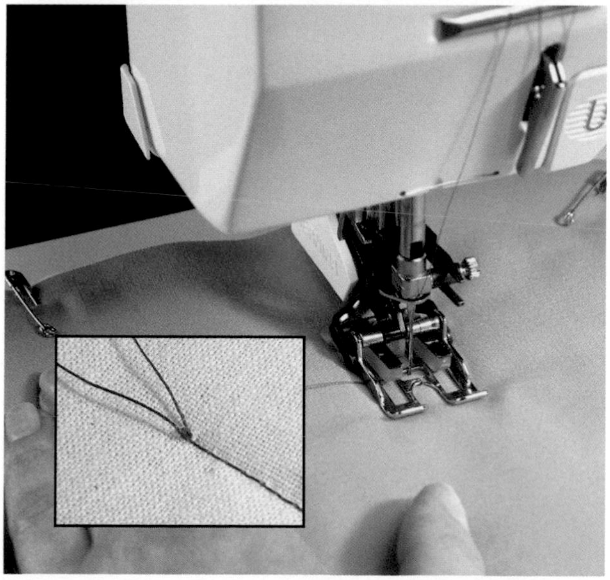

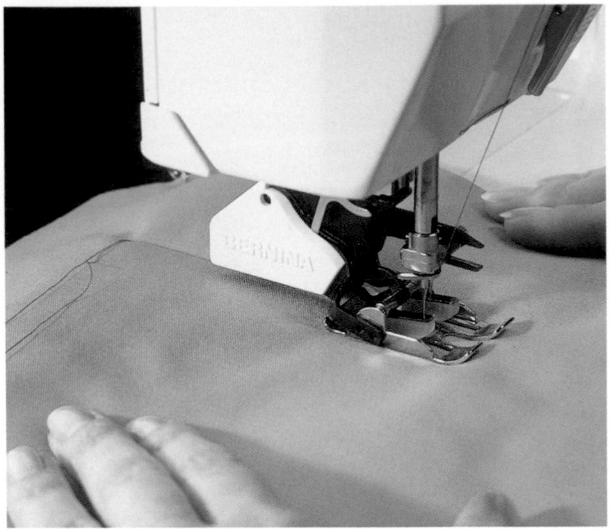

3 If you are going to do free-motion quilting, the feed-dogs will already be lowered, so simply begin to move the quilt sandwich and start to stitch. For machine-guided quilting, raise the feed dogs, adjust the stitch length back to 10 or 12 stitches per inch, and start stitching, releasing the threads with your left hand as you begin.

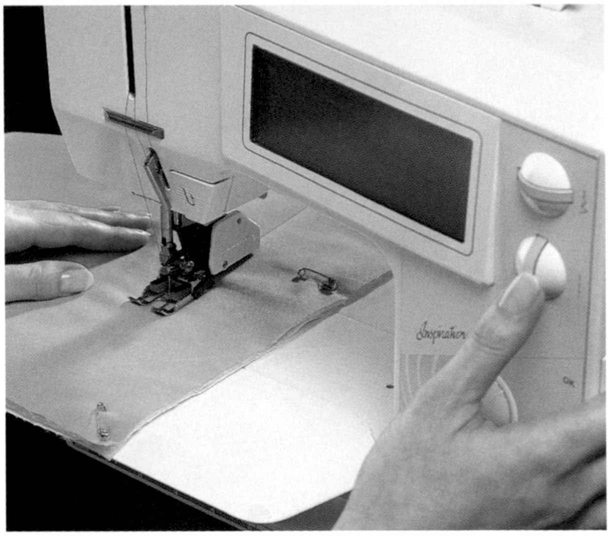

STOPPING

1 Continue stitching for a few inches more and end by following the same process described earlier. Stop with the needle in the down position. If you are doing machine-guided quilting, lower the feed dogs, set the stitch length to 0, and take a few stitches in place. For free-motion quilting, it is not necessary to adjust the stitch length or lower the feed dogs; simply take a few final stitches in place.

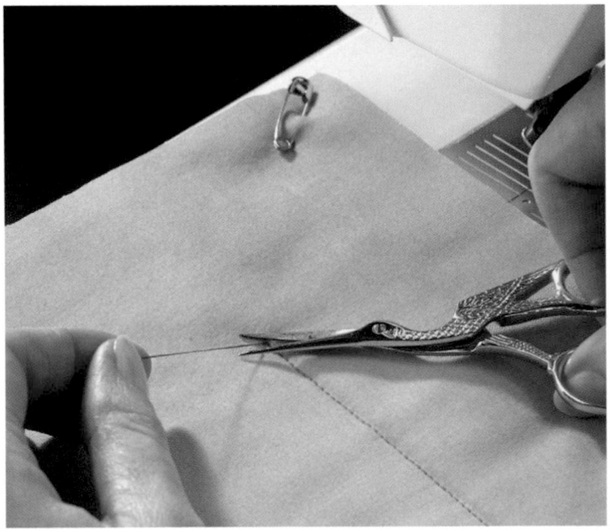

2 Lift the presser foot and remove the quilt sandwich from the sewing machine. Clip all threads close to the fabric. The knots will be quite small, and extra care should be taken not to cut them from the quilt.

SHORT STITCHES

This method can be used for either machine-guided or free-motion quilting. It is especially effective for continuous-line designs because the beginning and ending stitches are nearly invisible. It is also a very secure method of anchoring stitches. (To show yourself how secure short stitches actually are, try this: Use a seam ripper and see if you can remove several short stitches—you'll find that it is almost impossible!) Short stitches are also suitable for stitch-in-the-ditch quilting, outline quilting, channel quilting, and any other machine-guided technique for the same reasons.

STARTING

1 To practice starting with short stitches, place your quilt sandwich under the presser foot, approximately 1 inch to the left of your previous line of stitching, and bring the bobbin thread to the top. For machine-guided quilting, pull the top and bobbin threads to the left, lower the presser foot, and adjust the stitch length to approximately 20 stitches per inch. Insert the needle back into the quilt sandwich at the point where the bobbin thread came up. Hold the threads with your left hand and take several short stitches. For free-motion quilting, the stitch length is already set at 0, so simply move the quilt sandwich very slowly, so that the first several stitches you take are very small.

2 After you have made four to six short stitches, let go of the threads and continue stitching. For machine-guided quilting, use your left hand to guide the quilt sandwich and gradually increase the stitch length to 10 to 12 stitches per inch with your right hand as you continue stitching. For free-motion quilting, there is no need to adjust the stitch length; simply move the quilt sandwich more quickly to lengthen your stitches and continue. **Note:** The photo shows the stitching line from behind the walking foot.

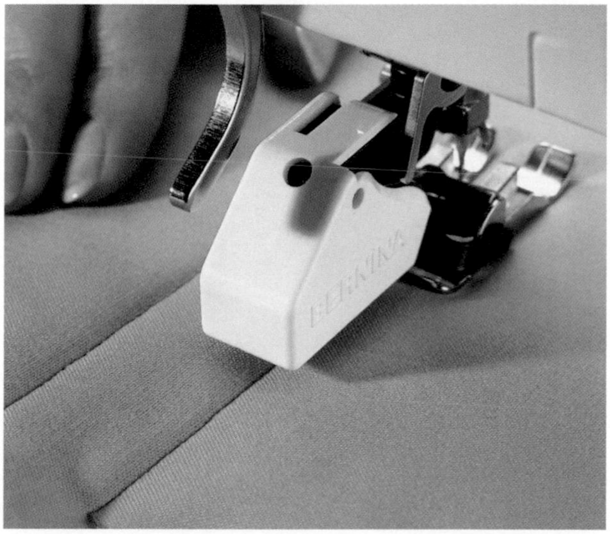

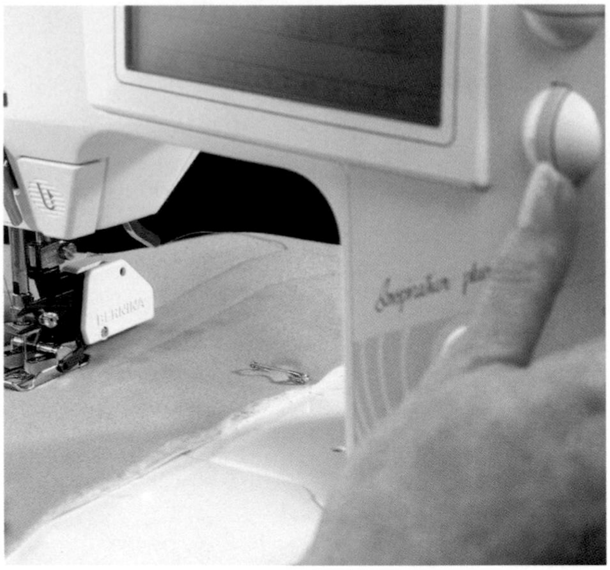

STOPPING

To stop with short stitches, pause approximately $\frac{1}{4}$ to $\frac{1}{2}$ inch before you wish to end your stitching line, and follow the same process described earlier. For machine-guided quilting, use your right hand to gradually adjust the stitch length back to approximately 20 stitches per inch, and take several short stitches to end the line. For free-motion quilting, slow down the speed at which you are guiding the quilt sandwich, take four to six more short stitches, and stop. Remove the quilt sandwich from the machine and clip the threads close to the fabric.

BACKSTITCHES

Backstitches are suitable for machine-guided quilting because the feed dogs remain in the raised position. Use this method of starting and stopping in an inconspicuous place on your quilting design, such as at the edge of the quilt, or in the ditch of a seam between two pieces in a pieced quilt.

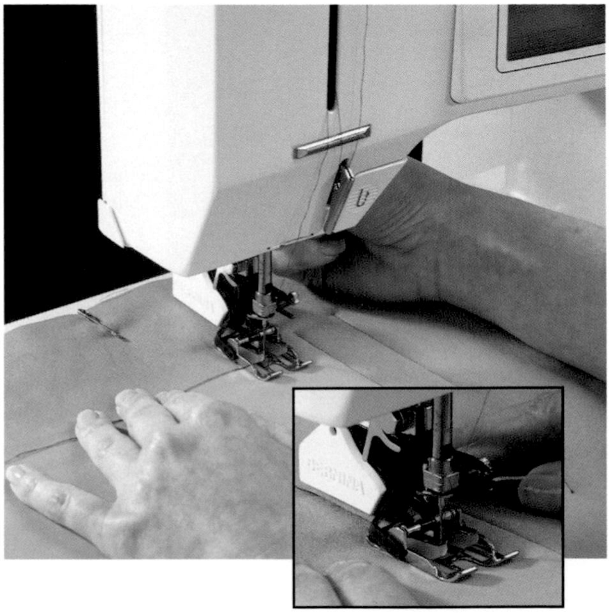

STARTING

To start with backstitches, place your practice quilt sandwich under the presser foot, and take one stitch to bring the bobbin thread to the top of the fabric. Then hold the top and bobbin threads to the left, and lower the presser foot. With the stitch length set at 10 to 12 stitches per inch, insert the needle where the bobbin thread came up, and take four stitches in reverse. Let go of the threads and continue quilting.

STOPPING

To end with backstitches, stop with the needle down in the quilt sandwich at the end of the stitching line and take four backstitches. Lift the presser foot, remove the quilt sandwich from the machine, and clip the threads at the end of the stitching line. Do not clip the beginning threads at this time.

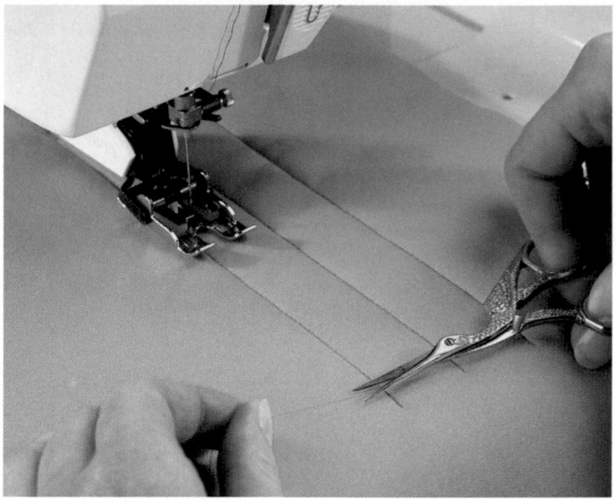

BURYING THREADS BY HAND

This technique can be used with any method of starting and stopping, as long as you do not clip the threads. It offers a way to hide the ends of thread invisibly and keep an even stitch length in your quilting lines. It is also a way to avoid getting small knots on the back side of a quilt, which can be very useful when the backing is a solid fabric.

1 To practice this technique, use the thread tails at the beginning of the previous line of stitching. Pull gently on either the top or bobbin thread, which will bring both threads to the same side of the quilt sandwich. Then hold the threads together and trim the ends evenly.

2 Thread a sharp, large-eyed needle with this pair of threads, and insert the needle into the quilting stitch at the end of the stitching line, guiding the needle into the batting layer for 1 or 2 inches along the line of quilting stitches. Bring the needle out through the top layer of fabric, and clip the threads close to the fabric. The tiny pinpoints of thread that are left will disappear into the batting layer of the quilt sandwich. Repeat this process for each pair of threads.

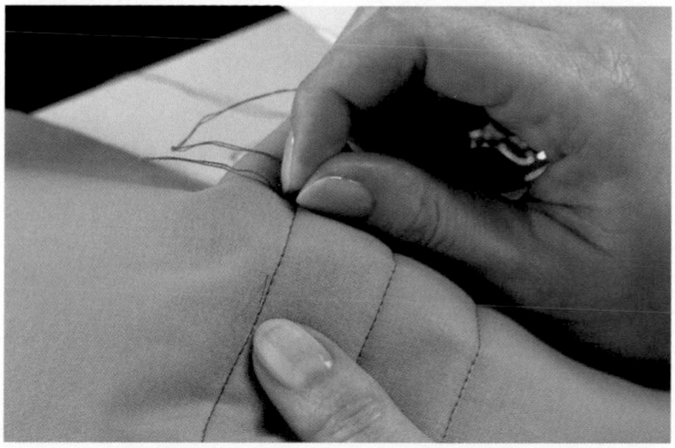

LESSON 4

Outline and Stitch-in-the-Ditch Quilting

Ideally, the amount of quilting in any quilt should be consistent over the entire surface. Stitch-in-the-ditch quilting offers one way to accomplish this easily. It also enables you to quilt from one area to another without a need to duplicate or stitch over another quilting motif. Stitching in the ditch is functional because it holds the layers together securely. And it can enhance the loft because the quilting stitches are tucked into the seams between pieces.

Outline quilting is very easy to do. It can be effective for highlighting or echoing the curved shapes in an appliqué or whole-cloth quilt. It also requires no marking. My lesson will show you how to do both techniques. In a short time, you'll discover how useful they can be for almost any quilt project.

JEANNETTE MUIR

TRY OUTLINE QUILTING ON THESE PROJECTS:

Calico Garden, page 160
Hospitality Table Runner, page 210

TRY STITCH-IN-THE-DITCH QUILTING ON THESE PROJECTS:

Aquatic Realm II, page 128
Charming Log Cabin, page 144
Network, page 192
Autumn Trellis, page 202
September Rose and Bud, page 226

Stopf.+Stickgar

LESSON 4

Outline and Stitch-in-the-Ditch Quilting

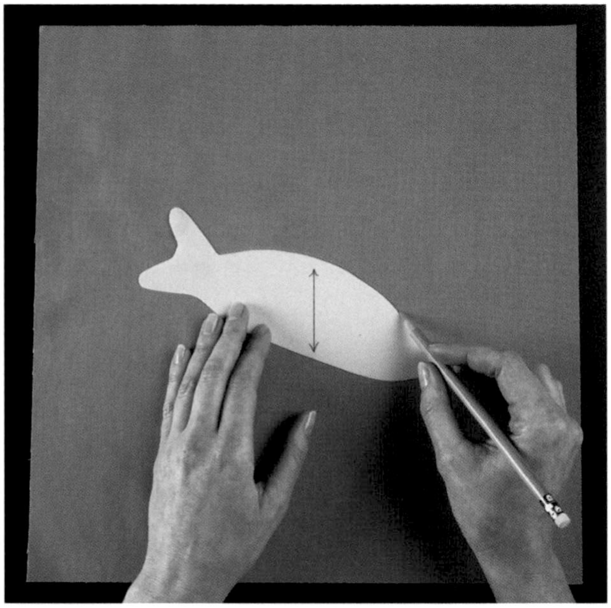

PREPARING A PRACTICE QUILT SANDWICH

For outline quilting: Cut a 14-inch square *each* of a light or medium solid fabric, batting, and backing fabric. Trace the fish pattern on page 48 onto template plastic, and mark the fish pattern on the right side of the fabric, aligning the grain line on the template with the straight grain of the fabric. Layer and baste the practice quilt sandwich. For more information on layering and basting, see page 19. **Note:** The markings in the following photos have been darkened slightly for visual clarity.

Get Set

Presser foot: even feed/walking foot

Top and Bobbin Threads: 100 percent cotton, in a darker color than the fabrics in your practice quilt sandwich

Needle: size 90/14

Stitch: straight

Stitch Width: 0

Stitch Length: 9–10 stitches per inch

Needle Position: centered

Feed Dogs: raised

Top Tension: normal for your machine

OUTLINE QUILTING

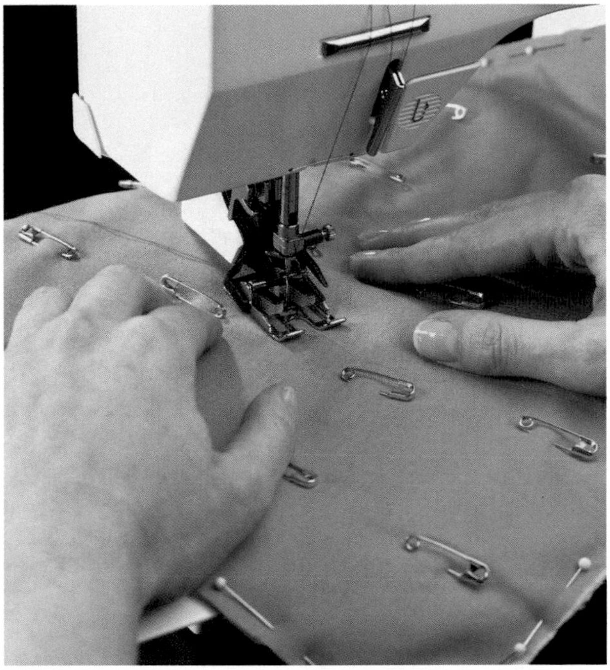

1 Leaving a 5- or 6-inch tail of both top and bottom threads, begin stitching on one side of the fish, using nine to ten stitches per inch. The tails of thread will be buried by hand after the quilting is complete. This method produces invisible beginnings and endings, which is helpful for creating smooth, continuous curves in outline quilting. Keep your arms relaxed and curve your fingers gently on the quilt sandwich on both sides of the presser foot, to avoid stretching or spreading the fabric. If your fingers create tension in front of the needle, your stitches will be too small, and if your fingers pull the fabric from behind the presser foot, they will be too long.

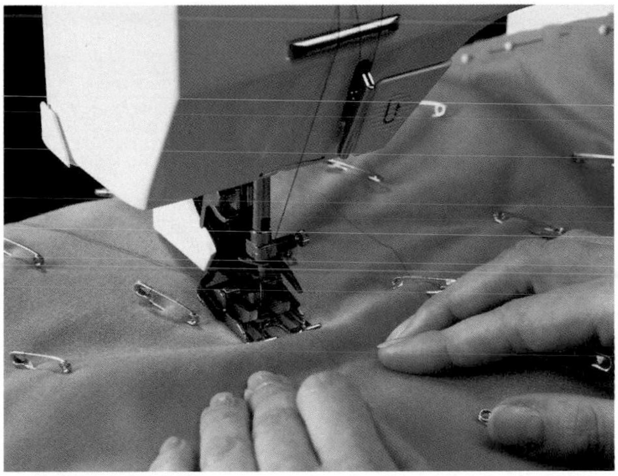

2 Gently push the quilt sandwich directly in front of the presser foot to create a little "speed bump." This will help ease the fabric underneath the needle, letting the walking foot and the feed dogs do the work of guiding the quilt sandwich. Continue keeping your fingers relaxed to avoid distortion or stress on the fabric.

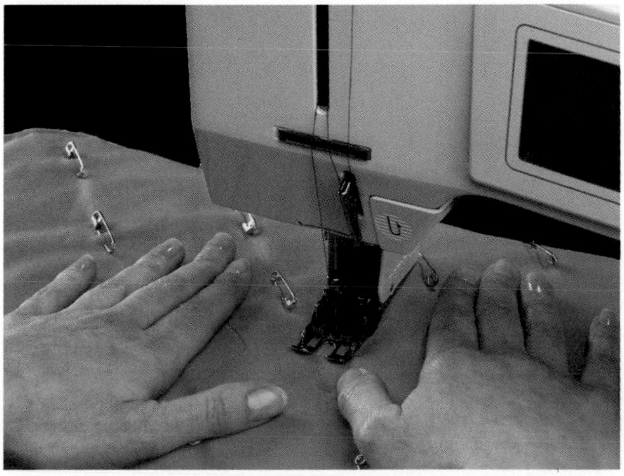

3 As you stitch around the curves on the sides of the fish, think of "putting the fabric where the needle is." For example, on this type of long, shallow curve, you can use the palms of your hands to pivot the fabric, gently moving the quilt sandwich while you continue stitching.

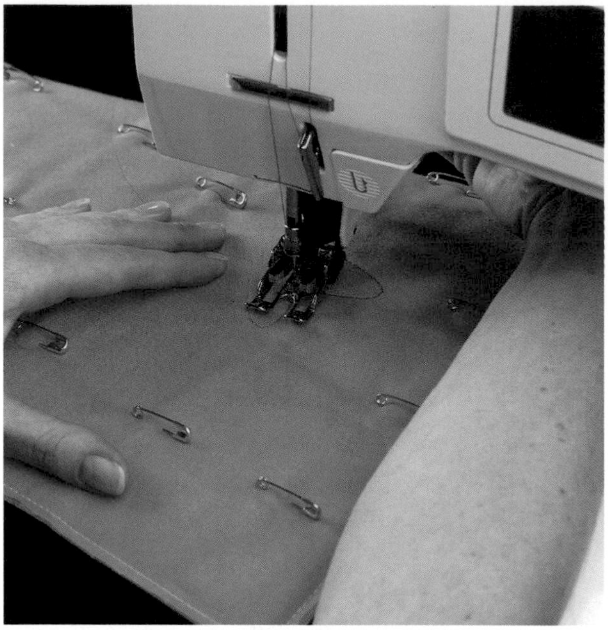

4 For small or tight curves like the tail of the fish, let the sewing machine needle help pivot the fabric. Lower the needle into the fabric, raise the presser foot, and move the quilt sandwich into position for the next curve. Then lower the presser foot and take just one or two stitches. Repeat this process as many times as needed to go around the curve, making sure the needle is lowered into the fabric each time you raise the presser foot. Continue stitching around the outline of the fish. When you reach the point where you started, remove the quilt sandwich from the machine and clip the threads, leaving approximately 6 inches free. Thread a sewing needle and bury all of the thread tails by hand in the layer of batting.

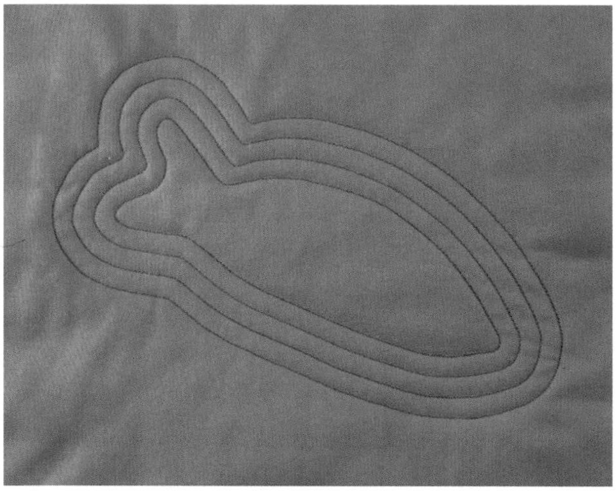

5 To quilt parallel lines around the outline of the fish, line up the edge of the walking foot with the previous line of stitching to space the lines of stitching at even intervals. Repeat Steps 1 through 4, until all of your curved outlines are smooth, with no angles or puckers. Bury the thread tails by threading them through a hand sewing needle and inserting them into the layer of batting for a few inches. Clip the end of each thread close to the quilt top. See photos on page 41 for more guidance on burying the thread ends.

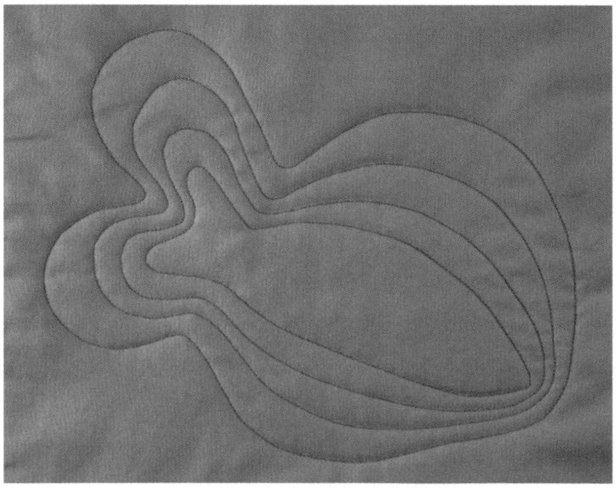

6 For another type of outline quilting, space the stitching lines at uneven intervals around the fish. While this kind of free-form stitching does not need to be marked, a chalk marker works well if you prefer to sew on drawn lines.

PREPARING A PRACTICE QUILT SANDWICH

1 **For stitch-in-the-ditch quilting:** Purchase ⅛ yard *each* of a light, medium, and dark fabric, or select fabrics from your scrap basket. From each fabric, cut a 2 × 23-inch strip. Sew the strips together with ¼-inch seams, as shown in Step 1 of the **Block Assembly Diagram.** Press each seam allowance toward the darker fabric.

2 Measure the width of the combined strips (approximately 5 inches) and cut four squares this size, as shown in Step 2 of the **Block Assembly Diagram.**

3 Sew the four squares together to complete a 9-inch Rail Fence block, as shown in Step 3 of the **Block Assembly Diagram.** Press each of the seam allowances to one side. Cut a 9-inch square of batting and backing fabric, and layer and baste the practice quilt sandwich with the Rail Fence block on top. For more information on layering and basting, see page 19.

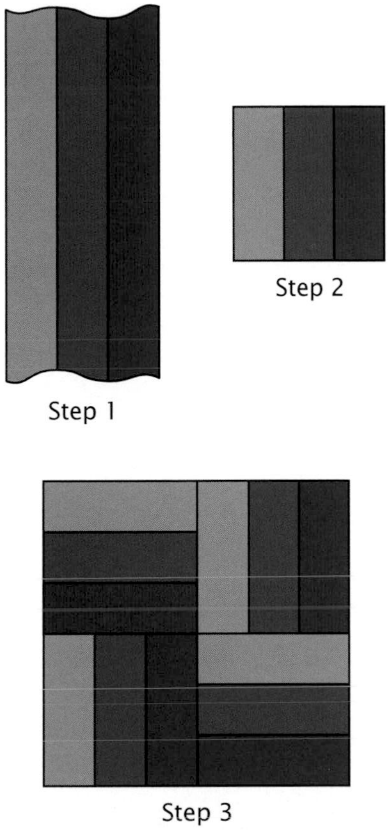

Block Assembly Diagram

STITCH-IN-THE-DITCH QUILTING

1 Lower the sewing machine needle into one of the seams at the outside edge of the Rail Fence block, and anchor the beginning stitches with one of the methods from Lesson 3. Stitch in the ditch of this seam on the side without the seam allowance. Sew from the edge of the block to the center of the block. Remember to form a speed bump to allow the walking foot and feed dogs to work together in guiding the fabric under the needle.

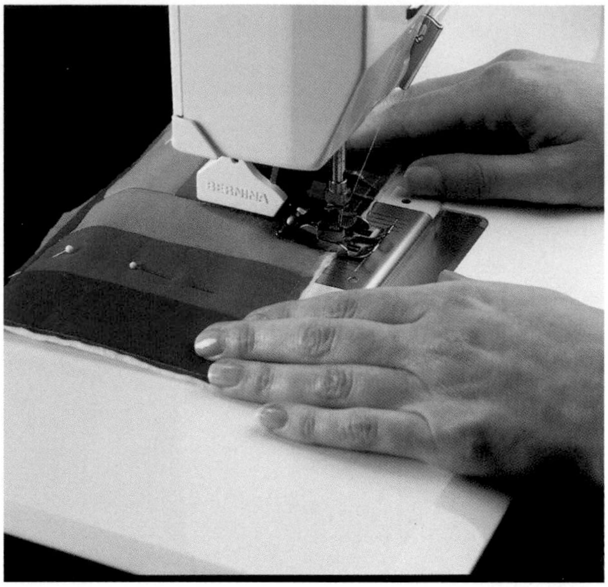

2 Lower the needle, raise the presser foot, and pivot the block 90 degrees while the needle is down. Continue stitching along the next ditch until you reach the other edge of the block. End this line of stitching with one of the starting and stopping methods from Lesson 3.

3 Quilt in the remaining ditches of the Rail Fence block in the same manner, beginning and ending each line of stitches with one of the methods from Lesson 3. **Note:** You can quilt in the ditches of rails of the same color fabric continuously across a block or an entire quilt, as I have done, or simply quilt in the ditch of each and every seam, without regard to the progression of the colors in the rails.

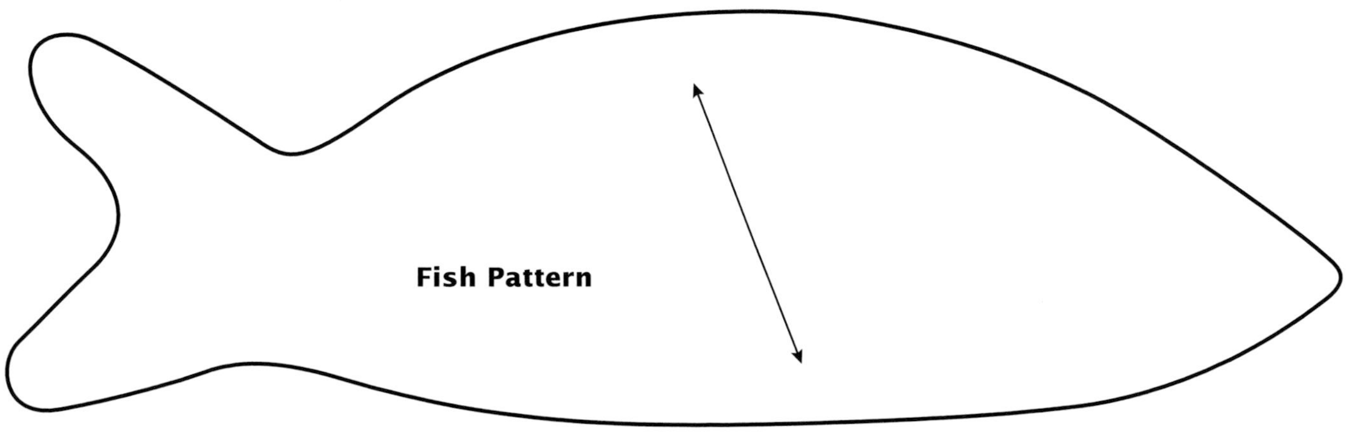

Great Ideas!

USE RUST-PROOF SAFETY PINS

I like to use 1-inch brass safety pins when I baste a quilt sandwich. My preference is for the brand sold by Crazy Ladies and Friends, Department R, 1604 Santa Monica Boulevard, Santa Monica, CA 90404 (phone: 310-828-3122). I think they're easier to fasten than many others I have tried.

TIPS FOR BETTER TENSION

For each of the practice quilt sandwiches in my lesson, I stitched around the outside edges. This is a good place to check the tension on your sewing machine, before you start to quilt. If a tiny pinprick of bobbin thread shows through to the top, loosen the top tension slightly on your machine just until the bobbin thread disappears. If the top thread shows through on the back side of the quilt and adjusting the machine tension does not help the appearance of your stitches, use the same thread color on both top and bottom to help disguise slight irregularities.

THREAD VARIATIONS

Try practicing stitch-in-the-ditch quilting on a block made with print fabrics. This will allow you to compare how it looks on both solids and prints. And when you're quilting a multicolored quilt, try using clear monofilament thread to make your stitches nearly invisible. Or change the top thread color as often as you like to keep it inconspicuous. And you can create interesting effects by using a multicolored thread that echoes the colors in your fabrics. While this type of thread is not truly invisible, it blends easily into many color combinations.

KWIK, KLIP IT!

There are a number of products available now to make the basting process easier, such as the Kwik Klip tool, which has little ridges that will hold the point of a safety pin above the surface of a quilt while you flip it closed. For more information about the Kwik Klip tool, contact Paula Jean Creations, 1601 Fulton Avenue, Sacramento, CA 95825 (or call 916-488-3480).

LESSON 5

Channel Quilting and Crosshatching

Channel quilting allows for easing in any fullness in a quilt and is especially useful for filling in small background areas. Straight or angled quilted channels make beautiful accents for appliqué shapes.

Crosshatched grids make very effective backgrounds for curved shapes in an appliqué quilt, and they can also add movement and balance to graphic, contemporary quilts. Crosshatching also requires minimal marking and is quick to quilt, which makes it easier to complete quilts in a minimum amount of time. My lesson offers several types of crosshatching and channel quilting. With a bit of practice, you may find them so enjoyable that you'll want to design your own unique patterns. As you try out the various grids and channels that follow, enjoy the process of quilting, and keep in mind that only practice makes perfect.

SHERRY SUNDAY

TRY CHANNEL QUILTING ON THESE PROJECTS:

Garden of Hearts, page 136
A Rose Garden, page 180
Amish Wall Quilt, page 218

TRY CROSSHATCHING ON THESE PROJECTS:

Aquatic Realm II, page 128
Calico Garden, page 160
A Rose Garden, page 180
Amish Wall Quilt, page 218

LESSON 5

Channel Quilting and Crosshatching

PREPARING A PRACTICE QUILT SANDWICH

For channel quilting and crosshatching: To prepare a practice quilt sandwich, cut a 14-inch square of light or medium solid fabric for the top. Cut a 14-inch square of batting and another 14-inch square of backing fabric. Place the backing fabric wrong side up on a flat surface, and lay the square of batting on top of it. Add the top fabric right side up over the batting. Pin-baste the three layers together by placing rust-proof quilter's safety pins at 3- to 4-inch intervals over the surface of the practice quilt sandwich, as shown in the photos on page 19. Make as few or as many practice quilt sandwiches as you like for practicing the techniques in this lesson. If you make more than one, consider using different types of batting in them, so you can begin to develop your own likes and dislikes while you stitch. **Note:** The markings in the following photos have been darkened slightly for visual clarity.

Get Set

Presser Foot: even feed/walking foot or a straight-stitch foot

Top and Bobbin Thread: 60-weight embroidery cotton, in a darker color than the fabrics in your practice quilt sandwich

Needle: size 80/12

Stitch: straight

Stitch Width: 0

Stitch Length: 10–12 stitches per inch

Needle Position: centered

Feed Dogs: raised

Top Tension: normal for your machine

CHANNEL QUILTING

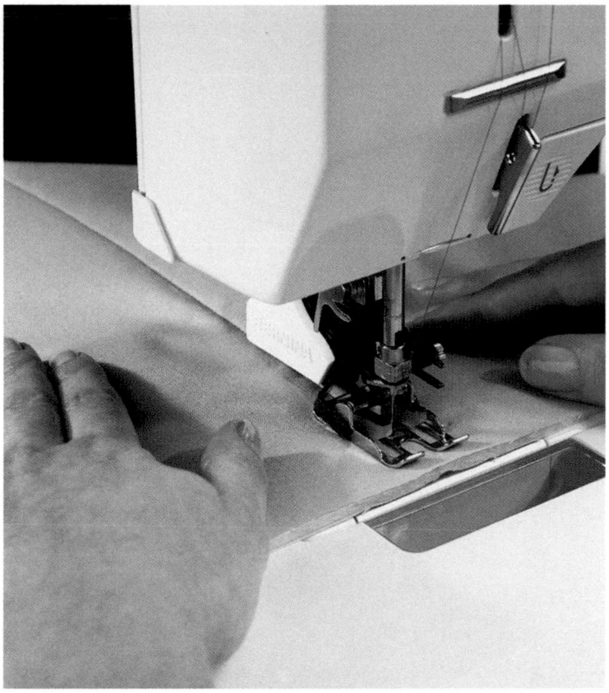

1 Use a quilter's see-through ruler and a Hera, a quilter's silver pencil, or other removable marker to mark a line across the center of the practice quilt sandwich. Place the quilt sandwich under the presser foot on this line, anchor the beginning threads with one of the techniques from Lesson 3, and stitch across the quilt sandwich, lining up the marked line with the needle before you begin to stitch. Don't hold onto the edges of the quilt sandwich or grip the fabric tightly; simply curve your fingers and place them gently on the quilt sandwich, allowing the feed dogs to do most of the work of moving the fabric. Anchor the ending stitches in the same manner. For more information on stopping and starting, see Lesson 3.

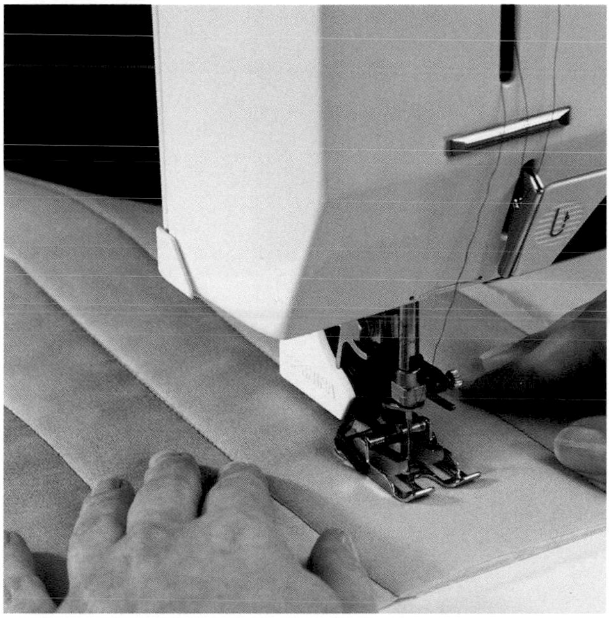

2 Mark and quilt another line of stitching parallel to the first one, approximately ¼ inch in from the edge of the fabric. Then mark a third line at the midpoint between the first two lines. Mark two more lines, each midway between this center line and the previous lines of stitching, for a total of five equally spaced lines in this half of the quilt sandwich. Quilt across all of these lines. If the fabric becomes distorted between the lines, use your thumbs and middle fingers to keep it evenly distributed as you stitch.

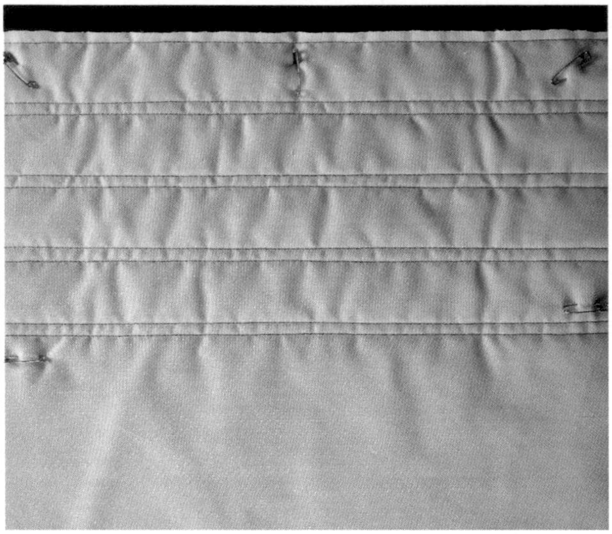

3 To create straight channels, do a line of stitches ¼ inch to the right of each of these lines.

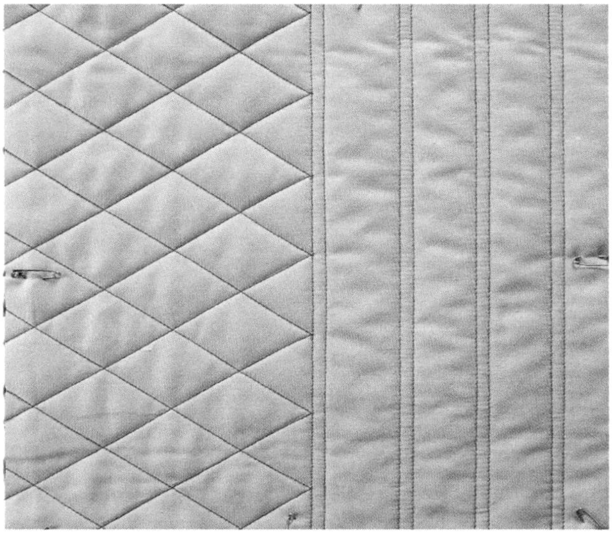

4 Now for some angled channels. In the other half of your practice quilt sandwich, place the 60-degree line on the quilter's see-through ruler at the center point, so that it is aligned with the center line of stitching. Mark this line from the center out to the edge of the fabric, and mark parallel lines at 1½-inch intervals on both sides of this line. Then rotate the quilt sandwich, and mark 60-degree angled lines that go in the opposite direction. Quilt all of these marked lines, anchoring the beginning and ending threads with one of the techniques from Lesson 3.

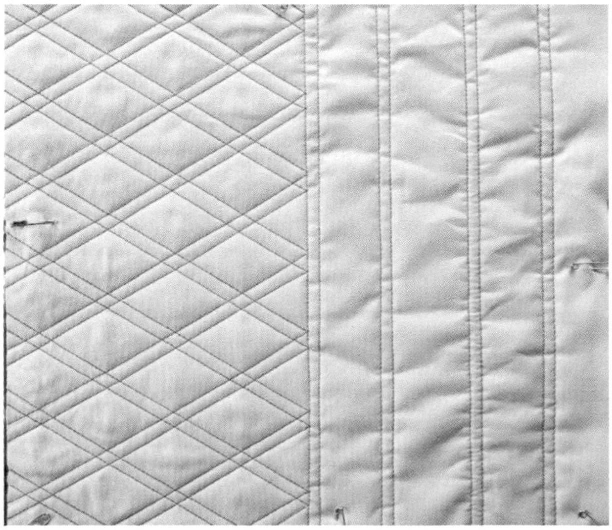

5 In the same manner as for straight channels, quilt a line of stitches ¼ inch to the right of each of these 60-degree lines. This creates a series of angled channels spaced at 1-inch intervals.

TRAPUNTO CORDING

You'll need a 5-inch trapunto needle with a blunt tip, a skein of soft, white bulky-weight yarn, and the practice quilt sandwich you have just completed.

1 Thread the trapunto needle with about 18 inches of the white yarn, and turn the practice quilt sandwich to the wrong side. Insert the needle into one of the straight channels, between the backing fabric and the batting, starting about 3 inches in from the edge of the quilt sandwich. (Although it is possible to insert the needle at the edge of the quilt sandwich, inserting it at this point approximates what it is like to work on a larger quilt.) Guide the needle as far as possible into the channel and bring it out again.

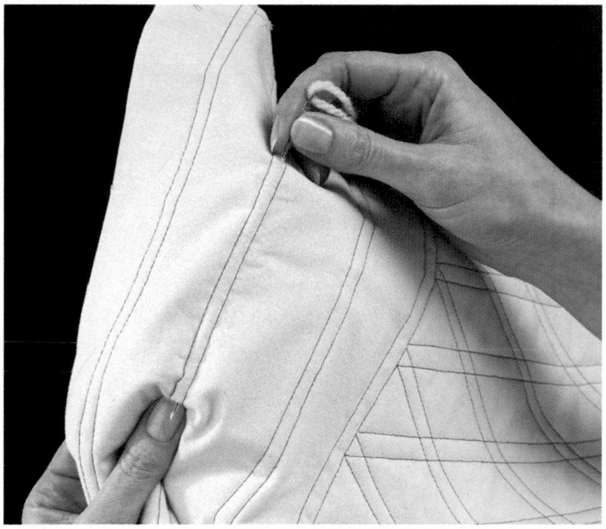

2 Insert the needle into the same hole again and continue sliding it through the channel, allowing a slight amount of yarn to remain visible above the backing fabric. This will keep the tension on the yarn even and keep it from stretching, so that when you reach the end of the channel and clip it, there will be enough yarn to fill the entire channel. When you bring the needle out at the edge of the quilt sandwich, tug gently on the yarn to make it disappear inside the channel, and clip the ends even with the edges of the quilt sandwich.

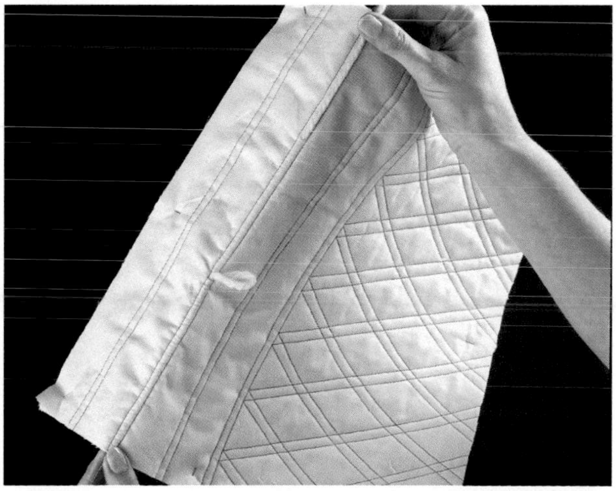

3 To hide the small holes left in the backing by the needle, use the tip of the trapunto needle and gently push the threads of fabric into place around each opening.

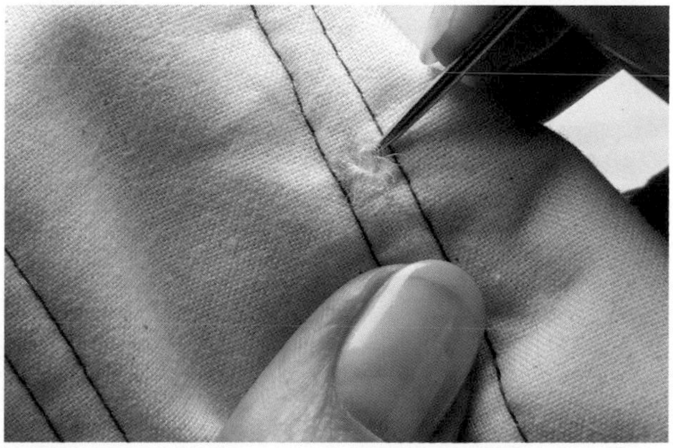

CROSSHATCHING

Prepare a separate practice quilt sandwich for each of the following techniques: 90-degree, 45-degree, and 60-degree grids. This will enable you to cover a larger space with each type of grid.

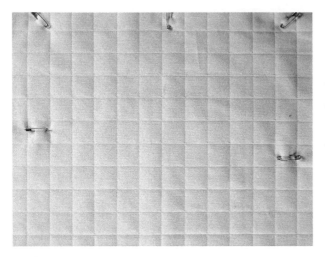

GRIDS

1 Use a quilter's see-through ruler and a Hera, a quilter's silver pencil, or other removable marker to mark a line across the center of another practice quilt sandwich. Move the ruler 1 inch to the right and mark a second line. Repeat this process until the quilt sandwich is filled with parallel lines spaced at 1-inch intervals. Then turn the quilt sandwich and mark parallel lines at 90-degree angles.

2 Quilt across the center of the quilt sandwich, anchoring the beginning and ending threads with one of the methods from Lesson 3. Turn the quilt sandwich 90 degrees and quilt through the center in the opposite direction. Then quilt the outermost line on all four sides of the quilt sandwich. This stabilizes the entire surface, making it easy to quilt in any portion of the quilt sandwich without creating puckers or distortions in the fabric.

3 Starting on any side of the quilt sandwich, quilt the line that lies midway between the center line of stitches and the outermost line of stitches on that side. Then turn the quilt 90 degrees and repeat this step. Work around all four sides in the same manner, turning the quilt sandwich after each line of stitches. This helps to ease any fullness in the fabric evenly over the entire quilt sandwich.

4 Follow the same process of quilting and rotating the quilt sandwich until all of the remaining lines are quilted. When you have finished, your 90-degree crosshatched grids will be even and smooth, without any puckers in the fabric.

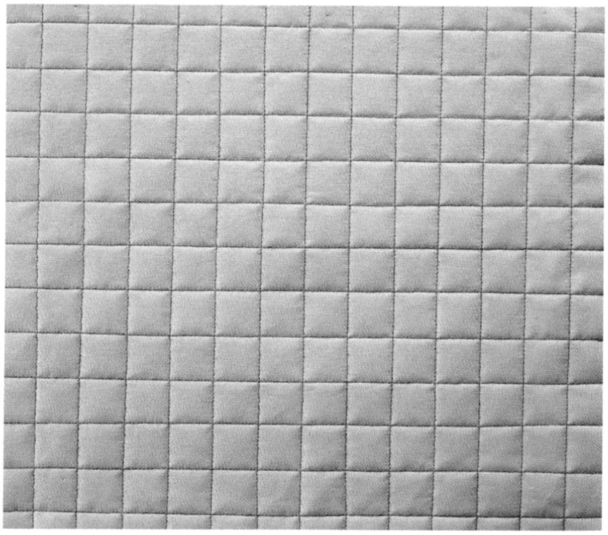

5 To quilt 45-degree crosshatched grids, the marking and stitching process is the same. The only thing that changes is the angle of the lines. To mark a 60-degree grid, line up the 60-degree line on a quilter's see-through ruler with the lower edge of a practice quilt sandwich, and mark lines in opposite directions. Quilt as shown in Steps 2 and 3.

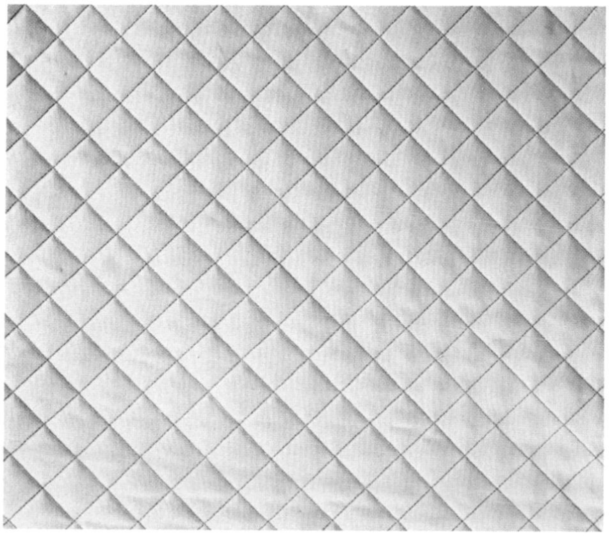

LINES THAT MEET MOTIFS

For this technique, I recommend using an appliqué block as the top layer of your practice quilt sandwich. You may choose any block design you like or use the templates for my block, which are provided on page 59. Refer to the letters on the pieces in the **Block Assembly Diagram** for the appliqué sequence.

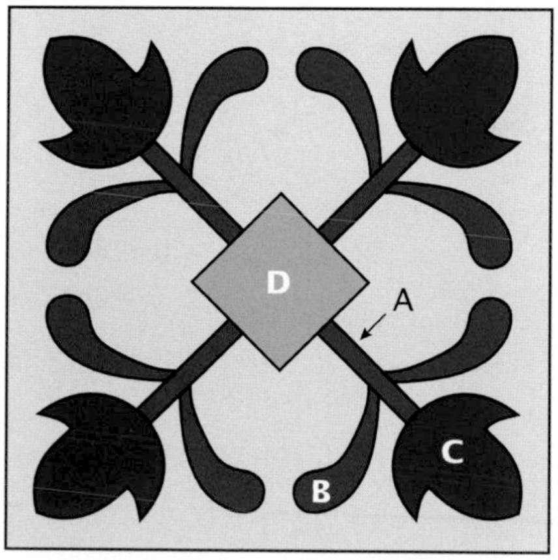

Block Assembly Diagram

1 Outline quilt around each of the appliqué shapes on the practice quilt sandwich. For more information on outline quilting, see Lesson 4. With a see-through ruler and a Hera or quilter's silver pencil, mark a 45-degree crosshatched grid as the background for the appliqué shapes.

2 Starting at the edge of the quilt sandwich, quilt any one of the 45-degree lines to within ⅜ inch of the first appliqué shape you encounter. Adjust the stitch length to 20 stitches per inch and quilt up to the outline stitching around the appliqué shape.

3 Lift the presser foot and cross over the appliqué shape, pulling the threads gently. Lower the presser foot on the other side of the appliqué shape and bring the bobbin thread to the top by taking a single stitch. Quilt a few more short stitches on this side of the motif, and then lengthen the stitch length to 10 to 12 stitches per inch. Continue quilting in the same manner, crossing over each appliqué shape as you come to it.

4 Quilt each of the remaining background grid lines in the same way. All "crossover" threads can be clipped close to the surface of the quilt sandwich after you are finished quilting.

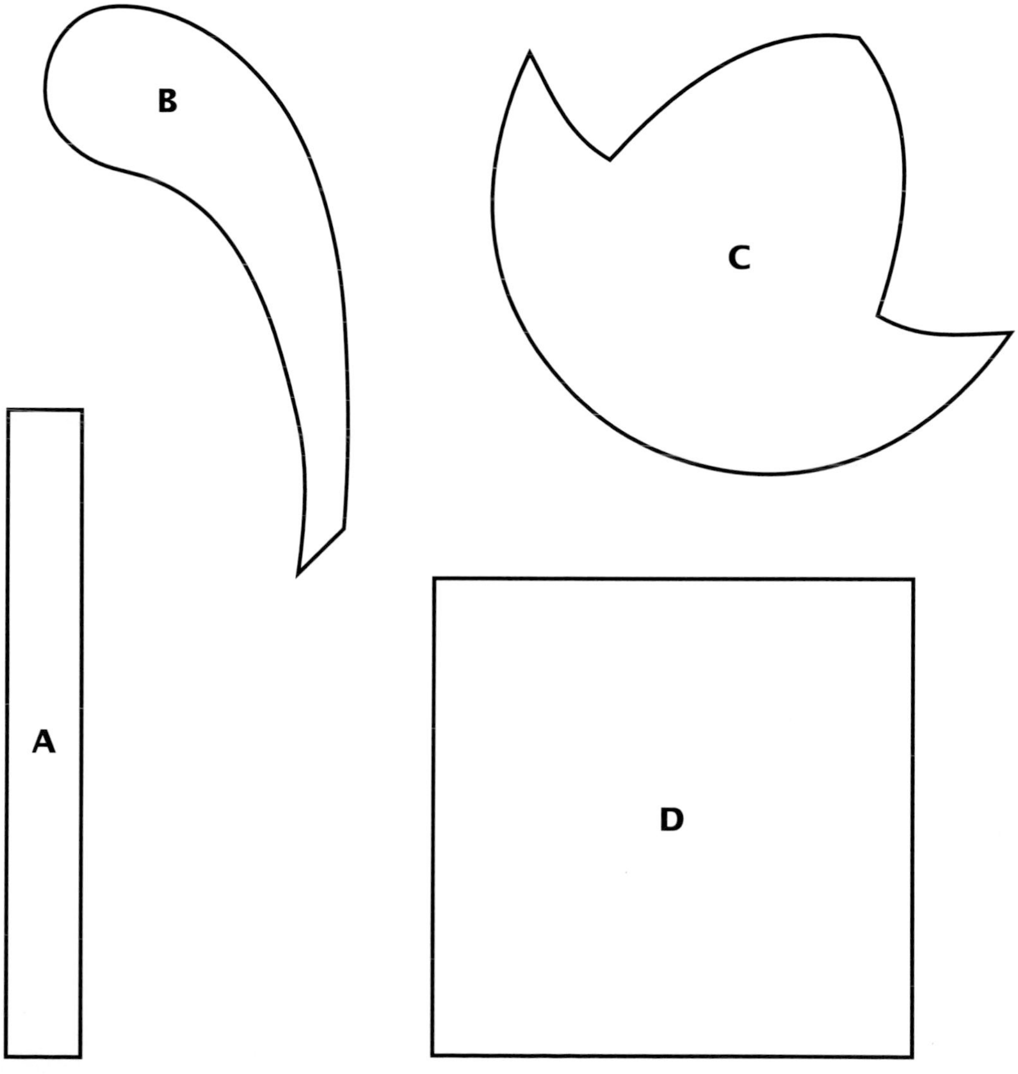

LESSON 6

Machine-Guided Curves and Points

Precision and accuracy are two of the biggest benefits of machine-guided quilting because the presser foot and feed dogs work together to produce even, consistent quilting stitches.

Designs with a lot of straight lines or gentle curves are particularly suited to machine-guided quilting because there is no need to turn a quilt frequently to stitch them. Flowers, feathered wreaths, circles, and motifs such as birds and fruits are better suited to free-motion quilting, where the feed dogs are inoperative.

My lesson is divided into two sections: the first on quilting machine-guided curves and the second on achieving perfect points. Think of these exercises as doodles, and enjoy stitching and watching your quilting skills improve at the same time.

JEANNETTE MUIR

TRY MACHINE-GUIDED CURVES AND POINTS ON THESE PROJECTS:

Aquatic Realm II, page 128

Network, page 192

LESSON 6

Machine-Guided Curves and Points

PREPARING A PRACTICE QUILT SANDWICH

1 **For machine-guided curves:** Cut a 14-inch square of a light or medium solid fabric for the top and 14-inch squares of batting and light fabric for the backing. With a chalk or mechanical pencil, mark a straight line 3¼ inches in from the edge on each side of the top fabric. Mark a diagonal line in each corner, going from the point where the guidelines cross each other outward to the corner of the fabric. **Note:** The markings in the following photos have been darkened slightly for visual clarity.

Get Set

Presser Foot: even feed/walking foot

Top and Bobbin Threads: 100 percent cotton in a color that is darker than the fabrics in your quilt sandwich.

Needle: size 90/14

Stitch: straight

Stitch Width: 0

Stitch Length: 9–10 stitches per inch

Needle Position: centered

Feed Dogs: raised

Top Tension: normal for your machine

2 With a permanent marker, trace Template A from page 69 onto template plastic or cardboard, and cut out the middle section, leaving that area open. Fold the top fabric in half in each direction to find the midpoint on each side and lightly finger press each fold. Place the template at the center on one side of the fabric, so that the straight edge of the template is even with the edge of the fabric and the vertical dashed lines on the template lie on the fold at the center of the fabric. With a chalk pencil or mechanical pencil, mark around each of the three curved edges of the template.

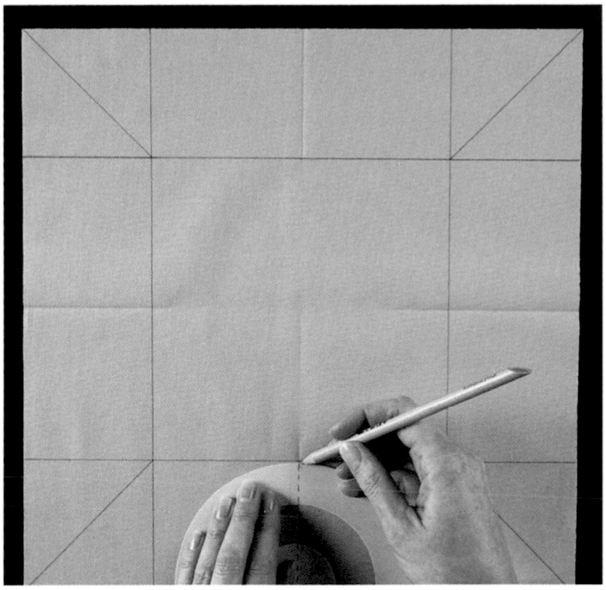

3 Continue using the template to mark around all four sides of the fabric, stopping wherever the lines meet the diagonal lines marked at the corners. To mark the very last curved line at each corner, slide the template over to one side, so that its outermost curve meets the smallest inner curve on the previously marked motif. Mark around the template, stopping at the diagonal line in the corner.

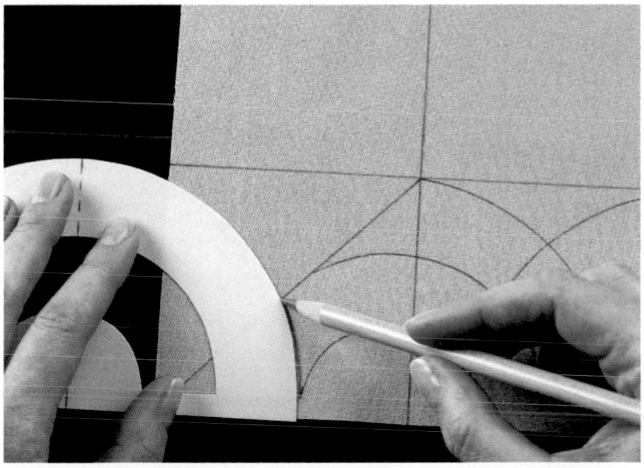

4 Layer and baste your practice quilt sandwich, spacing the pins evenly. For more information on layering and basting, see page 19.

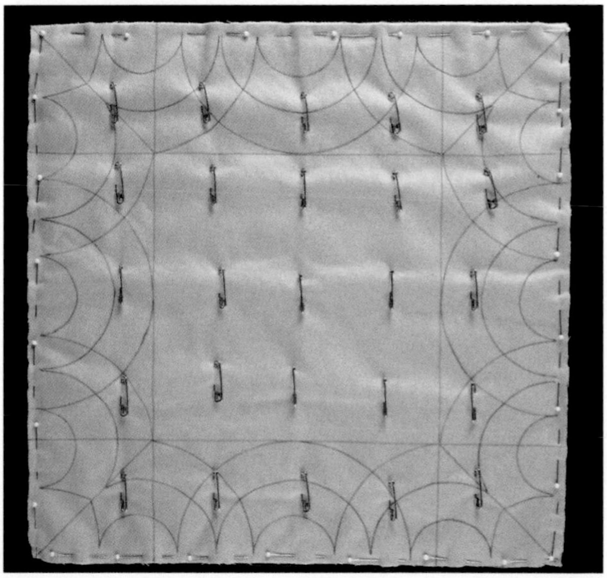

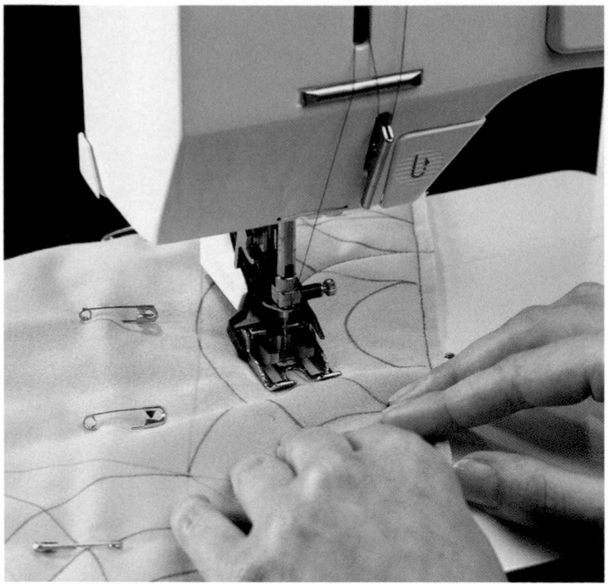

MACHINE-GUIDED CURVES

1 Place the presser foot at the center on one side of the practice quilt sandwich on the middle curve of the quilting motif. Anchor the threads at the edge of the quilt sandwich with one of the methods from Lesson 3. (On an actual project, the stitches at the edge of a quilt would be covered by binding.) Quilt exactly on the marked lines of the middle curve, gently pushing a little "speed bump" of fabric directly in front of the presser foot as you work. This will allow the presser foot and the feed dogs to work together, guiding the quilt sandwich smoothly through the sewing machine. Remember to unfasten and remove the safety pins approximately 2 inches before you come to them. Keep the quilt sandwich relaxed, without any distortion or stress on it, especially at the location of the needle. If too much finger tension is put in front of the needle, the result will be stitches that are too small. Pulling on the fabric from behind the presser foot will create stitches that are long and uneven.

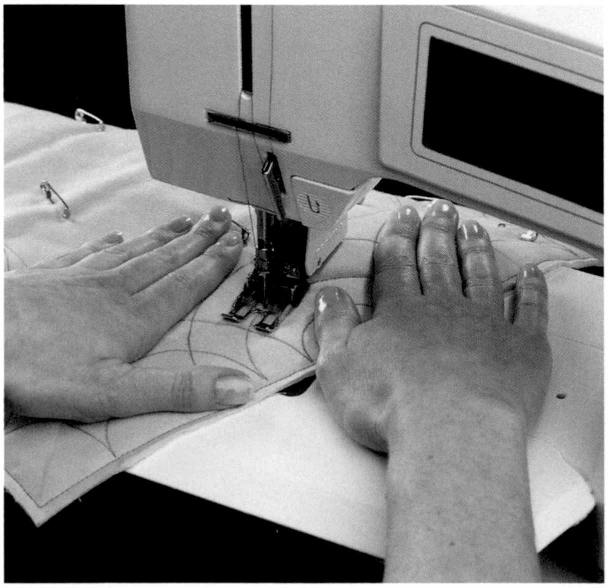

2 Because a sewing machine needle does not know that you want it to quilt curves, it's helpful to think in terms of "putting the fabric where the needle is." That makes it easy to maneuver long, shallow curves by simply using the palms of your hands to pivot the quilt sandwich gently, while you continue stitching.

3 Finish the line of stitching around the middle curve in the same way as you began, and remove the quilt sandwich from the machine. Check to see that your curves are smooth and even, with no angles or puckers. Then quilt the middle curve on the next motif in the same manner, but do not remove the quilt sandwich from the machine when you reach the edge of the fabric. Instead, lift the presser foot, pivot the fabric, and place the next curved line in position to stitch, and continue. You can quilt the middle curves of each motif around the entire quilt sandwich before ending at the first line you stitched.

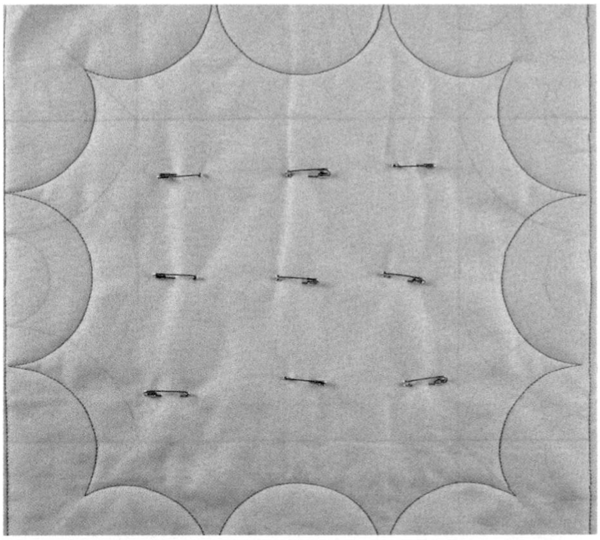

4 Use the sewing machine needle to help you pivot the quilt sandwich as you stitch around the small, inner curves. When you need to change the position of the quilt sandwich in order to keep stitching on a curve, simply stop, raise the presser foot, and move the quilt sandwich slightly, so that the needle is in position to continue stitching around the marked line. Then lower the presser foot, and take just one or two stitches. Repeat this step as often as necessary to quilt around very tight curves, remembering to keep the needle lowered whenever you raise the presser foot.

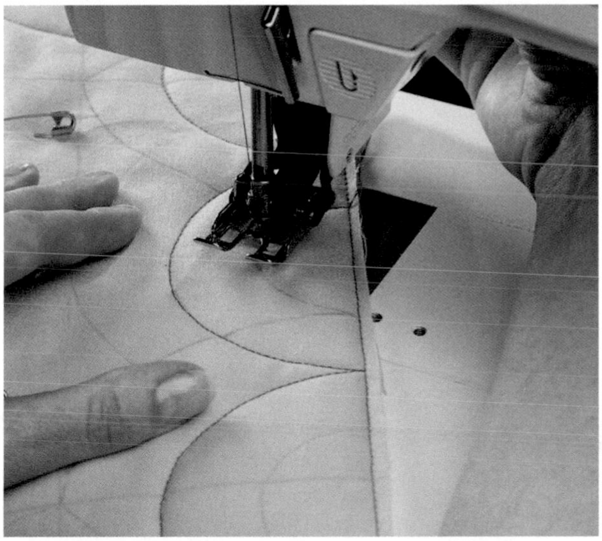

5 Quilt all of the remaining inner and outer curves individually.

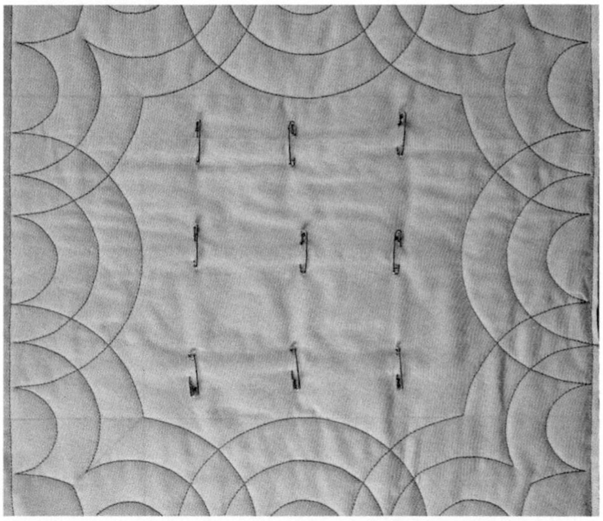

PREPARING A PRACTICE QUILT SANDWICH

For machine-guided points: The top of this quilt sandwich consists of a 9½-inch pieced quilt block made of one light and one dark solid fabric. You will need approximately ⅛ yard of *each* fabric to make this block and 10-inch squares of batting and backing fabric. The instructions are for rotary-cutting all of the pieces; ¼-inch seam allowances are included.

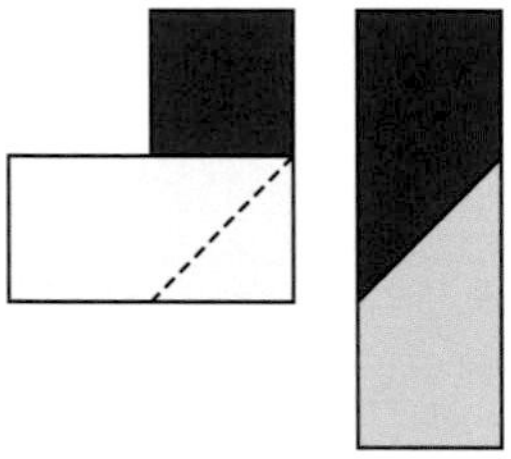
Step 3

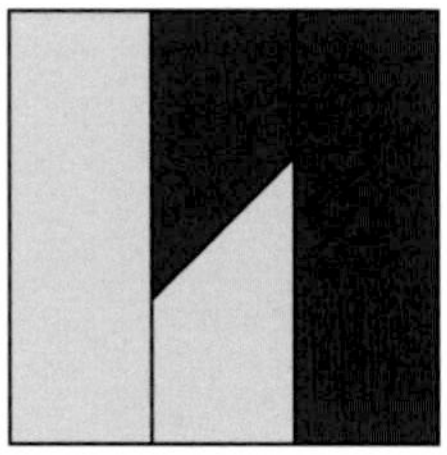
Step 4

Step 5

Block Assembly Diagram

1 From *each* of the light and dark solids, cut four 2 × 5-inch strips, for a total of eight strips.

2 From each fabric, cut four 2 × 3½-inch rectangles.

3 Place a light 2 × 3½-inch rectangle on top of a dark 3½-inch rectangle. Mark a seam line to join the two pieces at a 45-degree angle. Sew this seam, as shown in Step 3 of the **Block Assembly Diagram,** and trim the seam allowance to ¼ inch. Press the seam allowance toward the darker fabric. Repeat this step with the remaining three pairs of light and dark strips.

4 Sew one of the light/dark pieced strips between a light 2 × 5-inch strip and a dark 2 × 5-inch strip, as shown in Step 4. Repeat to make three more units like this one.

5 Sew the four pieced units together, rotating the direction of each unit, to complete the pieced block, as shown in Step 5.

6 With a permanent pen, trace Templates B and C on page 68 onto template plastic. Using Template B, mark a curved line from the center outward in each of the long light strips, referring to the **Block Assembly Diagram.** Using Template C, mark a curved line diagonally from the center outward in each of the short light pieces, as shown in the **Directional Stitching Diagram.** Layer and baste a practice quilt sandwich with this block as the top. For more information on layering and basting, see page 19.

MACHINE-GUIDED POINTS

1 Starting at the center on one side of the quilt sandwich, anchor a few beginning stitches with one of the methods from Lesson 3. Following the arrows in the **Directional Stitching Diagram,** stitch in the ditch of the center seam from point 1 across the entire block to point 2. For more information on stitching in the ditch, see Lesson 4. Lower the needle into the quilt sandwich exactly at point 2, and stop.

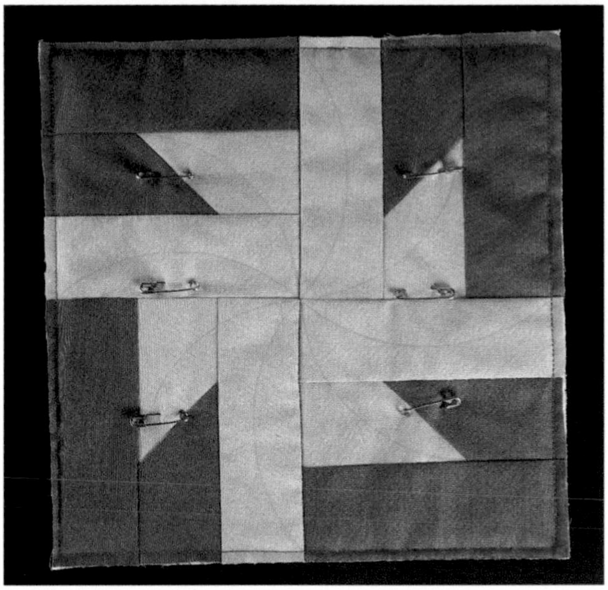

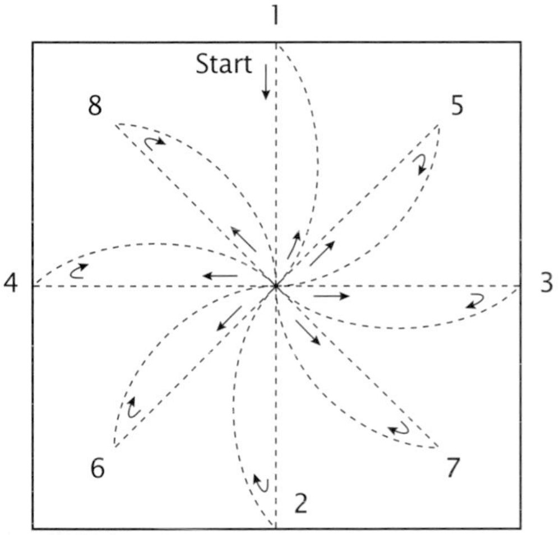

Directional Stitching Diagram

2 While the needle is down, use both hands to pivot the entire quilt sandwich sharply at the point, so that the needle is in position to stitch the next line on the **Directional Stitching Diagram.** Lower the presser foot and stitch the curved line from point 2 back to the center of the block, and stop with the needle down. Occasionally, when pivoting at a sharp angle such as this, the top thread on your sewing machine can become loose, creating a skipped stitch as you begin to stitch away from the pivot point. If this happens, take one stitch backward at the point, before continuing to stitch the next line of quilting stitches.

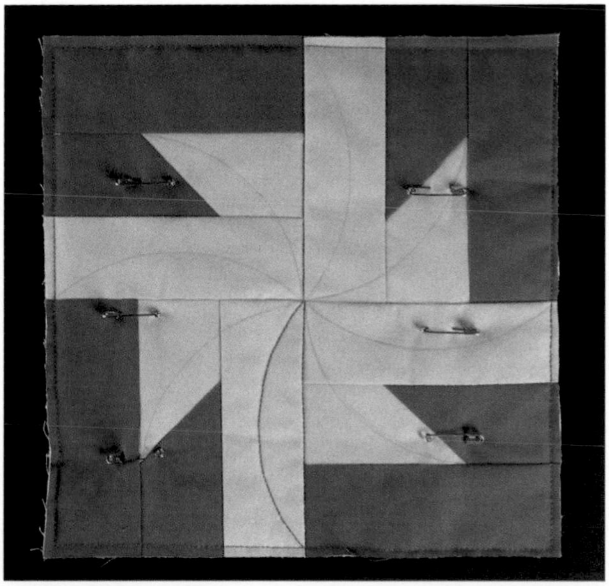

3 Continue to follow the arrows in the **Directional Stitching Diagram** on page 67, and use the palms of your hands to guide the fabric gently as you stitch across to point 3. Stop with the needle down at this point, raise the presser foot, pivot the quilt sandwich in the same manner as before, and stitch on the curved line to return to the center point. Stop with the needle down, raise the presser foot, and pivot the quilt sandwich to stitch straight across in the ditch of the seam, to point 4. Stop with the needle down at this point.

4 Continue stitching in the same manner, pivoting the quilt sandwich sharply at each point in the design and stitching in numerical order, until the design is completely quilted. The final line of stitching stops at the same point where you began. End your line of stitching with one of the methods from Lesson 3. After you're finished, stand back and admire your smoothly quilted gentle curves and sharply angled points.

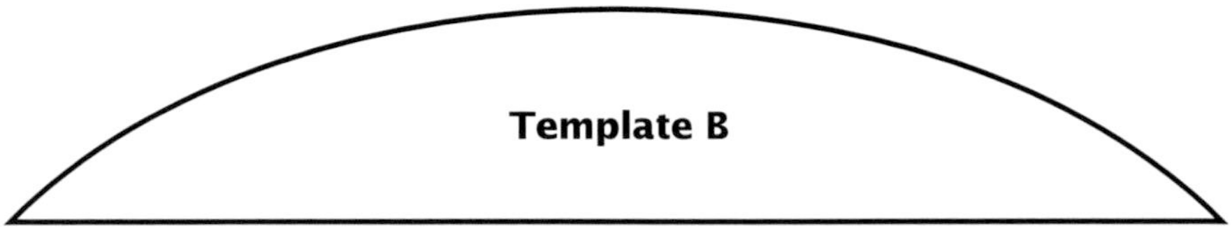

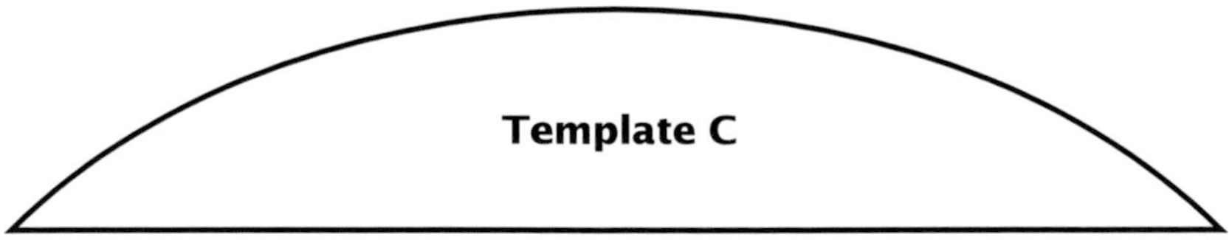

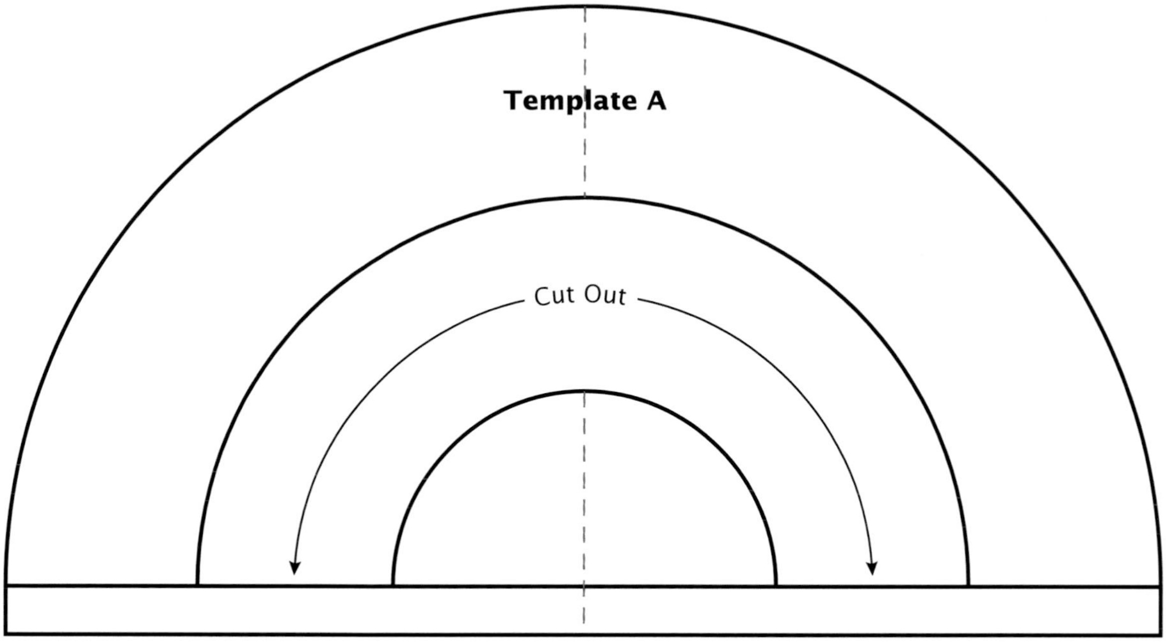

Great Ideas!

CORNER TABLES OFFER SUPPORT

My sewing machine is set into a corner console table that has a well in it, so that the throat plate is even with the surface around it. This allows me to sit high enough above the needle to look down on my work and lean on my elbows as much as possible. Another benefit is that a large quilt does not shift or fall onto the floor. And the stitching process is more relaxing, too.

CHANGE THROAT PLATE FOR FEWER PUCKERS

If you get puckers as you quilt, try using a single-stitch throat plate, which has a much smaller opening than a regular throat plate. Keep the needle in the center position whenever you use this type of throat plate to avoid breaking needles.

DECIDE WHEN TO MARK

The order in which you mark, layer, and baste a quilt sandwich is a personal preference. I like to mark most of my quilting designs after the quilt has been layered and pin-basted, so that the quilting designs do not get smudged; but if you prefer, it's perfectly fine to mark a quilt top before layering and basting the quilt sandwich.

LESSON 7

Free-Motion Curves and Points

Free-motion quilting is a lot like drawing with a pencil. It gives you the ability to stitch in any direction you like and "sketch" a design with your sewing machine needle and thread. The beauty of free-motion quilting lies in its very unpredictability. For example, lines of echo quilting around a heart shape remind me of ripples in a clear lake, since the lines are spaced irregularly. It's nice to strive for consistent free-motion stitches, but the overall effect of a design is more important than the regularity of each quilted line.

Learning to control the movement of the quilt sandwich to create an even stitch length is the key to mastering free-motion quilting. In my lesson, we will concentrate first on becoming comfortable with the all-over movement of a quilt sandwich and then focus on stitch length. After about 20 minutes of practice, you may find that free-motion quilting is becoming one of your favorite techniques.

ANNE COLVIN

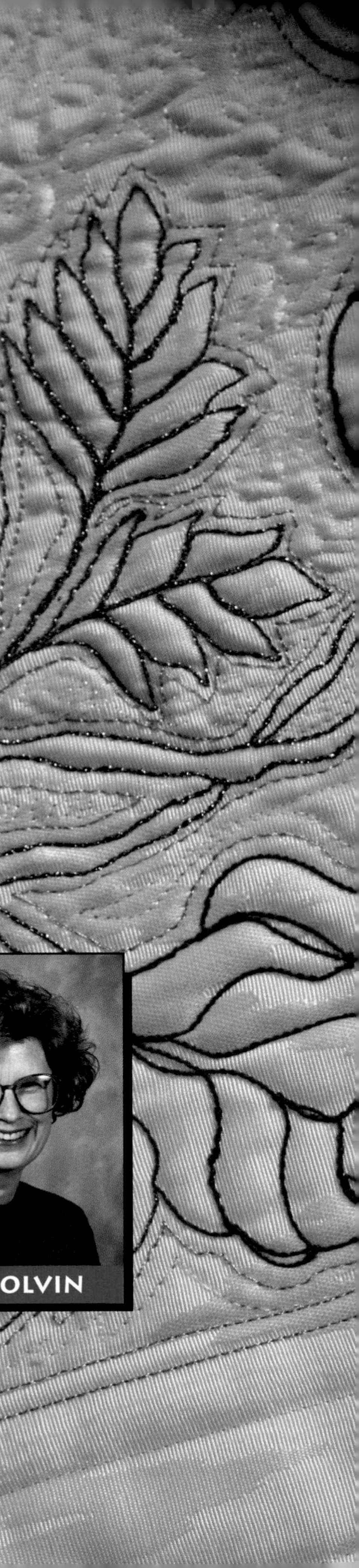

TRY FREE-MOTION CURVES AND POINTS ON THESE PROJECTS:

Garden of Hearts, page 136
A Quilted Vest, page 152
Calico Garden, page 160
Illusion #13, page 170
A Rose Garden, page 180
Autumn Trellis, page 202
Hospitality Table Runner, page 210
Amish Wall Quilt, page 218
September Rose and Bud, page 226

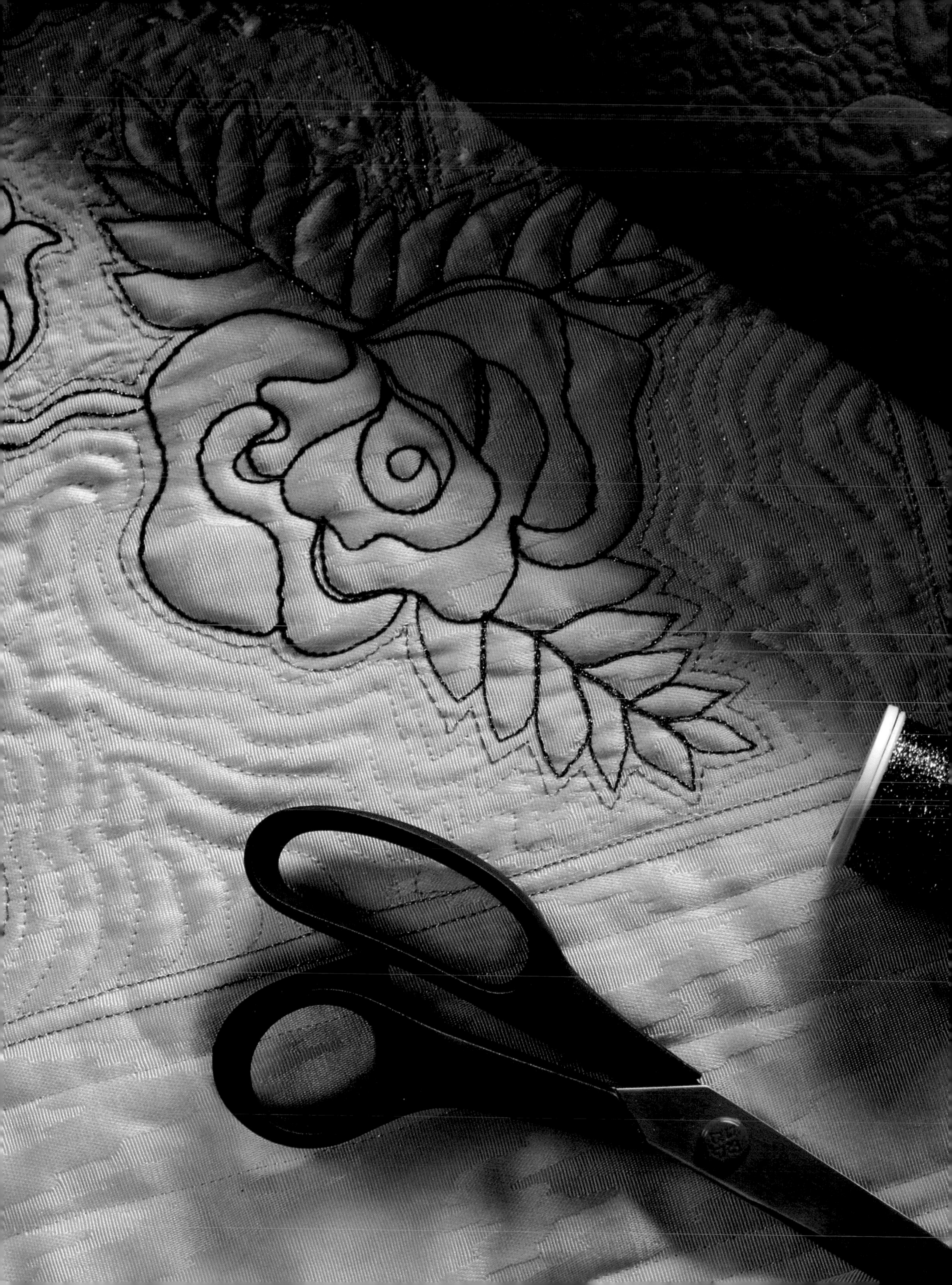

LESSON 7

Free-Motion Curves and Points

PREPARING A PRACTICE QUILT SANDWICH

For the warm-up: To prepare a practice quilt sandwich, cut a 14-inch square of light or medium solid fabric for the top. Cut a 14-inch square of batting and another 14-inch square of backing fabric. Place the backing fabric wrong side up on a flat surface, and lay the square of batting on top of it. Add the top fabric right side up over the batting. Pin-baste the three layers together by placing rust-proof quilter's safety pins at 3- to 4-inch intervals over the surface of the practice quilt sandwich, as shown in the photos on page 19. Make as few or as many practice quilt sandwiches as you like for practicing the techniques in this lesson. If you make more than one, consider using different types of batting in them, so you can begin to develop your own likes and dislikes while you stitch.

Get Set

Presser Foot: even feed/walking foot and darning foot

Top and Bobbin Thread: 100 percent cotton in a color that is darker than the fabrics in your practice quilt sandwich

Needle: size 80/12

Stitch Width: 0

Stitch Length: 9–10 for the walking foot; 0 for the darning foot

Needle Position: centered

Feed Dogs: raised for the walking foot; lowered for the darning foot

Top Tension: normal for your machine

A WARM-UP EXERCISE

1 Put the walking foot on your machine, place a practice quilt sandwich under the needle, and lower the foot. Bring the bobbin thread to the top, and insert the needle back into the quilt sandwich where the thread came up. Hold onto both threads and anchor a few beginning stitches with one of the methods from Lesson 3. Adjust your stitch length to nine to ten stitches per inch, and do a line of machine-guided stitches about 5 or 6 inches long. Then lower the feed dogs, adjust the stitch length back to 0, put on the darning foot, and do another straight line, this time in free motion. Guide the quilt sandwich lightly with your fingertips, and keep your hands flexed, as if you were playing the piano. Do not grip the fabric or hold onto the edges of it because that can make your hands sore and tired.

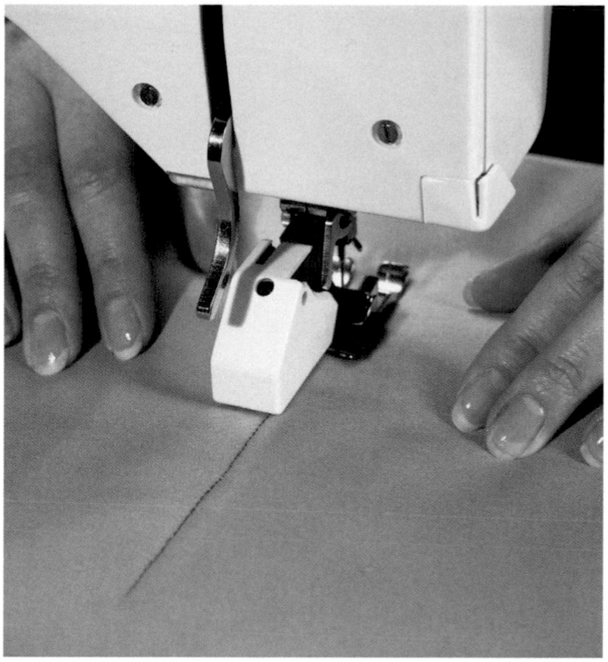

2 Raise the darning foot, pull the quilt sandwich gently away from the needle, and compare the two lines of stitches. If you find that your free-motion stitches are too long with respect to the machine-guided ones, it means that your hands were moving the quilt sandwich too quickly in relation to how fast the needle was moving up and down. Do a third line of stitching, this time taking care not to move your hands any more quickly than you did before. A faster needle speed will help your stitches become more even.

3 If some of the free-motion stitches look too short to you, it means that you were moving the quilt sandwich too slowly. To correct this, do a fourth line of stitching, moving the quilt sandwich more quickly, without changing the needle speed. It takes time to become comfortable guiding a quilt sandwich under the needle without the aid of the feed dogs, so be patient with yourself as you practice free-motion quilting.

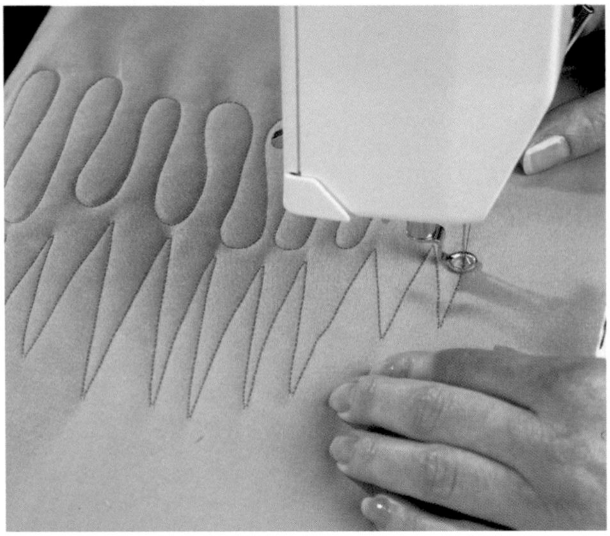

4 When you are comfortable with quilting toward yourself and guiding the fabric evenly, try doing some stitching from side to side. Concentrate on using your fingers lightly to move the quilt sandwich sideways. Think of letting the needle follow you as you stitch. Again, experiment to find the stitching speed as well as the speed for guiding the quilt sandwich that feel most comfortable to you.

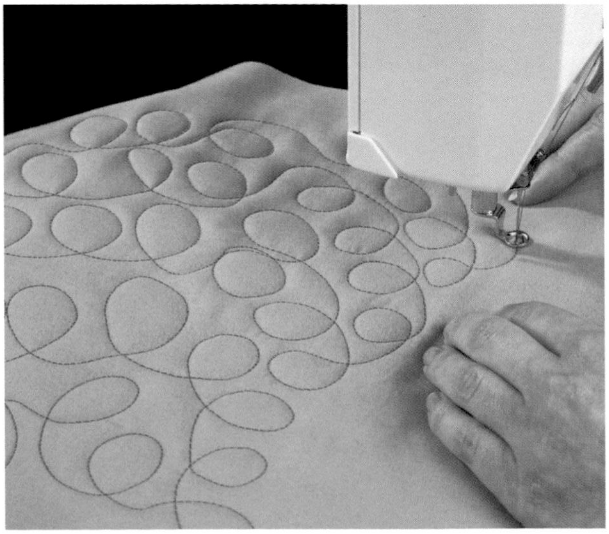

5 Next, try some circles on another practice quilt sandwich. Relax and have fun as you practice guiding the quilt sandwich in a circular motion. As you continue to practice quilting free-motion circles, you'll notice that your stitch length and the smoothness of your quilted lines are beginning to improve.

6 Now try signing your name or writing a message. Relax as you stitch and guide the quilt sandwich with easy, fluid motions. Practice until you are comfortable moving the quilt sandwich freely to quilt in any direction, even if this means covering several practice quilt sandwiches with stitches.

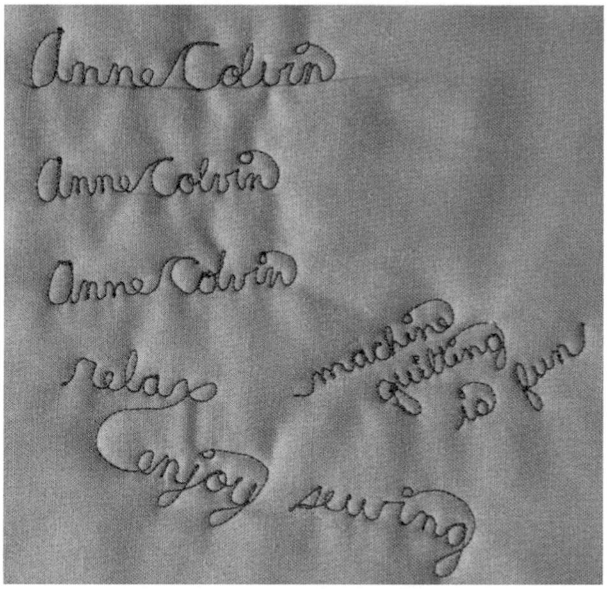

PREPARING A PRACTICE QUILT SANDWICH

For free-motion curves and points: Use a removable marker to trace the Leaf and Floral Quilting Design from page 159 onto a 14-inch square of light or medium solid fabric. Layer a practice quilt sandwich, pinning ten or more safety pins between the lines of the floral design. Place straight pins at right angles along the length of the longer stem. For more information on layering and basting, see page 19. **Note:** The markings in the following photos have been darkened slightly for visual clarity.

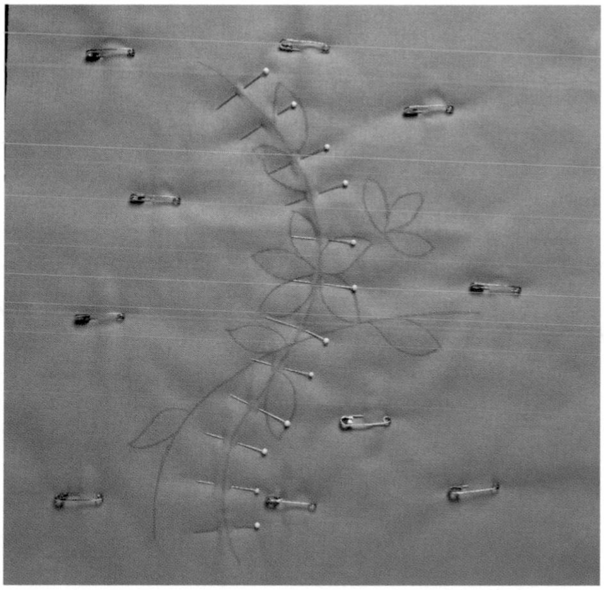

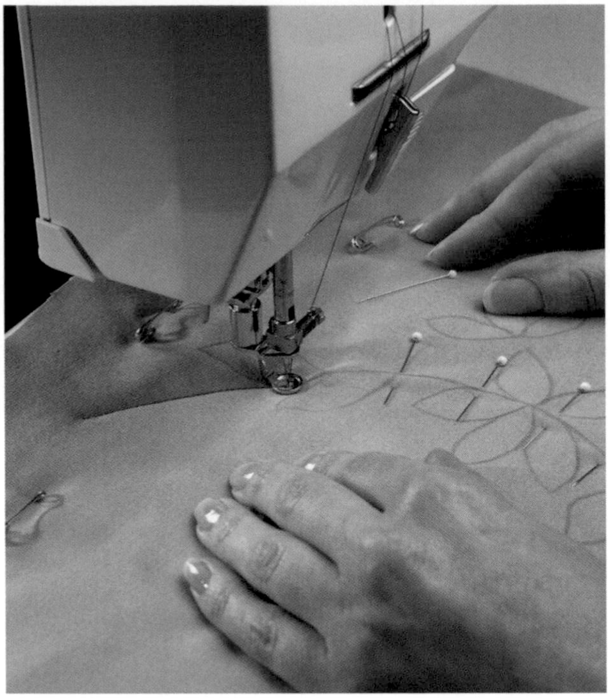

STEP BY STEP

1 Place the marked practice quilt sandwich under the darning foot, with the end of the pinned stem directly under the needle. Bring the bobbin thread to the top and anchor a few beginning stitches with one of the methods from Lesson 3. Quilt the stem, guiding the fabric gently with your hands on either side of the darning foot as you stitch. If your sewing machine will stitch over the straight pins, you may leave them in until you finish stitching the stem. If not, it's a good idea to remove the pins as you come to them to avoid bent pins and dulled or broken needles. End this line of stitching with one of the methods from Lesson 3. Place straight pins along the other stem, and quilt it in the same manner.

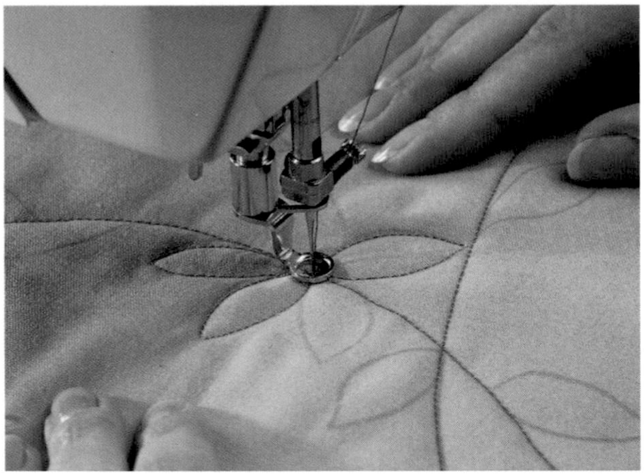

2 Quilt the flower petals, beginning at the center, and stitch over the center point as you complete each petal and go on to the next.

3 Take care when stitching lines between petals, so the stitches will come together neatly where they meet the stem.

4 Quilt each leaf separately, anchoring the beginning and ending threads with one of the methods in Lesson 3. Guide the quilt sandwich with your hands, so that the needle closely follows the marked lines of each leaf. Whichever method of starting and stopping you choose, the beginning and ending stitches of these leaves should be concealed in the stems.

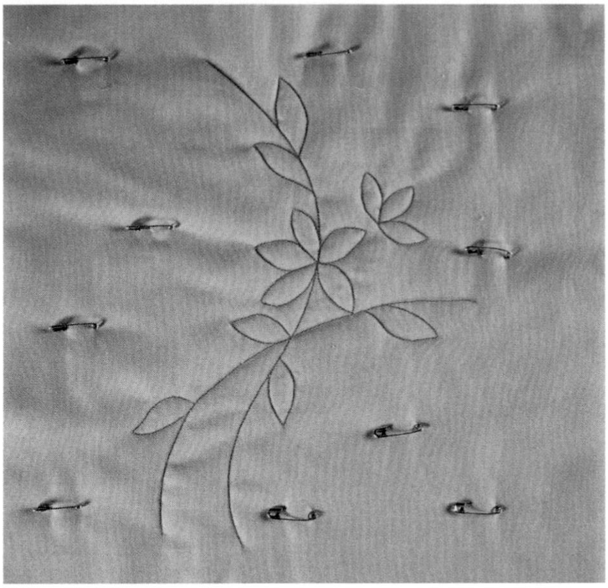

Great Ideas!

A WASHOUT MARKER FOR ANY FABRIC

My favorite removable marker is the E-Z Washout marking pencil because it always washes completely out when you soak the quilt in a solution of Orvus soap and water. One of the four pencil colors (pink, blue, white, and green) is sure to be easily visible on almost any fabric. And Orvus soap, originally intended as a soap for washing animal hair, is also good for virtually any fabric. For information about this pencil, contact E-Z International, 95 Mayhill Street, Saddle Brook, NJ 07663 (phone: 201-712-1234).

STIPPLE AND MEANDER QUILTING ACCENTS

As a complement to your finished free-motion floral design, consider covering the background of the practice quilt sandwich with stipple or meander quilting. Change the top thread to match your top fabric and the bobbin thread to match the backing fabric. Then fill in all areas around the design with stippling or meander stitching, covering the entire quilt sandwich. This practice project would make a lovely pillow top or a small wall quilt. For more information on stipple quilting, refer to Lesson 9. For more information on meander quilting, see Lesson 10.

LESSON 8

Free-Motion Continuous-Line Quilting

The term continuous-line quilting *refers to designs that have long, unbroken lines. These types of designs are easy to quilt with free-motion techniques because the individual elements are connected and require few stops and starts.*

My lesson will deal with how to select continuous-line designs; how to coordinate moving a practice quilt sandwich with the speed of the needle to produce even, consistent quilting stitches; how to follow the lines of a continuous-line design; and how to correct some of the most common stitching errors. You'll even find some ideas for adapting your own favorite quilting designs to free-motion continuous-line quilting.

As you practice the continuous-line techniques in my lesson, keep in mind that however long or short your stitches are, if they are even and they please you, your quilting is a success.

HARI WALNER

TRY FREE-MOTION CONTINUOUS-LINE QUILTING ON THESE PROJECTS:

Garden of Hearts, page 136
Autumn Trellis, page 202

No. 100
SWISS Art.
MADE 1171
No. 100
703

LESSON 8

Free-Motion Continuous-Line Quilting

SELECTING QUILTING DESIGNS

The best designs for continuous-line quilting are those with the least number of interruptions in the lines. Here are some basic guidelines for choosing the best designs for continuous-line quilting.

- Designs with unattached lines, like the ones in **Diagram 1,** require frequent stops and starts, which make machine quilting difficult and time-consuming. Designs like these are not suitable for continuous-line quilting.

- Designs with elements that are connected are suitable for continuous-line quilting because you can start quilting in one spot and continue the line of stitches until you complete the entire design. This saves a lot of time and produces a smoother appearance in a finished quilt. The dots in **Diagram 2** indicate the starting and ending points, and the arrows show the direction to begin stitching. To understand how each design is continuous, use a pencil or a pin to follow the lines of each design from the beginning dot all the way around, ending at the same dot.

Diagram 1

Diagram 2

Get Set

Presser Foot: darning foot
Top and Bobbin Thread: 100 percent cotton, in a darker color than the fabrics in your practice quilt sandwich
Needle: size 70/10
Stitch Width: 0
Stitch Length: 0
Needle Position: centered
Feed Dogs: lowered
Top Tension: normal for your machine

PREPARING A PRACTICE QUILT SANDWICH

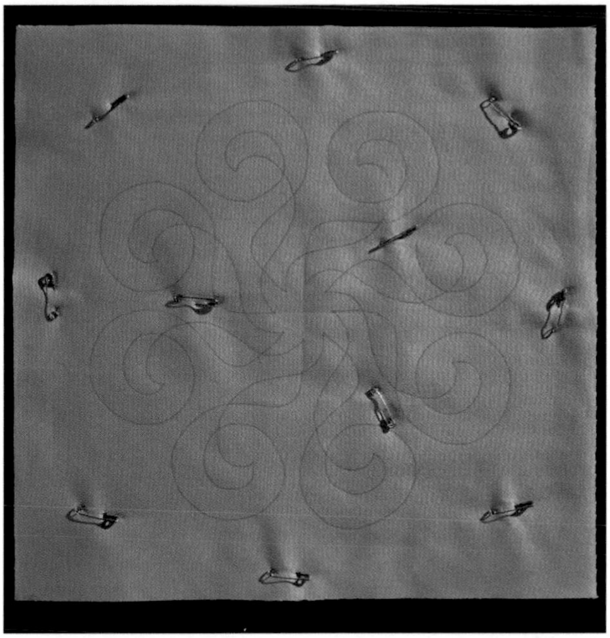

With a removable marker, trace the Continuous-Line Quilting Design from page 85 onto the right side of a 14-inch square of light or medium solid fabric, aligning the placement line with the center of the square of fabric. Turn the fabric 180 degrees and trace the design again, completing the continuous-line quilting design. Cut a 14-inch square *each* of batting and backing fabric, and layer and baste a practice quilt sandwich. For more information on layering and basting, see page 19. **Note:** The markings in the following photos have been darkened slightly for visual clarity.

STEP BY STEP

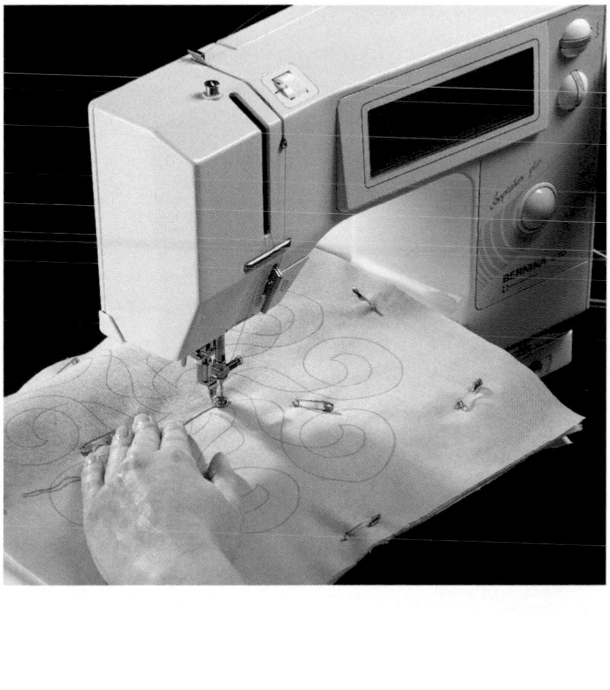

1 Insert the sewing machine needle at one of the center points on the marked design and bring the bobbin thread to the top. Take several tiny stitches to secure the beginning of the quilting line. Short stitches are the best method of starting and stopping for continuous-line quilting because they are more secure than backstitching, they avoid knots on the back of a quilt, and they are nearly invisible in a finished quilt. For more information on starting and stopping with short stitches, see Lesson 3.

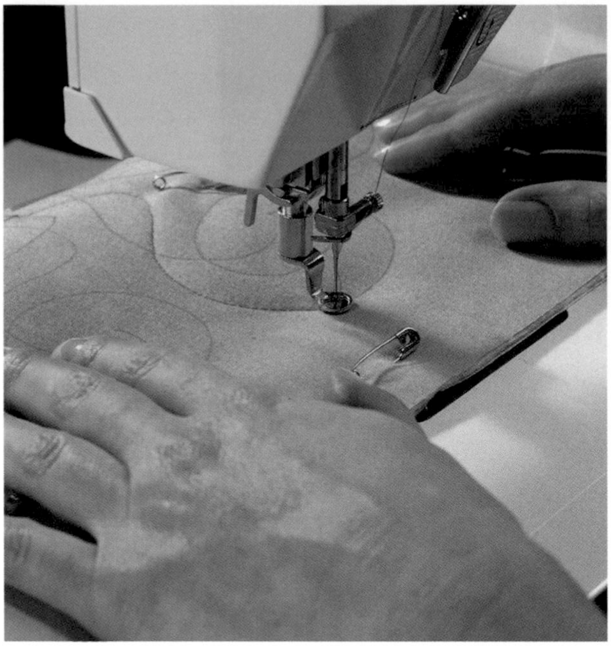

2 Stitch along the marked lines of the design. Refer to the arrows in the **Directional Stitching Diagram** on this page as you stitch, taking note that the stitching line crosses other marked lines in the design and comes back over them later. Do not veer away from the continuous line at these crossings. Continue stitching in the direction of the arrows, and think of feeding the design into the needle as you work. Keep your eyes approximately ⅛ to ¼ inch in front of the needle as you move the practice quilt sandwich under the needle. If you have difficulty remembering *not* to look at the needle, remind yourself that the needle only moves up and down, in and out of the same hole, while your quilt can move in any direction.

Directional Quilting Diagram

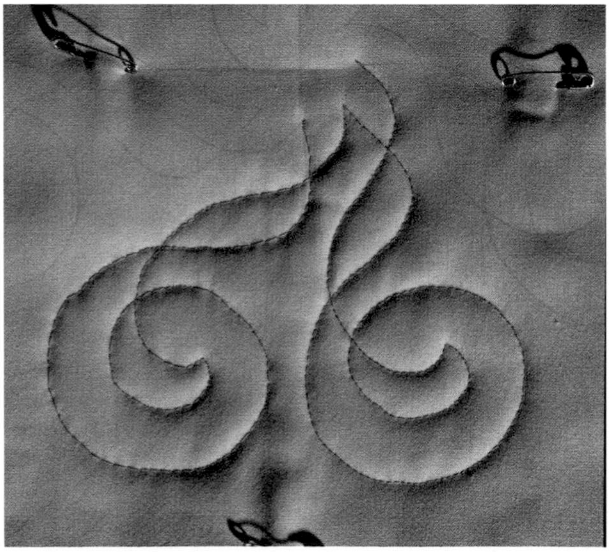

3 The rules of thumb for quilting a continuous-line design are like any other free-motion technique: The faster your needle speed, the shorter your stitches will be, and the faster you move your quilt, the longer your stitches will be. I do not like to specify any particular stitch length as "correct" because I think it is important that you find the combination of movement and stitching speed that makes you feel most comfortable. If your stitches look like the ones in the left portion of this photo, strive to keep your needle speed and hand movements consistent so that your stitches will be even, like the ones on the right.

4 When you come to any point in the marked design, pause—then take one more stitch and then continue to stitch. An "extra" stitch at each point will help to keep the points sharp and crisp, rather than rounded or uneven.

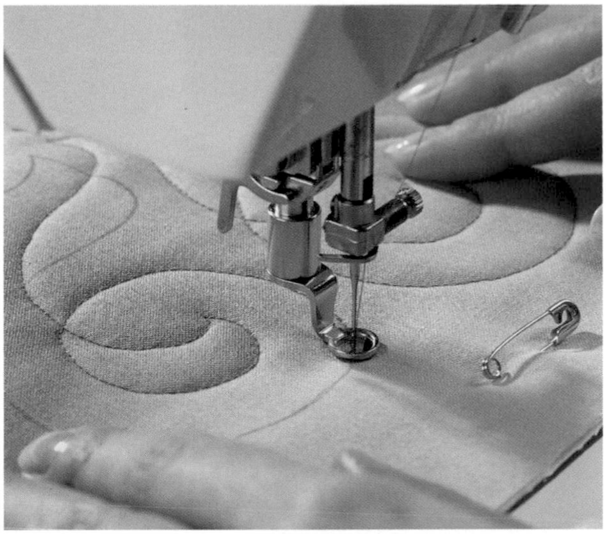

5 If you need to stop stitching to rewind a bobbin or for any other reason, stop at an intersection of lines or a point where it will be easy to reinsert the needle and resume stitching. Do not stop on a curve because it is difficult to continue the smooth flow in a line of stitches.

6 Continue stitching along the lines of the design. If you notice that your stitches are drifting far enough away from a marked line to detract from the design, a simple remedy will help you get back on track again. The moment that you realize you have made a mistake, stop stitching. Do not try to nudge the quilt sandwich back under the needle.

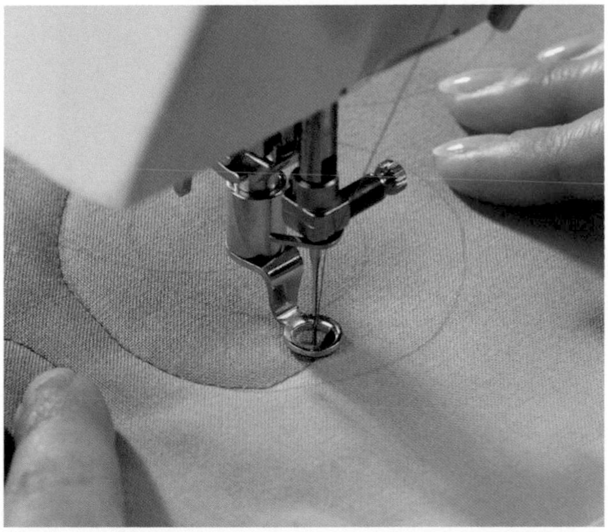

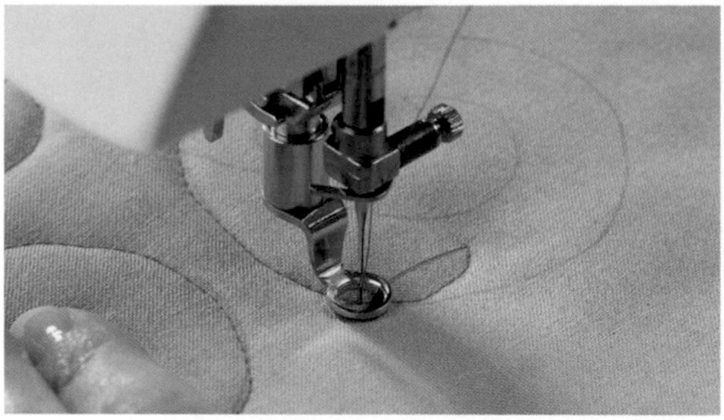

7 Lift the presser foot to release the top tension, and slide the quilt back, so that the needle lies directly over a point that is three or four stitches *before* you began to drift away from the marked line. Do not clip the long connecting thread at this time. Take three or four tiny stitches on top of your last several correct stitches, right up to the point where you began to stray from the marked line. This will secure them in place.

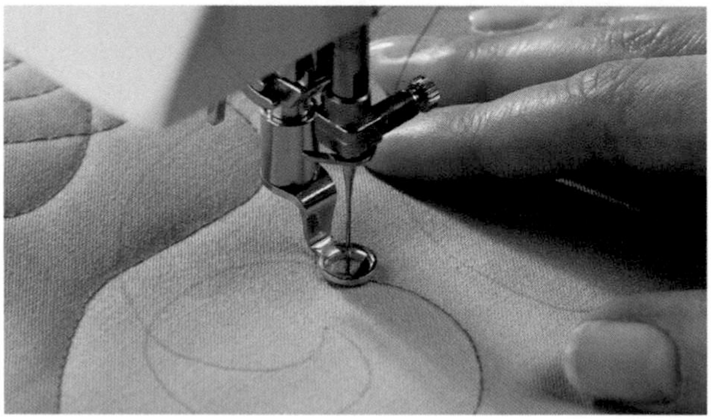

8 Continue stitching on the marked line approximately 2 or 3 inches beyond the area of the mistake, and stop with the needle down.

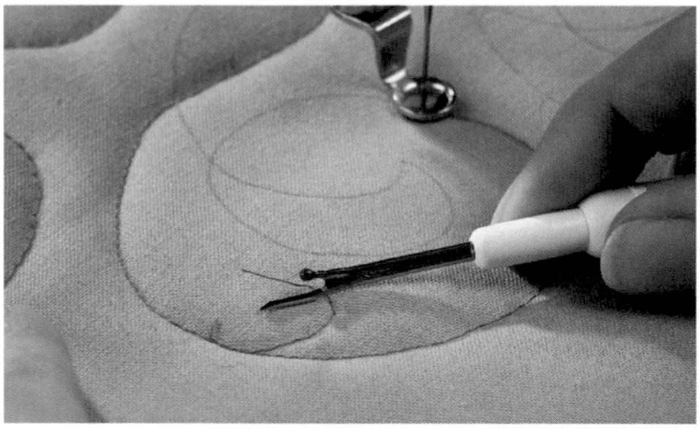

9 Clip the thread at the beginning and end of the mistake, and use a seam ripper to remove the mistake stitches. Your newly corrected stitching line will stay intact because of the stitches that overlapped each other at the correction point.

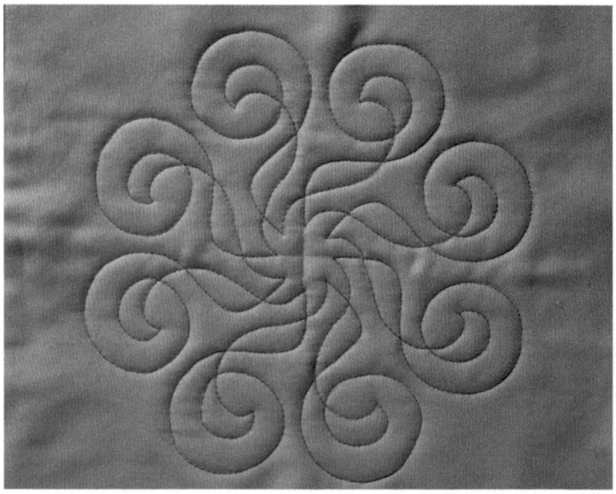

10 Stitch the rest of the design, and end with short stitches. Clip the thread tails close to the fabric in the practice quilt sandwich, and stand back to admire your work.

Turn this design 180 degrees to trace the other half.

Continuous-Line Quilting Design

Great Ideas!

MARK THE SAME WAY YOU STITCH

Whenever you mark a continuous-line design, mark it onto your quilt in the same order in which you will stitch it. Look at the stencil or design for a starting/ending dot and begin marking at that dot. Trace around the entire design, following the directional stitching arrows, and end where you began. That way, you will become familiar with the stitching sequence before you take the quilt to your machine.

CLIP THREADS LAST

When stitching more than one continuous-line design on the same quilt, you can move from one design to another easily. Start by securing the end of one quilted motif with tiny stitches. Then lift the presser foot and slide the quilt so that the starting point of the next design is under the needle. Lower the presser foot and quilt this design in the same manner. When you have completed all designs, clip all thread tails at one time.

BE PATIENT WITH YOURSELF

Continuous-line machine quilting is like any worthwhile skill. It takes a little time and practice to achieve results that make you happy. Experiment with different batts, needles, and threads, and remind yourself frequently that you are quilting for artistic expression and enjoyment. Don't allow a few little mistakes lead to frustration. Teach yourself continuous-line machine quilting techniques with the same patience you use when you are teaching others.

MY FAVORITE QUILTING FOOT

The Big Foot, made by Little Foot, Ltd., is a clear plastic foot that I like for quilting because it is easy to see through and around. It is shaped like a shallow bowl and holds the fabric down where the stitch is being made by the needle. For more information about this presser foot, contact Little Foot, Ltd., 605 Bledsoe NW, Albuquerque, NM 87101 (phone: 505-345-7647).

Great Ideas!

A WARM-UP FOR CONTINUOUS-LINE QUILTING

One of the things people worry about most in free-motion continuous-line quilting is how to coordinate moving a quilt sandwich with the movement of a sewing machine needle. There is an easy way to practice this. Place a piece of paper marked with a continuous-line design under your sewing machine needle. With the feed dogs lowered and the darning foot and the needle raised, begin to move the paper, so that the needle follows along the lines of the design. Do not press on the foot pedal. This process will familiarize you with how to guide a quilt sandwich in relationship to the needle—without ever taking a stitch.

PRACTICE ON PAPER

For practicing how to get even stitches as you quilt a continuous-line design, put a piece of paper marked with a continuous-line design under the needle. Lower the presser foot and stitch around the design with no top or bobbin thread in your machine. Remove the paper and look at it from the unmarked side. The perforations will show you how long your stitches will be. If they seem too long, it means that you have either moved the paper too quickly under the needle or pressed the foot pedal too slowly. If your stitches are too short, you have either run the machine too quickly or moved the paper too slowly.

MARK WITH YOUR SEWING MACHINE

Cut ten sheets of tracing paper a little larger than your quilting design. (For borders, make sure that the tracing paper is a bit wider than the border.) Trace the continuous-line quilting design onto one sheet of tracing paper, layer all the other sheets underneath it, and pin or staple them together. Remove the top and bobbin threads from your sewing machine, and insert a large, dull needle. Stitch on the marked lines of your design through all ten layers of paper. This will perforate all of the sheets and create ten identical quilting designs. Pin each sheet of tracing paper to your quilt where you want to stitch a design, and quilt through the paper.

LESSON
9

Stipple Quilting

Stipple quilting creates an interesting, crepe-like texture in a quilt. Good stippling looks like a maze, a meandering stream, or interlocking puzzle pieces. It is especially effective as a background pattern for appliqué shapes or quilted motifs.

The most common form of stipple quilting is vermicelli quilting, an overall pattern of curving lines that look similar to slender, intertwined pieces of vermicelli pasta. Because of the density of stitches, it is suitable for filling in small areas in a quilt.

Echo stipple quilting is a form of outline stitching done at very close intervals around various shapes. It works best in areas that have straight or well-defined edges, such as small appliqué designs and quilted motifs. In combination with trapunto, either type of stipple quilting can transform a quilt from the ordinary to the extraordinary, and whether it is done by hand or machine, good stipple quilting exemplifies the highest level of quilting skill.

DEBRA WAGNER

TRY VERMICELLI STIPPLE QUILTING ON THESE PROJECTS:

Garden of Hearts, page 136
A Quilted Vest, page 152
A Rose Garden, page 180
Autumn Trellis, page 202
Hospitality Table Runner, page 210
September Rose and Bud, page 226

TRY ECHO STIPPLE QUILTING ON THIS PROJECT:

Calico Garden, page 160

LESSON 9

Stipple Quilting

As you practice these techniques, keep in mind the following characteristics of good stipple quilting. Stipple stitches should appear indistinct against the background fabric and very small and close together with tightened tension to create a puckered texture. Traditionally, to qualify as true stippling, the spacing between lines should be no more than ⅛ inch. When the intervals between the stitching lines become larger than ⅛ inch, the correct term is actually *meander quilting.* However, the term *stippling* often applies to lines of stitching that are spaced from as much as ¼ to ½ inch apart. And finally, lines of stippling can come close but shouldn't cross each other.

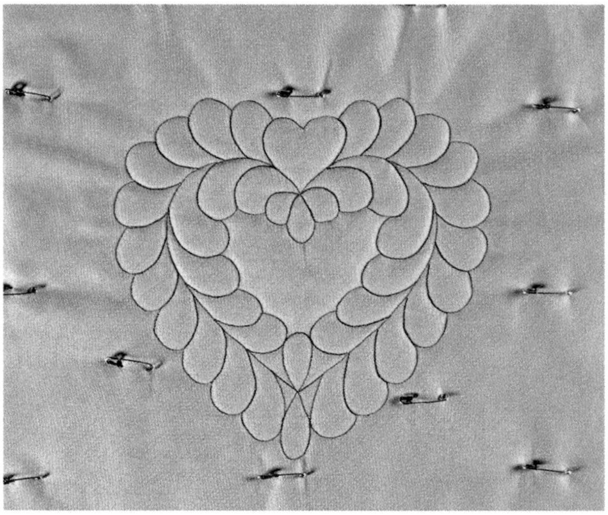

PREPARING A PRACTICE QUILT SANDWICH

For vermicelli stipple quilting: Cut a 14-inch square of a light or medium solid fabric for the top and 14-inch squares of batting and light fabric for the backing. Trace the Feathered Heart Quilting Design from page 95 onto the top fabric with a removable fabric marker. Layer and pin-baste your practice quilt sandwich. Free-motion quilt the entire feathered heart design. **Note:** The markings in the following photos have been darkened slightly for visual clarity.

Get Set

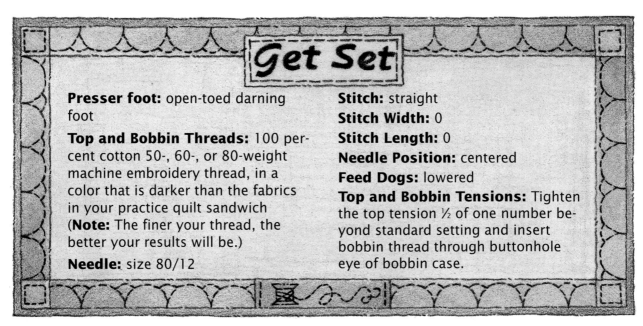

Presser foot: open-toed darning foot

Top and Bobbin Threads: 100 percent cotton 50-, 60-, or 80-weight machine embroidery thread, in a color that is darker than the fabrics in your practice quilt sandwich (**Note:** The finer your thread, the better your results will be.)

Needle: size 80/12

Stitch: straight

Stitch Width: 0

Stitch Length: 0

Needle Position: centered

Feed Dogs: lowered

Top and Bobbin Tensions: Tighten the top tension ½ of one number beyond standard setting and insert bobbin thread through buttonhole eye of bobbin case.

VERMICELLI STIPPLE QUILTING

1 Position your practice quilt sandwich so that the very edge of the inner area lies under the needle. Any part of the inner area will be fine to start, as long as the needle lies directly over one of the stitching lines of the feathered heart. Lower the presser foot, bring up the bobbin thread, and hold on to both thread tails. Begin by moving the quilt sandwich very slowly, and take four or five short stitches directly over a small portion of the previously stitched feathered heart. For more information about short stitches, see Lesson 3. Then allow your stitches to move out into the inner area approximately ¼ to ½ inch.

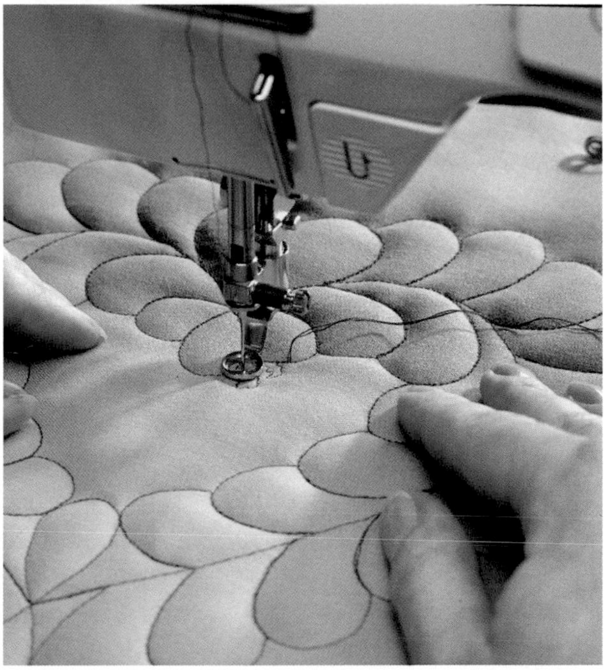

2 Continue stitching a ridge of stipple quilting approximately ½ inch wide that outlines the entire edge of the inner area. Keep your stitches small, and form random puzzle-piece shapes. Space your stitching lines approximately ⅛ to ¼ inch apart. Pull the quilt sandwich toward yourself and to the left as you work, rather than allowing the fabric to move behind the needle. This allows the stitches to fall in front of the needle, where you can see them easily and analyze the way your pattern is developing. Do not concentrate intensely on what you are doing—simply let it happen. When you have reached the place where you started, end with short stitches, and clip the threads close to the surface of the quilt sandwich.

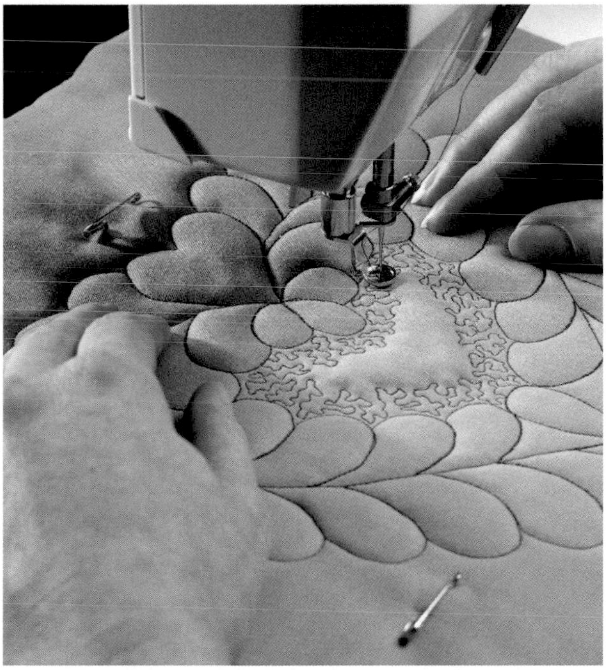

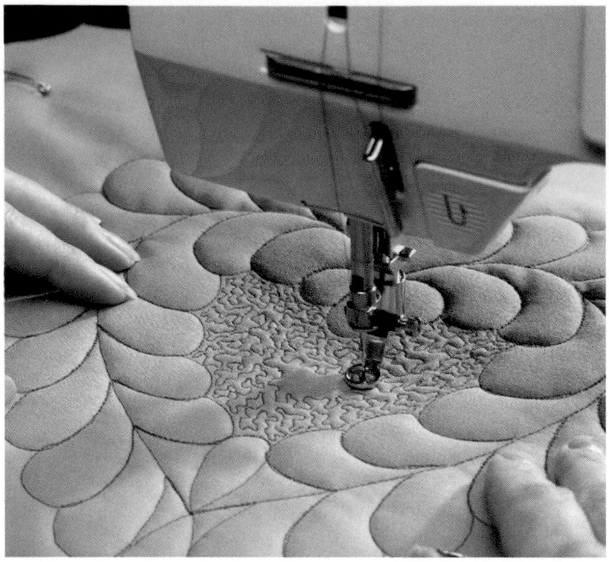

3 Fill in the rest of the inner area with vermicelli stipple quilting. Continue to make your stitching lines form puzzle-piece shapes, pulling the fabric toward you and to the left as you go. Work your way clockwise around the inner area. This avoids accidental pleats caused when stitching lines bump into each other. If you worked from one side of this inner area to the other, a pleat or pucker would be likely to form in the fabric wherever the needle encountered another line of stitching. Stipple stitches should form convoluted, interlocking puzzle-piece shapes that do not cross or touch each other.

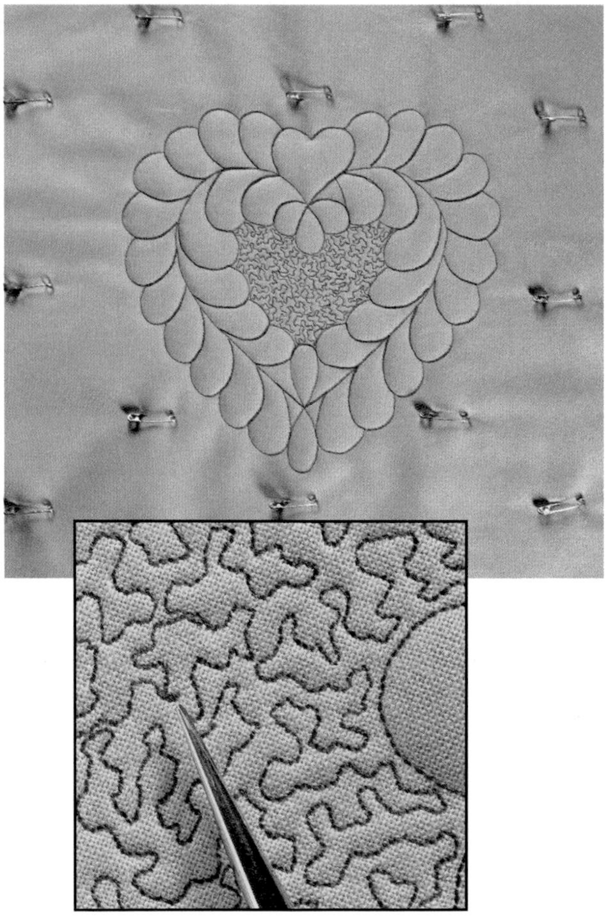

4 After you have filled the entire inner area with vermicelli stipple quilting, end by joining the end of your final stitching line to one of your previous lines of stitches using short stitches, as shown in the close-up photo. Trim the thread tails close to the surface of the quilt sandwich. Because stipple quilting can affect the drape and appearance of a quilt differently than other types of quilting, a good general rule to follow is to keep stippled areas under 2 inches square.

PREPARING A PRACTICE QUILT SANDWICH

For echo quilting, use an appliqué block as the top layer of your practice quilt sandwich. You may choose any appliqué block you like, or use my Fern Appliqué Pattern on page 95, which is suitable for an 8-inch block in a quilt. The inspiration for this pattern was an 1852 appliqué quilt by Mary Brown of Calvert, Maryland. Trace the pattern from page 95 and use whichever method of appliqué you prefer to appliqué it onto a 14-inch square of background fabric. If you wish, you can fuse the cut fabric shape in place on the background block to save time. Cut a 14-inch square *each* of batting and backing fabric and layer, and baste your practice quilt sandwich. For more information on layering and basting, see page 19. Outline quilt around the appliqué design as close as possible to the edge of the fabric. For more information on outline quilting, see Lesson 4. Then quilt a second line of stitches approximately ⅛ inch outside the first line.

ECHO STIPPLE QUILTING

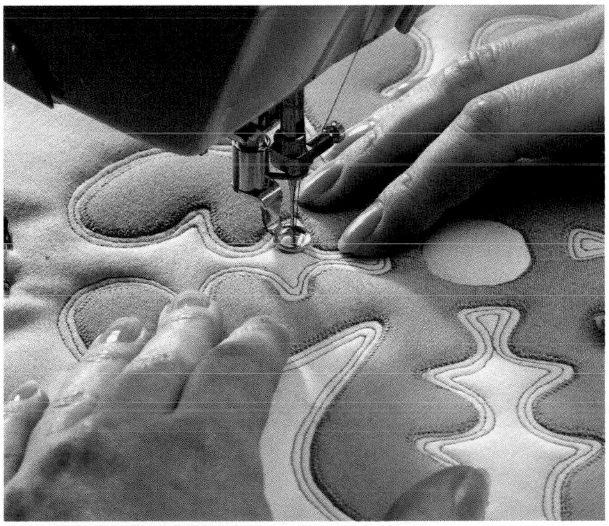

1 Start with one of the methods from Lesson 3, and stitch a line of echo stipple quilting stitches ⅛ inch away from the previous stitching line. I suggest that you avoid starting or ending at a point or corner because those are the most obvious to the viewer's eye. End this first line of echo stipple quilting at the point where you began, using one of methods from Lesson 3.

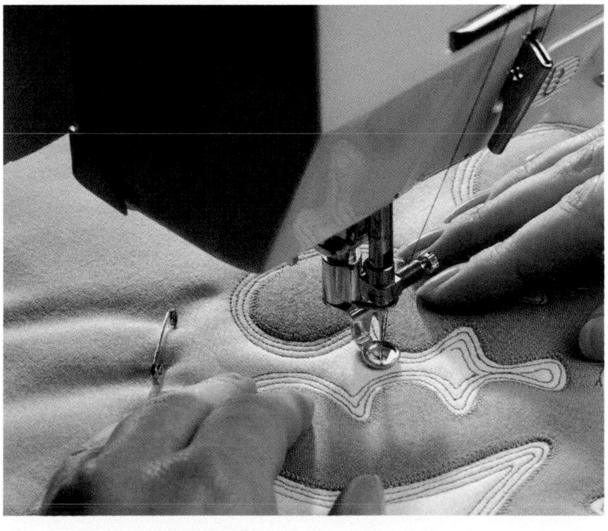

2 Without clipping the threads, raise the presser foot and needle, and do another line of echo stipple quilting approximately ⅛ inch away from the previous line. Begin with one of the methods from Lesson 3 to anchor this new line of quilting. Continue stitching around the entire appliqué shape and end as you began. **Note:** Each successive line of echo quilting you do will become slightly flatter and somewhat less curved than the previous line. This will make curves and angles become less defined the more lines of outline quilting you do.

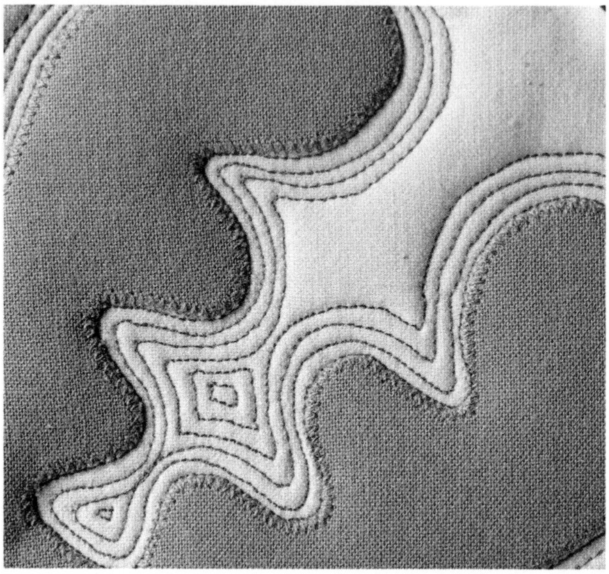

3 When you quilt between two appliqué shapes, two lines of echo stipple quilting may touch each other. This is called a "pool." When you have created one of these pools, continue doing lines of echo quilting inside it, until it is completely filled with concentric lines of stitches. Take care that these stitching lines do not overlap or cross each other. After you have finished all lines of echo stipple quilting in any given area of your quilt sandwich, clip the short tails of thread connecting the lines.

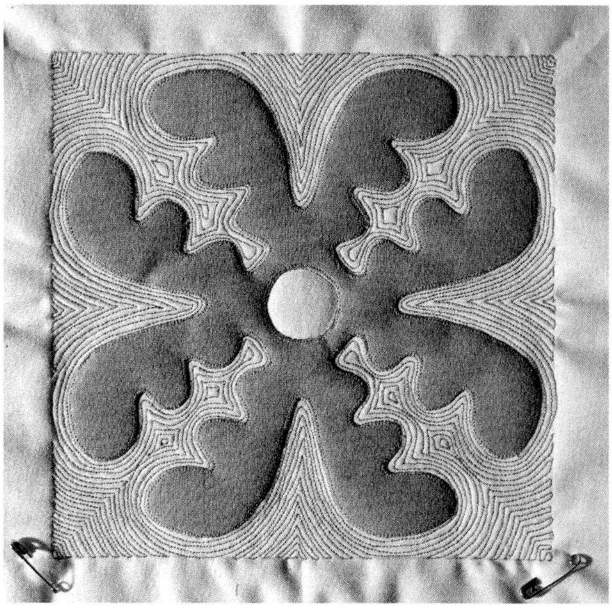

4 Whenever you stipple quilt in the outer portions of a quilt block, your stitching lines will run into the seams surrounding the block. Treat these areas just like a pool, and fill them in with concentric lines of stitches that radiate out to the seam line. To try this on your practice quilt sandwich, use a removable fabric marker and draw an 8-inch square around the appliqué shape to represent seam lines. Then fill in areas at each edge with pools of echo stippling.

One-Half of Fern Appliqué Pattern

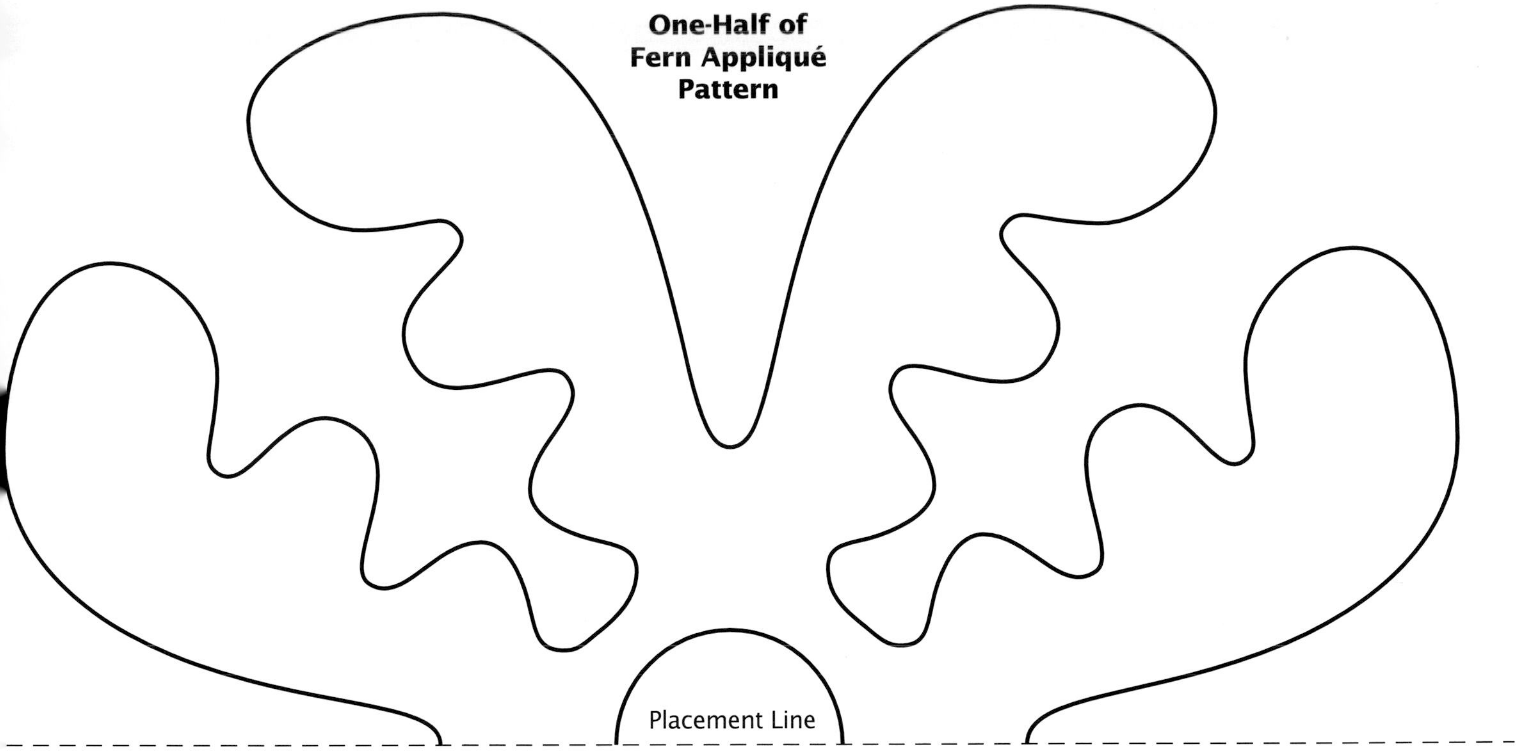

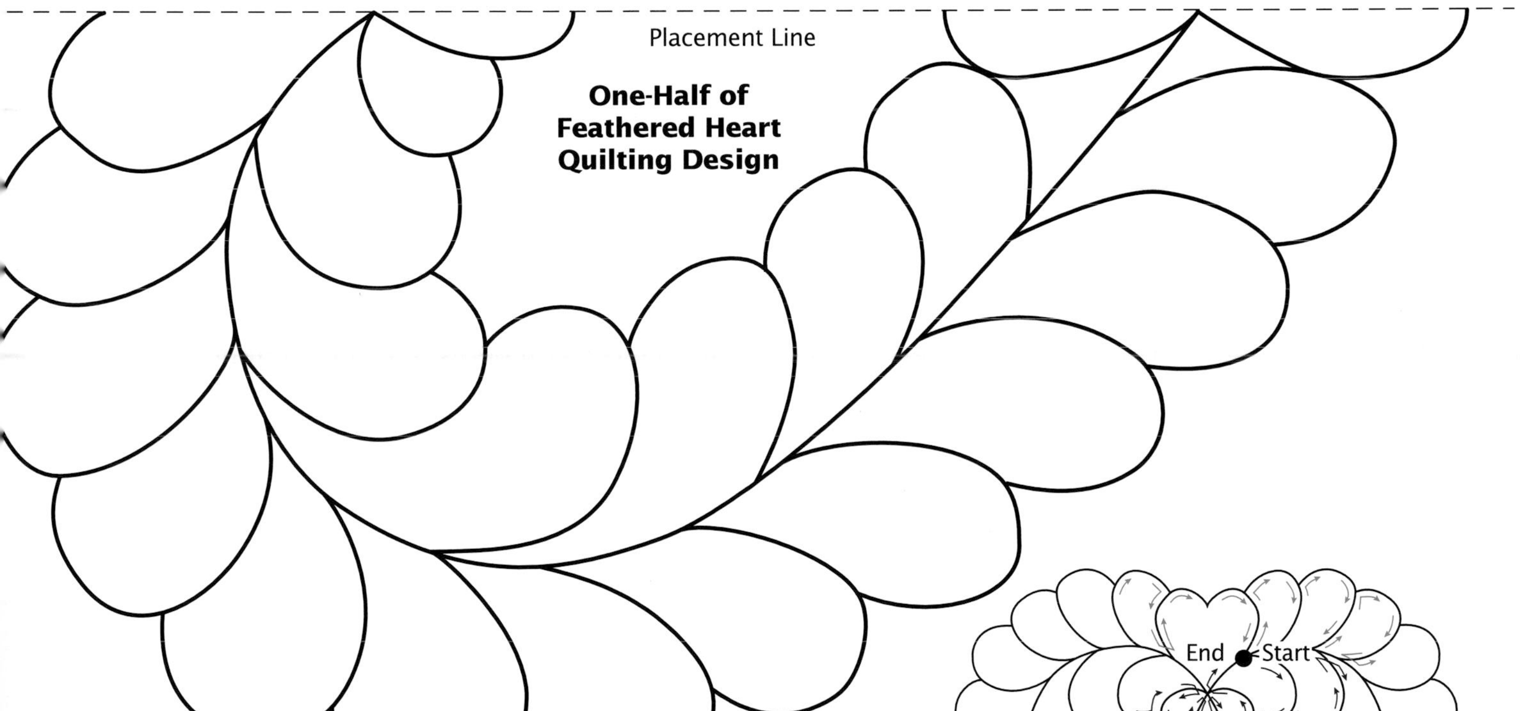

One-Half of Feathered Heart Quilting Design

Feathered Heart Quilting Design

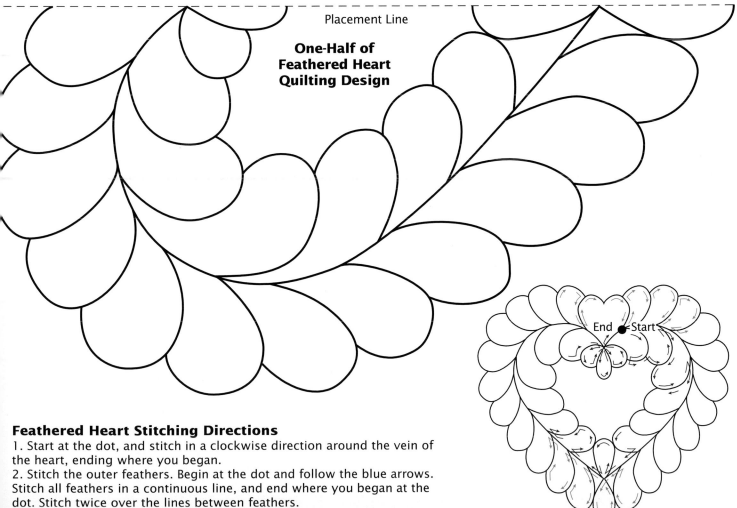

Feathered Heart Stitching Directions

1. Start at the dot, and stitch in a clockwise direction around the vein of the heart, ending where you began.
2. Stitch the outer feathers. Begin at the dot and follow the blue arrows. Stitch all feathers in a continuous line, and end where you began at the dot. Stitch twice over the lines between feathers.
3. Stitch the inner feathers. Begin at the dot and follow the pink arrows, stitching in a continuous line until you end at the dot, as before.

Troubleshooting Tips

■ **IF YOUR STITCHES ARE TOO LARGE AND UNEVEN,** with squared curves and lines that cross over each other, it means that you are running your sewing machine too slowly and moving your hands too quickly. To correct this, press harder on the foot pedal of your machine and slow down the movements of your hands. This type of look is striking in a quilt and you may wish to use it for special effect, but it does not qualify as stipple quilting.

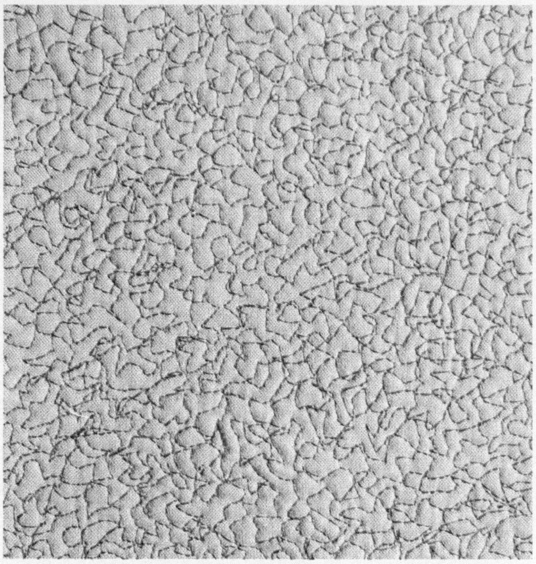

■ **IF YOUR STITCHES ARE TOO SMALL AND CLOSE TOGETHER,** they can cut the threads in your fabric and weaken it. If your lines of stitches look knotted and rough on the back side of your quilt sandwich, like the ones in these photos, you're creating an effect that is called "sanding" because the bobbin threads resemble grains of sand. The way to remedy this is to slow down the speed of your sewing machine needle and increase the speed at which your hands move the quilt sandwich.

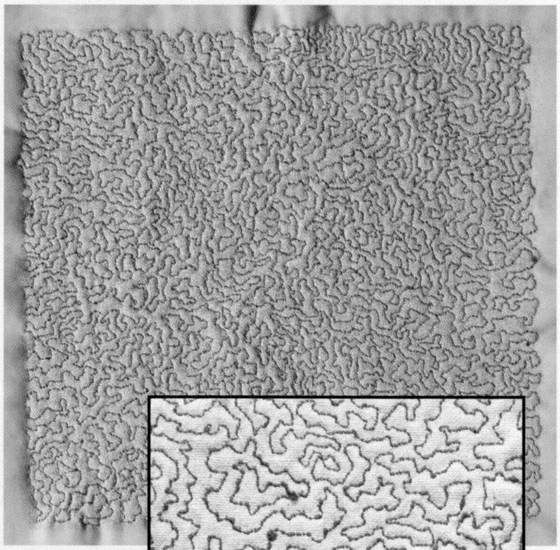

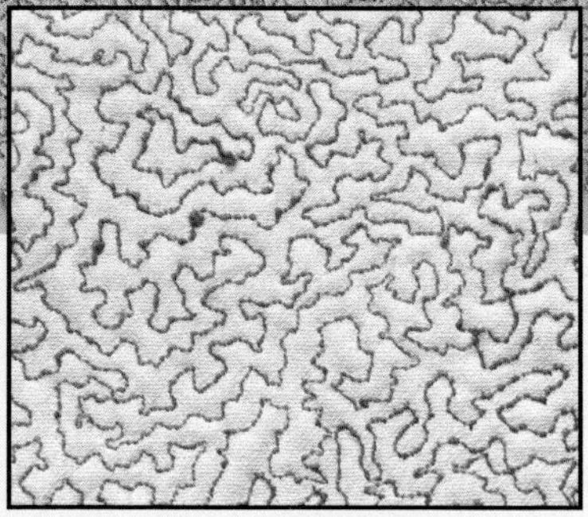

■ **IF YOUR STITCHES FORM A REGULAR PATTERN,** they will make your stipple quilting appear too uniform. The secret to good machine stippling is to make the stitches appear random. So if your stitches look like the ones in this photo, vary your hand movements often, keep your fingers relaxed, and change directions about every ¼ to ½ inch.

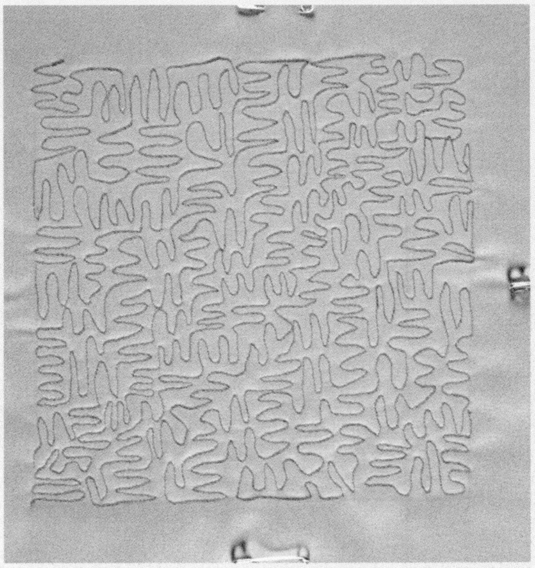

■ **IF THE LINES OF STIPPLE QUILTING ARE TOO SMOOTH,** their curves may appear too gentle rather than like the intricate swirls that characterize good stipple quilting. If your stitches look like these, it means that you are stitching too far in one direction before curving. Change your stitching direction approximately every ⅛ inch.

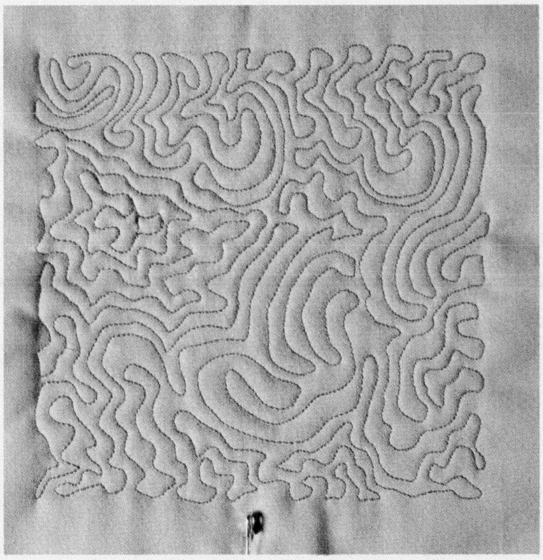

TIP: Another way to avoid distortion and puckering is to use low loft and cotton or polyester-blend batting and distribute stippled areas evenly throughout a quilt.

LESSON 10

Meander Quilting

Meander quilting is a free-flowing pattern of randomly stitched lines that can be used to fill either large or small spaces in a quilt. The stitching lines change direction frequently, and they do not duplicate themselves with regularity. The shapes of meander quilting can be as diverse as any found in nature; just as no two flowers or snowflakes look exactly alike, no two twists, angles, curves, or turns in meander quilting are ever identical.

Like its cousin, stipple quilting, meander quilting is a free-motion technique that is similar to drawing or doodling with a pencil. It is larger in scale than stipple quilting, however, with stitching lines that can range from ¼ to as much as 1 inch apart. There are many different types of meander quilting designs, and your interpretation of each one will be as individual and distinctive as your own signature.

For filling spaces between quilted motifs, any style of meander quilting is an excellent choice. It is ideal for holding the layers of a quilt together without taking away from the design of a quilt top, and it is a fast way to finish a quilt whenever time is at a premium.

As you gain experience with the meander quilting techniques in my lesson, take time to notice how your stitching lines are becoming more elaborate and taking on a style all your own.

CARYL BRYER FALLERT

TRY MEANDER QUILTING ON THIS PROJECT:

Illusion #13, page 170

LESSON 10

Meander Quilting

Use the following guidelines to evaluate your meander quilting stitches. Meander quilting is a randomly stitched free-motion technique that is not usually marked on a quilt top.

- Meander quilting can either appear indistinct against the background fabric or figure more prominently as an important design element of a quilt.
- The stitching lines in meander quilting can touch or even cross each other in some designs, while in others, they may never touch. Either way is acceptable, unlike stipple quilting, where lines do not cross each other.
- Meander quilting has a regularity of rhythm, without consisting of identical shapes.
- As long as the lines are spaced farther apart than ⅛ inch, which qualifies as stipple quilting, the scale of any meander quilting pattern can be whatever size you feel is appropriate for your project. If you wish to flatten an area of a quilt, small-scale meander quilting spaced at ¼-inch intervals works very well. For more open areas in a quilt, use larger, more graphic motifs such as the Caryl flower, or space the stitching lines of any type of meander quilting pattern up to 1 inch apart.

PREPARING A PRACTICE QUILT SANDWICH

For meander quilting: For each practice quilt sandwich you make, cut a 14-inch square of a light or medium solid fabric for the top and 14-inch squares of batting and light fabric for the backing. Layer and pin-baste your practice quilt sandwich. For more information on layering and basting, see page 19.

Get Set

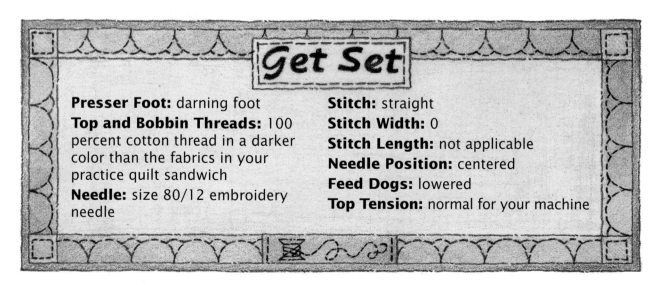

Presser Foot: darning foot
Top and Bobbin Threads: 100 percent cotton thread in a darker color than the fabrics in your practice quilt sandwich
Needle: size 80/12 embroidery needle
Stitch: straight
Stitch Width: 0
Stitch Length: not applicable
Needle Position: centered
Feed Dogs: lowered
Top Tension: normal for your machine

STEP BY STEP

1 Make a photocopy of the Serpentine Practice Pattern on page 104. Remove the thread from the top and bobbin of your sewing machine. Place this practice pattern so that the needle lies directly above the starting point. Lower the darning foot, and begin stitching at the starting point. Follow the directional stitching arrows, and take note of how your hands are moving as they guide the paper under the needle. Stitching on paper is the quickest and easiest way to become familiar and comfortable with the motions needed to stitch serpentine or any other type of meander quilting design.

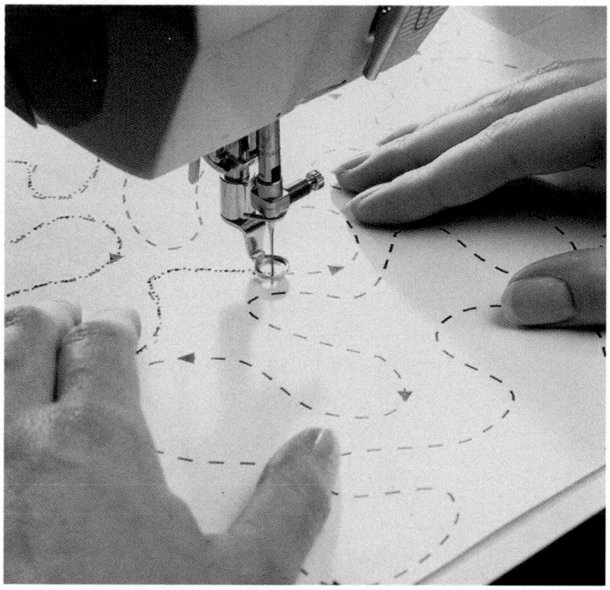

2 When you feel comfortable stitching the serpentine pattern, begin stitching. Start near the upper left corner and begin to stitch S-shaped curves, placing your thumbs and index fingers on either side of the presser foot to hold the fabric taut and smooth. Guide the fabric evenly and keep the needle moving at a steady speed. Remove the safety pins about 2 inches before you reach them. Think of your stitching lines as exaggerated S-shapes or jigsaw puzzle pieces that meander in every direction. Your stitch length will be determined by the speed of your hands and the speed of the needle. Continue stitching S-shaped curves until you fill the area between your thumbs and forefingers.

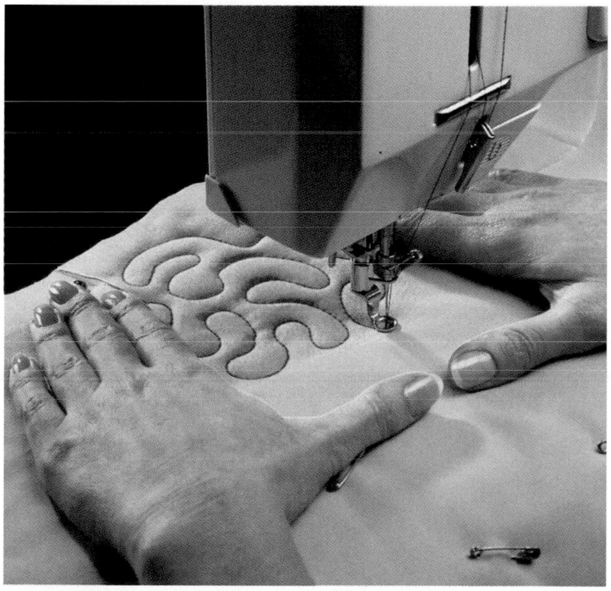

3 After you have filled the area between your thumbs and forefingers, pause to reposition your hands in front of the needle. Continue stitching as before, until this second area is filled. When you have filled 4 to 6 inches of space with stitches, stop and clip the top and bobbin threads from the starting point.

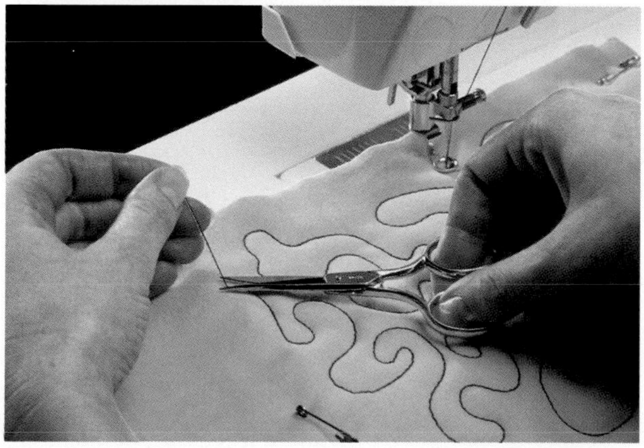

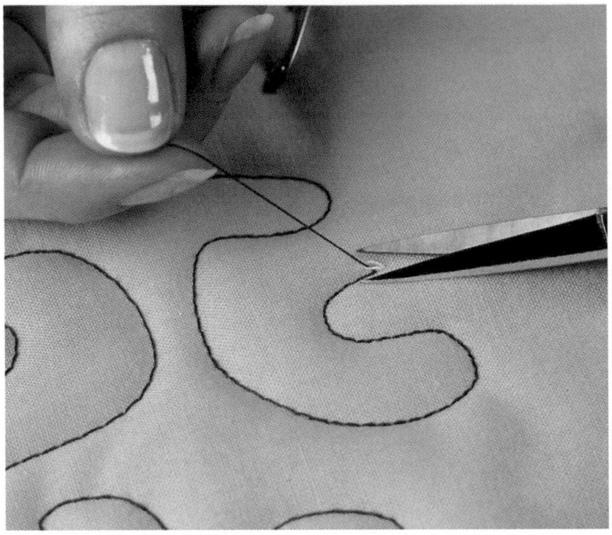

4 Cover the rest of the practice quilt sandwich with serpentine meander quilting stitches. If you need to stop stitching to change thread or when you wish to end your stitching line, gradually shorten the stitch length and take four or five short stitches. For more information on short stitches, see Lesson 3. Then take one more slightly longer stitch, which will pull a small loop of bobbin thread to the top. This allows you to clip both the top and bobbin threads, remove the bobbin thread easily, and eliminate having to turn a large quilt top over to end a line of stitching.

VARIATIONS

Meander quilting can take many forms, from the classic serpentine pattern to more graphic designs, such as flowers and leaves. Each of the following variations can be used to add interesting visual texture to a quilt. For some of them, you will find practice patterns on pages 104–107. Photocopy these patterns and stitch them on paper without thread, following the directional arrows. When you are comfortable with stitching on paper, switch to a practice quilt sandwich. When you finish, keep your practice quilt sandwiches as reference guides for future use. For intricate or graphic designs like echo quilting or spirals and crescents, no practice patterns are given. Use the photos as inspiration for stitching similar patterns or creating new designs.

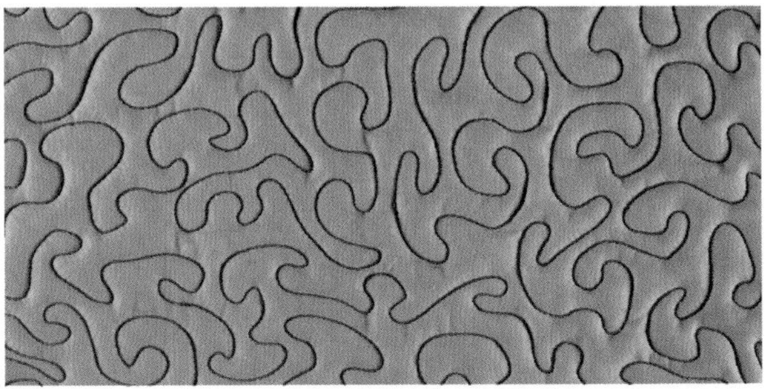

Serpentine or Jigsaw Puzzle (see page 104): Large-scale, random loops and curls are fast and easy to stitch. Jigsaw puzzle shapes are especially good for quilts with geometric patterns, such as the Log Cabin, because they do not distract from the surface design of the quilt.

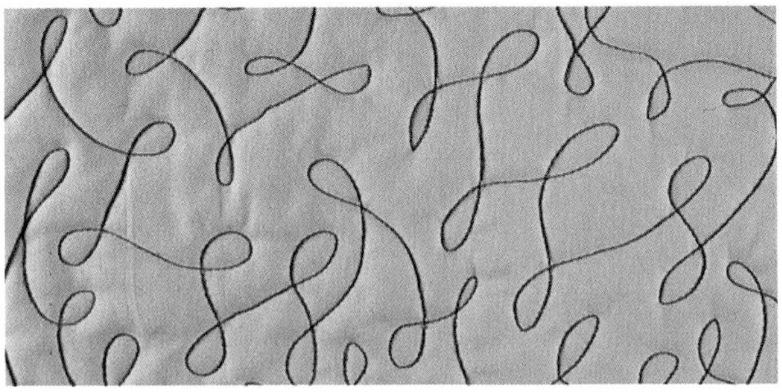

Loop-de-Loop (see page 105):This is one of the most recent meander quilting patterns I have learned. It is a series of connected capital L-shapes that alternate directions from loop to loop. Loop-de-loop meander quilting is quick to do and is an attractive way to anchor the layers of a quilt together.

Zigzags (see page 106): Straight-line meander quilting looks like a series of Z-shapes going in different directions. When stitching this angled design, stop at each point, raise the needle, and move the quilt sandwich ever so slightly before beginning to stitch in the next direction. This slight adjustment will avoid having the needle enter more than once into the same hole, which could create a knot on the back side of the quilt.

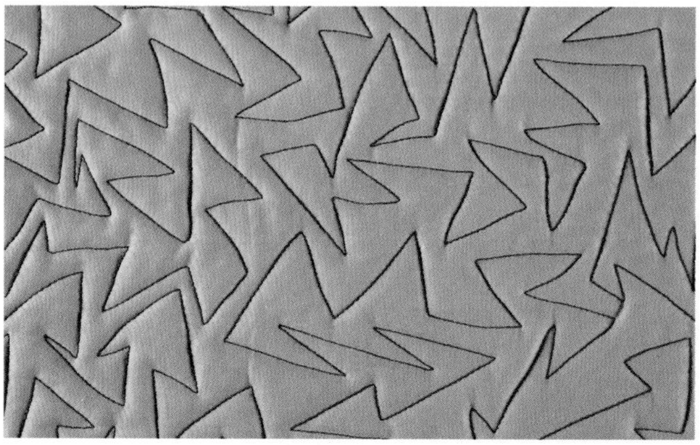

Caryl Flowers (see page 107): My floral design is a bit more planned than other types of meander quilting, but it is still used in the same way, as a filler for odd spaces in a quilt. It is particularly effective when combined with spiral and crescent shapes. You can stitch the entire design—even the spirals and crescents—without ever breaking your thread. Simply start at the lower left corner and follow the directional stitching arrows given on the practice pattern.

Spirals and Crescents: An all-over pattern of spirals and crescent shapes can become an important design element in a quilt, especially when combined with floral motifs. Use this pattern alone or combine with Caryl flowers. To enhance the visual effect of this pattern, use variegated thread in the top of your machine.

Echo Quilting: Outlining quilted designs or appliqué shapes with echo quilting can create visual interest in a quilt, especially when the lines are spaced unevenly. To qualify as echo meander quilting, the stitching lines should be spaced farther apart than ⅛ inch. There is no practice pattern for echo meander quilting; simply quilt a Caryl flower and then surround it with lines of echo quilting spaced at various intervals.

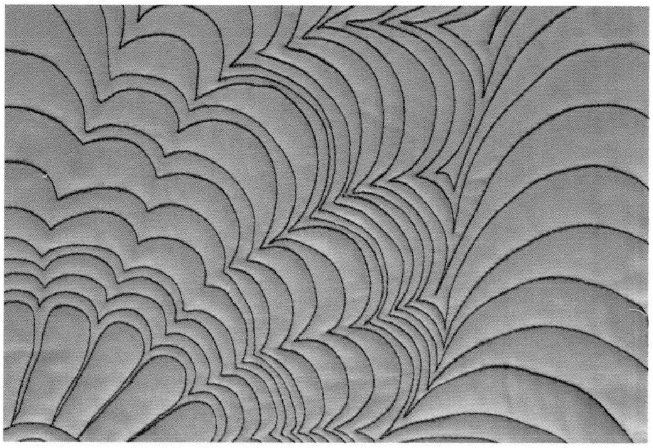

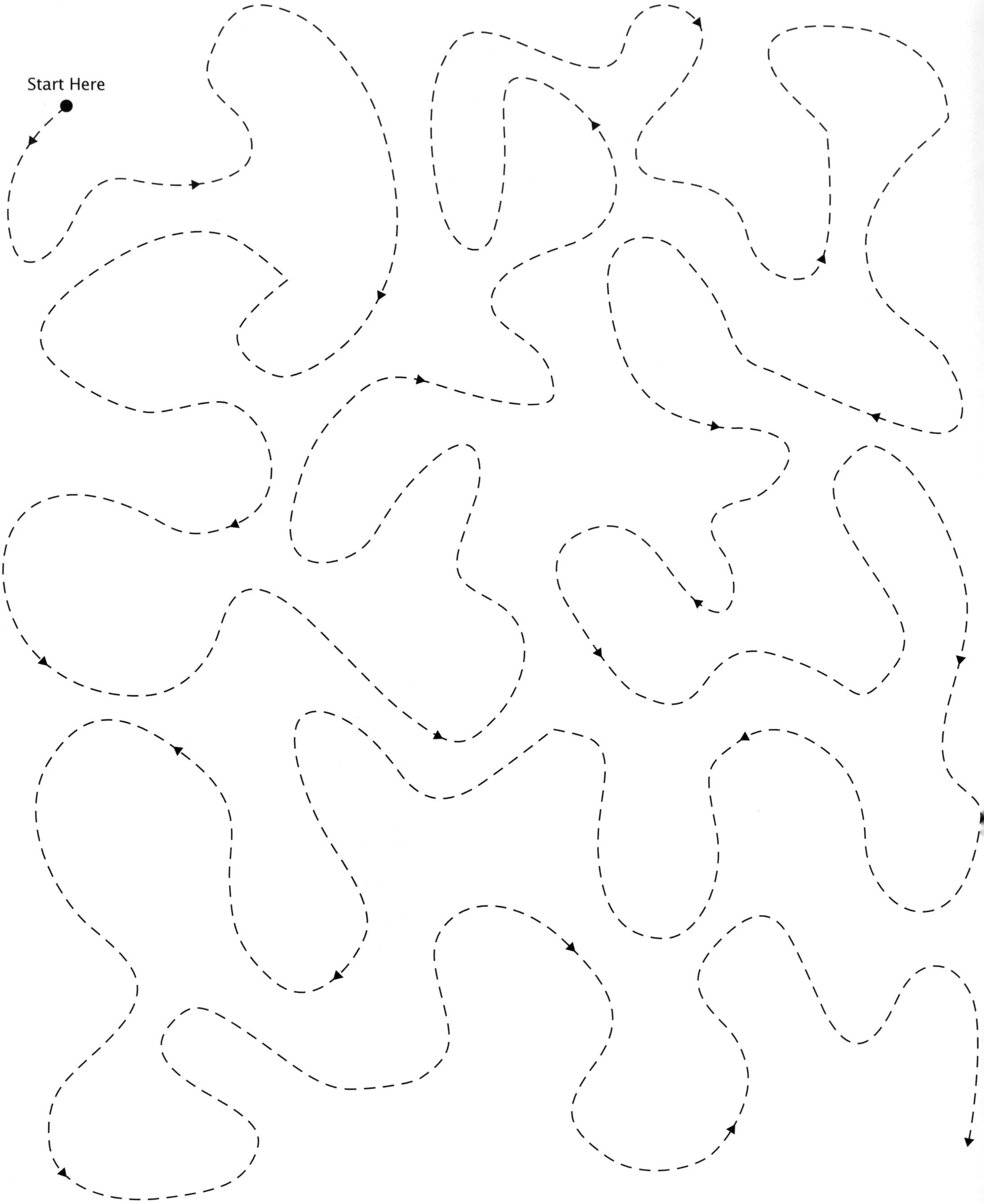

Serpentine Practice Pattern

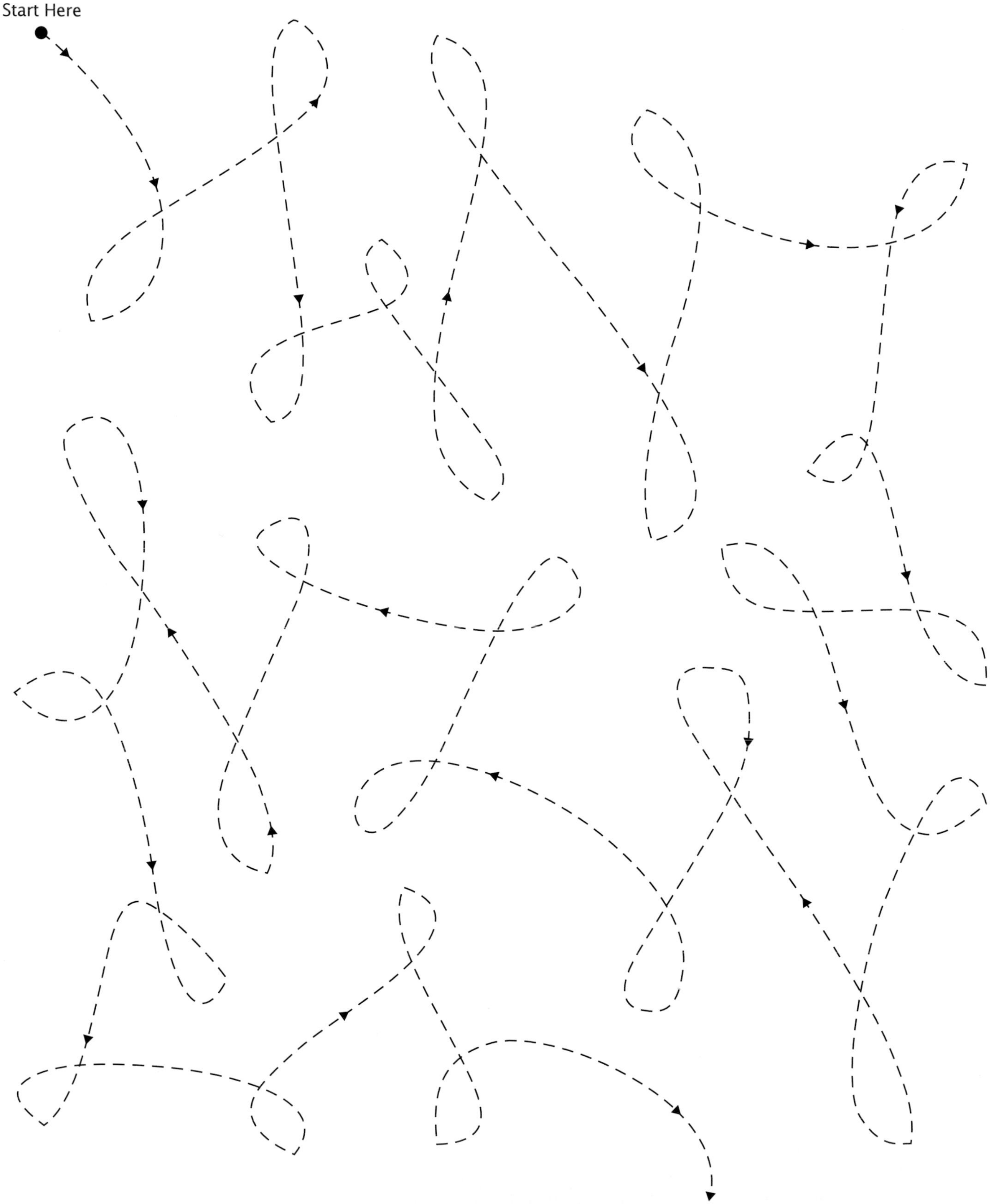

Loop-de-Loop Practice Pattern

Zigzag Practice Pattern

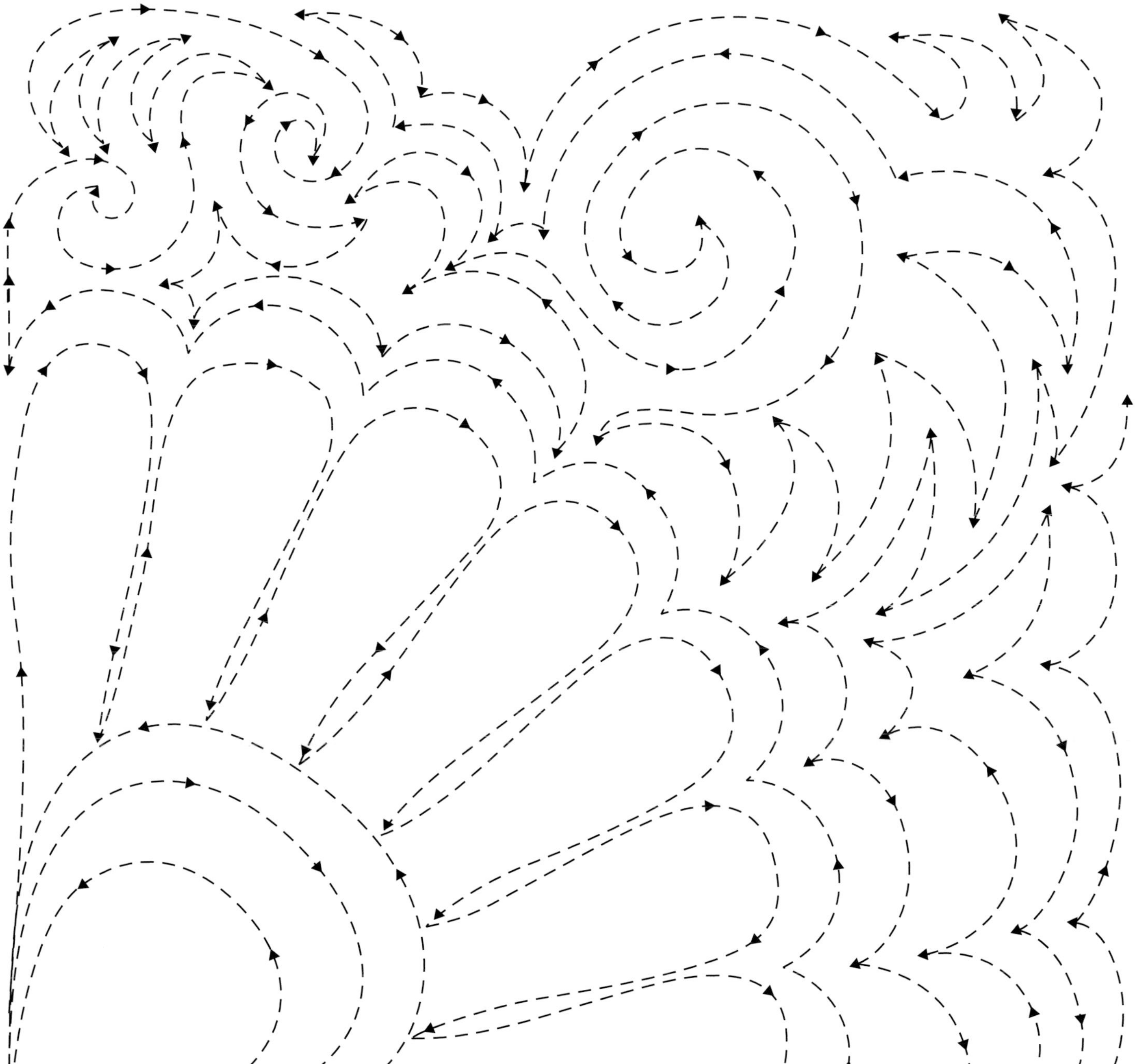

Caryl Flower Practice Pattern

LESSON 11

Machine Trapunto

The word trapunto *comes from the Italian language, where it originally referred to embroidery. For quilters it refers to quilting designs that have a raised look. Quilts that feature machine trapunto have a three-dimensional quality because light and shadow create a soft, sculptural quality in the stuffed areas. Trapunto adds depth and richness to the appearance of a quilt.*

Traditionally, trapunto involves quilting by hand and then making tiny slits or holes in the backing of a quilt to carefully stuff selected motifs with extra batting. The holes in the fabric are closed by gently moving the separated threads back into place with a needle or by stitching them closed with matching thread. This process is time-consuming and often leaves traces of holes on the back side of the quilt. My lesson will show you a quicker method for using water-soluble thread and specially placed extra layers of batting to do beautifull trapunto by machine. It's easy, and after a while, you may find that machine trapunto is sort of like eating peanuts—it's hard to stop!

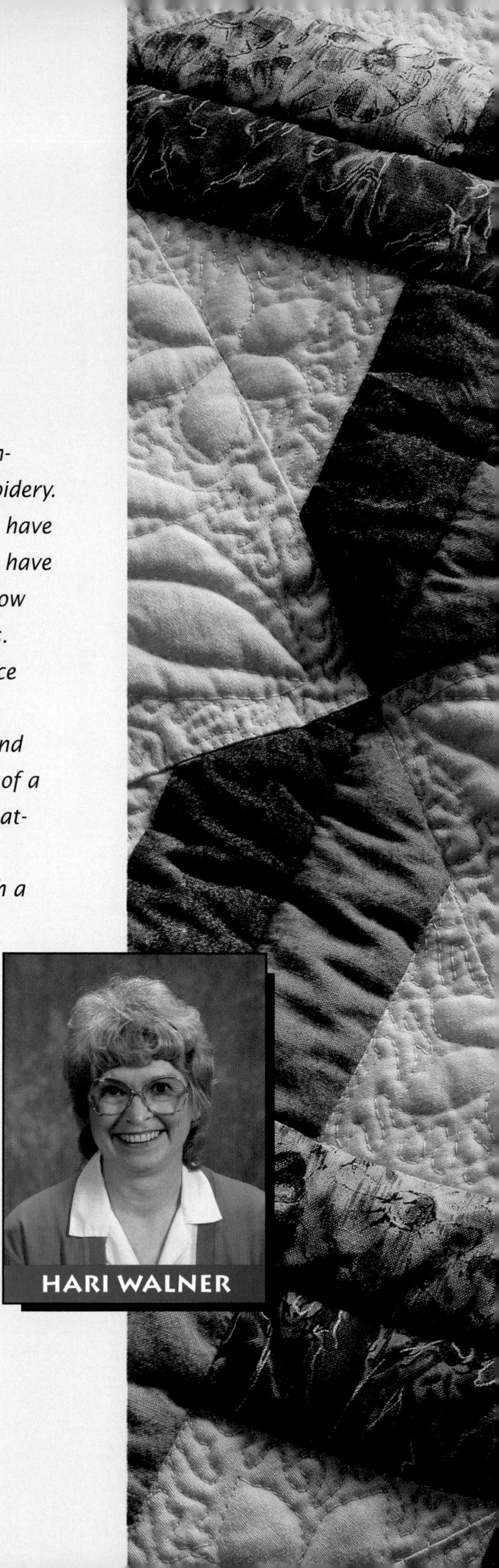

HARI WALNER

TRY MACHINE TRAPUNTO ON THESE PROJECTS:

Garden of Hearts, page 136
Autumn Trellis, page 202

Mettler
metrosene
No.

LESSON 11

Machine Trapunto

SELECTING QUILTING MOTIFS

Choosing designs for machine trapunto is easy if you keep these guidelines in mind.

■ Designs with open lines, as shown in **Diagram 1,** cannot be stuffed because they will not contain an extra layer of padding.

■ Designs with enclosed areas, like the ones in **Diagram 2,** are suitable for the raised look of machine trapunto because they can be stuffed with extra batting to create a raised appearance.

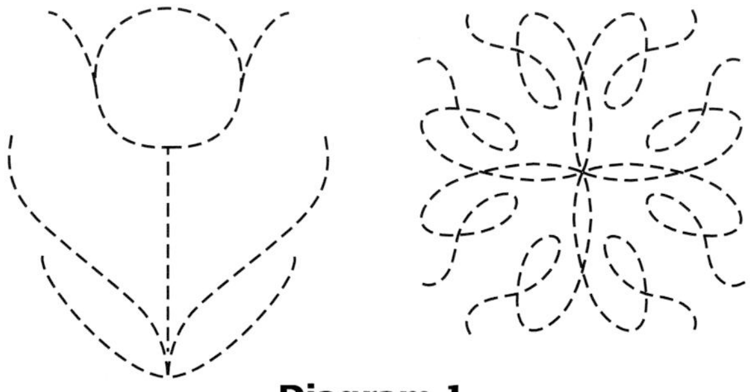

Diagram 1

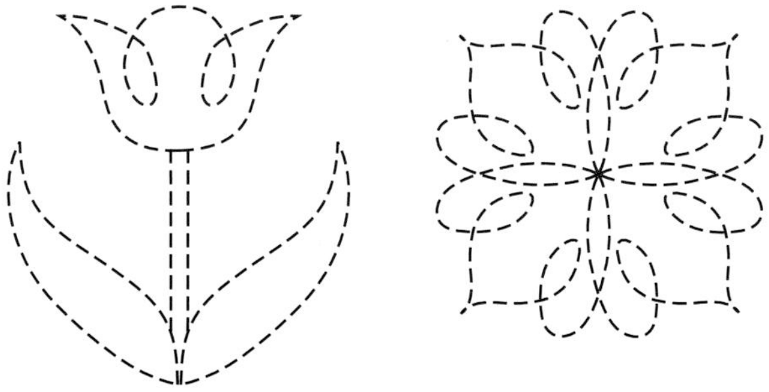

Diagram 2

Get Set

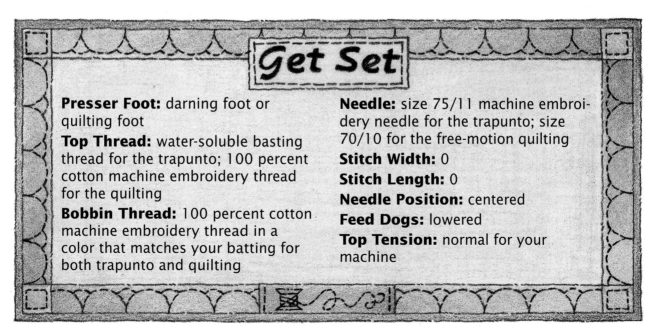

Presser Foot: darning foot or quilting foot

Top Thread: water-soluble basting thread for the trapunto; 100 percent cotton machine embroidery thread for the quilting

Bobbin Thread: 100 percent cotton machine embroidery thread in a color that matches your batting for both trapunto and quilting

Needle: size 75/11 machine embroidery needle for the trapunto; size 70/10 for the free-motion quilting

Stitch Width: 0

Stitch Length: 0

Needle Position: centered

Feed Dogs: lowered

Top Tension: normal for your machine

PREPARING A PRACTICE QUILT SANDWICH

You'll need water-soluble basting thread, one 8-inch square of thick polyester batting, water-soluble marker, pair of blunt scissors, and a container of water large enough to hold your practice quilt sandwich.

With a removable marker, trace the Primrose Quilting Design from page 114 onto the right side of a 14-inch square of light or medium solid fabric. Do not layer and baste the quilt sandwich at this time. **Note:** The markings in the following photos have been darkened slightly for visual clarity.

MACHINE TRAPUNTO

1 Layer the marked 14-inch square of fabric with an 8-inch-square piece of thick polyester batting, and pin them together with safety pins, so that the thick batting lies directly underneath the marked design. Do not add backing fabric at this time.

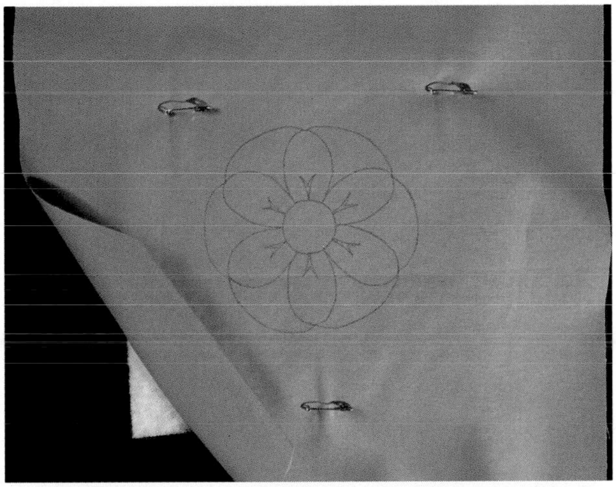

2 With water-soluble basting thread in the top of your machine and cotton thread in the bobbin, start at the dot and follow the arrows in **Directional Stitching Diagram 1** on page 112 to free-motion stitch the outline of the design. Do not stitch the inside lines. Clip the threads close to the fabric. For more information on free-motion quilting, see Lesson 7. Do not worry about getting perfect stitches for this step because the water-soluble thread will eventually be dissolved, and the cotton thread will remain inside the layer of batting.

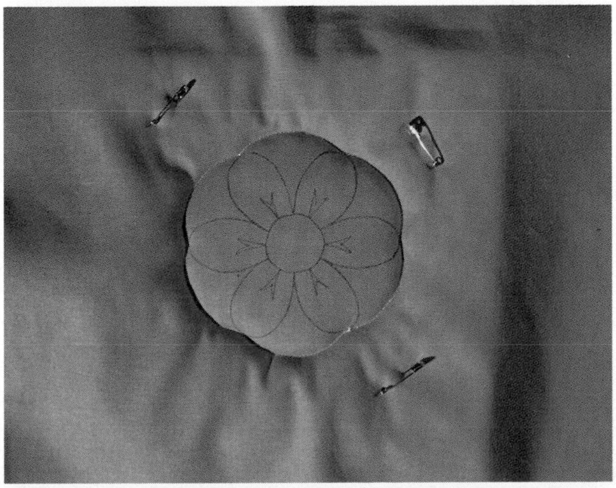

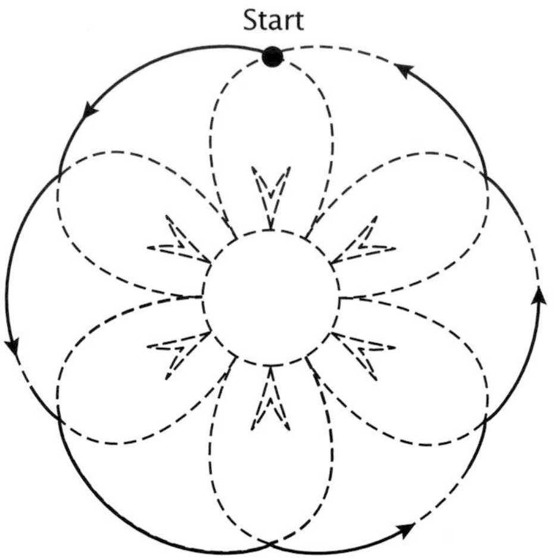

Directional Stitching Diagram 1

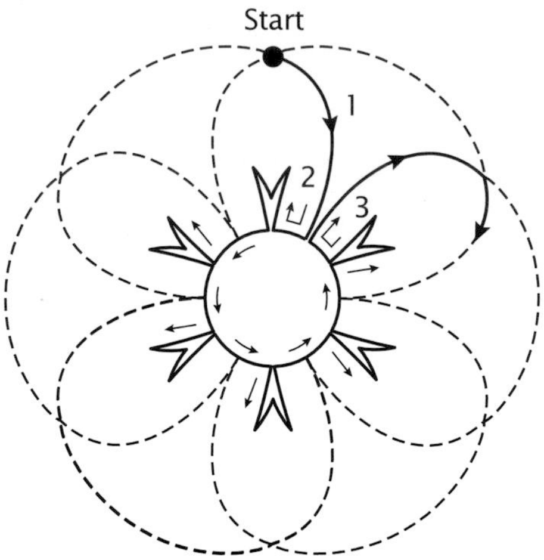

Directional Stitching Diagram 2

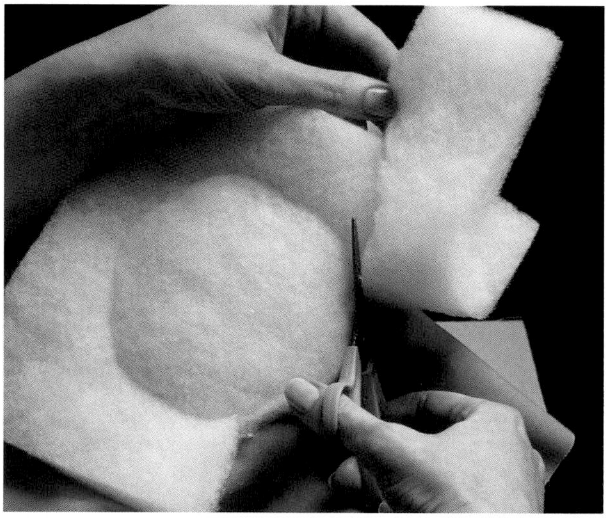

3 Turn the fabric over, and use a pair of blunt scissors to trim away the polyester batting from all areas that you do not wish to appear stuffed. For this Primrose design, cut the batting away just outside the outline stitching, trimming very close to your stitches and taking care not to cut the fabric. If you accidentally cut some of the stitches, however, do not worry. There needs to be just enough stitching to hold the thick batting in place while you complete the process of machine trapunto.

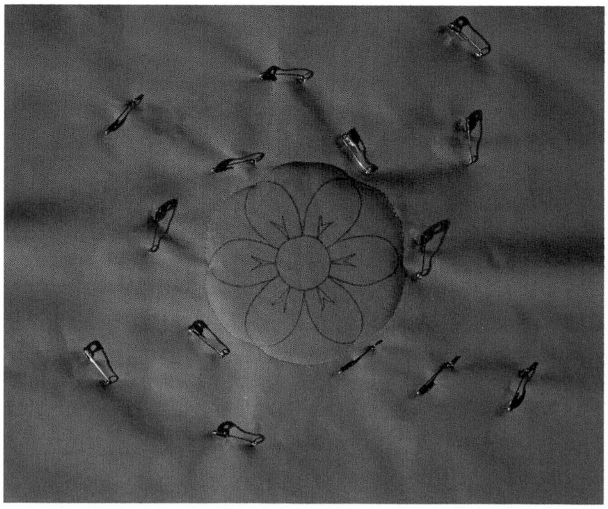

4 From this point on, proceed with the quilt sandwich as you normally would. Layer the fabric (with the thick batting stitched to it) with a 14-inch square *each* of regular batting and backing fabric. Pin-baste these three layers together very securely, especially in the area of the thick batting. This will help to eliminate puckers while you are quilting.

5 Rethread your machine with 100 percent machine embroidery thread in both the top and bobbin. Starting at the dot, follow the arrows in **Directional Stitching Diagram 2** to quilt the inside details in a continuous line. Then stitch back over the line of stitches you did in Step 2 (shown by the arrows in **Directional Stitching Diagram 1**) and end at the dot. Clip the threads close to the fabric. Sometimes you will be stitching on top of the water-soluble thread; do not worry if this second line of stitches does not exactly match because your first stitches will be dissolved in water.

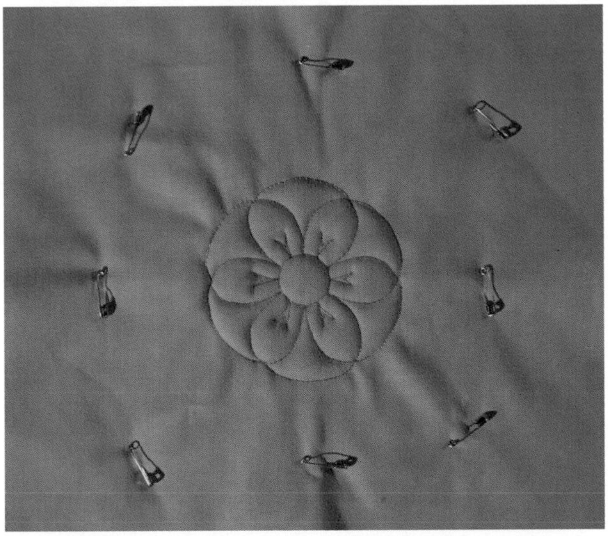

6 If you'd like to make the raised area of the design stand out even more, do a background of stipple quilting behind the trapuntoed area. For more information on stipple quilting, see Lesson 9.

7 When you have completed all of the stitching you want to do on this practice quilt sandwich, immerse it in clear, tepid water with no detergent or soap added. Wait a minute or two, and then agitate it by hand for a few seconds. This will dissolve the water-soluble thread as well as the lines made by your removable marker. Allow the quilt sandwich to dry, and smooth it into shape with your fingers, if necessary.

Primrose Quilting Design

Great Ideas!

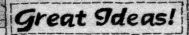

USE AN IRONING BOARD FOR SUPPORT

Try placing an ironing board behind or to the left of your sewing machine, and lower it to the height of your sewing table. Cover it with a large plastic bag, and you'll have an excellent surface for supporting the weight of your quilt while you are stitching.

OFFICE FINGERS FOR A BETTER GRIP

I like to use rubber office fingers on each finger to guide and control a quilt and help me stay relaxed while I stitch. I think that the Swingline brand fingers with "high tread" are the Michelins of the quilting world! These are available at any office supply store.

ADJUST TABLE HEIGHTS

Check to make sure that the table you place your sewing machine on is at the right height for you. The surface of my quilting table is 43½ inches, a height at which my arms can rest comfortably. It's also helpful to choose a table that is large enough to bear the weight of the quilt and keep it from dropping onto the floor.

USE SMALL PIECES OF THICK BATTING

When you do machine trapunto on a large quilt, cut pieces of thick batting that are just large enough to cover the back side of each of the motif(s) you are going to pad. Then trim these pieces of batting after you stitch each motif to help eliminate bulk. If you try to use a single large piece of thick batting, the quilt can become very unwieldy and difficult to manage at the sewing machine.

STAND WHILE YOU STITCH

I think it's easier to quilt standing up than sitting down, especially if I am working with a large quilt. Standing gives me better leverage, and I find it much easier to reach, refold, and reposition a quilt when I am not sitting. Standing also prevents backaches that can come from manipulating a heavy quilt for a long period of time.

LESSON 12

Tying Quilts by Machine

Tying is a quick, easy, and practical way of anchoring the three layers of a quilt together. Tying also goes by other names, such as tacking, tufting, and knotting, and it is popular for comforters, quilts that receive a lot of use and regular laundering.

The traditional tying method is to bring a threaded hand sewing needle down through the layers of a quilt and back up again, knot and clip the threads, and leave thread tails as a decorative element on the front or back surface. Machine tying can be as simple as using a zigzag stitch to create bar tacks, arrows, diamonds, and hourglass shapes. Free-motion techniques enable you to add decorative designs and embellishments, such as colorful buttons, for textural interest.

If you are new to quiltmaking, you might enjoy machine tying the first few projects you make, so that you can finish quickly and enjoy the feeling of completing a quilt in a short amount of time. If you already know how to quilt, you're sure to love the variety of looks that machine tying offers. Take some time to explore the assortment of machine-tying options in my lesson, and design some charm tacks and other embellishments that only you and your sewing machine can create.

CAROLINE REARDON

TRY MACHINE TYING ON THIS PROJECT:

Charming Log Cabin Quilt, page 144

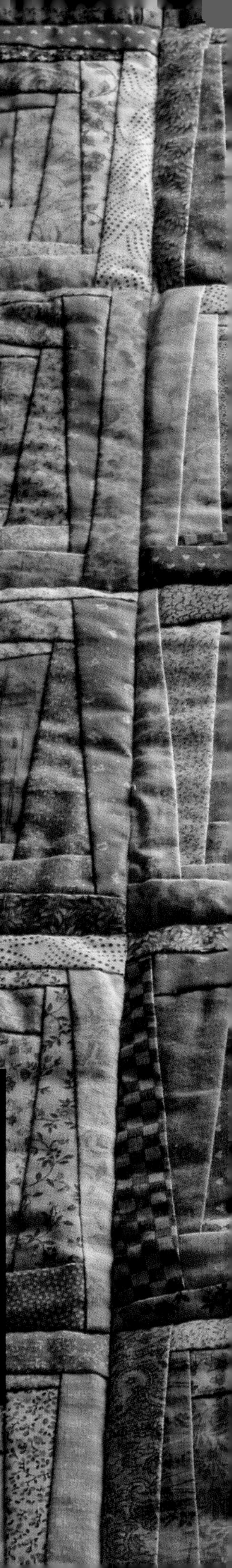

LESSON 12

Tying Quilts by Machine

PREPARING A PRACTICE QUILT SANDWICH

To prepare a practice quilt sandwich, cut a 14-inch square of light or medium solid fabric for the top. Cut a 14-inch square of batting and another 14-inch square of backing fabric. Place the backing fabric wrong side up on a flat surface and lay the square of batting on top of it. Add the top fabric right side up over the batting. Pin-baste the three layers together by placing rust-proof quilter's safety pins at 3- to 4-inch intervals over the surface of the practice quilt sandwich, as shown in the photos on page 19. Make as few or as many practice quilt sandwiches as you like for practicing the techniques in this lesson. If you make more than one, consider using different types of batting in them, so you can begin to develop your own likes and dislikes while you stitch.

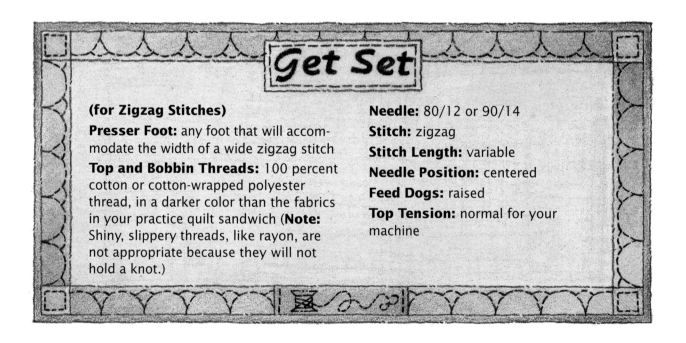

Get Set

(for Zigzag Stitches)

Presser Foot: any foot that will accommodate the width of a wide zigzag stitch

Top and Bobbin Threads: 100 percent cotton or cotton-wrapped polyester thread, in a darker color than the fabrics in your practice quilt sandwich (**Note:** Shiny, slippery threads, like rayon, are not appropriate because they will not hold a knot.)

Needle: 80/12 or 90/14

Stitch: zigzag

Stitch Length: variable

Needle Position: centered

Feed Dogs: raised

Top Tension: normal for your machine

ZIGZAG STITCHES

Note: Some of the zigzag stitches in the following photos have been enlarged for visual clarity.

BASIC BAR TACKS

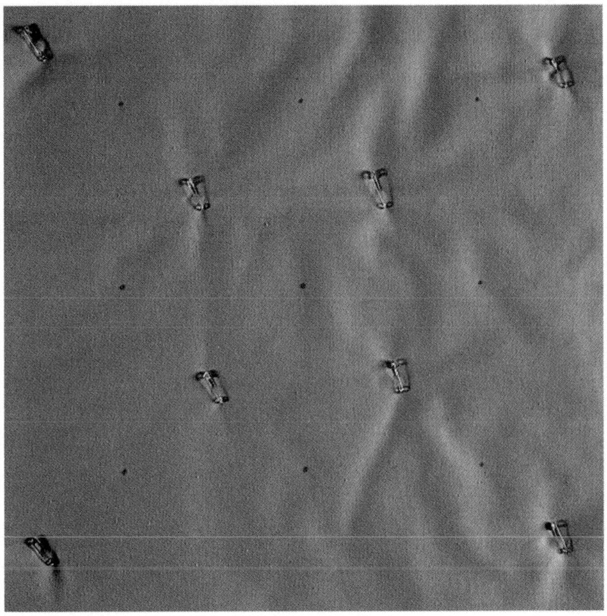

1 Use a removable marker or pencil to mark three rows of three dots each on the top fabric of your practice quilt sandwich, placing them at approximately 3- to 4-inch intervals. This spacing is ideal for allowing as much loft in the batting as posible, while anchoring the layers of a quilt securely. Take care to anchor your beginning and ending stitches securely for each of the tying methods in this lesson, so that they will not come loose. To do this, set both the stitch length and the zigzag control knob on your sewing machine to 0 and take three or four stitches in place. Use this method of starting and stopping for all techniques in this lesson.

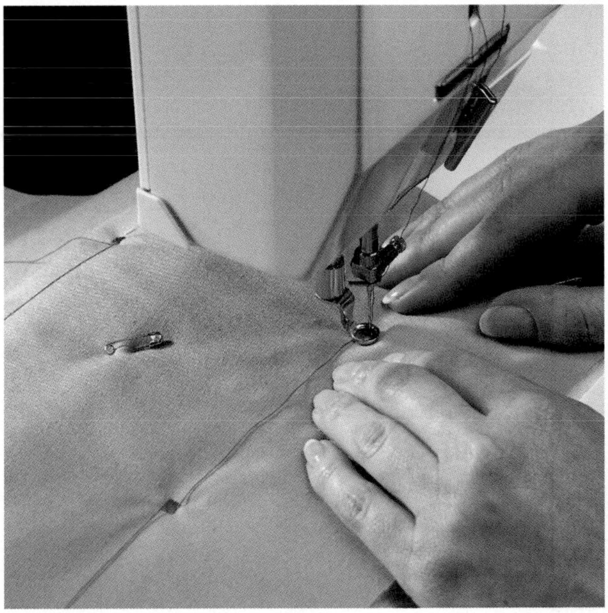

2 Set your stitch width to the widest setting and the stitch length to just a bit longer than 0. Do eight to ten zigzag stitches at one of the dots, and stop with the needle down. Reset your stitch length and zigzag width to 0, and take several stitches in place to secure the threads. This will create a bar tack of zigzags that lie very close together, yet not on top of each other. Do not clip the threads at this time; simply slide the quilt sandwich over to the next dot, pulling the top and bobbin threads along, so that the needle is positioned directly above the next dot. Do a bar tack at each of the remaining dots, and then clip all of the threads close to the surface of the quilt sandwich.

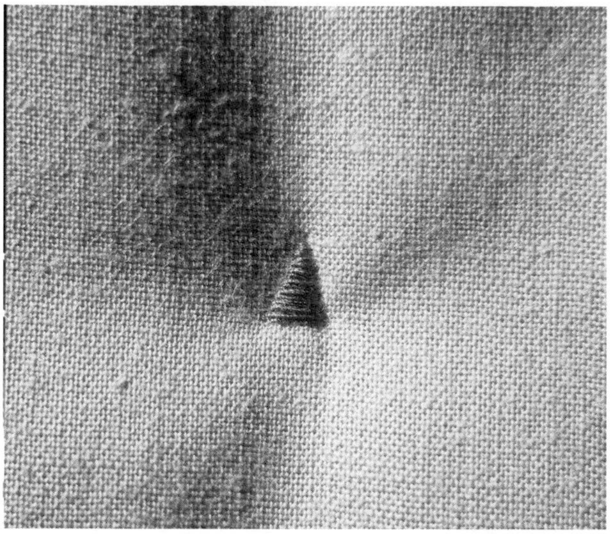

ARROWS

1 Somewhere near one edge of your practice quilt sandwich, mark three more dots, spacing them approximately 3 or 4 inches apart, in any configuration you like. At one of the dots, do a bar tack, but rather than changing to a wide zigzag stitch immediately after you anchor the beginning stitches, begin to turn the zigzag knob very slowly, gradually increasing the stitch width while you continue stitching. This will create an arrowlike effect, with very narrow stitches at one end increasing to wide zigzags at the other.

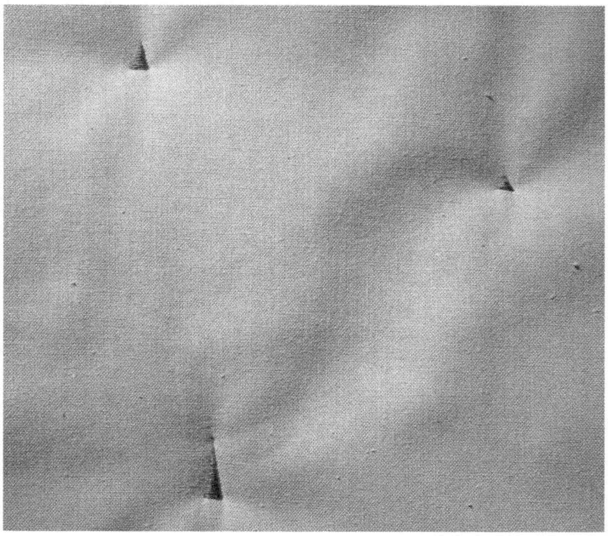

2 Practice stitching more arrows at each of the remaining two dots. Try creating a longer arrow by simply increasing the width of your zigzag more slowly after you anchor the beginning stitches. Stitch a shorter arrow by increasing the stitch length more quickly after anchoring the beginning stitches. Then compare all three arrows to decide which ones appeal to you most.

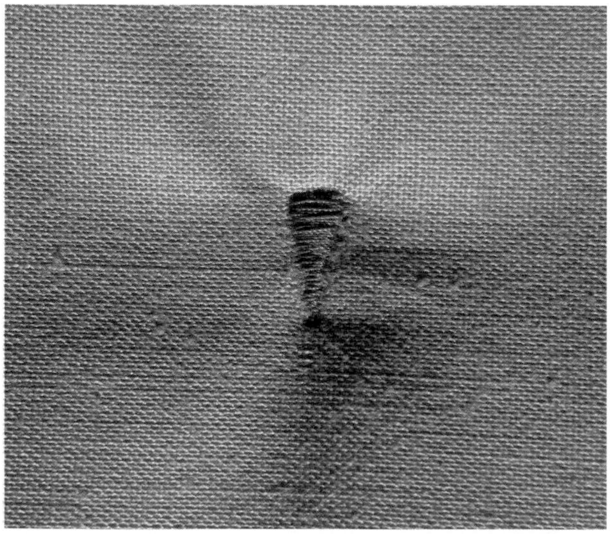

HOURGLASS SHAPES

1 Near another edge of your practice quilt sandwich, mark three more dots at approximately 3- or 4-inch intervals. At one of the dots, anchor a few beginning stitches, and immediately set your stitch width to the widest zigzag on your machine. Start stitching and decrease your stitch width quickly until your stitching reaches a small point, and stop. When you have reached this point, the half-hourglass shape will look like this.

2 To complete the hourglass shape, increase your stitch width at the halfway point by moving the zigzag control knob on your machine at the same rate of speed as before and continuing to stitch until you reach the widest zigzag on your machine. This creates a completed hourglass shape. When you have finished, anchor the ending threads in place as before, and clip the threads close to the surface of the fabric.

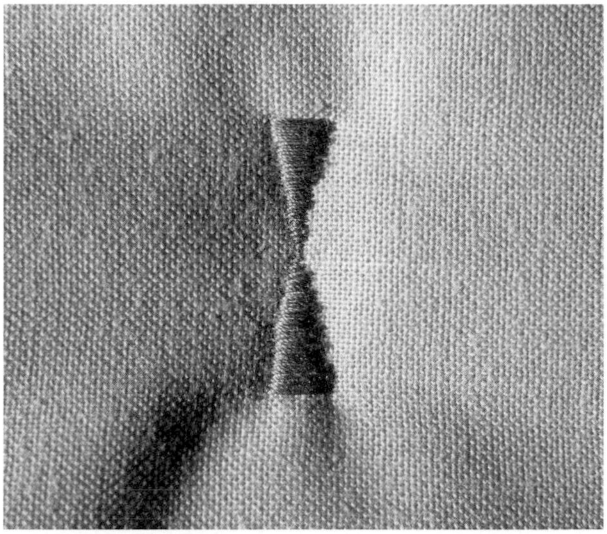

DIAMONDS

1 To stitch a diamond shape at one of the two remaining dots, start by anchoring a few beginning stitches. Then start to stitch, gradually increasing your stitch width to the widest zigzag on your machine, and stop with the needle down. This will look similar to a half-hourglass shape.

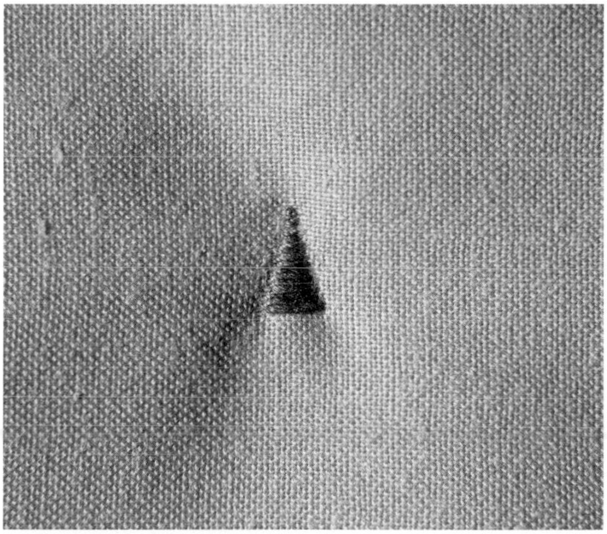

2 To create the second half of the diamond, decrease your stitch width at the same speed, until the second half of the diamond matches the first half.

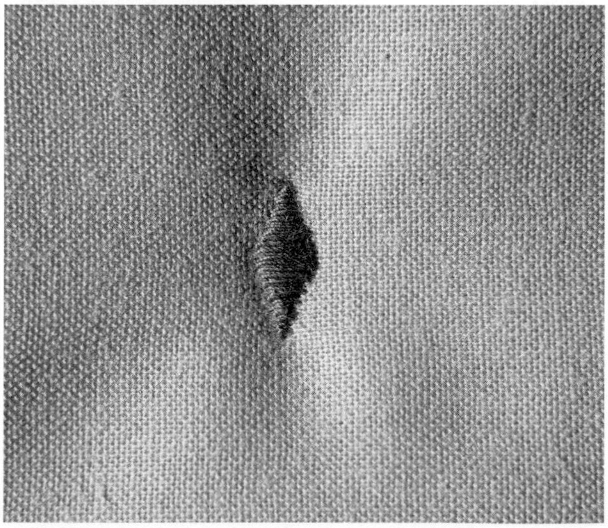

EMBELLISHMENTS

To create interesting texture and add more color to the surface of a quilt, embellishments like buttons and charm tacks are the perfect answer. They are suitable for quilts that will not receive hard wear. Buttons should be avoided for baby quilts, where safety is of prime importance, and for any quilt that will be used or cleaned frequently.

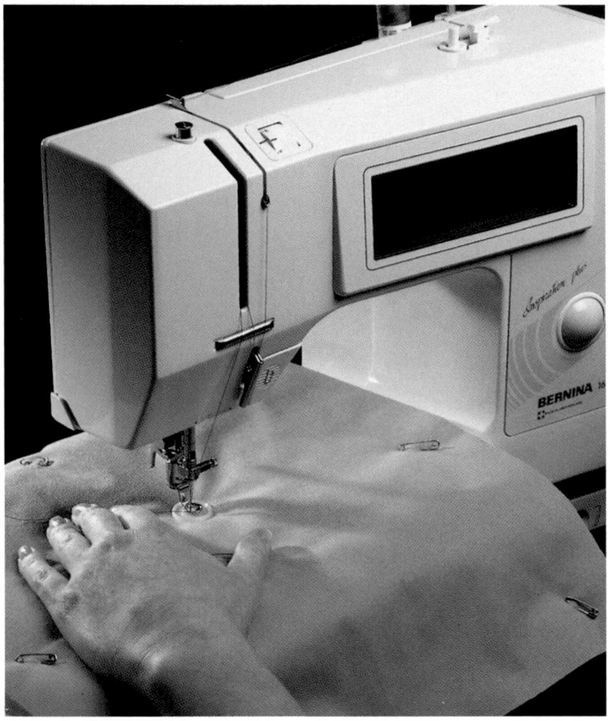

BUTTONS

You'll need a water-soluble fabric glue stick and assorted buttons in various sizes.

1 Dab a bit of glue from the glue stick onto the wrong side of a button and place it on your practice quilt sandwich, pinching the button and fabric between your fingers for a few seconds to make them stick together. Place the quilt sandwich under the presser foot, so that the holes in the button lie parallel to the front of your sewing machine. Then guide the needle into the left buttonhole by slowly turning the hand wheel while you adjust the position of the quilt sandwich to align the hole with the needle. Then lower the presser foot, adjust the stitch width and length to 0, take three stitches in place to anchor the beginning threads, and stop with the needle up.

Get Set

(for Buttons)

Presser Foot: button foot, open-toed appliqué foot, or any foot that will accommodate the width of a zigzag stitch

Top and Bobbin Threads: 100 percent cotton or cotton-wrapped polyester thread, in a darker color than the fabrics in your practice quilt sandwich; choose thread colors that contrast to the buttons you choose.

Needle: 80/12 or 90/14 (**Note:** The needle must pass easily through the holes in the buttons you use.)

Stitch: zigzag

Stitch Width: variable

Stitch Length: 0

Needle Position: centered

Feed Dogs: raised

Top Tension: normal for your machine

2 Adjust the width of the zigzag stitch on your machine so that the needle will fall directly into each of the holes in the button as it swings from side to side. Carefully stitch back and forth through the button holes four times, and stop with the needle down. Adjust the stitch width to 0, and stitch three times in place to secure the ending threads. Remove the quilt sandwich from your machine and clip the threads close to the button and close to the backing fabric. Practice this technique with several different buttons to become comfortable with adjusting the zigzag stitch to various widths.

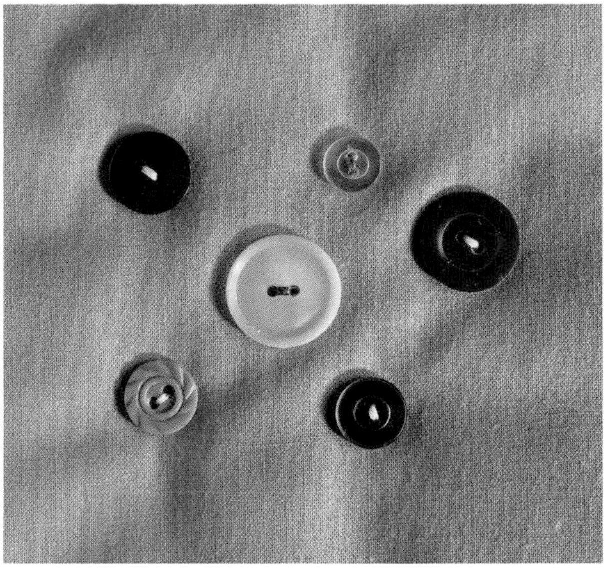

CHARM TACKS

Charm tacks are small, decorative shapes that are free-motion stitched onto a quilt to hold the three layers together. They add an element of fun to any quilt, and if their shapes are not perfectly formed or symmetrical, it only adds to their charm. On each of the designs on page 125, you'll find a starting dot and directional arrows indicating the stitching path for each motif.

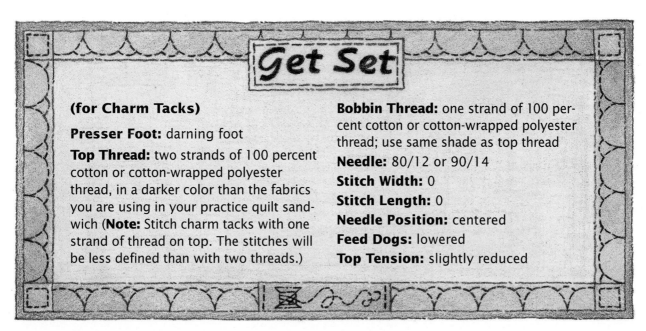

Get Set

(for Charm Tacks)

Presser Foot: darning foot

Top Thread: two strands of 100 percent cotton or cotton-wrapped polyester thread, in a darker color than the fabrics you are using in your practice quilt sandwich (**Note:** Stitch charm tacks with one strand of thread on top. The stitches will be less defined than with two threads.)

Bobbin Thread: one strand of 100 percent cotton or cotton-wrapped polyester thread; use same shade as top thread

Needle: 80/12 or 90/14

Stitch Width: 0

Stitch Length: 0

Needle Position: centered

Feed Dogs: lowered

Top Tension: slightly reduced

1 With a permanent fabric marker, trace the house pattern onto a small piece of tissue paper. Pin the tissue paper at the center of a practice quilt sandwich with straight pins. Place the starting dot directly under your sewing machine needle. Take three or four stitches in place, and then begin to stitch along the design lines. When you reach the small flower, stitch around the small, inner circle in a continuous motion. At the base of the small inner circle, continue stitching the outline of the larger circle, and then go on to the flower stem. Continue stitching around the entire house in a continuous line, anchoring your ending stitches at the lower right corner of the house. Clip the threads, leaving approximately 3-inch tails.

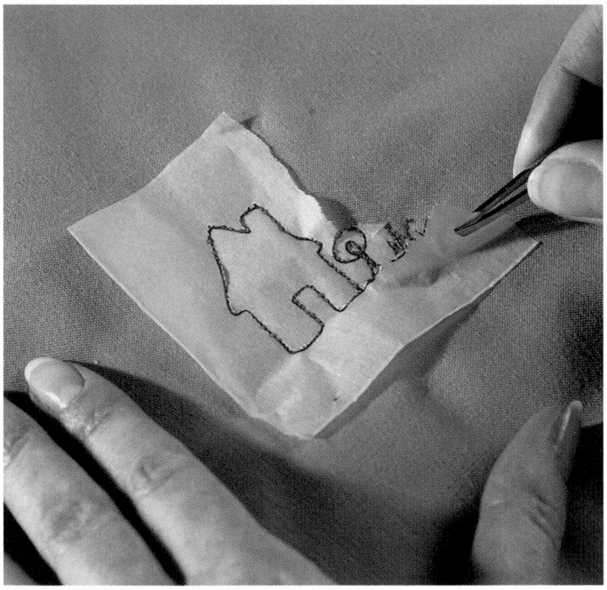

2 Carefully tear the tissue paper away from your stitches, and gently remove any remaining tissue paper with a pair of tweezers. Use a hand sewing needle to bury the threads in the layer of batting.

Charm Tacks

A DOZEN PROJECTS TO MACHINE QUILT

Aquatic REALM II

Jeannette Muir

Skill Level: Easy

Size: Finished quilt is 18 × 24 inches

The cool blues, greens, and purples in Aquatic Realm II mingle and flow like fish darting gently back and forth under the surface of a clear lake. Besides being a very convenient size to machine quilt easily, this small quilt is perfectly suited to be a doll quilt or a wall hanging.

TECHNIQUES YOU'LL NEED:

Starting and stopping, page 34
Stitch-in-the-ditch quilting, page 47
Crosshatching, page 56
Machine-guided curves and points, page 60

FABRICS AND SUPPLIES

As few as two fabrics can be used to make this quilt, although a wide variety of compatible prints creates more visual appeal. The quilt shown contains 16 different fabrics, 8 dark and 8 light prints in varying shades of blue, green, and purple. The inner border, which makes the vertical rows appear to "float," can be cut from any one of the light fabrics. Note that in this quilt, the light fabrics at the sides match the fabric in the inner border.

FABRIC
One 18 × 22½-inch piece ("fat quarter") *each* of eight different light prints for the vertical rows and inner border
One 18 × 22½-inch piece ("fat quarter") *each* of eight different dark prints for the vertical rows
¾ yard of a dark blue print for the outer border
¼ yard of a light print for the binding
⅝ yard of a dark print for the quilt back

MATERIALS
One crib-size Cotton Classic batting (45 × 60 inches)
Rotary cutter, ruler, and mat
Template plastic
Chalk marker
Removable fabric marker
Rust-proof quilter's safety pins

CUTTING

All of the pieces for this quilt are rotary cut. Note that the borders for this quilt are cut longer than needed; trim them to the correct length when adding them to the quilt.

From *each* of the eight light fabrics, cut:

Two 1¼ × 22-inch strips. From these strips, cut eight 1¼ × 3½-inch rectangles; there should be a total of 64 rectangles in the eight light fabrics.

From *each* of the eight dark fabrics, cut:

Two 1¼ × 22-inch strips. From these strips, cut eight 1¼ × 3½-inch rectangles; there should be a total of 64 rectangles in the eight dark fabrics.

From the dark blue fabric, cut:

Two 2¼ × 19-inch border strips

Two 2¼ × 21-inch border strips

From one of the light fabrics, cut:

Thirty-two 1¼-inch squares

Four 1½ × 22-inch border strips

From the light binding fabric, cut:

Three 2⅛ × 45-inch strips

From the dark print fabric for the quilt back, cut:

One 22 × 28-inch piece

From the crib-size batting, cut:

One 22 × 28-inch piece

PIECING THE VERTICAL ROWS

To create a pleasing color scheme for this quilt, try experimenting with various fabric strips on a design wall or on a piece of flannel that can be taped to a wall. This will allow you to step back and view each combination from a distance until you find the one that pleases you. In the quilt shown, fabrics are graded from dark to light. To achieve the same look in your quilt, start by first pairing the "darkest" dark fabric with the "darkest" light fabric. Then combine the "next darkest" dark strip with the "next darkest" light and continue, until finally the "lightest" dark is paired with the "lightest" light fabric. Use the quilt in the photo on page 128 as a guide to color placement.

STEP 1. Place a light strip over a dark strip and sew a diagonal seam line. Trim the seam allowance to ¼ inch, as shown, and press it toward the dark fabric. Sew the remaining light and dark strips together in the same manner, for a total of 64 light/dark pairs, as shown in **Diagram 1.** Press the seam allowances toward the darker fabrics.

STEP 2. Alternating lights and darks, sew together four pairs of light/dark strips, making sure that adjacent diagonal seams go in opposite directions, as shown in **Diagram 2.** Press the seams toward the darker fabric. Make a total of 16 of these vertical rows. At each end of each vertical row, place a contrasting light 1¼-inch square over the final rectangle and sew the seam diagonally, as shown. Trim the seam allowance to ¼ inch and press it toward the small triangle.

Diagram 1

Diagram 2

ASSEMBLING THE QUILT TOP

STEP 1. Sew the 16 vertical rows together, as shown in the **Quilt Assembly Diagram.** Press the seams open.

STEP 2. Sew a light inner border strip to each side of the quilt, as shown in the **Quilt Assembly Diagram,** and trim away the excess fabric. Press the seam allowances toward the borders.

STEP 3. Sew a light inner border strip to the top and bottom of the quilt, as shown. Trim away the excess fabric and press the seam allowances toward the borders.

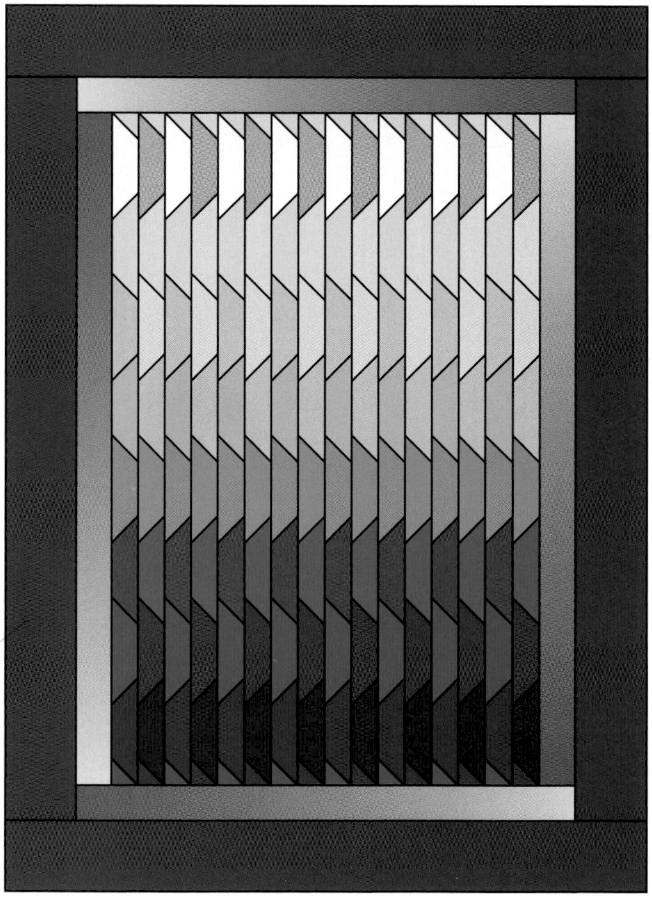

Quilt Assembly Diagram

STEP 4. Sew a dark blue outer border strip to each side of the quilt, as shown in the **Quilt Assembly Diagram.** Trim away the excess fabric and press the seam allowances toward the borders.

STEP 5. Sew a dark blue outer border strip to the top and bottom of the quilt. Trim away the excess fabric and press the seam allowances toward the borders.

STEP 6. Press the entire quilt top.

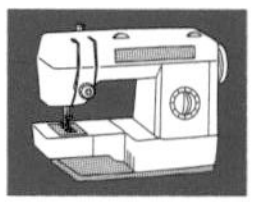

MACHINE QUILTING

STEP 1. Trace Template A and Template B from page 135 onto template plastic. Use Template A to mark the quilting design in the dark pieces in each vertical row, as shown in the **Quilting Diagram.** Position the placement line on the seam line as you mark, to alternate the direction of each curve.

STEP 2. Using a chalk marker, draw a 3-inch square and a diagonal line at each corner, as shown in the **Quilting Diagram.** In addition, mark the centers of each side and the top and bottom.

STEP 3. With a removable fabric marker, use Template B to mark the border quilting designs, as indicated in the **Quilting Diagram.** At the corners, trace around the template as usual, stopping at the diagonal line.

STEP 4. Layer the quilt back, batting, and quilt top and baste the center area thoroughly with safety pins, making sure to use straight pins around the entire perimeter of the quilt.

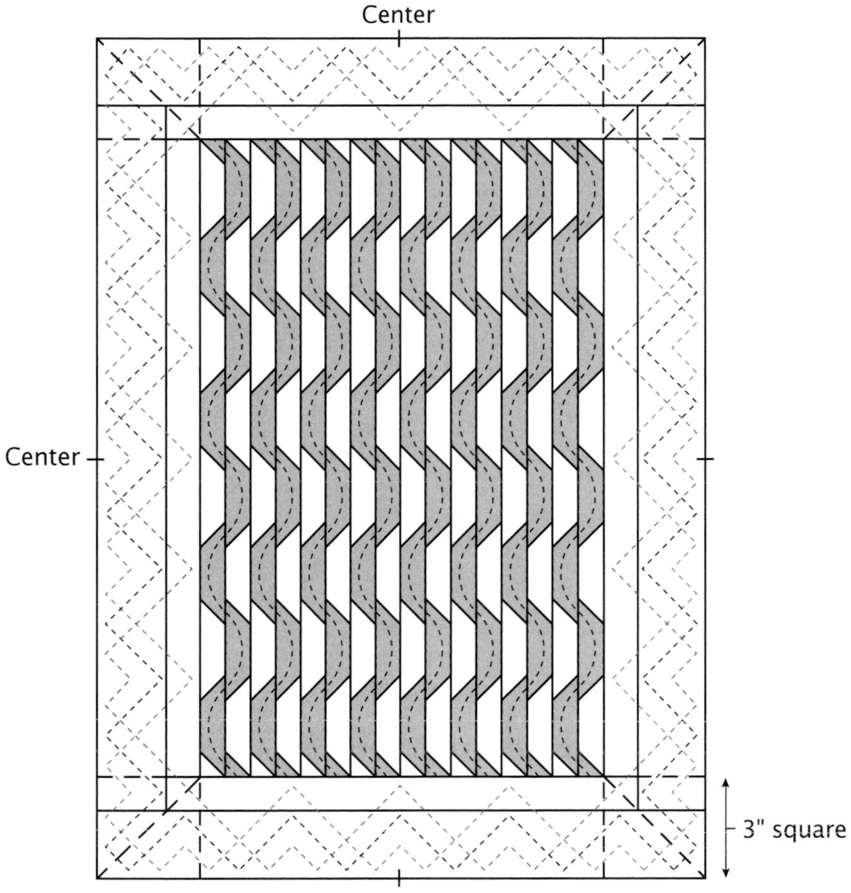

Quilting Diagram

STEP 5. Stitch around the entire quilt top 3⁄16 inch in from the edge of the fabric, removing the straight pins as you reach them. Check for desired stitch length and adjust thread tension at this time. If you can see bobbin thread on top of the quilt, loosen the top tension until it is no longer visible.

STEP 6. With the needle in center position, begin by hiding four or five tiny stitches in the ditch of the inner border. Then quilt the curved designs in each vertical strip, ending each line by stitching in the ditch of the inner border at the opposite edge of the quilt.

STEP 7. Quilt in the ditch around the inner edge of the inner border.

STEP 8. Machine quilt three individual lines or tracks of stitches in the border, as indicated by the red, gray, and blue lines on the **Quilting Diagram**. Start and end at the edges of the quilt top, so that these stitches will be covered by the binding.

STEP 9. Trim the quilt back and batting so that they are even with the edges of the quilt top.

APPLYING THE BINDING

STEP 1. Sew the binding strips together with diagonal seams. Trim these seams to ¼ inch and press them open.

STEP 2. Cut one end of the binding strip off at a 45-degree angle that faces the same direction as the seams. Fold the binding in half, wrong sides together, and press. "Walk" the binding around the edges of the quilt to make certain that the seams will not lie at the corners.

STEP 3. Position the binding at the edge on one side of the quilt sandwich, beginning approximately 5 inches away from a corner and leaving 5 or 6 inches of binding free. Start sewing the binding to the quilt with a ¼-inch seam.

STEP 4. Stop stitching exactly ¼ inch from the corner. Sew five or six backstitches into the seam allowance to secure the threads. Remove the quilt from the machine and clip the threads.

STEP 5. Fold the binding straight up and finger press the fold.

STEP 6. Fold the binding down, matching all edges, and finger press it in place. Insert the needle ¼ inch from the top edge, backstitch to the top, and continue stitching to the next corner. Repeat this process for all corners.

STEP 7. As you approach the beginning point, leave an additional 5 or 6 inches of binding unstitched. Remove the quilt from the machine and pin the unstitched ending portion of binding in place. Fold the binding straight up, matching the angle of the folded edge to the angle of the beginning of the binding, as shown in **Diagram 3.** Finger press this fold in place.

STEP 8. Unfold the binding. With a chalk pencil, mark along the fold and make an additional mark ½ inch beyond the fold. Open up the binding to a single layer and cut along this line.

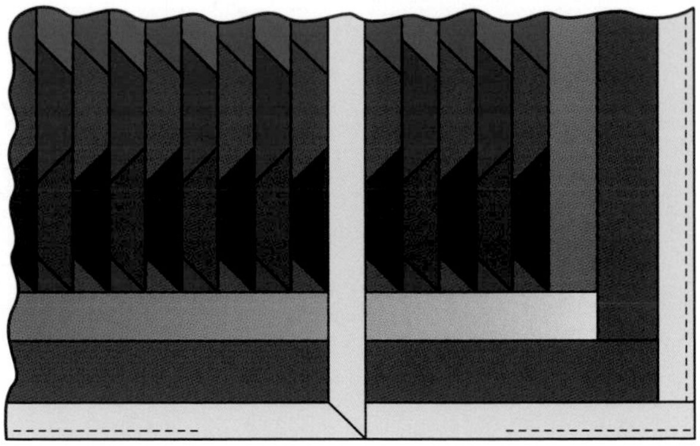

Diagram 3

STEP 9. Pin the two free ends of the binding right sides together and sew them with a ¼-inch seam. Press this seam open. Refold and press the binding.

STEP 10. Sew the final portion of the binding to the quilt.

STEP 11. Fold the binding to the back side of the quilt and hand sew it in place, mitering the fold at each corner and stitching it closed on both sides of the quilt.

Great Idea!

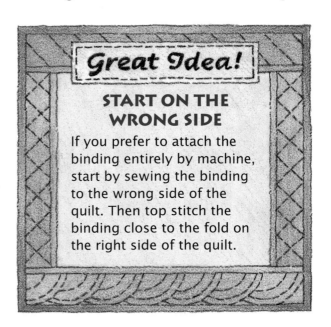

START ON THE WRONG SIDE

If you prefer to attach the binding entirely by machine, start by sewing the binding to the wrong side of the quilt. Then top stitch the binding close to the fold on the right side of the quilt.

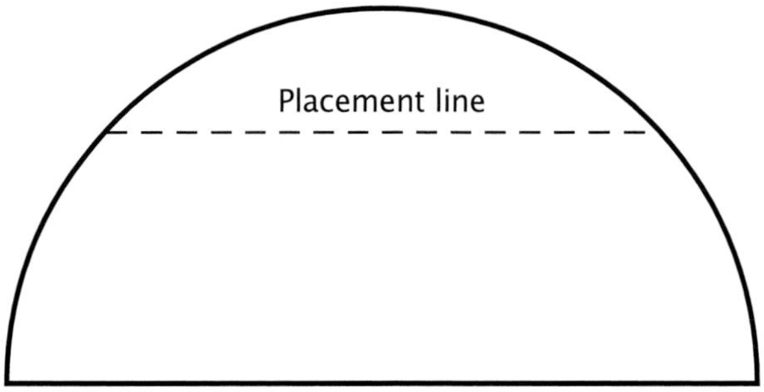

Template A

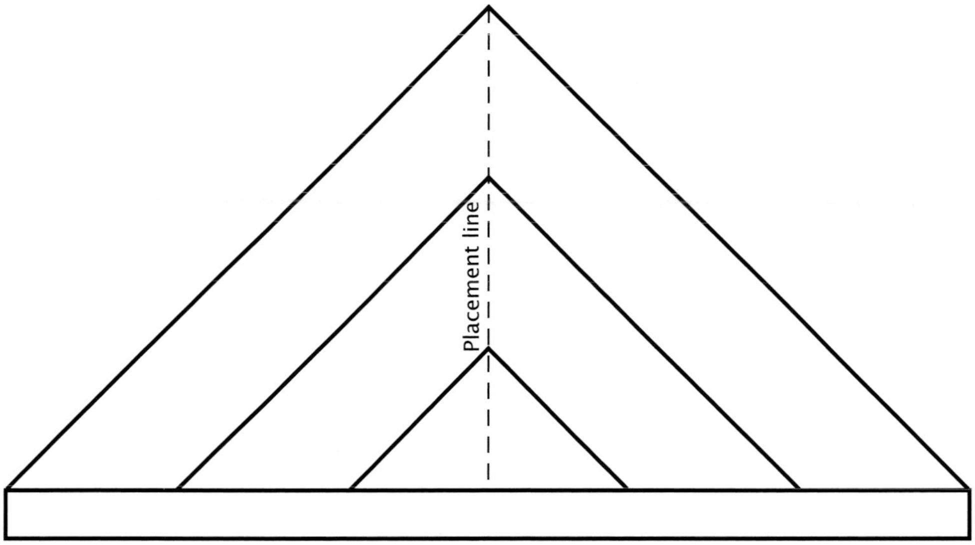

Template B

Garden OF HEARTS

Hari Walner

Skill Level: Easy

Size: Finished quilt is 38 × 45½ inches

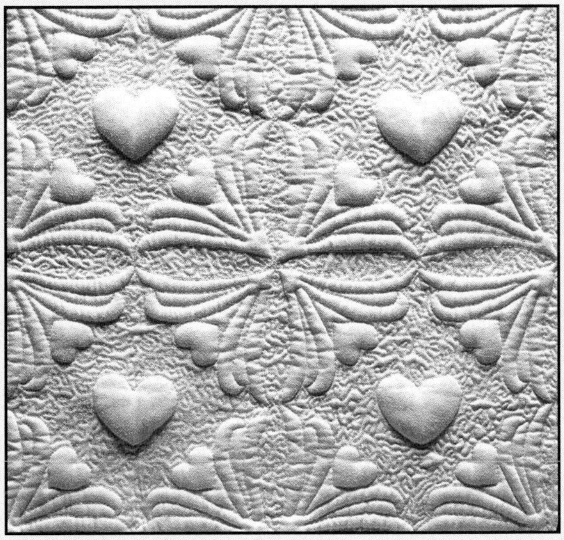

If you'd like to get right to the fun of machine quilting, Garden of Hearts is the perfect project to choose. Shell pink fabric gives the stitched hearts and leaves a soft sheen, and stipple quilting accentuates the raised look of the quilted designs.

TECHNIQUES YOU'LL NEED:

Starting and stopping, page 34
Outline quilting, page 45
Channel quilting, page 53
Free-motion curves and points, page 70
Free-motion continuous-line quilting, page 78
Vermicelli stipple quilting, page 91
Machine trapunto, page 108

FABRICS AND SUPPLIES

FABRIC

1¾ yards of light solid 100 percent cotton sateen fabric for the quilt top and binding
1½ yards of medium print fabric for the quilt back

MATERIALS

One crib-size cotton or cotton-polyester blend batting (45 × 60 inches)
One 49-inch square of high-loft polyester batting for the machine trapunto
Machine quilting thread in the same color as (or slightly darker than) the top fabric
Water-soluble basting thread for the machine trapunto
White or natural 100 percent cotton machine embroidery thread or regular sewing thread for the machine trapunto
Size #70 jeans/denim needle for quilting
Size #75 machine embroidery needle for basting with water-soluble thread for the machine trapunto
Rust-proof quilter's safety pins
Quilter's see-through ruler
Blunt scissors for cutting high-loft polyester batting
Removable fabric marker
Removable transparent tape

CUTTING

From the solid-colored cotton sateen fabric, cut:

One 42 × 50-inch rectangle for the quilt top

Five 2½ × 45-inch strips for the binding

From the medium print fabric, cut:

One 42 × 50-inch rectangle for the quilt back

From the high-loft polyester batt, cut:

Two 8 × 24-inch pieces for the top and bottom borders

Two 8 × 45-inch pieces for the side borders

Twelve 8 × 8-inch squares for the blocks

From the crib-size batting, cut:

One 42 × 50-inch rectangle

PREPARING AND MARKING THE QUILT TOP

STEP 1. If you plan to launder the finished quilt, prewash the top and backing fabrics. Press the top fabric and mist it with a light coating of spray sizing or spray starch. This will give the fabric added body and make it easier to mark with a removable fabric marker, because the marks will not sink into the fabric as deeply. This means that they will be easier to remove after you have finished quilting.

STEP 2. Lay the top fabric on a large, flat surface, and tape the edges with removable transparent tape, so that the fabric will not shift during the marking process. With a quilter's see-through ruler and a removable fabric marker, mark the fabric with twelve 7½-inch squares, as shown in **Diagram 1.** Mark a line ¾ inch away from the outside edges of these squares on all four sides.

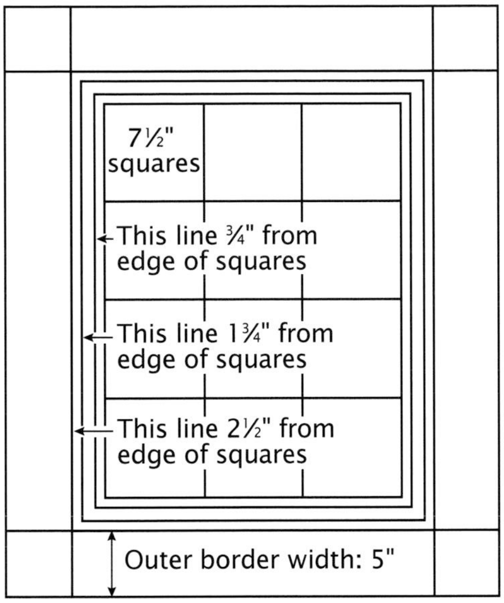

Diagram 1

Diagram 2

Mark a second line 1¾ inches away from the edges of the squares on all four sides, as shown. Mark a third line 2½ inches from the edges of the squares on all four sides, as shown, extending each of these lines at the corners to 5 inches beyond the point where they cross. Finally, mark the outer edges of the quilt to meet the previously marked lines, as shown.

STEP 3. With the removable fabric marker, trace the Block Quilting Pattern from page 143 in each of the 7½-inch squares. Make sure that the large center heart faces the same direction in all of the squares, as shown in **Diagram 2.**

STEP 4. Trace the Top and Bottom Border Quilting Pattern from page 142 onto the top and bottom borders, using four repeats, as in **Diagram 2.** Make sure that the scallops face toward the edges of the quilt.

STEP 5. Referring to **Diagram 2,** trace the Side Border Quilting Pattern from page 142 onto the side borders, using five repeats, as indicated by the dashed lines.

STEP 6. Trace one-fourth of the Block Quilting Pattern on page 143 at each of the border corners, positioning them as shown in **Diagram 2.** Note that the leaves on the corner motifs do not meet the leaves in the top/bottom/side motifs exactly. This difference is a small fraction of an inch, so it will be easy to adjust the leaves of the corner motifs to meet the leaves on the side/top/bottom borders when you are marking.

MACHINE TRAPUNTO AND STIPPLE QUILTING

STEP 1. Thread the sewing machine with water-soluble thread on top and natural colored machine embroidery or regular sewing thread in the bobbin. Attach a darning or quilting foot to the machine and lower the feed dogs.

STEP 2. Pin an 8-inch square of high-loft polyester batt to the wrong side of one of the blocks near the center of quilt top. With the fabric on top, stitch the high-loft batting to the block by free-motion stitching the lines of the block design, as shown in the **Block Directional Stitching Diagram** on page 140.

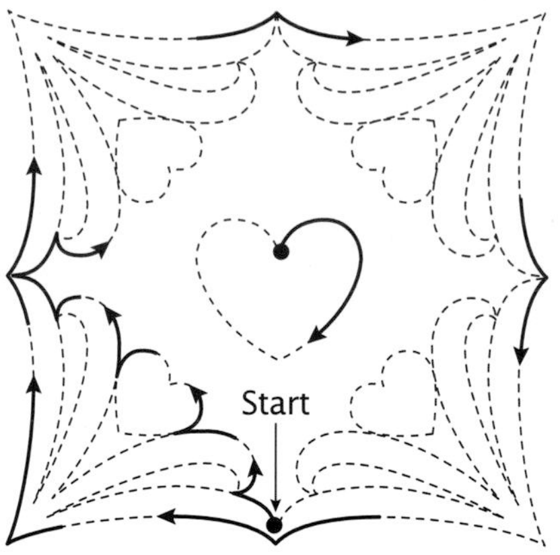

Block Directional Stitching Diagram

Begin stitching at the dots and stitch only the outlines of the block design and the heart; do not stitch any of the inside details at this time. With the blunt scissors, trim the high-loft batting to just outside your stitched lines. Repeat this process to stitch a square of high-loft batting to the wrong side of each of the remaining 11 blocks and trim each piece of high-loft batting in the same manner.

STEP 3. After you have stitched and trimmed all 12 blocks, pin the 8 × 45-inch pieces of high-loft batting to the wrong sides of the side borders. **Note:** This batt should be pinned right up to the edge of the blocks so that the area inside the straight inner border lines will appear raised. Stitch all of the marked lines in these borders in the same manner as for the blocks, referring to the **Border Directional Stitching Diagram** and continuing to use the water-soluble thread on top. Start by stitching the innermost straight line and working outward, using an even feed/walking foot and raising the feed dogs. Then return to free-motion quilting and stitch the curved outlines of the border motifs, starting at the dot and stitching around the entire quilt. After you have finished, trim away the high-loft batt just outside your stitched lines, as before.

STEP 4. Pin the two 8 × 24-inch pieces of high-loft batt to the wrong sides of the top and bottom borders, taking care to place the edge of the high-loft batt right next to the blocks, so that the areas inside the straight lines will appear raised. Stitch the high-loft batts in place, following the outlines of the design, as shown in the **Border Directional Stitching Diagram,** and trim away the excess batt close to your stitching, as before.

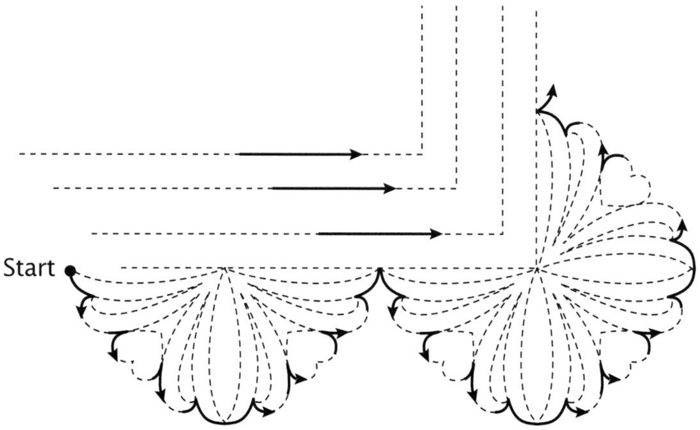

Border Directional Stitching Diagram

STEP 5. After you have trimmed away the high-loft batt from all areas that will not appear raised, the quilt top will be ready for layering. Place the backing fabric wrong side up on a flat surface and lay the batting over it. Place the quilt top over the batting and baste the three layers together securely with rust-proof safety pins placed at 2- to 3-inch intervals. Pinning very closely will help eliminate the puckering that can occur when quilting over the high-loft batting. For more information on layering and basting, see page 19.

STEP 6. Remove the water-soluble basting thread from the top of the machine, and take the machine embroidery or regular sewing thread out of the bobbin. Rethread the machine with regular machine quilting thread on top and in the bobbin.

STEP 7. Free-motion quilt the design lines in the blocks, starting at the dots, as shown in the **Block Quilting Diagram.** Begin with a block the near the center of the quilt and work outward toward the borders. Then quilt the straight inner lines of the borders, starting with the innermost line and working outward.

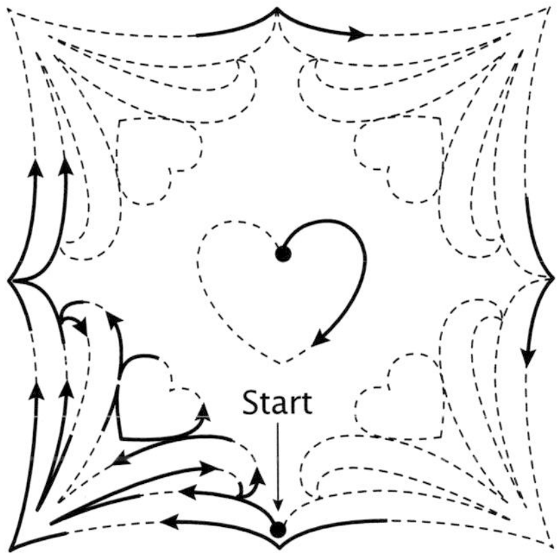

Block Quilting Diagram

STEP 8. Quilt the continuous-line designs in the borders, as shown in the **Border Quilting Diagram,** starting with the innermost straight line and working around all four sides of the quilt. Repeat for each of the remaining straight lines. For these straight lines, use an even feed/walking foot and raise the feed dogs. To quilt the curved border motifs, start at the dot and stitch around the entire design, as indicated by the arrows on the diagram. Do the inner curved lines first and then do the outer curved lines. Continue this process all the way around the quilt.

STEP 9. Do vermicelli stipple quilting around the stitched designs in the areas where you trimmed away the high-loft batting. This will make the quilting designs look even more raised.

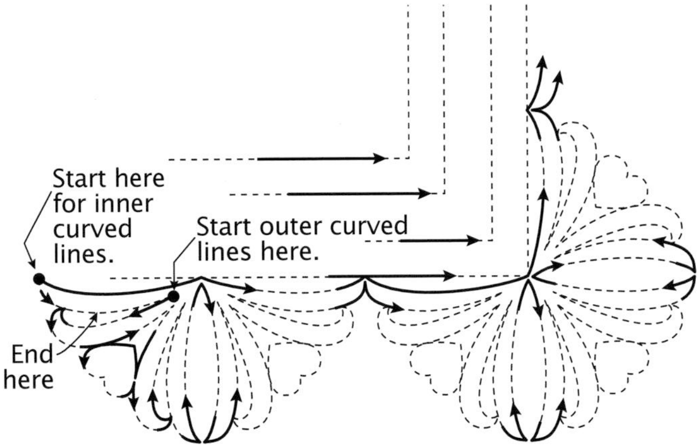

Border Quilting Diagram

APPLYING THE BINDING

For diagrams and more information on applying binding to a quilt, see page 240.

STEP 1. Trim the edges of the quilt back and batting even with the quilt top.

STEP 2. Sew the binding strips together with diagonal seams. Trim these seams to ¼ inch and press open. Fold the binding strip in half lengthwise, wrong sides together, and press.

STEP 3. Position the folded binding strip at the edge of quilt sandwich, with about 1 inch folded over at the beginning. Starting ½ inch from this fold, do three or four backstitches to secure the threads and stitch the binding to the quilt through all layers with a ¼-inch seam allowance.

STEP 4. Stop stitching ¼ inch from the corner. Backstitch, stop, and clip the threads. Fold the binding straight up and finger press the fold.

STEP 5. Fold the binding down, align raw edges with the quilt, and finger press in place. Beginning at the top edge, stitch to ¼ inch from the next corner. Repeat on all four sides of the quilt.

STEP 6. As you approach the beginning point, lay the end of the binding strip over the folded part at the beginning, and stitch across the fold.

STEP 7. Turn the binding to the wrong side of the quilt and stitch it in place by hand, mitering the corners.

STEP 8. Immerse the quilt in clear, tepid water to dissolve the basting thread. Let the quilt soak for a few moments and then agitate it by hand for 10 to 15 seconds. Remove it and lay it out on a flat surface to dry.

Side Border Quilting Pattern

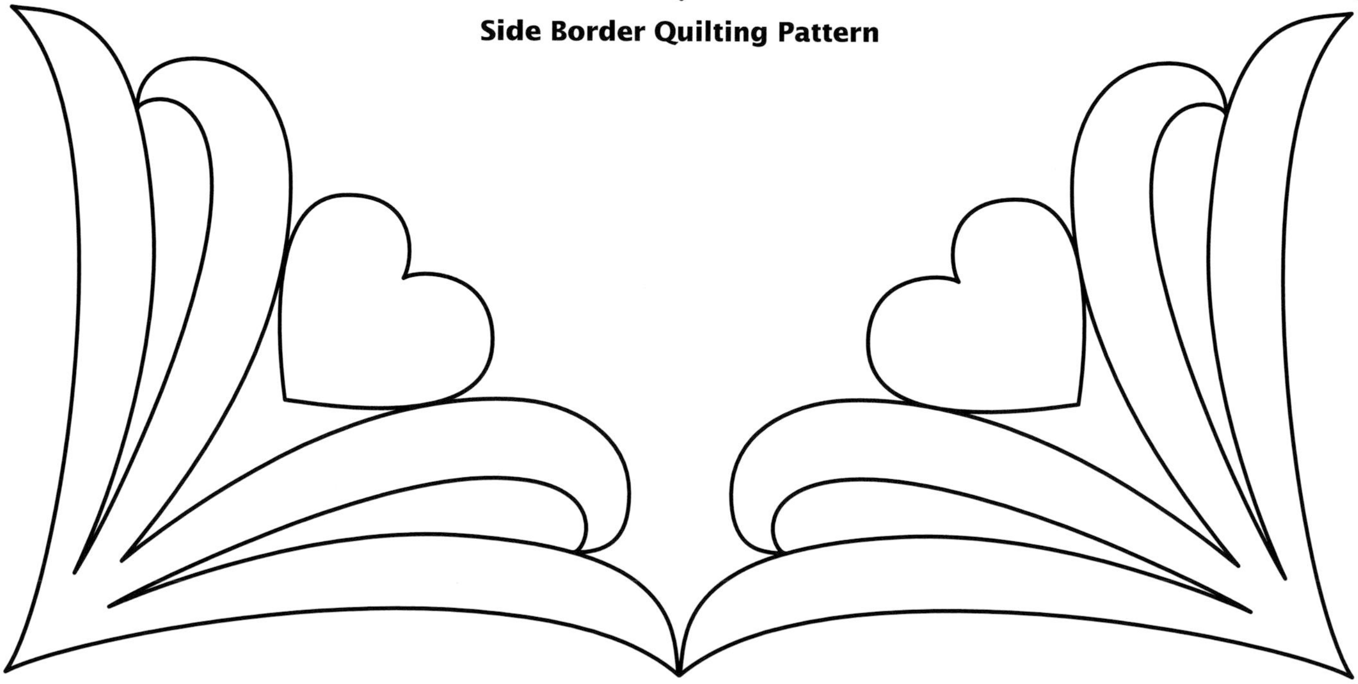

Top and Bottom Border Quilting Pattern

Block Quilting Pattern

Charming LOG CABIN

Caroline Reardon

Skill Level: Easy

Size: Finished quilt is 40 × 40 inches

Finished block is 6 inches square

Whisper-soft shades of pink and blue dance around pale yellow centers in this whimsical twist on the well-loved Log Cabin pattern. Traditionally made with straight "logs," the blocks in this baby quilt are slightly skewed, which gives them a playful look. And Caroline's placement of the darker halves of the blocks creates a subtle diamond shape at the center.

TECHNIQUES YOU'LL NEED:

Starting and stopping, page 34
Stitch-in-the-ditch quilting, page 47
Tying quilts by machine, page 116

FABRICS AND SUPPLIES

FABRIC

- ⅓ yard of pastel yellow solid for the block centers
- 2½ yards *total* of light blue, pink, and yellow print scraps for the blocks. If your scrap supply is limited, you may buy ⅛ yard of 20 *different* light scraps to get a wide variety of fabrics.
- 2½ yards *total* of medium blue, pink, and yellow print scraps for the blocks (or ⅛ yard of 18 *different* fabrics)
- 2¼ yards of medium blue print for the borders, quilt back, and binding

MATERIALS

- Crib-size polyester regular-loft batting (45 × 60 inches)
- 36 paper copies of the Paper Foundation Pattern
- Rotary cutter, ruler, and mat
- Monofilament thread for stitch-in-the-ditch quilting
- Two spools of medium blue cotton-covered polyester thread for piecing and the charm tacks
- Rust-proof quilter's safety pins
- One size #80 topstitching needle
- One large-eyed embroidery needle
- Thirty-six 3-inch squares of tracing paper

CUTTING

The measurements for foundation piecing are only approximate measurements, so it is important to use pieces of fabric that are large enough to cover each of the finished patches in the Log Cabin block and overlap the adjoining patch at least ¼ inch. If you use scraps of fabric, each one must measure at least 1¾ inches wide and ½ inch longer than the log it will cover.

From the yellow solid fabric, cut:

Thirty-six 3 × 3-inch squares

From the light blue, pink, and yellow print fabrics, cut:

Thirty-six 1¾ × 40-inch strips, or an equivalent amount of strips from scrap fabrics

From the medium blue, pink, and yellow print fabrics, cut:

Thirty-six 1¾ × 40-inch strips, or an equivalent amount of scrap fabrics

From the medium blue print fabric, cut:

Two 2½ × 36½-inch side border strips

Two 2½ × 40½-inch top and bottom border strips

One 44 × 44-inch square for the quilt back

Five 3¼ × 42-inch binding strips

From the crib-size batting, cut:

One 44 × 44-inch square

FOUNDATION PIECING

Piecing a quilt with paper foundations is an easy, highly accurate method that is fun to do. Use the following guidelines as you piece the Log Cabin blocks for this quilt.

- To prepare paper foundation patterns for this quilt, you can either trace the Paper Foundation Pattern on page 151 36 times on sheets of typing paper or make 36 photocopies of it on an accurate photocopy machine. If you use a photocopy machine, check the first copy to make sure there are no distortions before making more copies.
- The first piece of fabric is labeled 1 on the Paper Foundation Pattern on page 151. After that, the remaining numbers indicate the piecing order for the logs. The shaded areas indicate where to place the medium-value fabrics; make sure this shading is visible on all copies.
- Set the stitch length on your sewing machine to a very short length. Short stitches will perforate the paper, making it easy to remove the foundation paper after you have assembled the quilt.
- A presser foot with a centerline marking can be helpful for guiding the needle accurately along the stitching lines.
- Cover your ironing board with muslin to protect it from photocopy ink, which can transfer when you press each block.
- Working with a paper foundation is easier if you trim the paper to approximately ½ inch beyond the outer line.

PIECING THE LOG CABIN BLOCKS

For each Log Cabin block, you will need one yellow solid square, eight strips of light prints and eight strips of medium prints. Choose a variety of fabrics, so that no two are repeated within one block.

STEP 1. Place a yellow solid square underneath the center square #1 on the paper foundation, so that wrong side of the fabric lies next to the unprinted side of the paper. Pin them together with a straight pin from the paper side.

STEP 2. With right sides together, place a medium print strip on top of the yellow solid square, as shown in **Diagram 1,** so that it overlaps seam line 2 on the Paper Foundation Pattern by at least ¼ inch. Note that both fabrics are placed on the unprinted side of the Paper Foundation Pattern and that the greater portion of the medium print strip lies over the first patch, as shown. You can accurately gauge the position of this medium print fabric by holding the Paper Foundation Pattern up to a light source to see where the fabric is positioned.

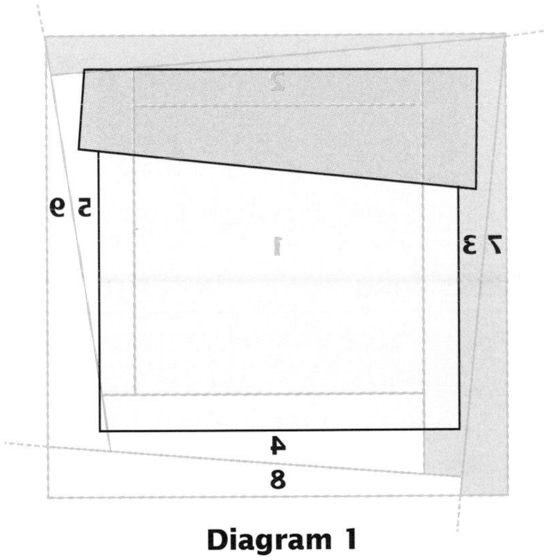

Diagram 1

STEP 3. With the paper side up, hold the fabrics securely, and carefully stitch through the foundation pattern and fabrics on seam line 2, beginning and ending this seam ¼ inch beyond the ends of the marked seam line, as shown in **Diagram 2** on page 148. Then remove the paper foundation from the machine and trim the fabric strip to approximately ¼ inch beyond the ends of the stitching line.

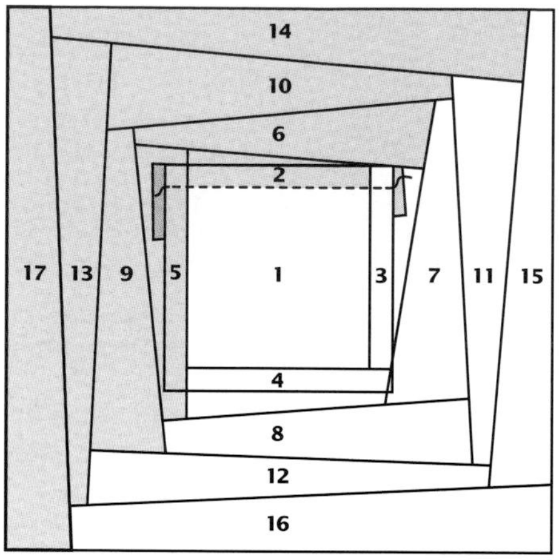

Diagram 2

STEP 4. Turn the Paper Foundation Pattern over, so that the fabrics face you and open them up. With a hot, dry iron, press the fabrics flat along the seam line. Bend the paper foundation out of the way, and trim away any extra fabric to leave a ¼-inch seam allowance, as shown in **Diagram 3.**

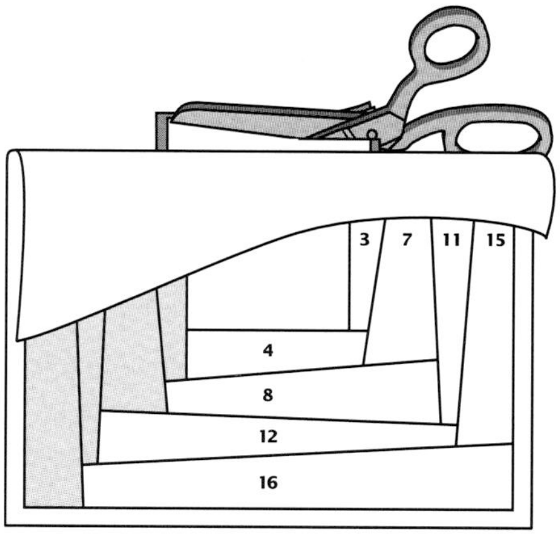

Diagram 3

STEP 5. Rotate the Paper Foundation Pattern, and add a light print fabric in the same manner, stitching on seam line 3. Open the fabric and press this seam line. Trim the extra fabric to leave a ¼-inch seam allowance. Paying attention to the shaded areas that indicate placement of light and medium print fabrics, continue adding fabrics to the pattern until all patches are covered, as shown in **Diagram 4.**

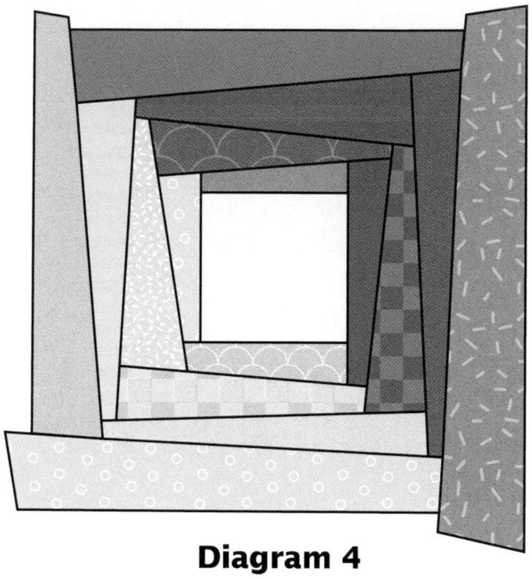

Diagram 4

STEP 6. Place the completed Log Cabin block paper side up on a cutting mat. With a rotary cutter, trim the paper and fabric along the outer lines of the Paper Foundation Pattern, as shown in **Diagram 5.** Do not remove the paper at this time.

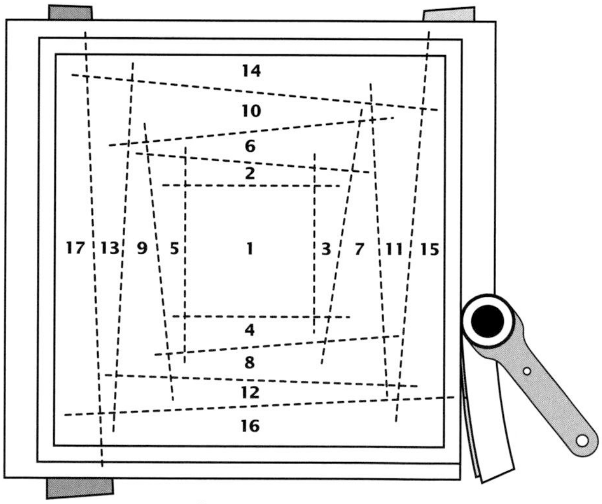

Diagram 5

STEP 7. Repeat Steps 1 through 6 to make a total of 36 Log Cabin blocks.

ASSEMBLING THE QUILT TOP

STEP 1. Arrange the blocks as shown in the **Quilt Assembly Diagram,** taking care to position the dark and light halves of the blocks as shown. Using a very short stitch, sew the blocks into horizontal rows, taking care to match the seam lines printed on the foundation patterns. After you complete the horizontal rows, press the seam allowances in alternating directions from row to row. Then sew the rows of the quilt top together, aligning the seams, and press the seam allowances between rows in the same direction. Carefully tear away all foundation paper from the back of the quilt top, using tweezers or a soft toothbrush to remove any paper fragments.

STEP 2. Match the midpoint of one 2½ × 36½-inch side border strip to the midpoint on one side of the quilt top, as shown in the **Quilt Assembly Diagram.** With right sides together, pin the border to the quilt top at 2- to 3-inch intervals and sew it to the quilt

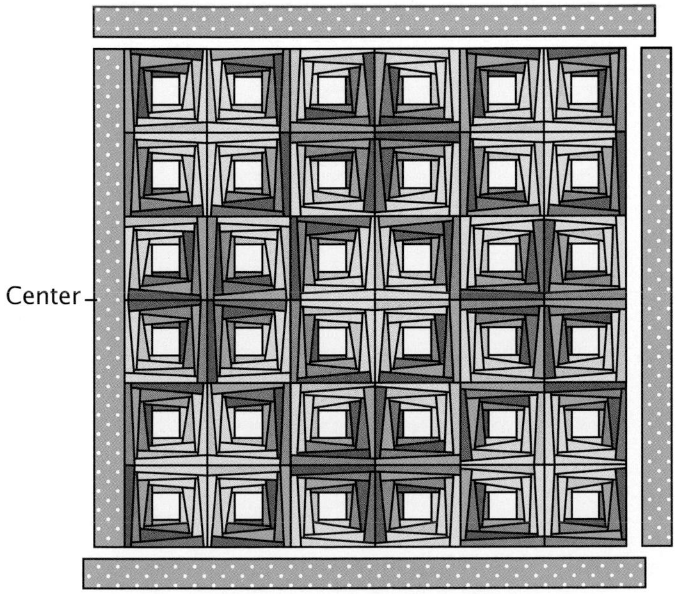

Quilt Assembly Diagram

top, as shown. Repeat for the opposite side. Press the seam allowances toward the border side strips. Sew the top and bottom border strips to the quilt top and press the seam allowances toward the borders.

STEP 3. Press the completed quilt top.

LAYERING AND BASTING

STEP 1. Trim the selvages from the backing fabric and lay the quilt back wrong side up on a flat surface. Stretching the fabric slightly, tape or pin it to the flat surface. Center the batting over the quilt back and smooth out any wrinkles. Place the quilt top right side up over the batting. The batting and backing should extend approximately 2 inches beyond the edges of the quilt top on all sides.

STEP 2. Baste the layers together with safety pins at approximately 4-inch intervals and remove the pins or tape from the quilt back.

STEP 3. Roll the edges of the quilt back over the edges of the quilt top, encasing the batting, and pin them through all layers. This will keep the batting from raveling or shedding during the quilting process.

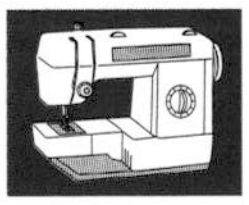

MACHINE QUILTING

STEP 1. Using a walking foot and monofilament thread, machine quilt in the ditch along all of the block seam lines and the border seam lines. Start by quilting along the center seams in both directions and then work outward.

STEP 2. Change to a darning foot and a size #80 topstitching needle and disengage the feed dogs on your sewing machine. Thread the top of the machine with two strands of medium blue cotton or cotton-polyester thread and matching thread in the bobbin. If your machine does not have two spool spindles, set one spool of thread to the back of your machine.

STEP 3. Select the charm tack motifs you like from page 125 and trace them onto 36 3-inch squares of tracing paper. Position a charm tack over the yellow center patch of each Log Cabin block and machine quilt the motifs you have chosen, leaving a 2-inch tail of thread on both top and back of the quilt. Remove the charm tack tracing paper patterns and finish by inserting the tails of thread into the batting with a large-eyed embroidery needle.

APPLYING THE BINDING

For diagrams and more information on applying binding to a quilt, see page 240.

STEP 1. Trim the backing and batting even with the edges of the quilt top.

STEP 2. Sew the binding strips together with diagonal seams. Trim the seams to ¼ inch and press them open.

STEP 3. Fold the binding strip in half lengthwise, wrong sides together, and press.

STEP 4. Position the raw edges of the folded binding strip at the edge of the wrong side of the quilt, with approximately 1 inch folded over at the beginning. Starting ½ inch from this fold, do three or four backstitches to secure the threads and start stitching the binding to the quilt through all layers with a ½-inch seam allowance.

STEP 5. Stop stitching ½ inch from the corner, backstitch to secure the threads, and stop. Remove the quilt from the machine and clip the threads. Fold the binding straight up, and finger press the fold.

STEP 6. Fold the binding down again, aligning the raw edges with the edge of the quilt, and finger press it in place. Beginning at the top edge, stitch to ½ inch from the next corner. Repeat this process on all four sides of the quilt.

STEP 7. As you approach the point where you began stitching, lay the end of the binding strip over the folded part at the beginning of the binding. End the binding seam by stitching across the fold.

STEP 8. Turn the binding to the front side of the quilt and stitch it in place by hand with a blind stitch, or you can use your machine's blind hemstitch with a very short stitch length and a narrow zigzag stitch.

STEP 9. Miter the corners by folding them out and back again; take a few stitches by hand to secure the fold.

Great Idea!

DOUBLE SPOOLS FOR GREATER SECURITY

If a spool of monofilament thread will not fit on the spool spindle of your sewing machine, try this trick. Place a narrow spool of regular sewing thread over your spool spindle and then place the monofilament spool, upside down, over it. This will keep the spool of monofilament thread securely in place.

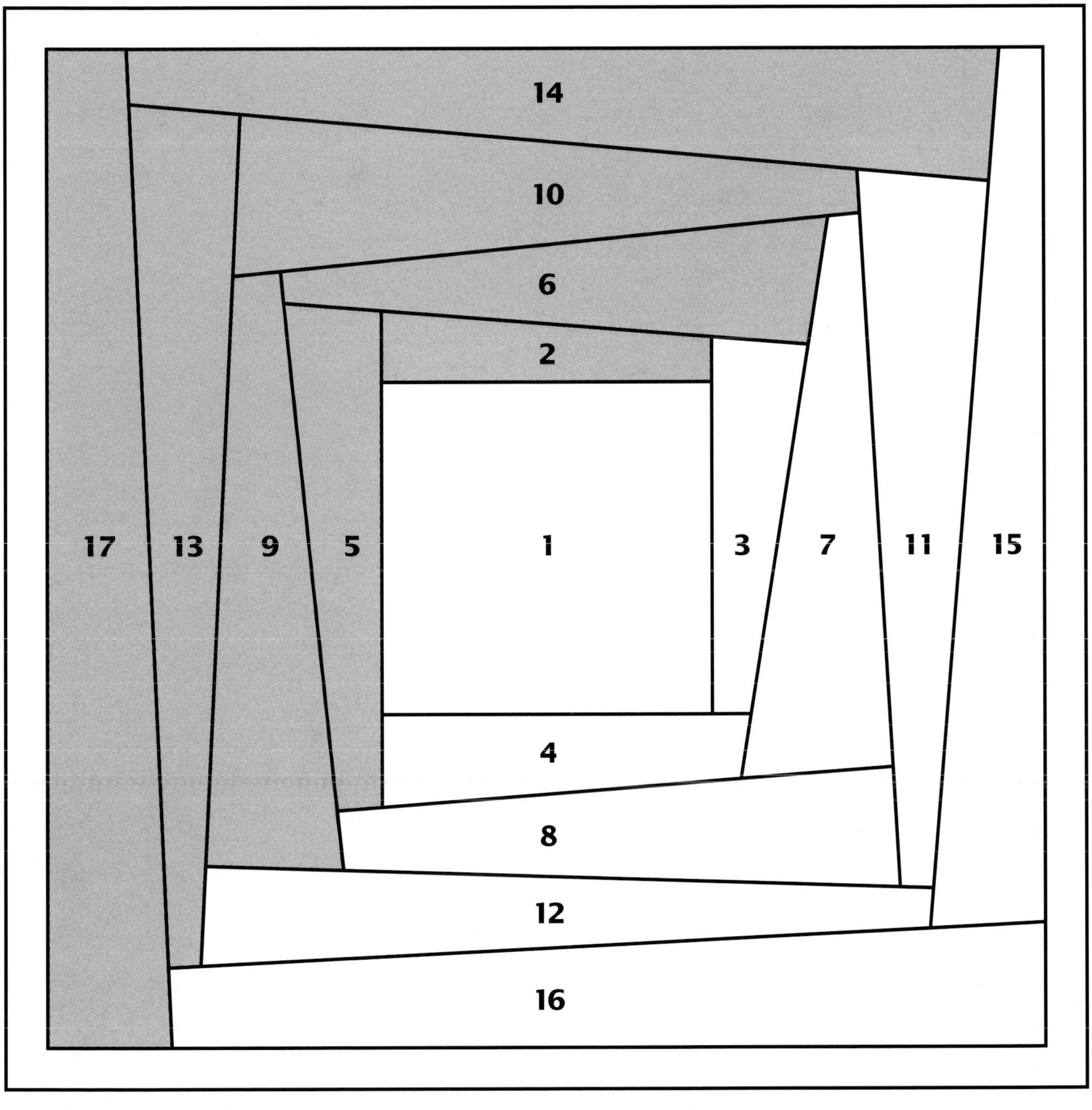

Paper Foundation Pattern

A Quilted VEST

Anne Colvin

Skill Level: Easy

Size: Up to size large vest pattern

To show off your newly acquired machine quilting skills, why not make something you can wear? Just select an easy-to-sew commercial vest pattern you like, a bright solid fabric to highlight your quilting stitches, and a coordinating print for the inside of the vest, and you'll have a versatile garment to wear almost anywhere.

TECHNIQUES YOU'LL NEED:

Starting and stopping, page 34
Free-motion curves and points, page 70
Vermicelli stipple quilting, page 91

FABRICS AND SUPPLIES

The following yardages are for a size large vest that is up to 30 inches long. If you make a vest in another size, adjust yardages accordingly.

FABRIC
3 yards of solid red fabric for the outside of the vest and the binding
2 yards of a red print fabric for the vest *lining*

MATERIALS
Crib-size cotton batting (45 × 60 inches)
Contrasting thread for the floral design
Thread to match the red solid fabric for stipple quilting
Removable fabric marker (test for visibility and removability before marking vest fabric)
Any commercial vest pattern that has basic pattern pieces: a left/right front piece, and a back piece
Rust-proof quilter's safety pins

CUTTING

Note: Wait to cut the actual outlines of the vest until after the quilting is completed.

From the red print lining fabric, cut:

One 1 × 44-inch strip on the crosswise grain for covering the seam allowances

From the red solid fabric, cut:

Approximately 200 inches of 2-inch-wide bias binding strips

MARKING AND CUTTING THE VEST

STEP 1. Lay the pattern pieces for your vest on the right side of the red solid fabric, allowing 4 to 5 inches between them, as shown in **Diagram 1.** Place the grain line arrows along the lengthwise grain of the fabric. With a removable fabric marker, trace around each pattern piece and cut them out 2 inches *beyond* the marked lines. Cut out the binding strips, as shown.

STEP 2. Mark the Leaf and Floral Quilting Design from page 159 on all three pieces, connecting designs, as shown in **Diagram 2.** Reverse the design where necessary to make the stems flow in the right direction. Make sure that the designs lie at least 2 inches in from the marked edges of each vest piece.

STEP 3. Lay the cut and marked vest fronts and back on the batting. Cut a piece of batting for each portion of the vest, taking care to cut even with the edges of each vest piece.

STEP 4. Lay the red print fabric for the vest lining wrong side up on a flat surface. Place the marked vest fronts and back right sides up on the lining fabric. Cut a piece of lining fabric for each vest front and back, taking care to cut along the edges of each vest piece.

STEP 5. Place the three lining pieces wrong side up on a flat surface and lay a matching piece of batting on top. Add the solid front and back pieces, right sides up, as shown in **Diagram 3,** and pin-baste the layers together with safety pins.

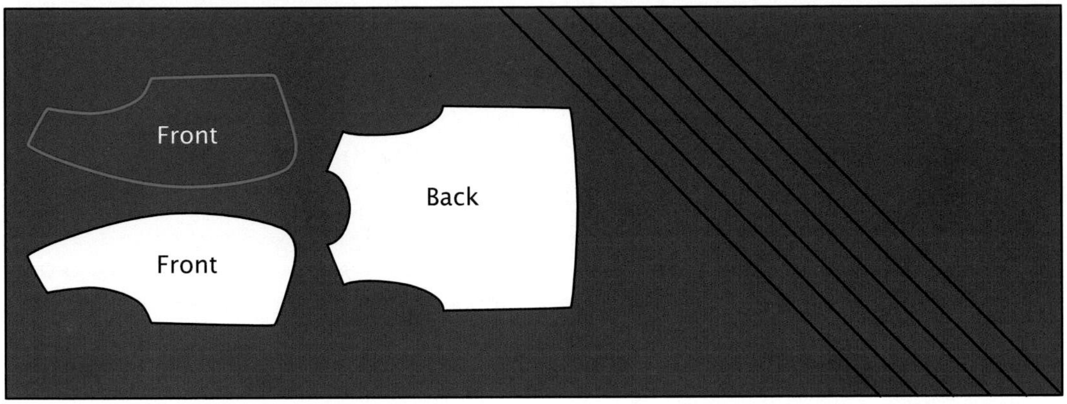

Diagram 1

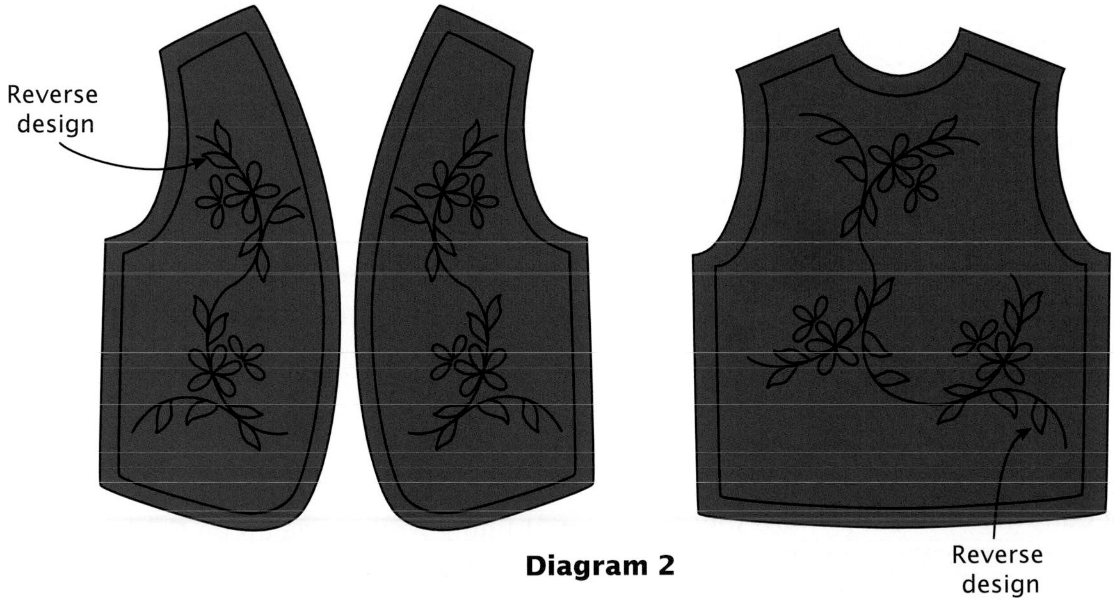

Diagram 2

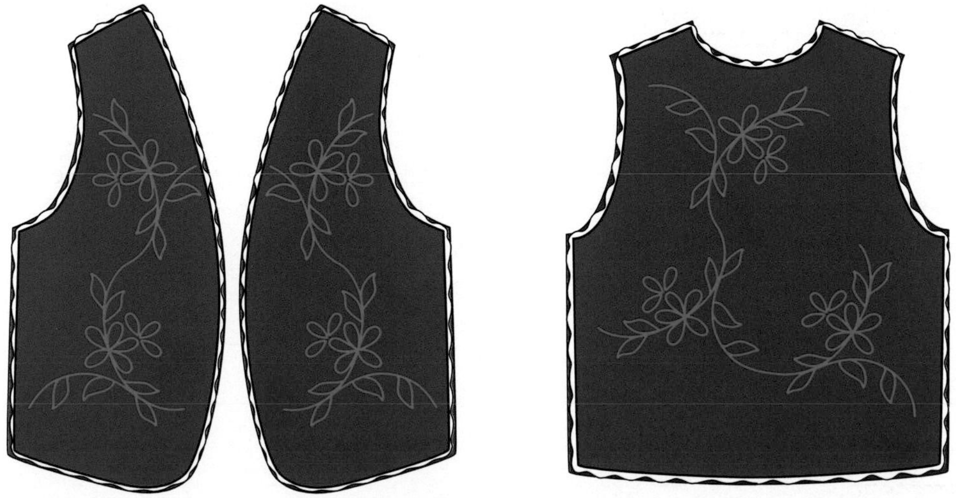

Diagram 3

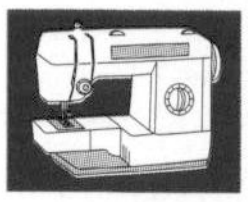

MACHINE QUILTING

STEP 1. Quilt the leaf and floral designs on the right side of each front and back piece, as shown in the **Quilting Diagram.** Use contrasting thread to highlight the leaves and flowers.

STEP 2. Using thread to match the vest fabric, fill in the background of each piece with stipple quilting, as shown in the **Quilting Diagram.** This stipple quilting should extend to approximately 1 inch beyond the marked edges to allow for possible shrinkage.

STEP 3. Wash each of the vest pieces or soak them in clear water until all markings are removed and place them on a flat surface to dry.

STEP 4. Pin the pattern pieces on each of the quilted pieces, taking care to keep the quilting lines of the floral design at least ½ inch from the edges of the pattern pieces, so they will not lie too close to the neckline or armholes. Cut along the outer lines of each pattern piece.

ASSEMBLING THE VEST

Refer to your vest pattern for the seam allowance width in your pattern pieces before beginning the following steps.

STEP 1. Trim the shoulder and side seam allowances to ¼ inch.

STEP 2. Pin the vest fronts to the vest back at the shoulders, right sides together. Lay the 1 × 44-inch strip of lining fabric over one of the shoulder seams, so that the right side of the strip lies next to the red print on the inside of the front, as shown in **Diagram 4.** Align the cut edges and trim the strip even with the ends of the shoulder seam.

STEP 3. Stitch the shoulder seam through all layers and trim away some of the thickness from it. Press the seam toward the vest back. Turn under the edge of the 1-inch-wide strip ¼ inch and lay it over the seam. Pin it in place and blindstitch it by hand, as shown in **Diagram 5.** Repeat Steps 2 and 3 for the other shoulder seam.

STEP 4. Pin the side seams of the vest right sides together and place a 1-inch-wide

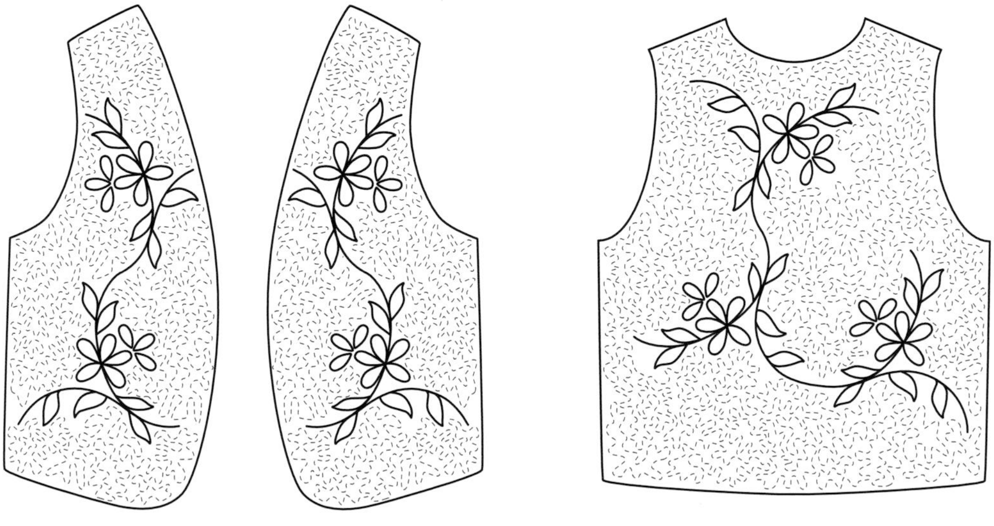

Quilting Diagram

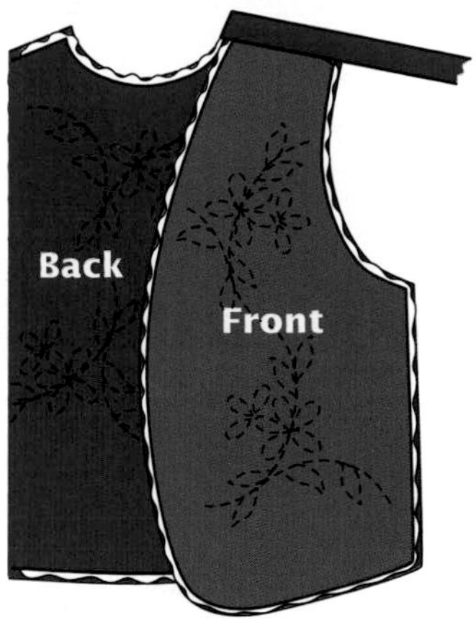

Diagram 4

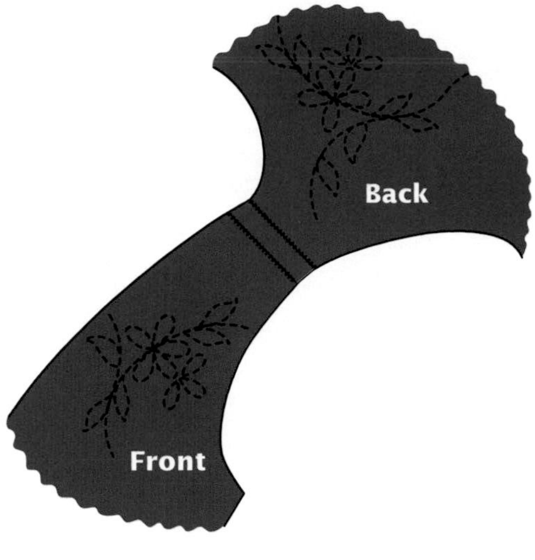

Diagram 5

strip of lining fabric over each of them in the same manner as the shoulder seams. Stitch these seams through all layers, and blindstitch the strips in place by hand in the same manner as in **Diagram 5.**

STEP 5. Because the edges of this vest are covered with binding, it will be necessary to trim the seam allowances of the neck, center fronts, bottom, and armholes to ¼ inch.

APPLYING THE BINDING

STEP 1. Sew the bias binding strips together with diagonal seams and trim the seam allowances to ¼ inch. Press these seams open.

STEP 2. Fold the entire binding strip in half lengthwise, with wrong sides together and press. Cut the short ends of the binding strip so that they are at 90 degree angles to the long edges.

STEP 3. Place the raw edges of the binding strip at one armhole, so that the short end of the binding overlaps the side seam by ¼ inch, as shown in **Diagram 6.**

STEP 4. Using a ¼-inch seam and starting approximately 3 inches from the beginning of the binding strip, begin sewing the binding to the armhole of the vest, as shown in **Diagram 7.** When you have stitched about 3 inches, stop and backstitch. Without removing the vest from the machine, turn the stitched portion of the binding to the inside of the vest to make sure that it will fold comfortably, yet snugly

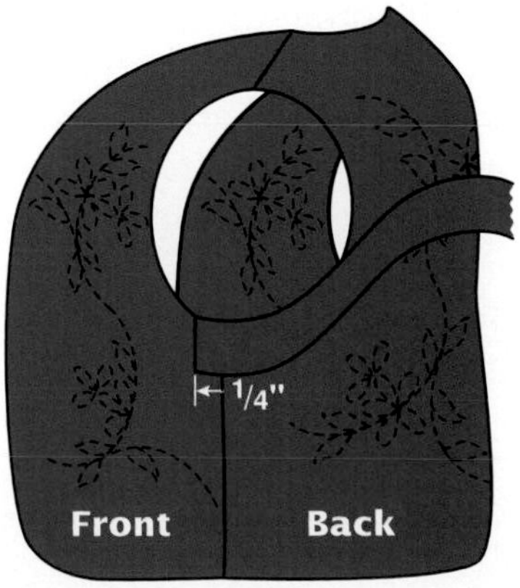

Diagram 6

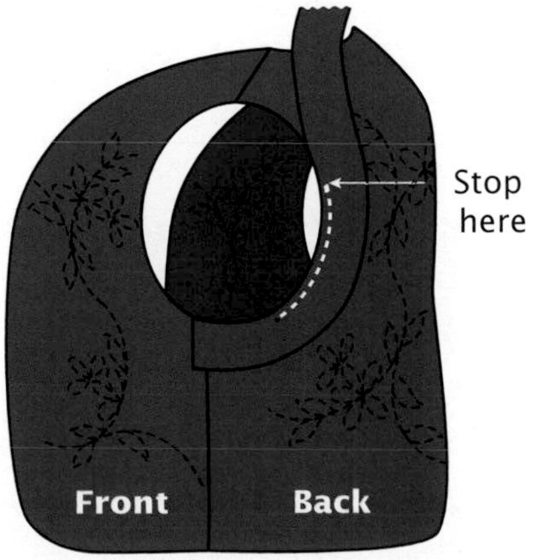

Diagram 7

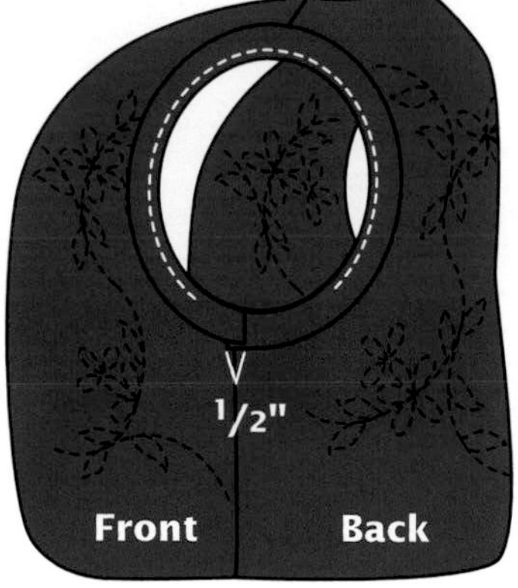

Diagram 8

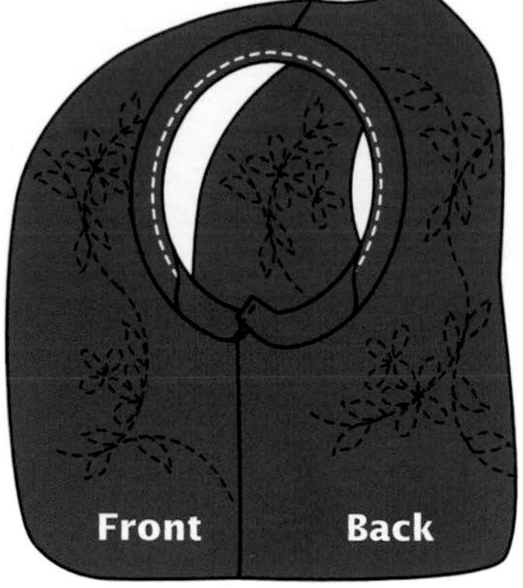

Diagram 9

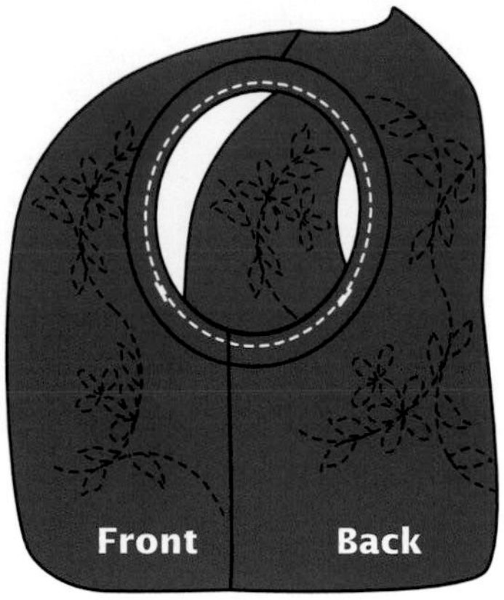

Diagram10

over the seam allowance without creating ripples or puckers. If there is too much or not enough binding to turn to the inside of the vest, it is easy to remove the stitching you have just done, and adjust the width of your seam allowance.

STEP 5. Stitch the binding around the armhole, stopping approximately 3 inches before you reach the side seam again. Remove the vest from the machine and lay the end of the binding strip over the beginning of the binding and trim the end so that it overlaps the beginning by ½ inch, as shown in **Diagram 8.**

STEP 6. Open up both ends of the binding, place the short ends right sides together, and stitch a ¼-inch seam, as shown in **Diagram 9.** Finger press this seam open.

STEP 7. Fold the binding in half again and stitch the final portion of the seam, as shown in **Diagram 10.**

STEP 8. Fold the binding to the inside of the vest and handstitch it in place with a blind stitch.

STEP 9. Repeat Steps 3 through 8 to apply binding to the other armhole and the outer edges of the vest in the same manner. If your vest pattern has angled corners at the lower front edges, refer to page 241 for more information about mitering corners.

STEP 10. To finish the vest, add buttonholes and buttons as desired.

Great Idea!

SHEDDING LIGHT ON THE SUBJECT

Use Halogen bulbs in any light source you have, whenever possible. Their clear, natural light does not change the colors of the fabric you are working on, which sometimes happens with fluorescent lighting. Halogen bulbs are cool and long-lasting, which makes them worth their higher price. For halogen bulbs, check lighting stores or hardware stores.

Leaf and Floral Quilting Design

Calico GARDEN

Debra Wagner

Skill Level: Intermediate

Size: Finished quilt is 32½ inches square

Finished blocks are 4½ inches square

Bright calicoes and understated neutrals bloom alongside each other in this colorful patchwork and appliqué garden. Based on a 1951 design by quiltmaker Florence Peto, the open areas between the pieced and appliquéd blocks are perfect for showcasing delicate echo stipple quilting and diagonal crosshatched grids.

TECHNIQUES YOU'LL NEED:

Starting and stopping, page 34
Outline quilting, page 45
Crosshatching, page 60
Free-motion curves and points, page 70
Echo stipple quilting, page 93

FABRICS AND SUPPLIES

FABRIC

1¾ yards of beige solid for the appliqué blocks, setting triangles, and borders
Thirty-five to forty 13-inch squares (or an equivalent amount of smaller scraps) of assorted prints, including shades of blue, brown, pink, coral, red, beige, and green, for the blocks and borders; any remaining fabric will be used for appliqué
1 yard of a medium multicolored print for the quilt back and the rod pocket
⅓ yard of green print for the binding

MATERIALS

Crib-size cotton or cotton-polyester blend batting (45 × 60 inches)
Rotary cutter, ruler, and mat
Paper-backed fusible web
Removable fabric marker or quilter's pencil
Rust-proof quilter's safety pins
Freezer paper
100 percent cotton, 50-weight machine embroidery threads for machine appliqué. These threads should match the appliqué pieces.
Cotton machine embroidery thread in 50-, 60-, or 80-weight for quilting. This thread should match the beige background fabric.
Invisible monofilament thread for quilting pieced areas of the quilt

CUTTING

The cutting instructions that follow are for quick-cutting with a rotary cutter and ruler. All measurements include ¼-inch seam allowances. **Note:** Cut strips across the entire 13-inch square. It will be helpful to start by cutting just enough pieces for one block; then assemble that block to test your seam allowances for accuracy. If your block does not measure 5 inches square, you can make the necessary adjustments before cutting the pieces for the other blocks.

From the beige solid, cut:

One 7⅝ × 44-inch strip. From this strip, cut two 7⅝-inch squares; cut each square in half diagonally in both directions for a total of eight side setting triangles.

Two 4⅛-inch squares. Cut each of these squares in half diagonally for a total of four corner setting triangles.

Four 4¾ × 44-inch strips for the borders. Cut two of the strips to measure 4¾ × 19⅝ inches and cut the remaining two strips to measure 4¾ × 28⅛ inches.

One 5½ × 44-inch strip for the appliqué blocks. Cut this strip into four 5½-inch squares; these squares are larger than necessary, to allow for distortions that may be caused by machine appliqué—trim them to 5-inch squares after the appliqué is completed.

Eight 2½ × 44-inch background strips for the pieced borders. From one of these strips, cut eight 2½-inch squares

From the assorted print fabrics, cut:

One 2 × 13-inch strip from *each* of the 35 to 40 assorted fabrics for the Nine Patch blocks and borders. From each of these strips, cut five 2-inch squares; you will need a total of 137 squares—these strips will yield more than the required number of squares, giving you a wide assortment of fabrics to choose from.

From the medium multicolored print, cut:

One 36-inch square for the quilt back
One 8 × 32-inch strip for the rod pocket

From the green print, cut:

Four 1¾-inch binding strips

From the crib-size batting, cut:

One 36-inch square

PIECING THE NINE PATCH BLOCKS

For each Nine Patch block, you will need nine 2-inch squares. To vary the color placement in each block, combine fabrics so that there is a high level of contrast between pieces, referring to the quilt photo on page 160 for guidance.

STEP 1. Sew together three sets of three 2-inch squares to make three rows. Press these seams open.

STEP 2. Sew the three rows together to complete the Nine Patch block, as shown in **Diagram 1,** and press the seams open. Repeat to make a total of 9 Nine Patch blocks.

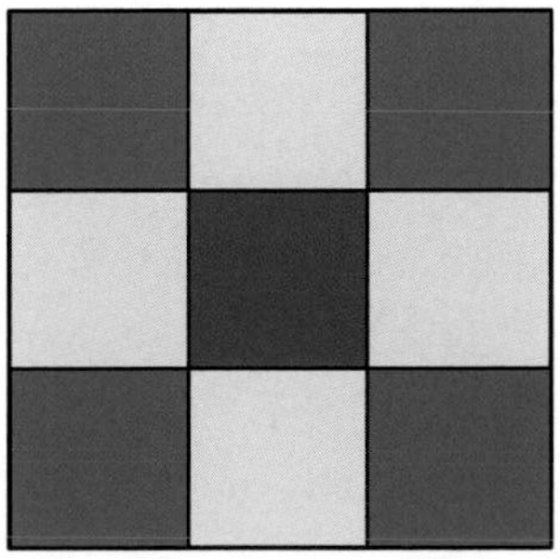

Diagram 1

APPLIQUÉING THE FLORAL BLOCKS

Each of the four appliqué blocks in the center area of the quilt features a different design. The following instructions are for basic machine appliqué using the pattern pieces on page 168. **Note:** The pattern pieces are in reverse position, so that they will lie in the correct positions after the appliqué is finished. The pieces for each block are numbered to indicate the stitching sequences. Choose any combination of fabrics you like for each design, using the quilt photo for reference.

STEP 1. Trace the appliqué pieces for Blocks A, B, C, and D onto the paper side of the paper-backed fusible web, making sure to leave at least ½ inch of space between each of the pieces. **Note:** Any area of an appliqué piece that overlaps another piece is shown in medium gray on the pattern pieces. When cutting out these pieces, be sure to add a ¼-inch extension to any area that will lie underneath another appliqué piece.

STEP 2. Cut the appliqué pieces apart, taking care not to tear the fusible web from the paper backing as you cut.

STEP 3. Place the appliqué pieces, web side down, on the wrong side of the fabrics you have chosen for each block and press them with an iron on the cotton setting. Move the iron in an up and down motion to avoid scorching the paper.

STEP 4. Let the fabric, paper, and fusible web cool. Cut out each appliqué piece along the marked lines, making sure to include all ¼-inch extensions.

STEP 5. Peel away the paper backing from the fabric side of each piece. Arrange the appliqué pieces for Blocks A, B, C, and D at the center of the four 5½-inch beige solid background squares, as shown in **Diagram 2.** Start with piece #1 for each design and place the remaining pieces on the fabric in numerical order, making sure that all of the pieces will lie within a 4½-inch space when the appliqué is completed. Any extra fabric in the background squares will be trimmed away after the appliqué is finished.

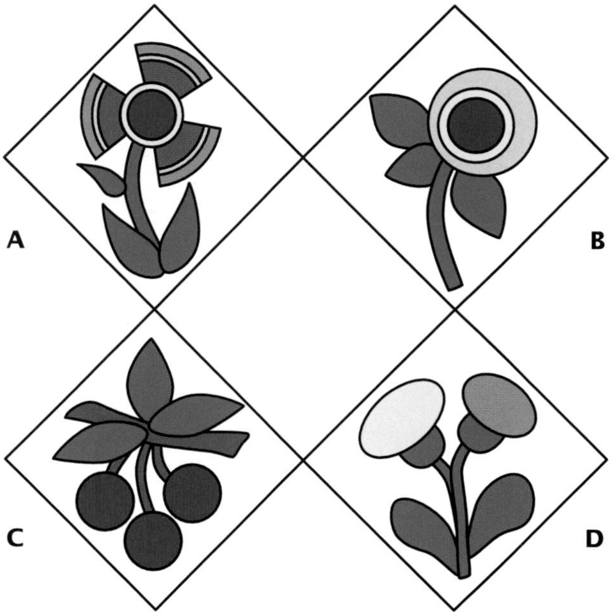

Diagram 2

STEP 6. When the pieces are in the proper positions for each of the four blocks, press them onto the background squares with an iron set on the cotton setting.

STEP 7. Press the shiny side of a 5½-inch square of freezer paper onto the wrong side of each background square. This will act as a stabilizer for the machine appliqué stitches.

STEP 8. Using a zigzag stitch that is 2 mm wide and 1 mm long and thread to match each fabric, stitch the appliqué pieces for each of the four blocks in numerical order onto the background squares.

STEP 9. After you have completed all of the appliqué for each block, remove the square of freezer paper from the wrong side of the background squares. Press the finished blocks from the right side and trim the background squares to 5 × 5 inches.

ASSEMBLING THE QUILT TOP

STEP 1. Sew the Nine Patch blocks, the appliqué blocks, and the side and corner setting triangles into diagonal rows, as shown in the **Quilt Assembly Diagram.** Press the seam allowances toward the Nine Patch blocks.

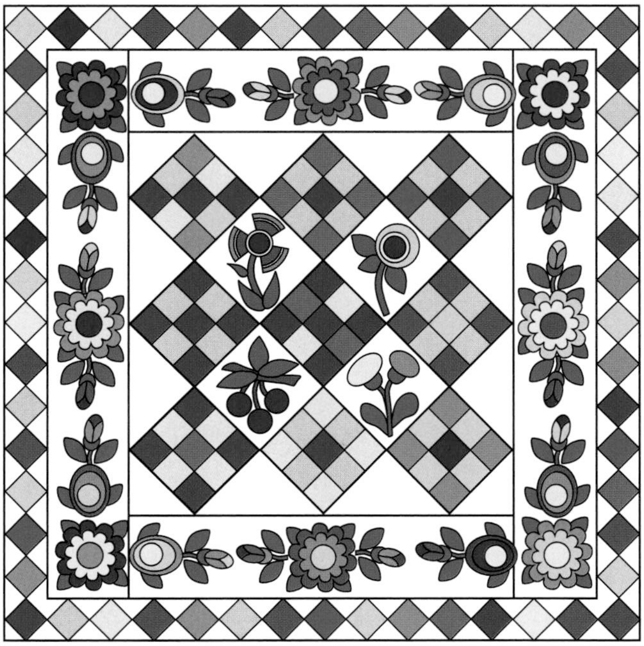

Quilt Assembly Diagram

STEP 2. Sew the two 4¾ × 19⅝-inch beige solid inner borders to the top and bottom edges of the quilt top, as shown in the **Quilt Assembly Diagram.** Press the seam allowances toward the borders.

STEP 3. Sew the two 4¾ × 28⅛-inch beige solid inner borders to the side edges of the quilt top, as shown in the **Quilt Assembly Diagram.** Press the seam allowances toward the borders.

APPLIQUÉING THE INNER BORDERS

STEP 1. Trace the appliqué pattern pieces for the inner borders from page 169 onto the paper side of the fusible web.

STEP 2. Using the quilt photo for reference, appliqué the top, bottom, and side borders, placing the pieces as indicated in the **Quilt Assembly Diagram.**

PIECING THE OUTER BORDERS

STEP 1. Sew twenty 2-inch squares to one long side of a 2½ × 44-inch beige background strip, as shown in **Diagram 3.** These squares should be approximately ¼ inch apart. Press this seam open.

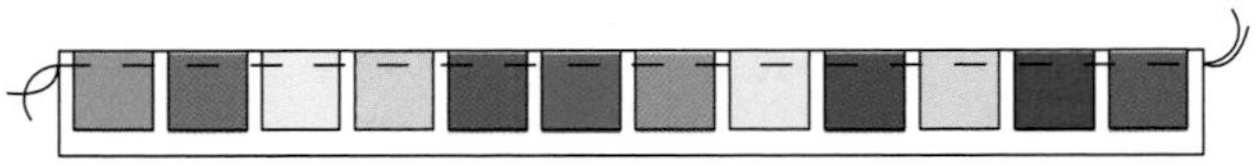

Diagram 3

STEP 2. Sew another 2½ × 44-inch background strip to the opposite side of these squares, as shown in **Diagram 4.** Press this seam open.

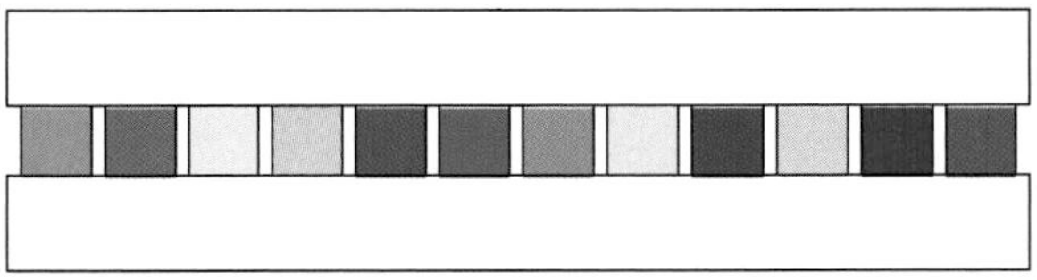

Diagram 4

STEP 3. Rotary cut this pieced unit into 20 rows of three 2-inch squares each, as shown in **Diagram 5,** making sure that the horizontal seams are perpendicular to the cut edges as you cut. **Note:** There will be a small amount of waste fabric between these rows. Repeat Steps 1 through 3 twice to make a total of 56 of these pieced rows.

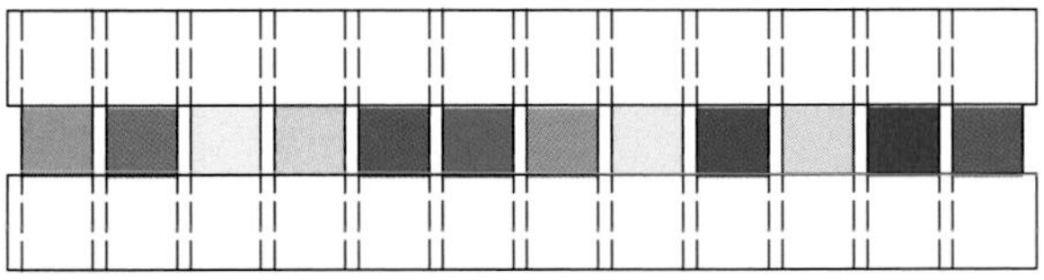

Diagram 5

STEP 4. Sew 13 of the pieced rows together, offsetting them by one square each, as shown in **Diagram 6.** Repeat to make another pieced border unit of 13 rows. Sew together two more pieced border units of 15 rows each, referring to the diagram. To complete each of the pieced border units, sew a 2½-inch beige solid square to the ends, as shown. Press these seams open.

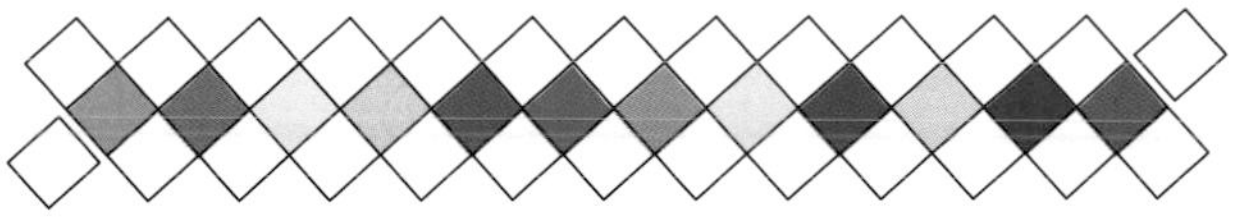

Diagram 6

STEP 5. Trim each of the four pieced border units so that the straight edges are ¼ inch beyond the points of the center squares, as shown in **Diagram 7.**

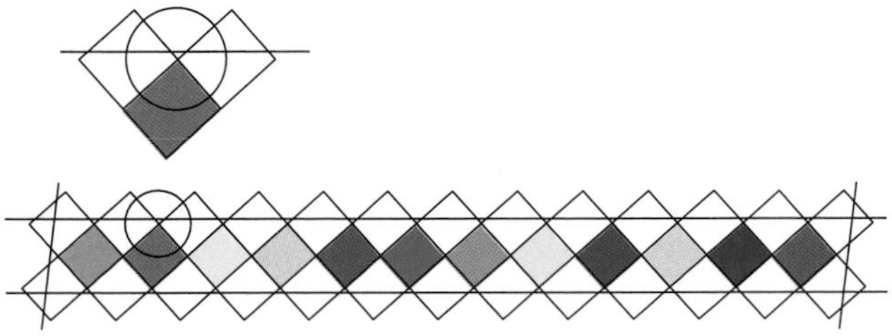

Diagram 7

ADDING THE PIECED OUTER BORDERS TO THE QUILT TOP

STEP 1. Sew a 13-row pieced border unit to the top and bottom edges of the quilt top, referring to the **Quilt Assembly Diagram** on page 164. Press these seam allowances toward the appliqué borders.

STEP 2. Sew a 15-row pieced border unit to the side edges of the quilt top, as shown in the **Quilt Assembly Diagram.** Press these seam allowances toward the appliqué borders.

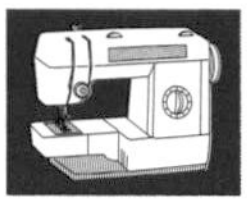

MACHINE QUILTING

STEP 1. With a removable fabric marker or quilter's pencil, mark a grid of diagonal lines spaced at ¾-inch intervals in all of the beige solid background areas, as shown in the **Quilting Diagram. Note:** These grid lines will go through the middle of the squares in the Nine Patch blocks and the squares in the borders.

STEP 2. Layer the quilt back, batting and quilt top; baste the layers together with safety pins. For more information on layering and basting, see page 19.

STEP 3. Using thread to match each of the fabrics in the appliqué shapes on top and thread to match the backing fabric in the bobbin, free-motion outline quilt around each of the appliqué shapes in Blocks A, B, C, and D and around the appliqué shapes in the borders.

STEP 4. Change to monofilament nylon thread on top and cotton machine embroidery thread to match the backing fabric in the bobbin, and do narrowly spaced rows of echo quilting in the backgrounds of Blocks A, B, C, and D.

Quilting Diagram

STEP 5. Continuing to use monofilament thread on top and machine embroidery thread in the bobbin, quilt all of the diagonal crosshatched grids, as shown in the **Quilting Diagram.**

MAKING THE ROD POCKET

STEP 1. Hem the short edges of the 8 × 32-inch multicolored strip by turning up ½ inch at each end and blind stitching it in place by hand.

STEP 2. Fold the strip in half lengthwise, wrong sides together, and press. Align the raw edges of the rod pocket with the top edge of the quilt back. Baste the pocket to the quilt back, and blindstitch the bottom edge of it to the quilt back, as shown in **Diagram 8.**

Diagram 8

APPLYING THE BINDING

For diagrams and more information on applying binding to a quilt, see page 240.

STEP 1. Trim the edges of the quilt back and batting even with the edges of the quilt top.

STEP 2. Sew the binding strips together with diagonal seams. Trim these seams to ¼ inch and press them open.

STEP 3. Fold the binding strip in half lengthwise, wrong sides together, and press.

STEP 4. Position the raw edges of the folded binding strip at the edge of quilt sandwich, with approximately 1 inch folded over at the beginning. Starting ¼ inch from this fold, do three or four backstitches to secure the threads and start stitching the binding to the quilt through all layers with a ¼-inch seam allowance.

STEP 5. Stop stitching ¼ inch from the corner, backstitch to secure the threads, and stop. Remove the quilt from the machine and clip the threads. Fold the binding straight up and finger press the fold.

STEP 6. Fold the binding down again, aligning the raw edges with the edge of the quilt, and finger press it in place. Beginning at the top edge, stitch to ¼ inch from the next corner. Repeat this process on all four sides of the quilt.

STEP 7. As you approach the point where you began stitching, lay the end of the binding strip over the folded part at the beginning of the binding. End the binding seam by stitching across the fold.

STEP 8. Turn the binding to the wrong side of the quilt and stitch it in place by hand with a blind stitch. Miter the corners by folding them out and back again, taking a few stitches to secure the fold.

Great Idea!

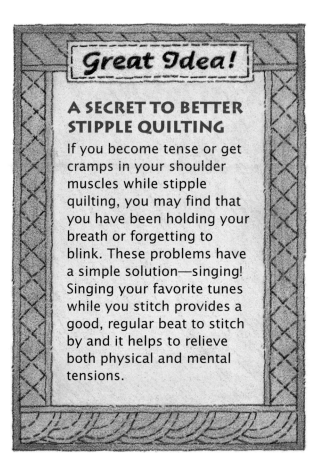

A SECRET TO BETTER STIPPLE QUILTING

If you become tense or get cramps in your shoulder muscles while stipple quilting, you may find that you have been holding your breath or forgetting to blink. These problems have a simple solution—singing! Singing your favorite tunes while you stitch provides a good, regular beat to stitch by and it helps to relieve both physical and mental tensions.

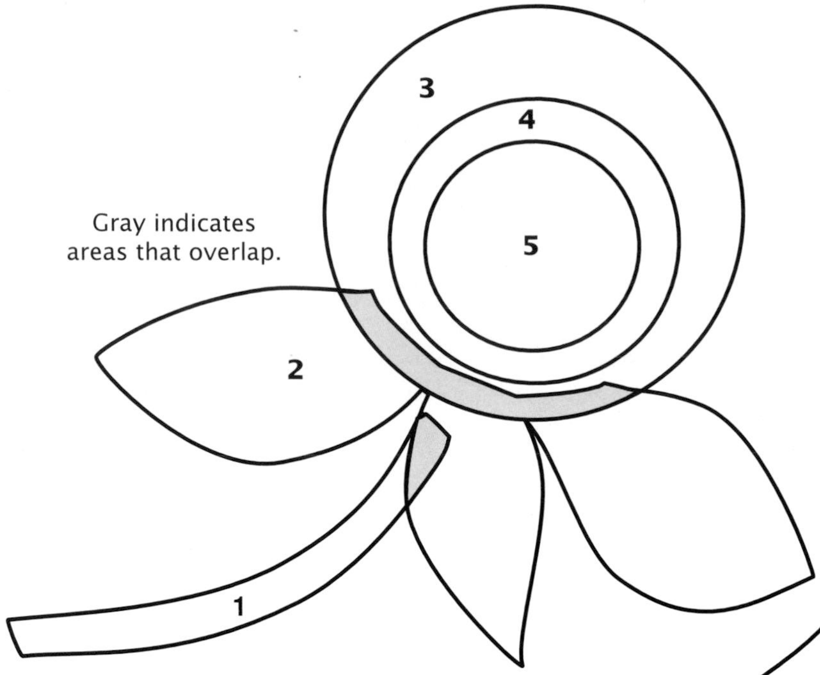

Gray indicates areas that overlap.

Block B Pattern Pieces

Gray indicates areas that overlap.

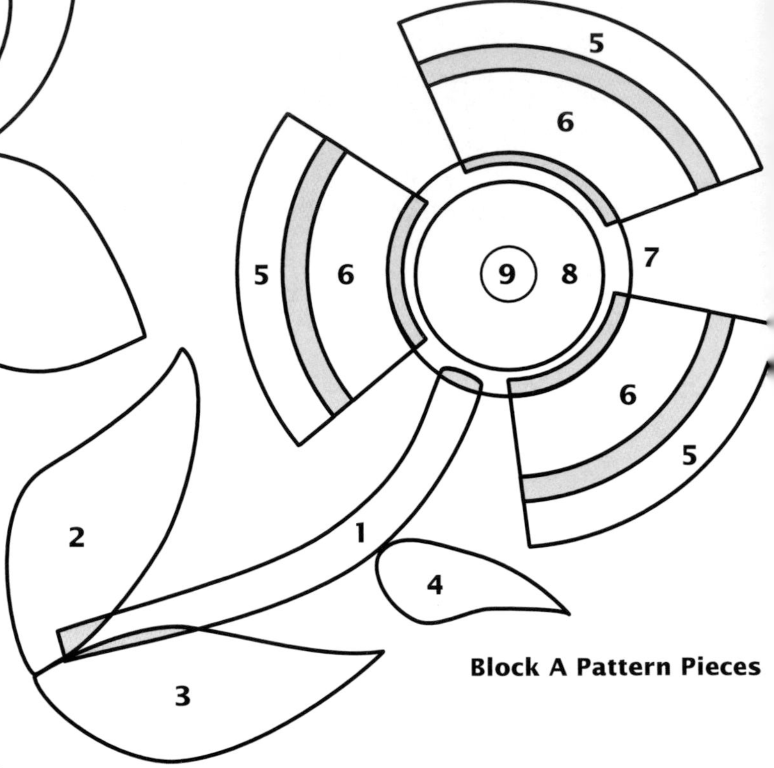

Block A Pattern Pieces

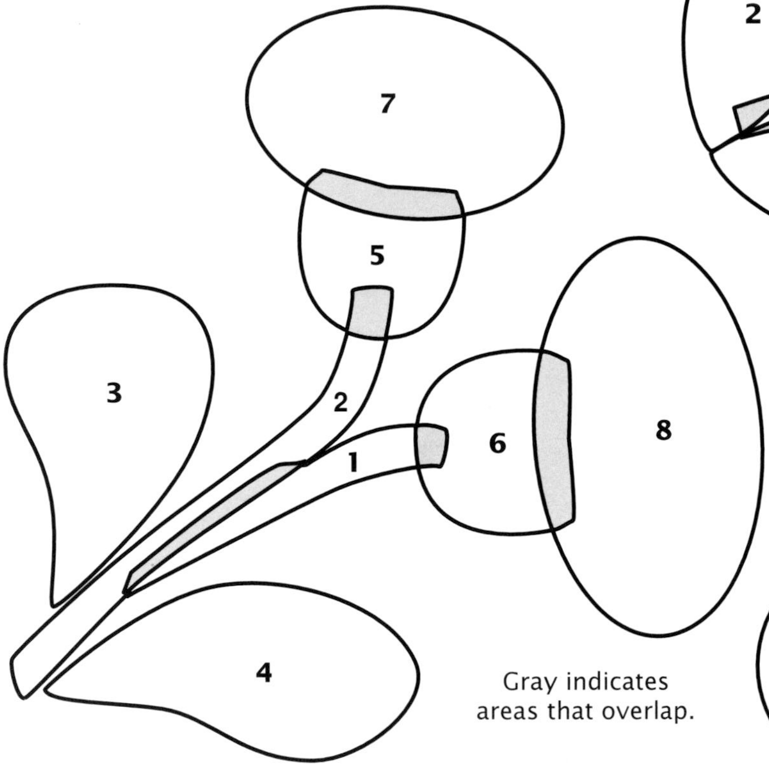

Gray indicates areas that overlap.

Block D Pattern Pieces

Block C Pattern Pieces

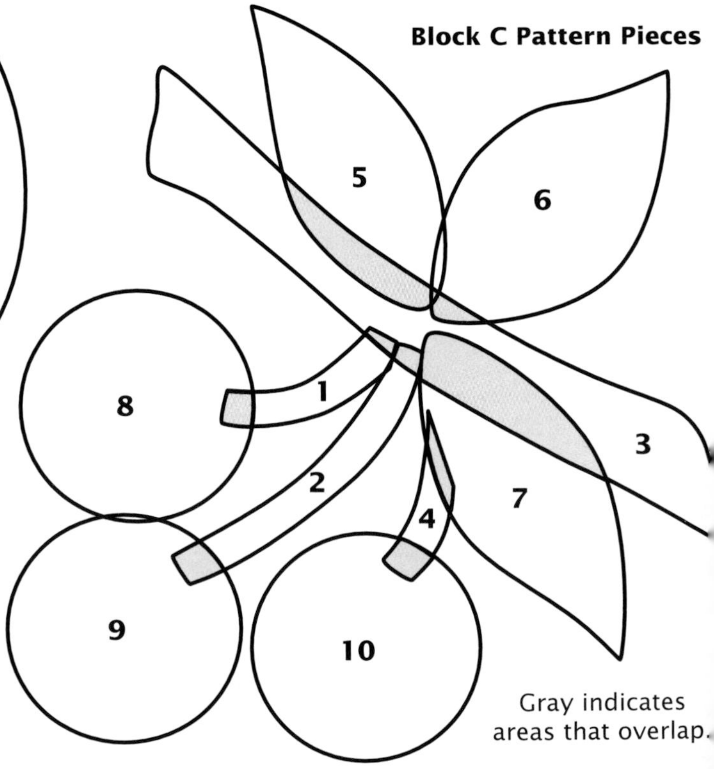

Gray indicates areas that overlap.

Top, Bottom, and Side Border Appliqué Pattern Pieces

Illusion
#13

Caryl Bryer Fallert

Skill Level: Intermediate

Size: Finished quilt is 48 × 64 inches

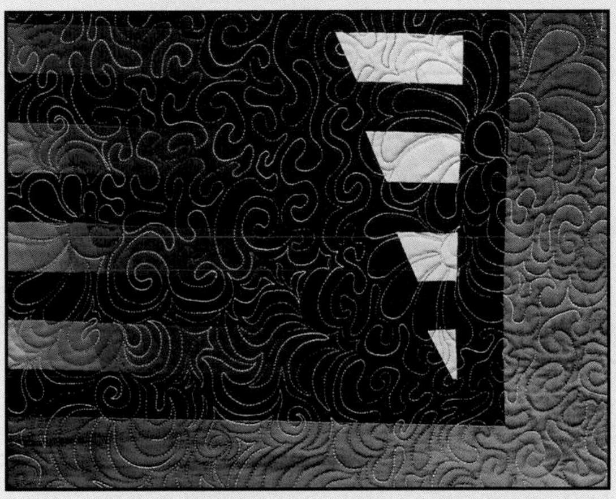

This stunning quilt is easier than it seems at first glance! It starts with simple pieced triangles, which are then cut apart and sewn back together in alternating strips. This yields a design with the illusion of more than one triangle occupying the same space, with a diamond at the center. The luminous quality of Caryl's quilt comes from her use of many different fabrics in graduated colors and values.

TECHNIQUES YOU'LL NEED:

Starting and stopping, page 34
Free-motion curves and points, page 70
Meander quilting, page 98

FABRICS AND SUPPLIES

The fabrics in the center portion of this quilt are graduated in shades that go from very dark to very light, which creates an interesting interplay of light and dark. The more fabrics you use, the more color and depth the final design will have. For each color gradation, you may use as many as 15 fabrics, as in the quilt shown, or select as few as 6 fabrics. **Note:** The more fabrics you use, the more left over fabric you will have.

FABRIC

1/4 yards *each* of at least six different fabrics in the following color gradations: Very dark purple graded to white Very dark purple graded to red and then to orange and to yellow Very dark purple graded to blue and then to green and to yellow
2 yards of fabric for the outer borders. This may be a solid, print, or painted fabric (as in the quilt shown); it may also be pieced from fabrics left over from the triangles.
3½ yards of black solid fabric for the inner borders, binding, and hanging sleeve
3 yards of fabric for the quilt back. This may be a solid, print, or painted fabric.

MATERIALS

Twin-size cotton or cotton-polyester blend batting (72 × 90 inches)
Rotary cutter, ruler, and mat
Light gray, medium gray, and black threads for piecing
Spools of variegated pearl cotton thread for quilting
100 percent cotton thread to match the backing fabric
Quilter's see-through ruler or yardstick
Large sheets of paper
Rust-proof quilter's safety pins
No. 2 pencil
Colored pencils
Scotch brand Magic Tape

CUTTING

From *each* of the fabrics used for the three different color gradations, cut:

Two or more strips 1½ up to 3 inches wide along the lengthwise grain of each fabric, for ease of sewing. If you decide to work with only 6 fabrics, cut your strips the maximum 3 inches wide. If you use a selection of many different fabrics, the strips may be cut narrower. The quilt shown has 15 fabrics in one of the color gradations, in strip widths that vary from 1½ to 2 and 2½ inches wide.

Two 4 × 52-inch strips

Two 4 × 72-inch strips

From the black solid fabric, cut:

Two 2 × 81-inch strips for the side inner borders

Two 2 × 40½-inch strips for the top and bottom inner borders

Four 2 × 81-inch strips for the binding

One 9 × 81-inch strip for the hanging sleeve

Two triangles, using paper foundations as pattern pieces, as described under "Making the Paper Foundations"

From the fabric for the quilt back, cut:

Two 34½ × 52-inch pieces

MAKING THE PAPER FOUNDATIONS

STEP 1. Cut two 35½-inch squares of paper and fold each square in half. Cut each of these folded squares diagonally, from the outside corners to the folded center points. You will now have two large triangles and four smaller triangles, as shown in **Diagram 1.**

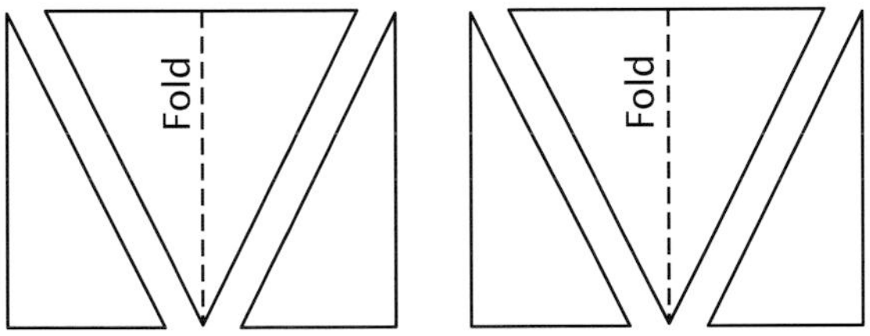

Diagram 1

STEP 2. Cut along the center fold lines of the two large triangles, creating a total of eight identical triangles, as shown in **Diagram 2.** These eight triangles will become the paper foundations for piecing the triangles in various color gradations.

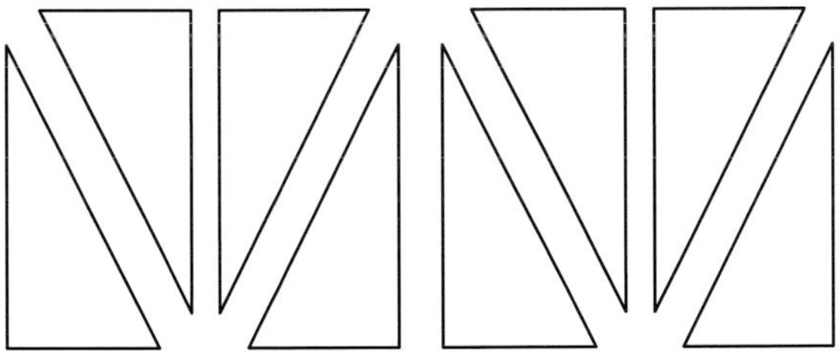

Diagram 2

STEP 3. On six of these paper foundations, use a pencil and a ruler or yardstick to mark parallel lines at 3-inch intervals, as shown in **Diagram 3. Note:** These marked lines will be used as guidelines only, *not* as seam lines, for sewing strips of fabric onto the paper. They will allow you to make sure that your stitched strips are going to lie straight in the finished quilt.

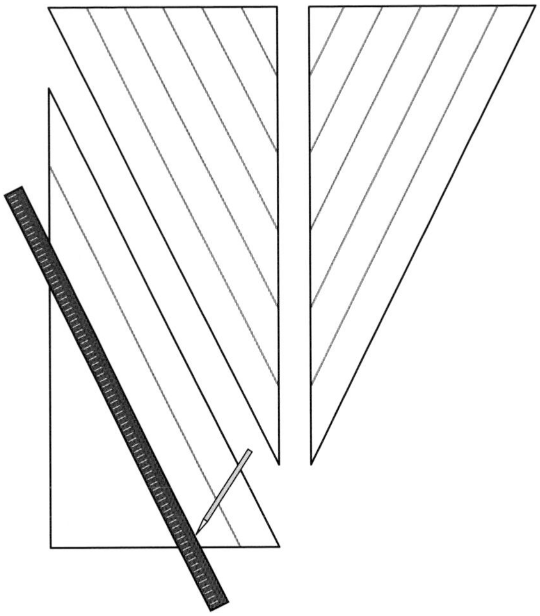

Diagram 3

PIECING THE TRIANGLES

STEP 1. Lay out your strips of fabric so that they are grouped according to the three color gradations listed under "Fabrics and Supplies." This will help in stitching them onto the paper foundations in the correct sequences to create the illusion of transparent, overlapping triangles.

STEP 2. Lay the darkest strip in one of your color gradations wrong side up on a flat surface. Place the diagonal edge of one paper foundation on top of the strip, so that at least ¼ inch of fabric extends beyond the edge of the paper foundation, as shown in **Diagram 4** on page 174. **Note:** Place the marked side of the paper foundation facing down. Use a piece of tape to hold this strip of fabric in place, if necessary.

STEP 3. Turn the paper foundation over and tape the next strip in your sequence of colors on top of the first strip, right sides together, as shown in **Diagram 5** on page 174, and tape it in place. **Note:** The marked

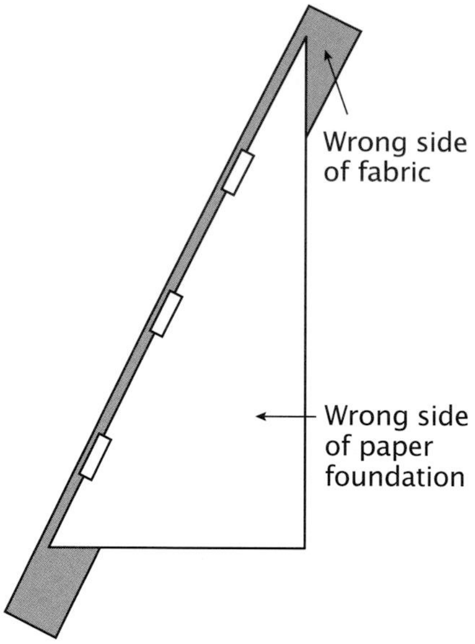

Diagram 4

side of the paper foundation is now facing up. Using a stitch length of approximately 25 stitches per inch, sew the strips together with a ¼-inch seam allowance, as shown. Use the marked guidelines on the paper foundation as you sew, to ensure that your seam is straight. Using a very short stitch length will allow you to sew over a wide range of fabric colors and values without having to change thread for each seam. It will also perforate the paper thoroughly, so that you can remove it easily later.

STEP 4. Open up the two strips and press the fabric flat with a steam iron.

STEP 5. Continue sewing strips onto the paper foundation in the same manner until it is covered. Be sure to keep your gradation of dark to light in the proper sequence, because this is what will create the illusion of light in your finished quilt. As you sew each strip, remember that there must be fabric extending at least ¼ inch beyond the edges of the paper foundation on all sides. Use the guidelines on the paper foundation to help keep your seams straight.

STEP 6. After you have covered the paper foundation with fabric strips, use a rotary cutter and ruler to trim the fabric on all sides to ¼ inch from the edges of the paper, as shown in **Diagram 6.** This will create the seam allowances for sewing the pieced triangles together. Using a pencil in a color that will show on the fabrics, mark a dot on the fabric at the corner point on each side of the paper foundation.

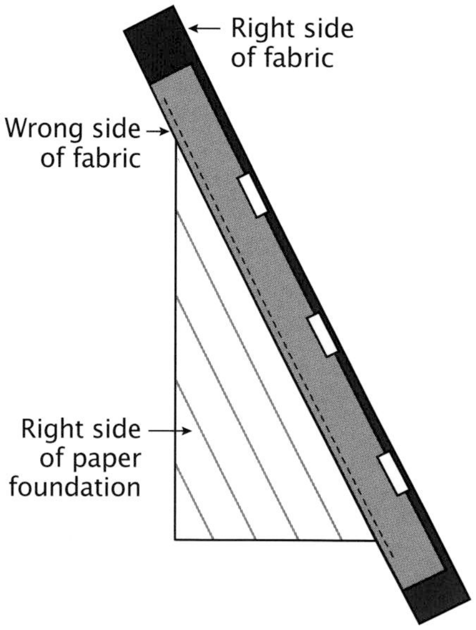

Diagram 5

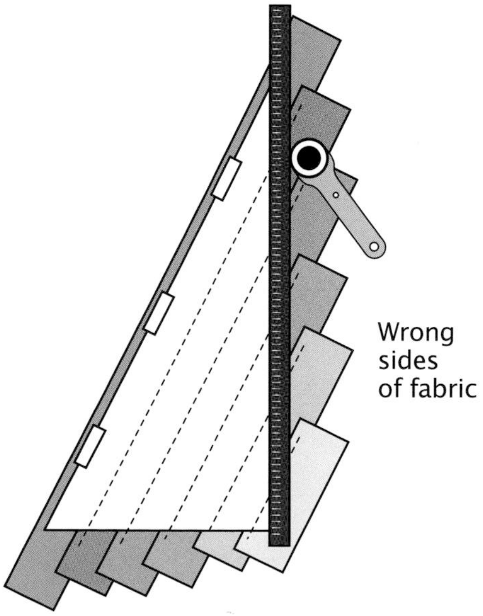

Diagram 6

STEP 7. Make three pairs of pieced triangles, as shown in **Diagram 7.** Note that they are mirror images of each other. Make two triangles that go from white to very dark purple. Make two triangles that go from very dark purple to blue to green and then to yellow. Make two triangles that go from very dark purple to red to orange and then to yellow.

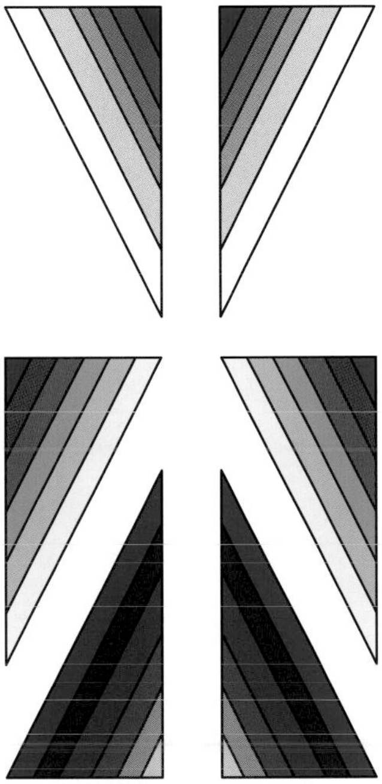

Diagram 7

STEP 8. Place the two remaining paper foundations on top of the black solid fabric, as shown in **Diagram 8,** and tape, if necessary. Rotary cut out the two black solid triangles. **Note:** Take care to add a ¼-inch seam allowance to each side as you cut.

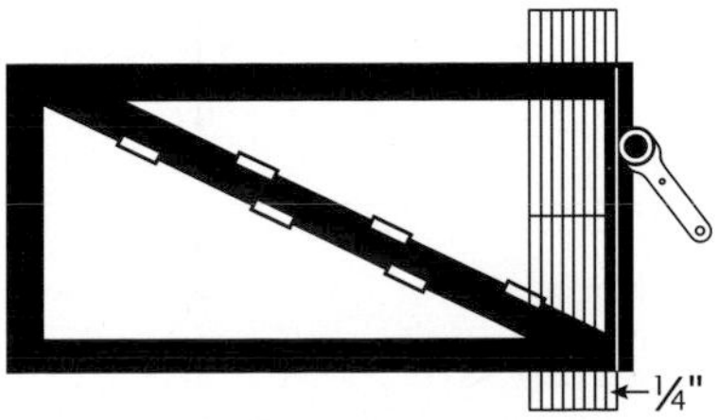

Diagram 8

ASSEMBLING THE CENTER PORTION OF THE QUILT

STEP 1. Sew the two triangle units that are graduated from white to very dark purple to the two black solid triangles, creating a pieced square, as shown in **Diagram 9.** Press these seam allowances open and remove the paper from the wrong sides of the pieced triangles.

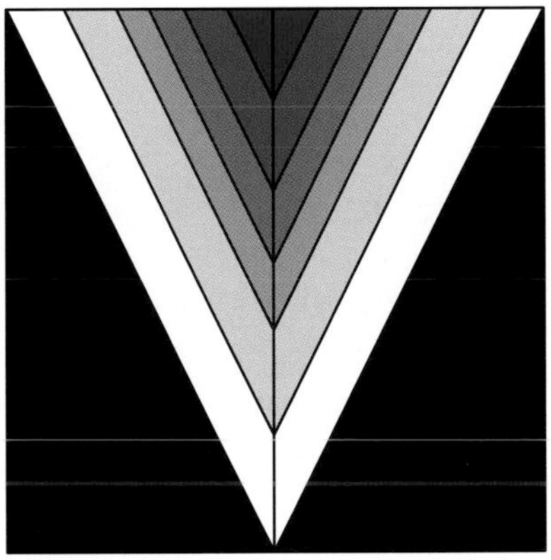

Diagram 9

STEP 2. Sew together the two pieced triangles that are graduated from very dark purple to red, orange, and yellow to the two pieced triangles that are graduated from very dark purple to blue, green, and yellow, creating two pieced rectangles, as shown in **Diagram 10.** Press these seams open.

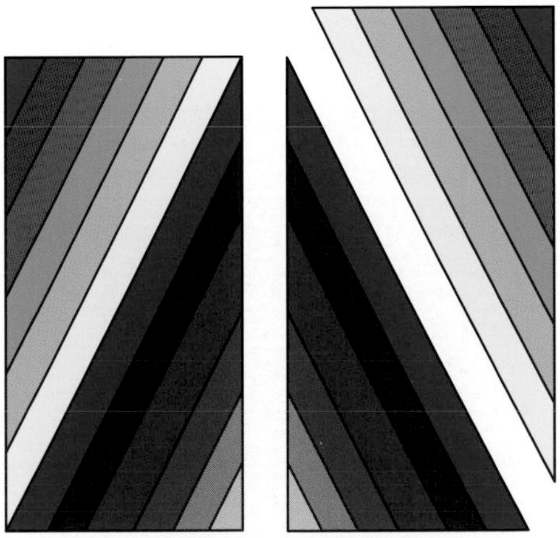

Diagram 10

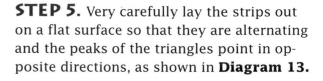

STEP 3. Sew these pieced rectangles together, creating a pieced square, as shown in **Diagram 11.** Press these seams open and remove the paper from the wrong side of each pieced triangle.

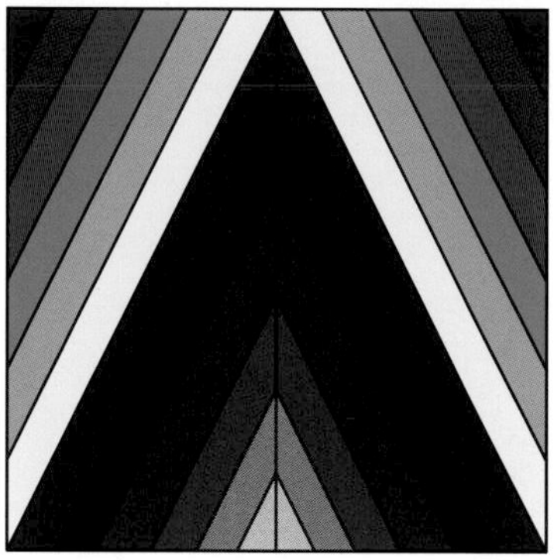

Diagram 11

STEP 4. With a rotary cutter and see-through ruler, cut each of these pieced squares into 2-inch strips, as shown in **Diagram 12.**

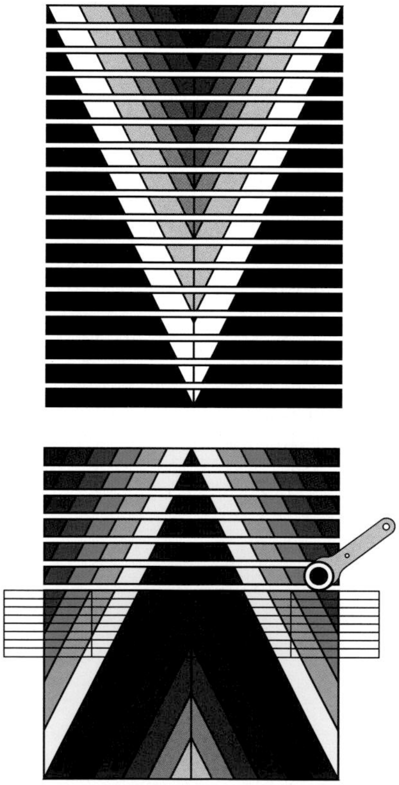

Diagram 12

STEP 5. Very carefully lay the strips out on a flat surface so that they are alternating and the peaks of the triangles point in opposite directions, as shown in **Diagram 13.**

Diagram 13

STEP 6. Beginning at the base of one triangle, pin the first two strips right sides together, taking care to match the peak of the triangle to the midpoint of the other strip. Sew these strips together and press the seam allowance open. Sew the successive strips together in the same manner, taking great care to keep them in the proper sequence. This completes the center portion of the quilt, as shown in the **Quilt Assembly Diagram.**

Quilt Assembly Diagram

ADDING THE BORDERS

STEP 1. Sew a 2 × 81-inch black inner border strip to each side of the quilt, referring to the **Quilt Assembly Diagram.** Trim the excess fabric even with the edge of the quilt and press the seam allowances toward the borders.

STEP 2. Sew a 2 × 40½-inch black inner border strip to the top and bottom of the quilt, as shown in the **Quilt Assembly Diagram.** Trim the excess fabric even with the edges of the quilt and press the seam allowances toward the borders.

STEP 3. Sew a 4 × 52-inch outer border strip to the top and bottom edges of the quilt, as shown in the **Quilt Assembly Diagram,** matching the midpoints of the borders to the midpoints of the top and bottom edges of the quilt. Begin and end each seam ¼ inch in from the edge of the quilt top.

STEP 4. Sew a 4 × 72-inch outer border strip to the side edges of the quilt, as shown in the **Quilt Assembly Diagram,** matching the midpoints and beginning and ending each seam ¼ inch in from the edge of the quilt top.

STEP 5. To miter the corner seams, place two adjacent outer border strips right sides together and mark a 45-degree diagonal seam line from the outer edge of the strip to the inner corner of the quilt top. Stitch from the outer corner to the inner corner of the border strip, as shown in **Diagram 14.** Repeat at the other three border corners.

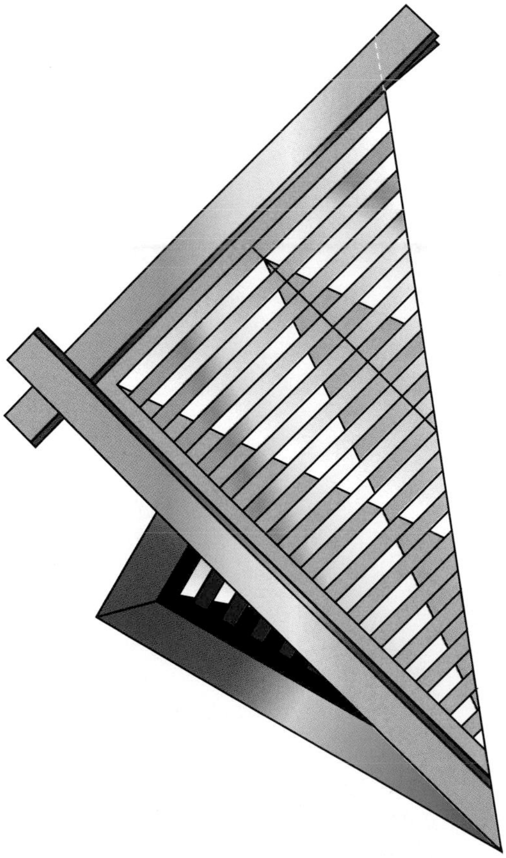

Diagram 14

STEP 6. With a rotary cutter and ruler, trim the fabric of each corner seam to ¼ inch, as shown in **Diagram 15.** Press these seam allowances open.

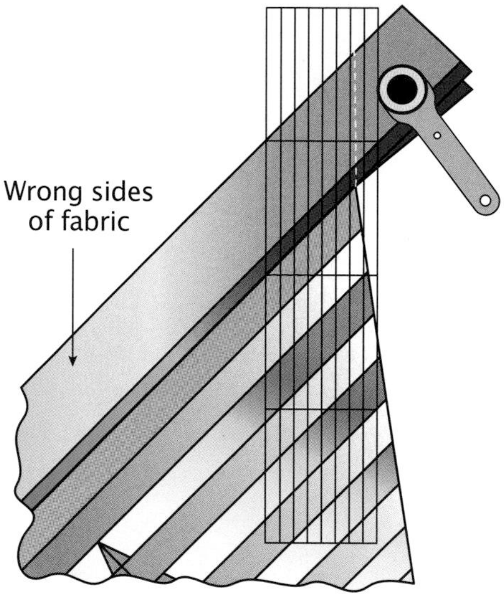

Diagram 15

LAYERING AND BASTING

STEP 1. Sew the two 34½ × 52-inch pieces of fabric for the quilt back together along the long edges and press the seam allowance open.

STEP 2. Layer the quilt back, batting, and quilt top, so that the seam of the backing fabric lies horizontally, and pin baste them together with safety pins placed at 3- to 4-inch intervals. For more information on layering and basting, see page 19.

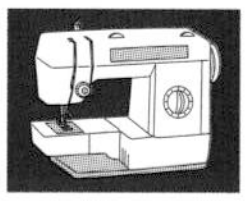

MACHINE QUILTING

With pearl cotton in the top and thread to match the backing fabric in the bobbin of your sewing machine, begin at the center of the quilt, working outward, and do meander quilting over the entire surface. Remove the safety pins as you go.

PREPARING A HANGING SLEEVE

STEP 1. Fold over 1 inch twice at the short ends of the black solid 9 × 81-inch strip and stitch hems in them by machine. Press these folds.

STEP 2. With wrong sides together, fold this strip in half lengthwise and press.

APPLYING THE BINDING

STEP 1. Fold the four 2 × 81-inch binding strips in half lengthwise, wrong sides together, and press.

STEP 2. Sew a binding strip to the left and right sides of the quilt, using a ¼-inch seam allowance.

STEP 3. Trim the ends of these binding strips even with the top and bottom edges of the quilt.

STEP 4. Fold these binding strips to the back side of the quilt and stitch them in place by hand with a blind stitch.

STEP 5. Lay the hanging sleeve along the top edge on the back side of the quilt and tape it in place along the fold.

STEP 6. Stitch a binding strip to the top and bottom edges of the quilt with ¼-inch seam allowances. The binding strips will extend at least 1 inch beyond the quilt top on each edge. The raw edges of the hanging sleeve will be sewn in this seam.

STEP 7. Fold the ends of the binding strips toward the quilt. Fold the strips to the back side of the quilt and stitch them in place by hand with a blind stitch.

STEP 8. Stitch the folded edge of the hanging sleeve to the quilt back with a blind stitch.

Great Ideas!

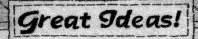

VERSATILE VARIATIONS

You can achieve another interesting look for this quilt by using a single gradation going from white to gray to dark gray to black. This produces the same kind of interplay between light and dark, while creating a stunningly dramatic monochromatic quilt. You can also make this quilt by using any color gradation you like and repeating it three times when piecing the triangles.

QUILT TO MUSIC

To learn to quilt smooth curves, I recommend holding a practice session while you listen to your favorite music or watch a good movie on video. To prepare a practice quilt sandwich, start with a 2-yard piece of muslin and a yard of batting. Fold the muslin in half around the batting, and pin the layers together with safety pins placed at 3- or 4- inch intervals. Sit down at your sewing machine and spend approximately two to three hours making free-flowing circles, serpentines, and loop-de-loop meander quilting patterns. By the end of that time, you will have trained your hands to draw smooth curves with thread.

THOUGHTS ON THREADS

Use the following guidelines to help choose threads for creating various effects with meander quilting.

- If you do not want the thread to show very much in a quilt, choose a thread color that matches the quilt top.
- If the fabrics in a quilt include a wide range of colors and values and you do not want the thread to show, use clear nylon filament as the top thread and match the color of the bobbin thread to the backing fabric.
- If you do want the thread to show on the top of a quilt, select a color that contrasts with the quilt top, both in color and value.
- If you want the thread in a quilt to make a very strong statement, use a heavier thread, like 30-weight topstitching thread or one of the many decorative threads now available.
- If you want the thread to show on the back side of a quilt, use a regular sewing thread in the bobbin and choose a shade that contrasts with the backing fabric.
- If you do not want the thread to show on the back side of a quilt, use nylon filament in the bobbin.

A Rose GARDEN

Sharee Dawn Roberts

Skill Level: Intermediate

Size: Finished quilt is 39½ inches square

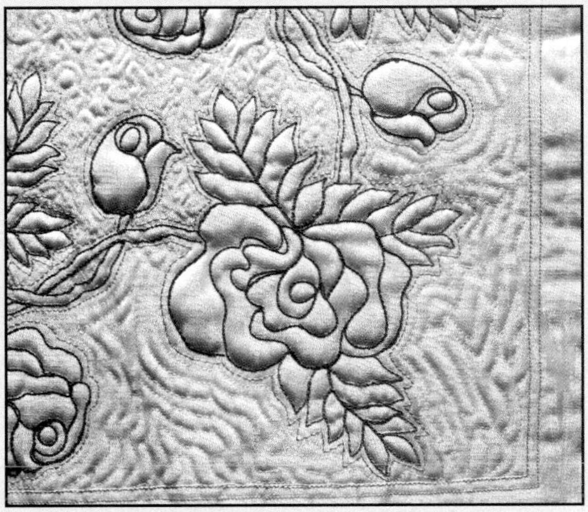

I*f the lazy, carefree days of summer are your favorite season, this elegant wall quilt will delight you. To emphasize the iridescent shimmer of wings in midflight, choose a colorful variegated metallic yarn and give a lustrous sheen to the flower petals with silky rayon floss.*

TECHNIQUES YOU'LL NEED:

Starting and stopping, page 34
Channel quilting, page 53
Crosshatching, page 56
Machine-guided curves and points, page 60
Free-motion curves and points, page 70
Vermicelli stipple quilting, page 91

FABRICS AND SUPPLIES

FABRIC

- 1⅞ yards of off-white moiré taffeta for the quilt top and the binding
- 1⅜ yards of off-white cotton fabric for the quilt back

MATERIALS

- Crib-size lightweight cotton or cotton-polyester blend batting (45 × 60 inches)
- 3 dark seed beads for the birds' eyes
- Fray Check
- Needle-nose bottle for dispensing Fray Check
- Tracing paper, graph paper, or bond paper
- Fine-point black permanent marker
- Soft lead pencil
- Water-soluble fabric marker
- Specialty threads for quilting: Madeira Glamour, colors 2582 and 2590; Madeira metallic no. 15, color gold 27; Rhode Island rayon ribbon floss, color 24; Madeira Supertwist, color 380; YLI fine metallic, color 50; Sulky Sliver, color 8040; and Sulky 30-weight rayon, colors 1071, 1057, 1051, and 1039
- Metafil needle
- See-through ruler
- Compass
- Pencils and string, or a yardstick compass
- Safety pins

CUTTING

From the off-white moiré taffeta, cut:
One 43-inch square for the quilt top
One 18-inch square for the binding

From the off-white cotton fabric, cut:
One 43-inch square for the quilt back

From the crib-size batting, cut:
One 43-inch square

MARKING THE BORDER DESIGNS

The quilting designs for this quilt are stitched by a technique called bobbin drawing. This means that decorative threads that are too thick to go through the eye of a sewing machine needle are wound onto the bobbin, and cotton thread is used on top.

All quilting is done from the back side of the quilt. This technique opens up a wide range of beautiful threads for machine quilting and means that all markings are done on the quilt back, rather than the quilt top.

STEP 1. Lay the 43-inch square of fabric for the quilt back right side up on a flat surface. With a soft lead pencil and a see-through ruler, mark a 31½-inch square at the center, as shown in **Diagram 1.** Fold the

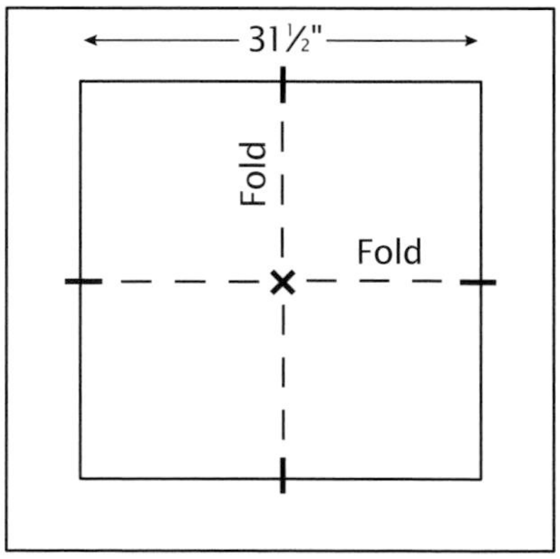

Diagram 1

square in half horizontally and vertically to find the exact center. Mark an X at that point and a small line at the midpoint on each side, as shown.

STEP 2. Using permanent marker, mark a 14 × 8¼-inch rectangle on a piece of tracing paper, graph paper, or bond paper. Enlarge the Rose Border Quilting Design on page 191 140 percent and trace it onto this rectangle, marking the X in the upper right hand corner, as shown in **Diagram 2.** This will be the quilting template for the entire quilt top.

Diagram 2

STEP 3. Place the quilting template on a light box and place the quilt back, right side facing up, on top. Position the fabric over the quilting template, so that the rose border design fits inside the bottom right corner of the marked 31½-inch square, and make sure that the X on the quilting template is still in the upper right hand side, as shown in **Diagram 3.** With a soft lead pencil, trace the rose border design lightly onto the fabric.

STEP 4. Rotate the fabric a quarter turn and position the quilting template at the next lower right corner of the 31½-inch square. Trace the rose border design onto the fabric with a soft lead pencil, as before. Continue marking each corner in the same manner, as

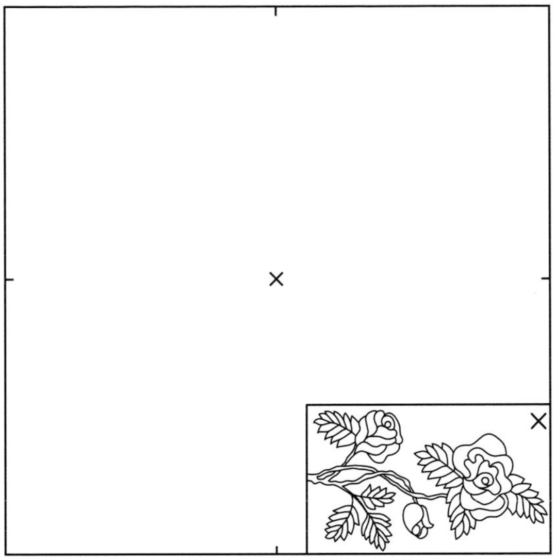

Diagram 3

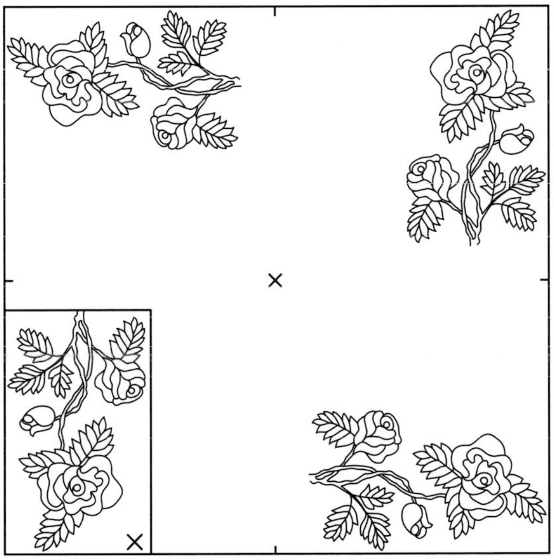

Diagram 4

shown in **Diagram 4.** The largest flower will always face the corner, as shown.

STEP 5. Pivot the quilting template, so that the X is now in the lower left corner. Then place the quilting template under the lower left corner of the quilt back, so that the large flower on the template lies directly beneath the large flower that is already marked on the fabric. This will allow you to mark the stems, smaller flowers, and leaves and connect them to the marked large flower, as shown in **Diagram 5.**

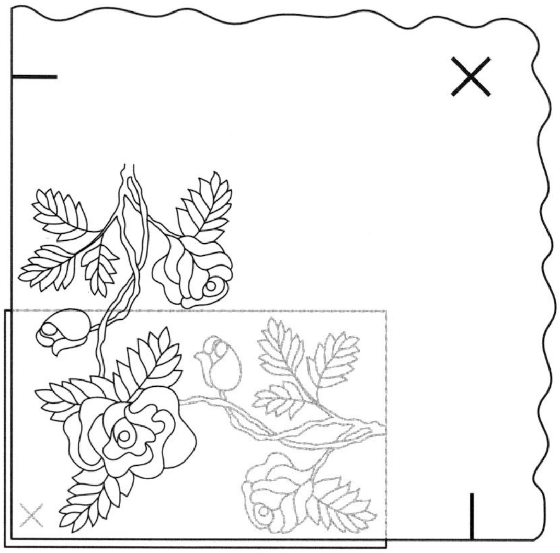

Diagram 5

STEP 6. Repeat Step 5 to mark the stems, smaller flowers, and leaves at the remaining three corners of the quilt top, as shown in **Diagram 6.**

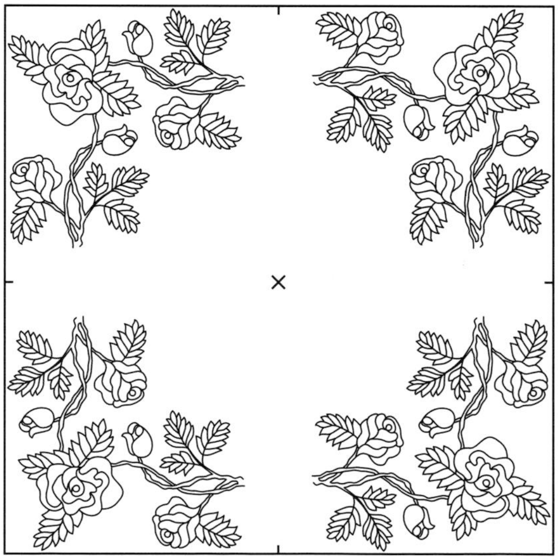

Diagram 6

STEP 7. Trace the largest flower at the center on each side of the 31½-inch square, as shown by the red lines in **Diagram 7,** and connect the vines to the flower.

Diagram 7

MARKING THE CENTER DESIGN

STEP 1. To mark the three birds at the center of the quilt, draw a 15½-inch circle on a large piece of tracing paper, graph paper, or bond paper. Tape sheets of paper together, if necessary, to create a large enough space for this circle. Use a compass that has an extension; pencils and a string; or a Yardstick Compass, which is a tool widely available at quilt shops, fabric stores, or art supply stores. This tool has two arms that slide over a yardstick. One arm has a point at the end that can be placed at the exact center point of a circle, and the other arm will hold a marker to draw a circle at any measurement on the yardstick.

STEP 2. Cut the circle out, fold it in half, and crease the fold line.

STEP 3. Fold the circle in half again to find the quarter points and crease this fold.

STEP 4. Make a small mark at each of the creases to mark the quarters of the circle and mark the center with an X, as shown in **Diagram 8.**

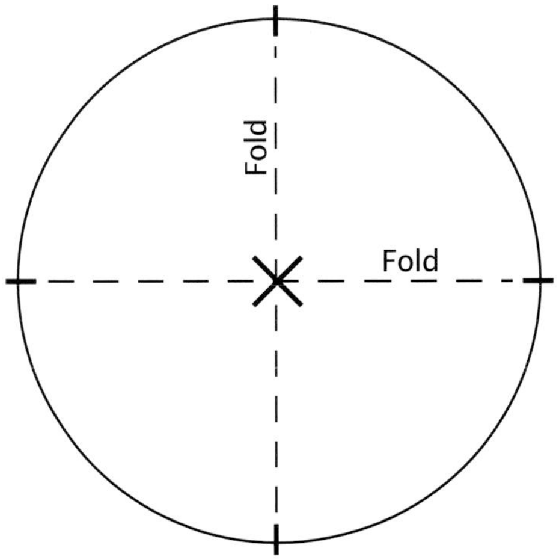

Diagram 8

STEP 5. Pin the paper circle to the center of the quilt back, inserting a straight pin through both X marks to position it as shown in **Diagram 9,** and trace around the outside with a soft lead pencil. Remove the paper circle from the fabric.

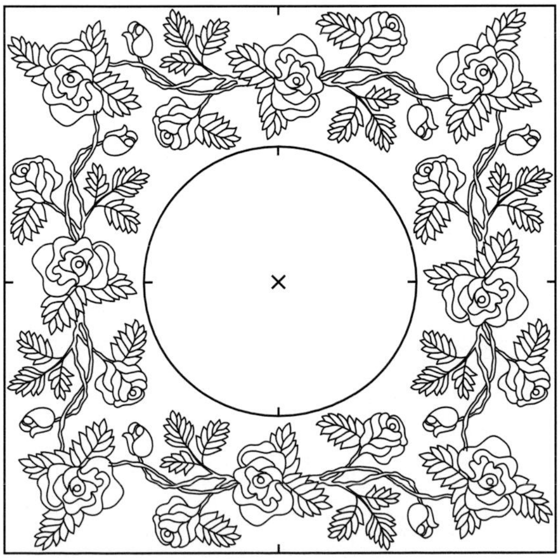

Diagram 9

STEP 6. To mark the bird designs evenly on the paper circle, I recommend using a nonmathematical paper-folding method I learned from *Patchwork Patterns,* by Jinny Beyer. Start by folding the circle in half, and then fold it into three even wedges, as shown in **Diagram 10,** disregarding all previous fold marks.

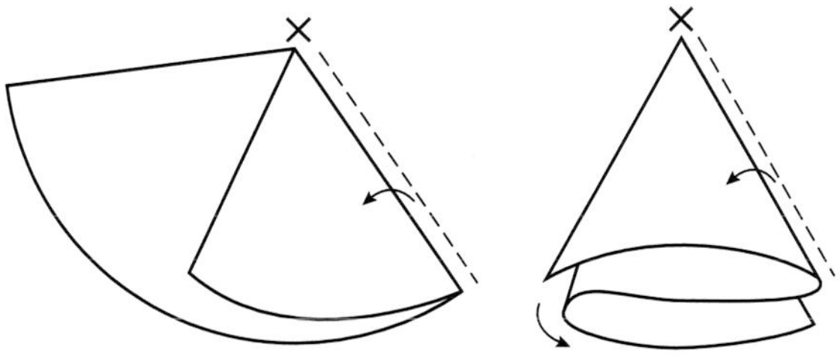

Diagram 10

STEP 7. Make a crease at each fold and open up the paper circle to check that there are three even wedges, as shown in **Diagram 11.**

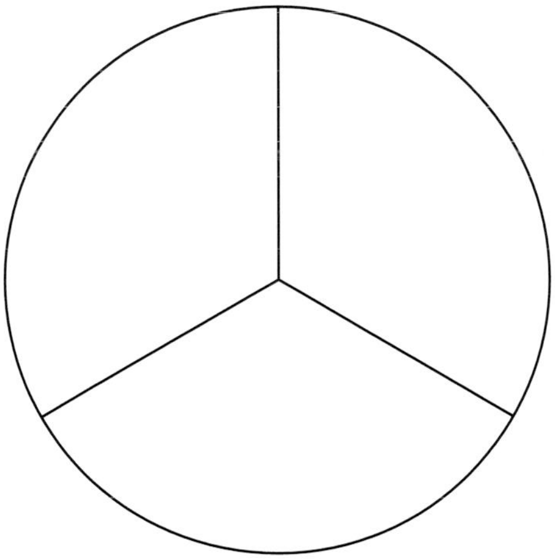

Diagram 11

STEP 8. With a fine-point black permanent marker, trace the **Bird Quilting Design and Directional Stitching Diagram** from page 190 onto a piece of tracing paper. Place the paper circle over this marked design so that the bird's wing tips and tail lie equal distances from the creases and edge of the circle, as shown in **Diagram 12**. Trace the bird design onto the paper circle with a permanent marker. Then trace the bird design into the two adjacent sections of the paper circle, as shown. **Note:** When you are tracing the bird into the third section, be sure to turn the bird design marked on the tracing paper wrong side up, so that the third bird will be a mirror image of the other two. This will make the beak of the third bird face the center X in the correct position. When you have finished tracing the third bird, use the permanent marker to darken your lines to match the lines of the first two birds.

Diagram 12

STEP 9. To transfer the marked bird design to the quilt back, tape the paper circle on the light box, and place the quilt back on top. Rotate the quilt back until the quarter marks on the paper circle line up with the marks at the midpoint on each side of the quilt back. Trace the bird designs onto the quilt back, using a soft lead pencil.

STEP 10. Layer the quilt top, batting, and quilt back. Working with the marked quilt back facing up, baste the layers together with safety pins at 3- to 4-inch intervals. For more information on layering and basting, see page 19.

MACHINE QUILTING

BOBBIN DRAWING

STEP 1. Fill a bobbin with Madeira Glamour color 2590 thread. Set the bobbin on the winding pin and wind a strand of thread around it several times. Then hold the spool in your left hand and pinch the strand of thread between your fingers to give it tension while you press on the foot pedal and wind the thread onto the bobbin. After you insert the filled bobbin into the bobbin case, loosen the bobbin tension to allow the thread to pull easily.

STEP 2. Lower or cover the feed dogs on your sewing machine, and put on a darning foot. Insert a Metafil needle, and thread the top of the machine with Sulky 30-weight rayon color 1057 thread. Tighten the top tension to approximately two numbers higher than normal for your machine.

STEP 3. Starting at point A on the **Bird Quilting Design and Directional Quilting Diagram** on page 190, take a single stitch to pull the bobbin thread up and hold both the top and the bobbin threads to the back of the darning foot as you begin to free-motion quilt around the outline of the bird's wings and tail feathers. Take fairly long stitches and "slide" around the tips of the wings as you quilt, rather than pivoting sharply. At point B, stitch back over the previous line of stitching to point C, and continue stitching the next feather. Repeat the same stitching sequence for each bird.

STEP 4. To end any line of stitching when you are bobbin drawing, take three or four short stitches, trim both the top and bobbin threads close to the surface of the fabric, and add a drop of Fray Check. Heavy decorative threads will not unravel, so there is no need to bury any thread tails by hand.

STEP 5. Using the same two threads, start at dot A on **Directional Stitching Diagram 1** and follow the numbers to stitch the bird's throat and beak in one continuous line, traveling from one line to the next without stopping, whenever possible. Do not stitch the top of the head at this time. Repeat the same stitching sequence for each bird.

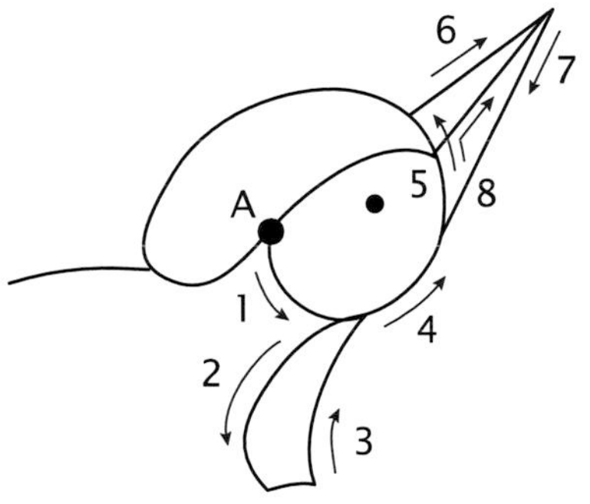

Directional Stitching Diagram 1

STEP 6. Change to Sulky 30-weight rayon color 1039 thread on top and fill a bobbin with the Rhode Island rayon ribbon floss color 24. Starting at point A in **Directional Stitching Diagram 2,** bring the bobbin thread to the top and begin stitching the bird's body and the top of the head and wing in a continuous line, as shown. Again, stitch over previous lines of stitching, when necessary, to keep from having to stop and cut threads. End the lines of stitching with short stitches, as before. Repeat the same stitching sequence for each bird.

STEP 7. To stitch an outline around the center circle, as shown in **Quilting Diagram 1,** raise or engage the feed dogs, put on a regular presser foot, and change to Sulky 30-weight rayon color 1071 thread on top. Fill the bobbin with Madeira metallic no. 15 color gold 27 thread. Stitch the outline of the large circle, as shown. To create an echo effect, do a second line of stitching

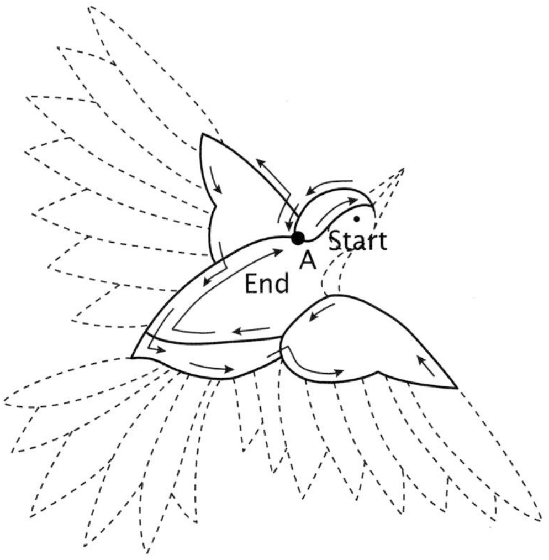

Directional Stitching Diagram 2

¼ inch inside the first, as indicated by the red lines in **Quilting Diagram 1.**

STEP 8. Refer to **Quilting Diagram 1** and use the following threads to complete the bobbin drawing portion of the quilting process. For stitching the vines, use Sulky 30-weight rayon color 1057 on top and Madeira Glamour color 2590 in the bobbin. For the leaves, change to Sulky 30-weight rayon color 1051 on top and Madeira Glamour color 2582 in the bobbin. For the roses, use Sulky 30-weight rayon color

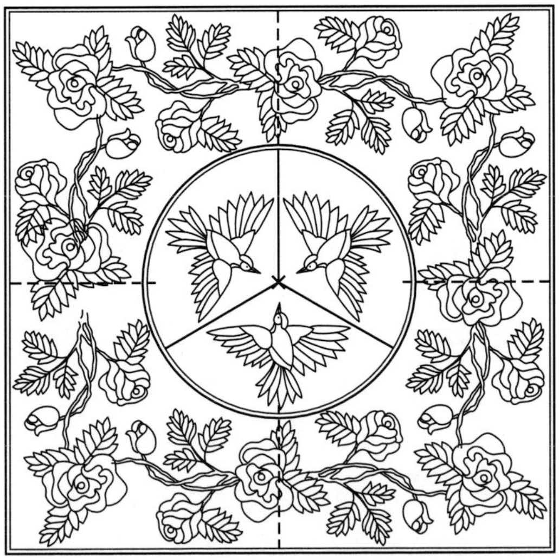

Quilting Diagram 1

1039 on top and Rhode Island rayon ribbon floss color 24 in the bobbin.

STEP 9. To quilt the outer edges of the borders, as shown in **Quilting Diagram 1,** change to Madeira metallic no. 15 color gold 27 in the bobbin and Sulky 30-weight rayon color 1071 on top. Stitch around the marked lines of the 31½-inch square. Do a second line of stitching ¼ inch inside the first, as indicated by the red lines in **Quilting Diagram 1.**

QUILTING FROM THE TOP

After you have completed all of the bobbin drawing, turn the quilt over and complete the remainder of the quilting with the quilt top facing up.

STEP 1. Disengage the feed dogs and put on the darning foot again. Fill the bobbin with Sulky 30-weight rayon color 1071 thread and tighten the bobbin tension back to normal for your machine. Lower the top tension slightly and thread the needle with Madeira metallic no. 15 color gold 27 thread.

STEP 2. Free-motion quilt ¼ inch outside all of the bobbin drawing designs, including the birds, vines, leaves and roses, as indicated by the red lines in **Quilting Diagram 2.**

STEP 3. Note: For all of the remaining quilting, use Sulky 30-weight rayon color 1071 thread in the bobbin. With a water-soluble fabric marker, draw curved lines radiating from the tips of the birds' feathers, as indicated by the red lines in the **Center Quilting Diagram.** These lines cross each other in the areas where the birds are close together. Stitch them with YLI fine metallic color 50 on top and stipple quilt in the center of the quilt, using Madeira Supertwist color 380 thread on top.

Quilting Diagram 2

Center Quilting Diagram

STEP 4. Change to Sulky Sliver color 8040 thread on top to stipple quilt the area inside the rose borders, as shown in the **Rose Border Quilting Diagram.** Use Madeira Supertwist color 380 to echo quilt outside the roses, as shown.

Rose Border Quilting Diagram

STEP 5. The last five lines of quilting occur in the area outside the marked 31½-inch square. Raise the feed dogs and put on a regular presser foot. With a see-through ruler and a water-soluble fabric marker, mark the following five lines for the outside border. Mark the first line ½ inch outside the edge of the rose border design, as shown in the **Outer Border Quilting Diagram.** Mark another line 1 inch from that line, another 1½ inches away, another line ¼ inch from that line, and a final line ¾ inch away. Quilt along these marked lines using Sulky Sliver color 8040 thread.

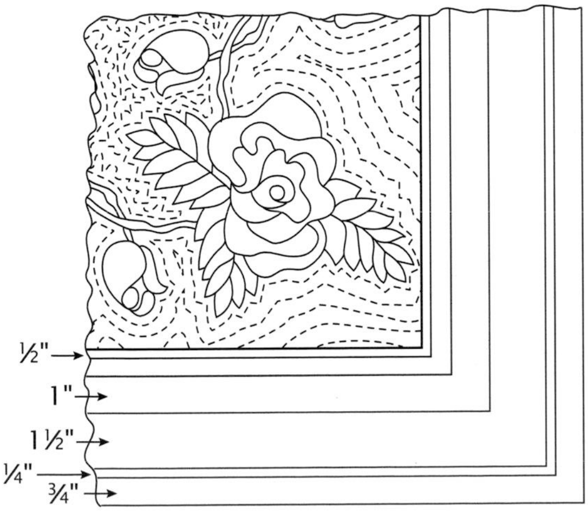

Outer Border Quilting Diagram

STEP 6. Hand sew a seed bead eye on each of the three birds.

APPLYING THE BINDING

For more information on applying binding to a quilt, see page 240.

STEP 1. From the 18-inch square of off-white moiré taffeta, prepare 4½ yards of continuous double-fold bias, by marking parallel lines at 2¼-inch intervals, sewing the edges together into a tube, and cutting the strips apart, as shown in **Diagram 13.**

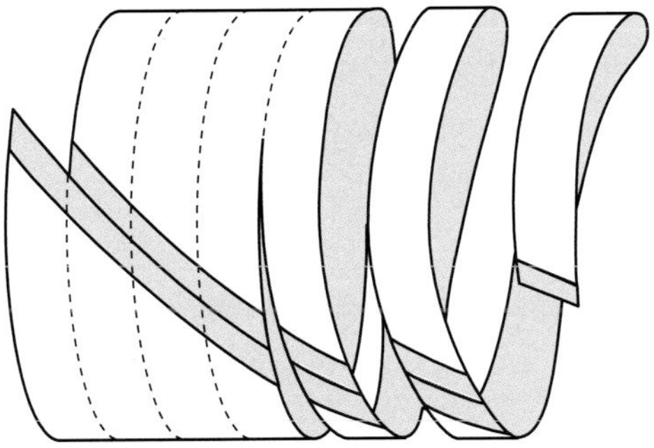

Diagram 13

STEP 2. Trim the edges of the backing and batting even with the quilt top.

STEP 3. Fold the binding strip in half lengthwise, wrong sides together, and press.

STEP 4. Place the folded binding strip at the edge of quilt sandwich, with approximately 1 inch folded over at the beginning. Starting ½ inch from this fold, do three or four backstitches and stitch the binding to the quilt with a ½-inch seam allowance.

STEP 5. Stop stitching ½ inch from the corner, backstitch, and stop. Remove the quilt, and clip the threads. Fold the binding up, and finger press the fold.

STEP 6. Fold the binding down again, aligning the raw edges with the edge of the quilt, and finger press it in place. Beginning at the top edge, stitch to ½ inch from the next corner. Repeat this process on all four sides of the quilt.

STEP 7. As you approach the point where you began stitching, lay the end of the binding strip over the folded part at the beginning of the binding. End the binding seam by stitching across the fold.

STEP 8. Turn the binding to the wrong side of the quilt and stitch it in place by hand with a blind stitch.

STEP 9. Miter the corners by folding them out and back again, taking a few stitches to secure the fold.

Bird Quilting Design and Directional Stitching Diagram

Rose Border Quilting Design
Enlarge 140%

Network

Jeannette Muir

Skill Level: Intermediate

Size: Finished quilt is 48 inches square

The four units that make up this dramatic quilt are very easy to piece. All you need is a bit of time and patience to create a bold network of indigo, purples, blues, and greens. If your scrap bag overflows with these shades, why not expand the design and make a bed-size quilt?

TECHNIQUES YOU'LL NEED:

Starting and stopping, page 34
Stitch-in-the-ditch quilting, page 47
Machine-guided curves and points, page 60

FABRICS AND SUPPLIES

As many fabrics as you like can be used to make this quilt. Choose light, medium, and dark fabrics from your scrap collection or use the quilt photo for color guidance in purchasing fabrics. If you work with three prints, you will need 1½ yards of a light print, ½ yard of a medium print, and ½ yard of a dark print. The following yardages are based on using more than three compatible prints. Use the yardages listed or "fat quarters" (approximately 18 × 22 inches) for greater economy.

FABRIC
½ yard *each* of four light blue, purple, and green prints for the blocks and units
½ yard *each* of four medium blue or green prints for the blocks and units
½ yard *each* of four dark blue or purple prints for the blocks and units
½ yard of dark gray-blue print for the inner border
4½ yards of navy print for the outer border and the quilt back
½ yard of blue-purple print for the binding

MATERIALS
Twin-size cotton batting (72 × 90 inches)
Rotary cutter, ruler, and mat
Freezer paper
Permanent fabric marker
Chalk marker or pencil
Template plastic
Neutral thread for piecing
Quilter's rust-proof safety pins
Thread to blend with prints for quilting

CUTTING

The following instructions are for rotary cutting. In some cases, the measurements include ¼-inch seam allowances, while in others there will be more than a ¼-inch seam allowance. Wherever this is the case, the seam allowances or fabric strips will be trimmed after the seams have been stitched.

From the light blue, purple, and green prints, cut:

Sixteen 4-inch squares for Block A
Sixteen 2 × 3½-inch strips for Block A
Twenty 2 × 3½-inch strips for Block B
Sixteen 5-inch squares for Unit C
Thirty-two 3 × 5-inch strips for Unit C
Forty-eight 3½ × 5-inch strips for Unit D

From the medium blue and green prints, cut:

Twenty 3½-inch squares for Block B
Twenty 2 × 3½-inch strips for Block B

From dark blue and purple prints, cut:

Thirty-two 2 × 5-inch strips for Block A
Four 2-inch squares for Block A
Five 2-inch squares for Block B
Thirty-two 2 × 5-inch strips for Unit C
Forty-eight 3 × 5-inch strips for Unit D

From the dark gray-blue print, cut:

Two 1¾ × 42-inch inner border strips
Two 1¾ × 44-inch inner border strips

From the navy print, cut:

Two 3½ × 45-inch outer border strips
Two 3½ × 49-inch outer border strips
Two 26½ × 52-inch pieces for the quilt back

From the blue-purple print, cut:

Five 2¼ × 44-inch binding strips

From the twin-size batting, cut:

One 52-inch square

PIECING BLOCK A

STEP 1. To prepare paper foundations for the corner units of Block A, cut sixteen 3½-inch squares of freezer paper and make two stacks of eight squares each. On the top square of each stack, use a pencil to mark a 3-inch square and mark a dot 1½ inches in from the top right corner in both directions, as shown in **Diagram 1.**

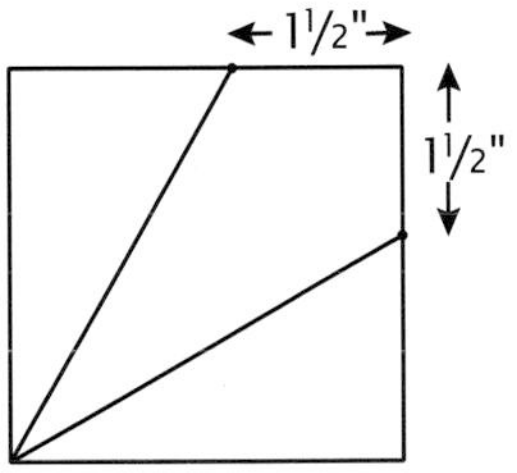

Diagram 1

STEP 2. With no thread in the top or bobbin of your sewing machine, set the stitch length to 12 to 15 stitches per inch and insert a size 90 needle. Stitch on the diagonal lines through all layers of each stack of paper foundations. Use a rotary cutter to trim each stack of paper foundations to exactly 3 inches square on the marked lines.

STEP 3. Using a dry iron on the cotton setting, press the shiny side of a paper foundation onto the wrong side of a light blue or purple print square, making sure that at least ¼ inch of fabric shows beyond all sides of the paper square, as shown in **Diagram 2.** This fabric will be trimmed to a ¼-inch seam allowances later, after these seams are stitched.

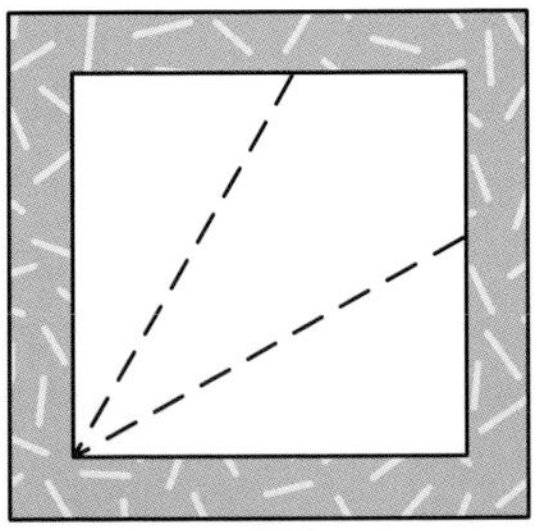

Diagram 2

STEP 4. Place a dark blue or purple 2 × 5-inch strip right sides together diagonally over the light blue or purple print square, making sure that the stitching line on the paper foundation is covered by at least ¼ inch of the dark fabric and that the strip extends beyond the edge of the paper, as shown in **Diagram 3.** To check this, hold the paper foundation and fabrics up to a light or window. With the paper foundation on top, stitch this seam directly on the stitching line.

STEP 5. Holding the paper foundation out of the way, trim the seam allowance to ¼ inch from the seam line, as shown in **Diagram 4,** and press it toward the dark strip.

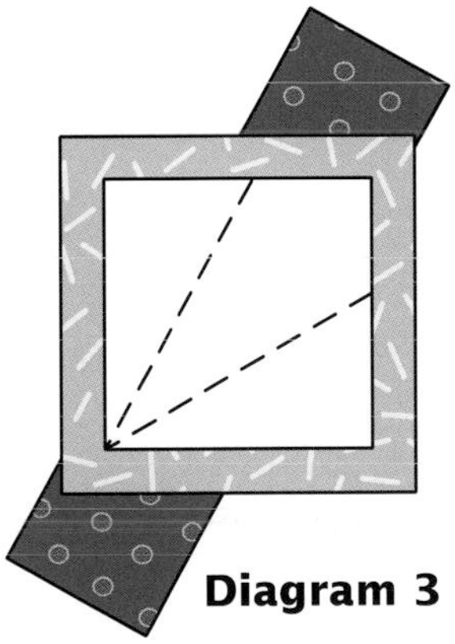

Diagram 3

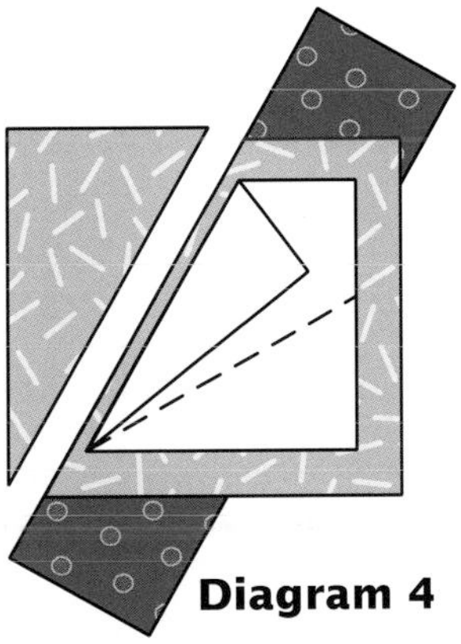

Diagram 4

STEP 6. Repeat Steps 4 and 5 to add another dark blue or purple strip to the other side of the paper foundation. Make a total of 16 corner units for Block A, as shown in **Diagram 5**. When you have finished piecing these units together, trim the fabrics to ¼ inch outside all edges of the paper foundations.

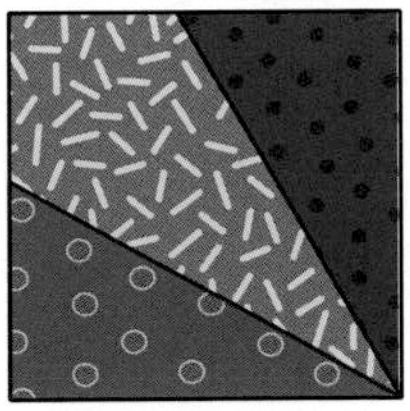

Diagram 5

STEP 7. Sew together two rows of two pieced units and a light blue or purple strip, referring to **Diagram 6.** Press the seam allowances toward each strip. **Note:** Use the edges of the paper foundations as guidelines for stitching these seams, or remove the paper foundations from behind the pieced units and use a presser foot that sews an accurate ¼-inch seam allowance.

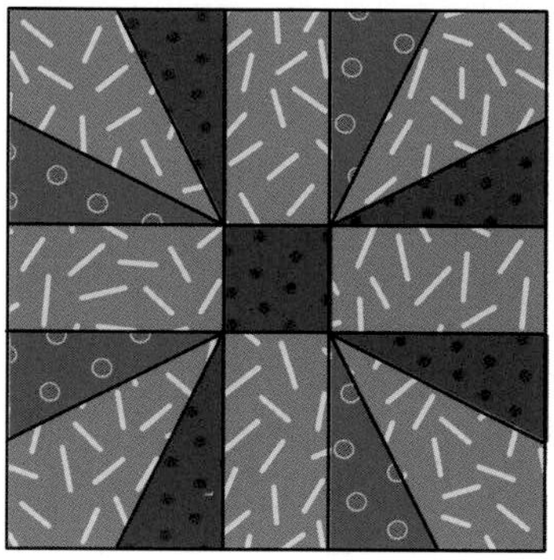

Block A
Diagram 6

STEP 8. Sew together a row of two light blue or purple strips and a dark blue or purple 2-inch square, again referring to **Diagram 6.** Press the seam allowances toward the light blue or purple strips.

STEP 9. Sew the three rows of Block A together, as shown in **Diagram 6.** Press the seam allowances toward the light blue or purple strips. Repeat steps 3 through 8 to make a total of four of Block A.

PIECING BLOCK B

Note: No paper foundations are needed for piecing this block.

STEP 1. Sew together two rows of two 3½-inch medium blue or green squares with a light blue or green 2 × 3½-inch strip between them, referring to **Diagram 7.**

STEP 2. Sew together one row of two 2 × 3½-inch light blue or green strips with a dark blue or purple 2-inch square between them, referring to **Diagram 7.**

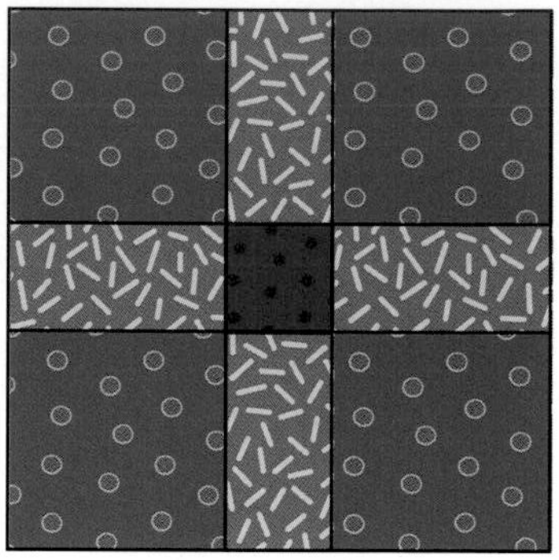

Block B
Diagram 7

STEP 3. Sew the three rows of Block B together, as shown in **Diagram 7.** Repeat Steps 1 to 3 to make a total of five of Block B.

PIECING UNIT C

STEP 1. To prepare paper foundations for Unit C, cut sixteen 5-inch squares of freezer paper and make two stacks of eight squares each. On the top square of each stack, use a pencil to mark a 4½-inch square. Mark a dot 1½ inches in from the corners on each side of the square, as shown in **Diagram 8.** Mark diagonal lines connecting these dots.

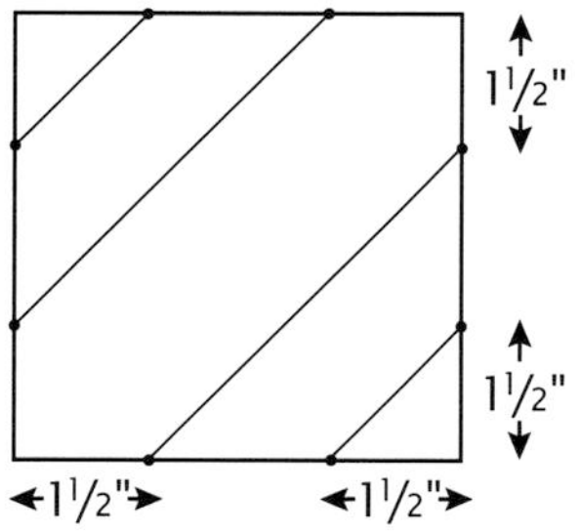

Diagram 8

STEP 2. With no thread in the top or bobbin of your sewing machine, set the stitch length to 12 to 15 stitches per inch and insert a size 90 needle. Stitch on the diagonal lines through all layers of each stack of paper foundations. Use a rotary cutter to trim each stack of paper foundations to exactly 4½ inches square.

STEP 3. Press a paper foundation to the wrong side of a light blue, green, or purple 5-inch square of fabric. Place a dark blue or purple 3 × 5-inch strip over the light fabric, right sides together, so that the dark fabric extends at least ¼ inch beyond the longer seam line, as shown in **Diagram 9.** Stitch the seam directly on the stitching line. Peel back the paper foundation and trim the fabrics to exactly ¼ inch from the seam line, referring to **Diagram 4** on page 195.

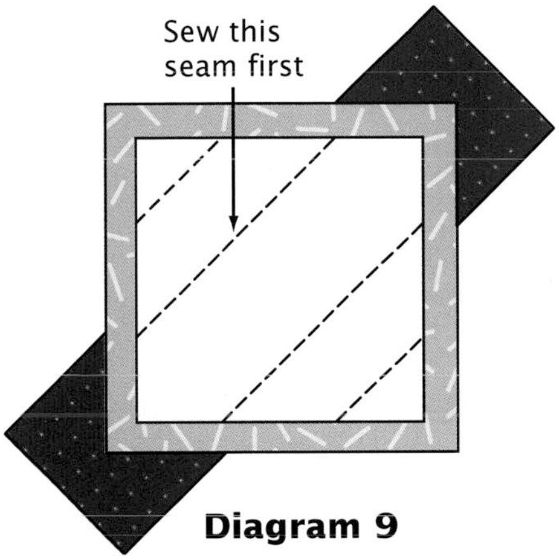

Diagram 9

STEP 4. Open up the fabrics and finger press the seam flat.

STEP 5. In the same manner, continue adding light and dark strips to cover the paper foundation, creating Unit C, as shown in **Diagram 10.** Trim the fabrics to exactly ¼ inch from the edges of the paper foundation on all sides. Do not remove the paper foundations; they will be used later as guidelines for sewing the quilt together. Repeat Steps 3 through 5 to make a total of 16 of Unit C.

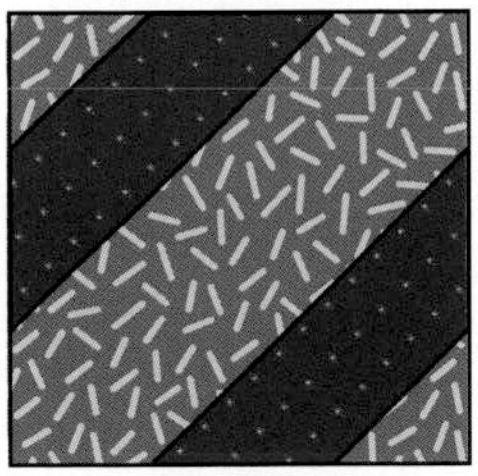

Unit C
Diagram 10

PIECING UNIT D

STEP 1. To prepare paper foundations for the side portions of Unit D, cut twenty-four 3½ × 5-inch pieces of freezer paper and make three stacks of eight pieces each. On the top square of each stack, use a pencil to mark a 3 × 4½-inch rectangle. Mark a dot 1½ inches down from the top edge on the left side of each rectangle, as shown in **Diagram 11.** Mark another dot 1½ inches in from the left corner on top of the rectangle and mark diagonal lines to connect the dots, as shown.

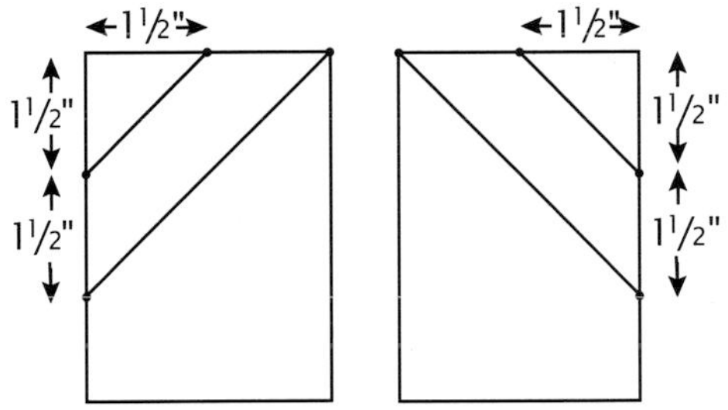

Diagram 11

STEP 2. Cut 24 more 3½ × 5-inch pieces of freezer paper and repeat Step 1, this time marking the diagonal lines on the opposite sides of the rectangles, as shown above.

STEP 3. With no thread in the top or bobbin of your sewing machine, set the stitch length to 12 to 15 stitches per inch and insert a size 90 needle. Stitch on the diagonal lines through all layers of each stack of paper foundations. Use a rotary cutter to trim each stack of paper foundations to rectangles measuring exactly 3 × 4½ inches.

STEP 4. Press one of the foundation papers to the wrong side of a 3½ × 5-inch strip of light blue, purple, or green fabric, checking to make sure that at least ¼ inch of fabric extends beyond all sides of the paper foundation.

STEP 5. Place a dark blue, purple, or green 3 × 5-inch strip over the light fabric, right sides together, as shown in **Diagram 12,** checking that the long edge of the dark fabric extends at least ¼ inch beyond the longer of the two seam lines. Stitch this seam, open up the fabrics, and finger press them flat.

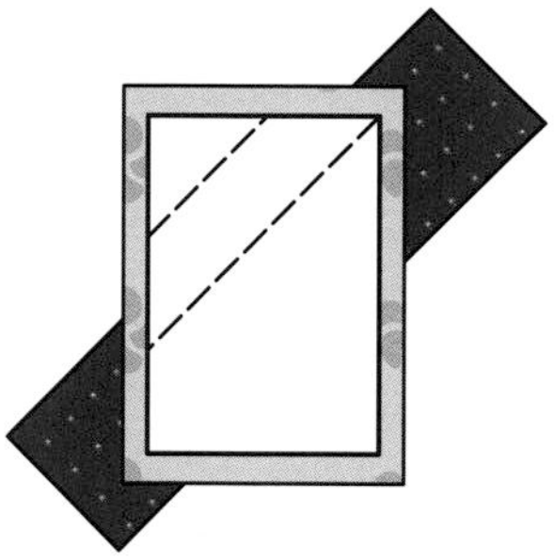

Diagram 12

STEP 6. Peel back the paper foundation and trim the seam allowances to ¼ inch, referring to **Diagram 4** on page 195.

STEP 7. Sew a light 3 × 5-inch strip to the other side of the dark strip. Finger press them open. Trim all fabrics to ¼ inch from the edge on all sides of the paper foundation. Repeat Steps 4 through 7 to make a total of 48 of Unit C. **Note:** Half of the pieced units have the diagonal strip of dark fabric facing in one direction and half in the opposite direction, as shown in **Diagram 13.**

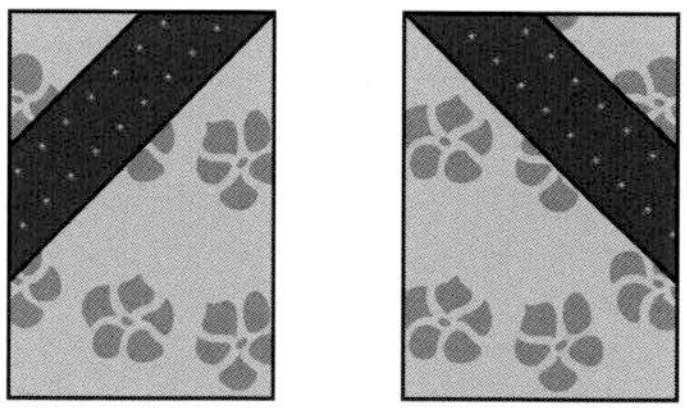

Diagram 13

STEP 8. Sew a medium blue, purple, or green 2 × 5-inch strip between two of the pieced units, creating Unit D, as shown in **Diagram 14.** Press the seam allowances toward the pieced units. Repeat Steps 4 to 8 to make a total of 24 of Unit D.

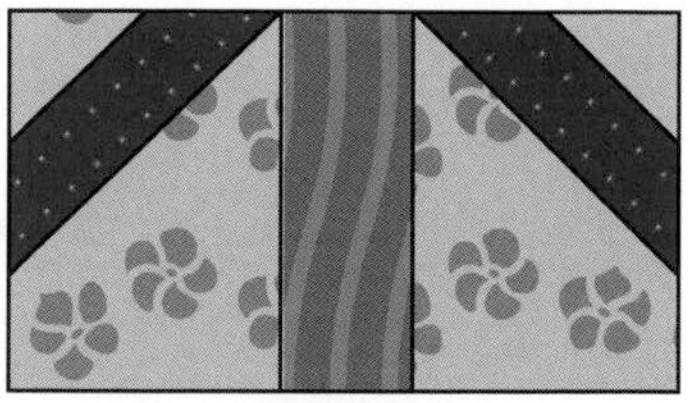

Unit D
Diagram 14

ASSEMBLING THE QUILT TOP

STEP 1. Lay out Blocks A and B and Units C and D in seven rows, as shown in the **Quilt Assembly Diagram.**

STEP 2. Sew the blocks and units into seven rows. Press the seam allowances in opposite directions.

STEP 3. Referring to the **Quilt Assembly Diagram,** sew the seven rows of the quilt top together, pressing the seam allowances between rows in the same direction.

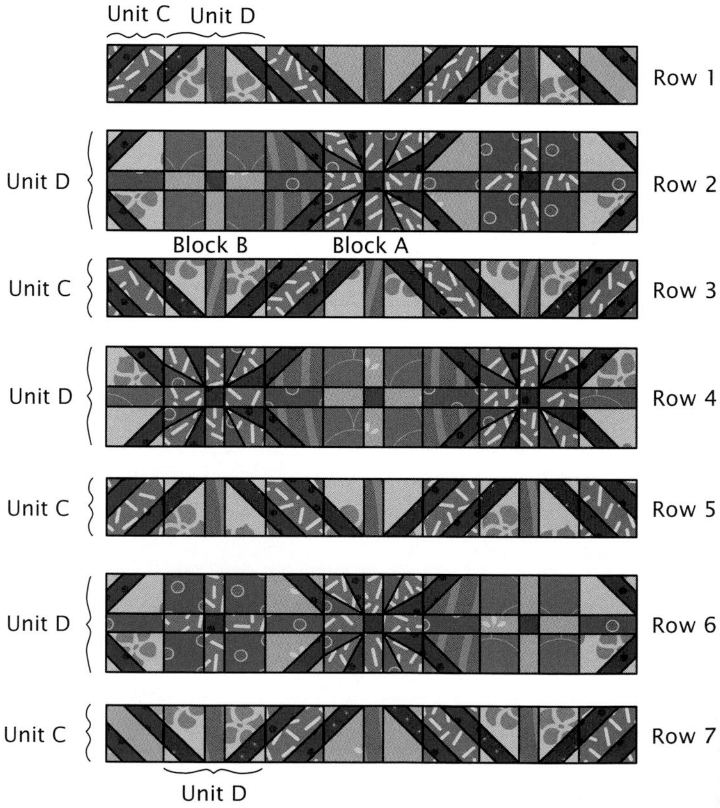

Quilt Assembly Diagram

COMPLETING THE QUILT TOP

STEP 1. Sew a dark gray-blue print 1¾ × 42-inch inner border strip to two opposite sides of the quilt top. Press the seams toward the border strips. Trim excess fabric from the end of the border strip even with the quilt top.

STEP 2. Sew a dark gray-blue print 1¾ × 44-inch inner border strip to the top and bottom of the quilt top. Press the seams toward the border strips. Trim excess fabric from the end of the border strip even with the quilt top.

STEP 3. Sew a navy print 3½ × 45-inch outer border strip to two opposite sides of the quilt top. Press the seams toward the border strips. Trim excess fabric from the end of the border strip even with the top.

STEP 4. Sew a navy print 3½ × 49-inch outer border strip to the top and bottom of the quilt top. Press the seams toward the border strips. Trim excess fabric from the end of the border strip even with the top.

STEP 5. Remove the selvage edges from the two navy print pieces for the quilt back. Sew the two pieces together with a ¼-inch seam and press this seam open.

STEP 6. Layer the quilt back, batting, and quilt top together. Baste the center area with safety pins and use straight pins around the perimeter of the quilt. For more information on layering and basting, see page 19.

STEP 7. Stitch around the entire quilt top 3/16 inch in from the edge of the fabric, removing the straight pins as you reach them. Check for desired stitch length and adjust thread tension at this time. If you can see bobbin thread on top of the quilt, loosen the top tension until it is no longer visible.

MACHINE QUILTING

STEP 1. Mark straight and diagonal lines at the corners of the inner and outer borders, as shown in the **Border Quilting Diagram** on page 200.

STEP 2. Mark straight lines at 5-inch intervals in the remainder of the inner and outer borders, as shown in the **Border Quilting Diagram.** Mark a guideline 2 inches in from the inner edge of the inner border, as shown.

STEP 3. With a permanent marker, trace Template A on page 201 onto template plastic, taking care to mark the dashed guidelines as well as the outlines.

STEP 4. Using a chalk marker or removable fabric marker, trace around Template A between each of the marked 5-inch segments. Then superimpose the dashed guidelines on Template A over the marked border guidelines and mark around Template A again. Make adjustments as needed.

STEP 5. When you reach the corner areas, stop marking wherever Template A reaches the marked diagonal line in both directions, as shown in the **Border Quilting Diagram.**

STEP 6. Block A and the areas surrounding it are quilted in the ditches of the seams, as shown in **Block A Quilting Diagram** on page 200. Note that in the center square of Block A, the lines of quilting form a small diamond shape; if desired, you may mark these lines before beginning to quilt.

STEP 7. Block B and the areas surrounding it are quilted in a configuration of concentric straight lines spaced at 1-inch intervals, as shown in **Block B Quilting Diagram** on page 200. Mark these lines with a chalk marker.

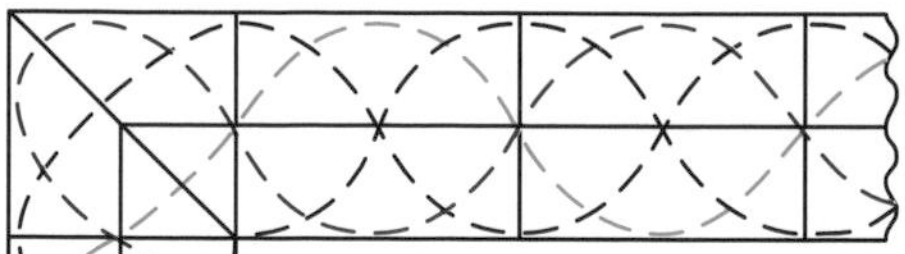
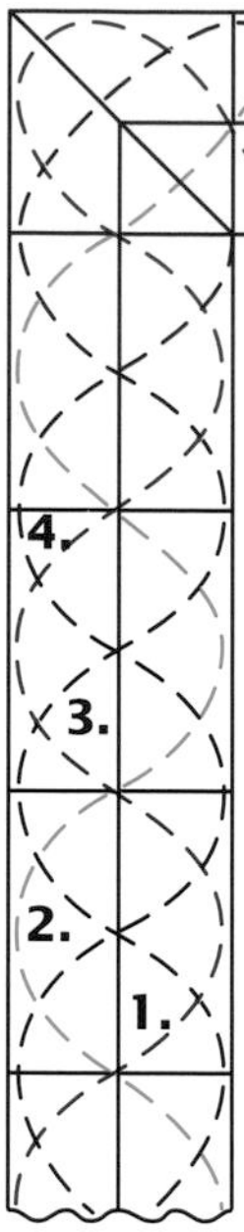

Border Quilting Diagram

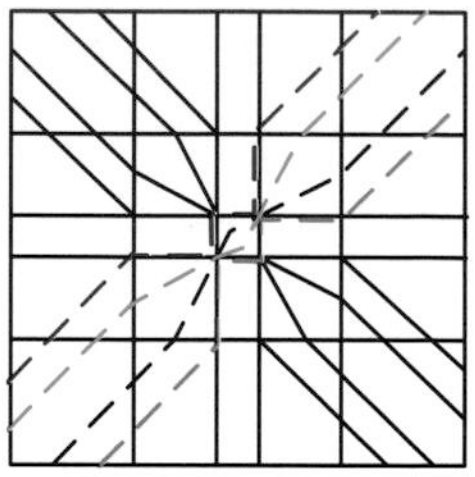

Block A Quilting Diagram

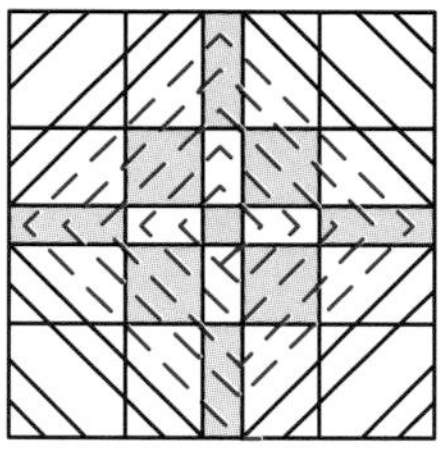

Block B Quilting Diagram

STEP 8. Begin quilting in the borders, starting at a place where two lines will cross, and leave 5- to 6-inch tails of thread to hide in the batting by hand. First, quilt the line of stitches labeled 1, as indicated by the red dashes in the **Border Quilting Diagram**.

STEP 9. When you return to the point where you started, switch to quilting line 2, as indicated by the blue dashes in the **Border Quilting Diagram**.

STEP 10. When you have finished this second track of stitches, quilt line 3, as indicated by the green dashes, and finally, line 4, as indicated by black dashes in the **Border Quilting Diagram.** Bury all thread tails in the batting by hand.

STEP 11. Quilt Block A and the surrounding areas by starting at a convenient point in one of the ditches, leaving 5- to 6-inch thread tails and stitching in the ditch of the seams, as indicated by the red, blue, green, and black dashes in the **Block A Quilting Diagram**.

STEP 12. Quilt Block B and the surrounding areas by starting where two lines meet at the center and stitching in concentric lines, as indicated by the red dashes in the **Block B Quilting Diagram**. Make sure that the needle is down each time you pivot the fabric and that the area surrounding the needle is always relaxed. Bury all thread tails in the batting by hand.

APPLYING THE BINDING

STEP 1. Sew the five binding strips together with diagonal seams and trim the seam allowances to ¼ inch. Press these seams open. For more information on diagonal seams, see page 241.

STEP 2. Cut one end of the binding strip off at a 45-degree angle that faces the same direction as the seams. Fold the binding in half, wrong sides together, and press. Check to make sure that the seams will not lie at the corners.

STEP 3. Position the binding at the edge of quilt sandwich, beginning 5 inches away from a corner and leaving 5 or 6 inches of binding free. Start sewing the binding to the quilt with a ¼-inch seam allowance.

STEP 4. Stop stitching ¼ inch from the corner. Sew five or six backstitches into the seam allowance to secure the threads. Remove the quilt, and clip the threads.

STEP 5. Fold the binding up, and finger press the fold. For more information on folding binding straight up, see page 241.

STEP 6. Fold the binding down, matching all edges, and finger press it in place. Insert the needle ¼ inch from the top edge, backstitch to the top, and continue stitching to the next corner. Repeat for all corners.

STEP 7. Leave the last 5 or 6 inches of binding unstitched. Remove the quilt, and smooth the unstitched binding in place. Fold the binding straight up, matching the angle of the folded edge to the angle of the beginning of the binding strip, as shown in **Diagram 15.** Finger press this fold in place.

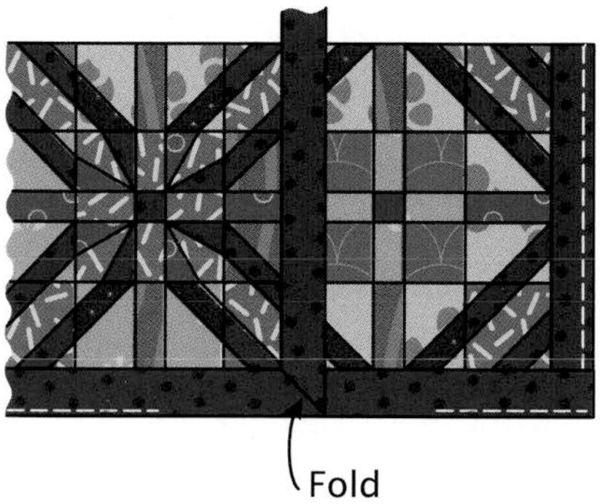

Diagram 15

STEP 8. Unfold the binding. Mark a line along the diagonal fold and mark a second line ½ inch beyond the first line, as shown in **Diagram 16.** Open the binding up to a single layer and extend the marking on the second diagonal line. Cut across the binding strip on this line.

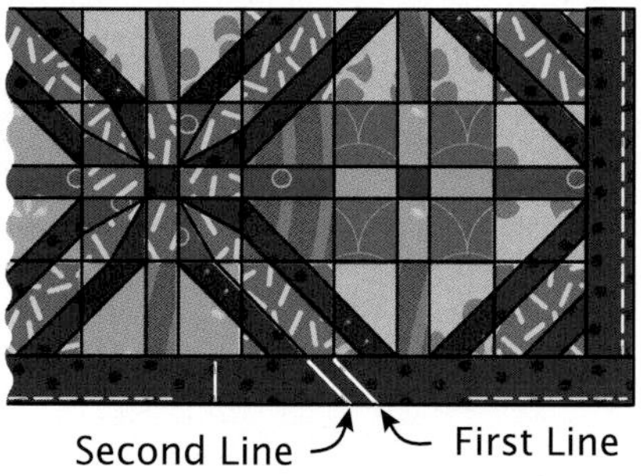

Diagram 16

STEP 9. Pin the two free ends of the binding right sides together and sew them with a ¼-inch seam allowance. Press this seam allowance open. Refold and finger press the binding. Sew the final portion of the binding to the quilt.

STEP 10. Fold the binding to the back side of the quilt and sew with a blind stitch, mitering the fold at each corner and stitching the miters closed.

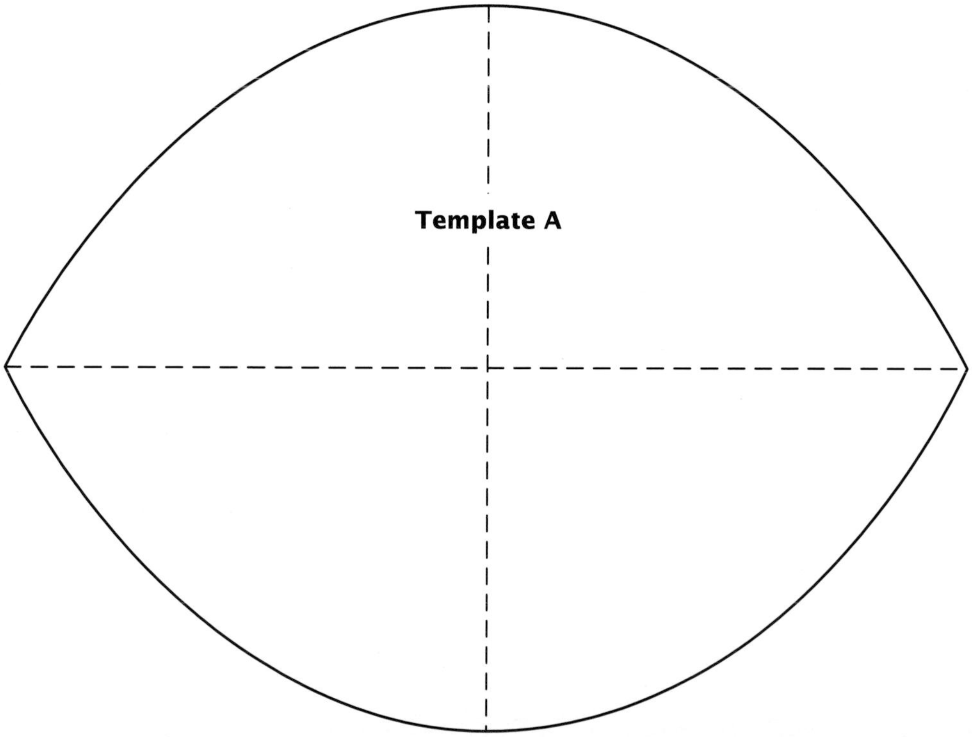

Autumn TRELLIS

Hari Walner

Skill Level: Easy

Size: Finished quilt is 72 × 88 inches

Finished block is 8 inches

Quilted flowers and leaves wander in and out of the peach and teal bars of this easy-to-piece Autumn Trellis quilt. Hari started by designing a continuous-line motif for the plain blocks and then created a simple pieced block to complement them. She used ultra-loft polyester batting to add to the three-dimensional effect of her quilt.

TECHNIQUES YOU'LL NEED:

Starting and stopping, page 34
Stitch-in-the-ditch quilting, page 47
Free-motion curves and points, page 70
Free-motion continuous-line quilting, page 78
Vermicelli stipple quilting, page 91

FABRICS AND SUPPLIES

FABRIC

- 3½ yards of ivory cotton sateen fabric for the pieced and quilted blocks
- 1½ yards of a medium rust print for the pieced blocks
- 1½ yards of a dark rust print for the pieced blocks
- 1½ yards of medium teal print for the pieced blocks
- 2 yards of a dark teal print for the pieced blocks and the binding
- 5¼ yards of light solid fabric for the quilt back

MATERIALS

- One full-size, ultra-loft polyester batting (81 × 96 inches)
- Light neutral-colored thread for piecing
- Machine embroidery thread to match the ivory sateen fabric for quilting
- Removable fabric marker

CUTTING

The solid squares for this quilt are rotary cut. The measurements include ¼-inch seam allowances. Prewash and iron all fabrics before cutting; when pressing, I suggest spritzing them with spray sizing to give them more body and make accurate cutting easier.

From the ivory sateen fabric, cut:
Thirty-two 8½-inch squares
268 A triangles (see page 208)

From the medium rust print, cut:
67 B pieces (see page 208)
67 C pieces (see page 208)

From the dark rust print, cut:
67 B pieces
67 C pieces

From the medium teal print, cut:
67 B pieces
67 C pieces

From the dark teal print, cut:
67 B pieces
67 C pieces
Nine 2 × 44-inch binding strips

From the light solid backing fabric, cut:
Two 38¼ × 92-inch pieces

From the full-size batting, cut:
One 76 × 92-inch piece

PIECING THE TRELLIS BLOCKS

STEP 1. Sew an ivory sateen A triangle to a medium teal print B piece, as shown in the **Trellis Block Diagram.** Sew a medium rust print C piece to the pieced unit, as shown. Repeat to make a total of 67 of these pieced units.

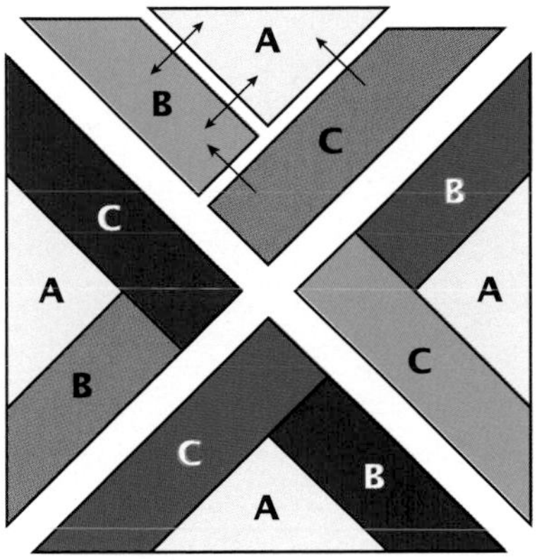

Trellis Block Diagram

STEP 2. Sew an ivory A triangle to a dark teal print B piece, as shown in the **Trellis Block Diagram.** Sew a medium teal print C piece to this unit, as shown. Repeat to make a total of 67 of these pieced units.

STEP 3. Sew an ivory A triangle to a dark rust print B piece, as shown in the **Trellis Block Diagram.** Sew a dark teal print C piece to the pieced unit, as shown. Repeat to make a total of 67 of these pieced units.

STEP 4. Sew an ivory A triangle to a medium rust print B piece, as shown in the **Trellis Block Diagram.** Sew a dark rust print C piece to this unit, as shown. Repeat to make a total of 67 of these pieced units.

STEP 5. Sew together the four pieced units of each Trellis block, taking care to keep the colors in each block in the same positions. Repeat to make a total of 67 Trellis blocks.

ASSEMBLING THE QUILT TOP

STEP 1. Sew together two horizontal rows of nine pieced blocks each, as shown in rows 1 and 11 of the **Quilt Assembly Diagram** on page 206, taking care to keep the colors in each block in the same position.

STEP 2. Sew together five rows of pieced and plain blocks, as shown in rows 2, 4, 6, 8, and 10 of the **Quilt Assembly Diagram.** Press the seams in alternating directions.

STEP 3. Sew together four rows of pieced and plain blocks, as shown in rows 3, 5, 7, and 9 of the **Quilt Assembly Diagram.** Press the seams in alternating directions.

STEP 4. Sew the 11 rows of the quilt together, taking care to position each row as shown in the **Quilt Assembly Diagram.** Press all seams in the same direction. Press the completed quilt top.

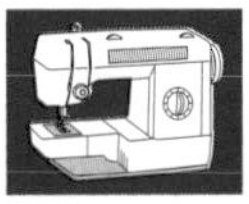

MACHINE QUILTING

STEP 1. Mark the Block Quilting Design on page 209 in the plain blocks, as shown in the **Quilt Assembly Diagram** on page 206. Note that this design will overlap into the ivory triangles on adjoining blocks.

STEP 2. Mark the Large Flower Quilting Design on page 208 where the ivory A triangles meet to form squares in the border, as shown in the **Quilt Assembly Diagram.**

STEP 3. Mark the Small Flower Quilting Design on page 208 in the A triangles at the edge of the border, as shown in the **Quilt Assembly Diagram.**

STEP 4. Sew together the two 36½ × 92-inch pieces of backing fabric, and press the seam allowance open.

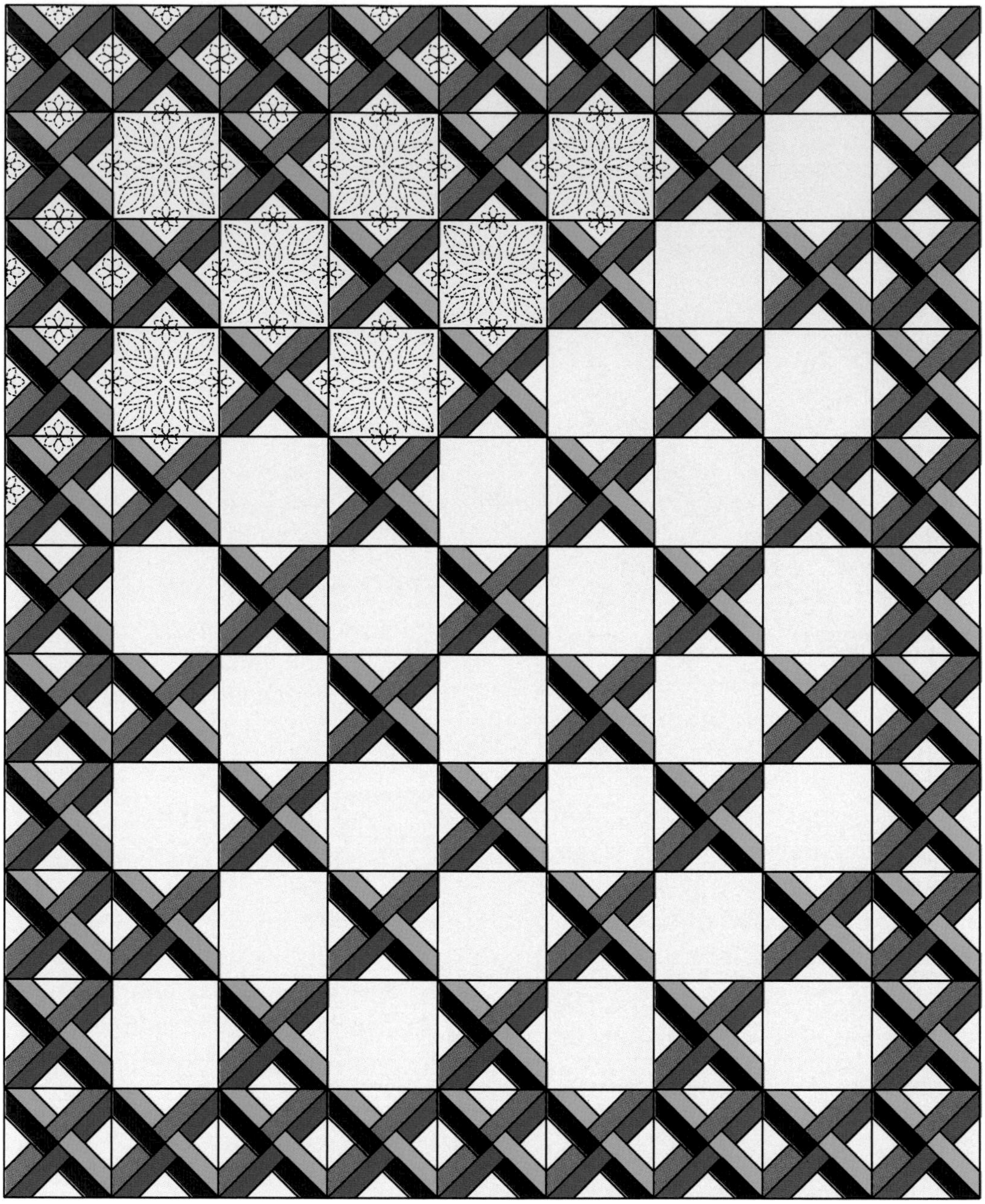

Quilt Assembly Diagram

STEP 5. With the backing fabric wrong side up and the seam allowance running vertically, layer and baste the quilt together. For more information on layering and basting, see page 19.

STEP 6. Stitch in the ditch diagonally through the center of each pieced block in both directions, starting at one edge of the quilt and continuing to the other edge.

STEP 7. Free-motion quilt all of the marked designs, referring to the **Directional Stitching Diagram** on the opposite page the starting dots and directional arrows.

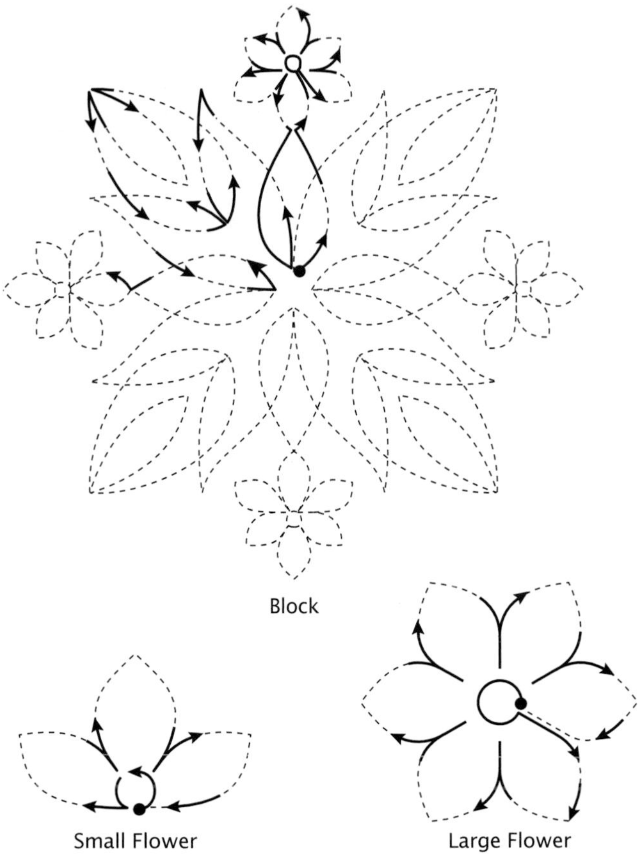

Directional Stitching Diagram

APPLYING THE BINDING

For diagrams and more information on applying binding to a quilt, see page 240.

STEP 1. Trim the edges of the backing and batting even with the edges of the quilt top.

STEP 2. Sew the binding strips together with diagonal seams. Trim the seams to ¼ inch, and press them open.

STEP 3. Fold the binding strip in half lengthwise, wrong sides together, and press.

STEP 4. Position the raw edges of the folded binding strip at the edge of quilt sandwich, with approximately 1 inch folded over at the beginning. Starting ½ inch from this fold, do three or four backstitches to secure the threads, and start stitching the binding to the quilt through all layers with a ½-inch seam allowance.

STEP 5. Stop stitching ½ inch from the corner, backstitch to secure the threads, and stop. Remove the quilt from the machine, and clip the threads. Fold the binding straight up, and finger press the fold.

STEP 6. Fold the binding down again, aligning the raw edges with the edge of the quilt, and finger press it in place. Beginning at the top edge, stitch to ½ inch from the next corner. Repeat this process on all four sides of the quilt.

STEP 7. As you approach the point where you began stitching, lay the end of the binding strip over the folded part at the beginning of it. End the binding seam by stitching across the fold.

STEP 8. Turn the binding to the wrong side of the quilt, and stitch it in place by hand with a blind stitch.

STEP 9. Miter the corners by folding them out and back again, taking a few stitches to secure the fold.

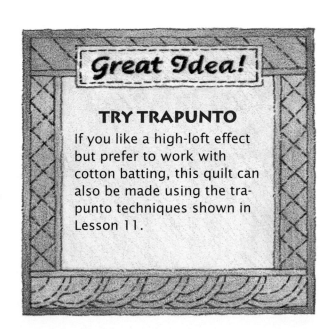

Great Idea!

TRY TRAPUNTO

If you like a high-loft effect but prefer to work with cotton batting, this quilt can also be made using the trapunto techniques shown in Lesson 11.

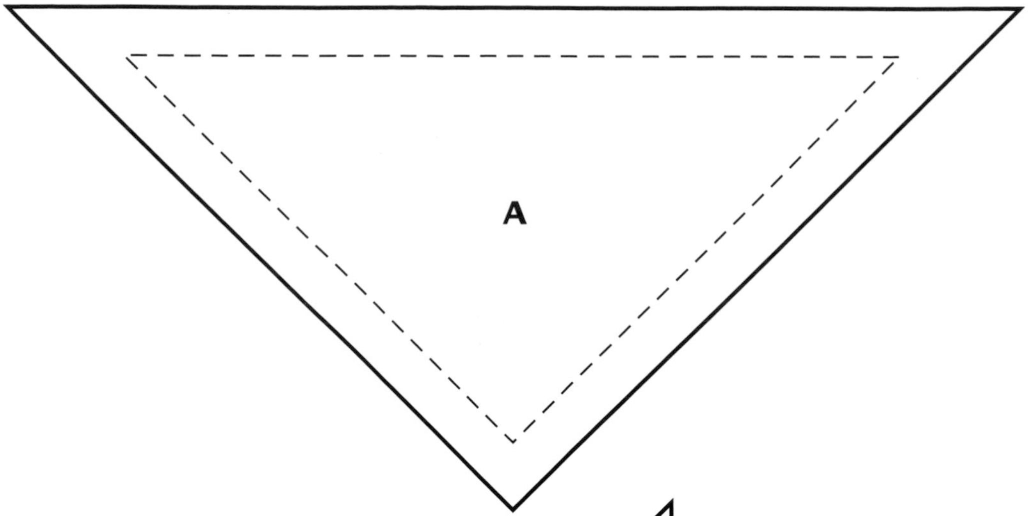

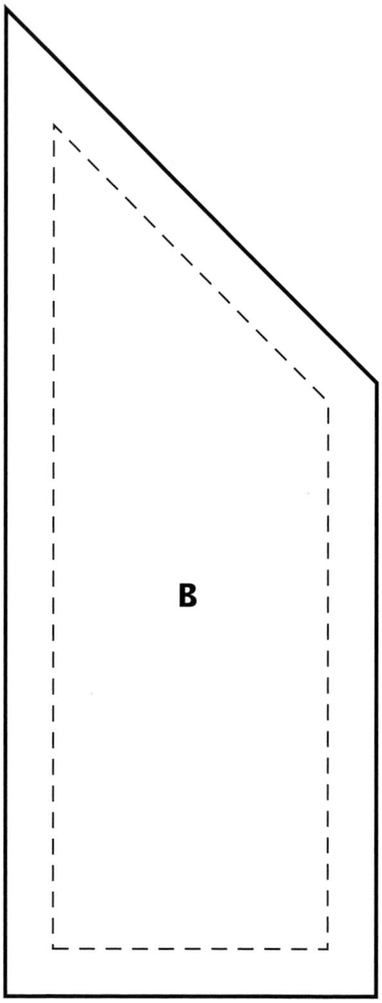

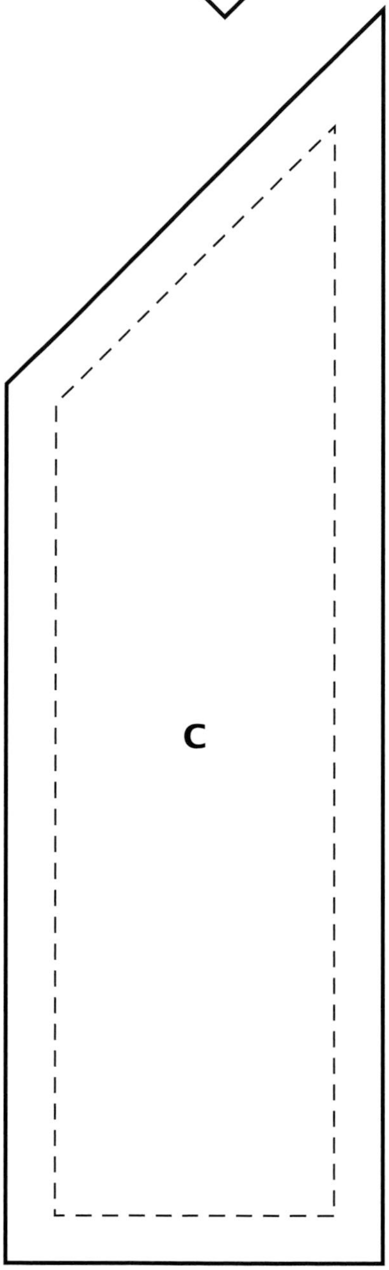

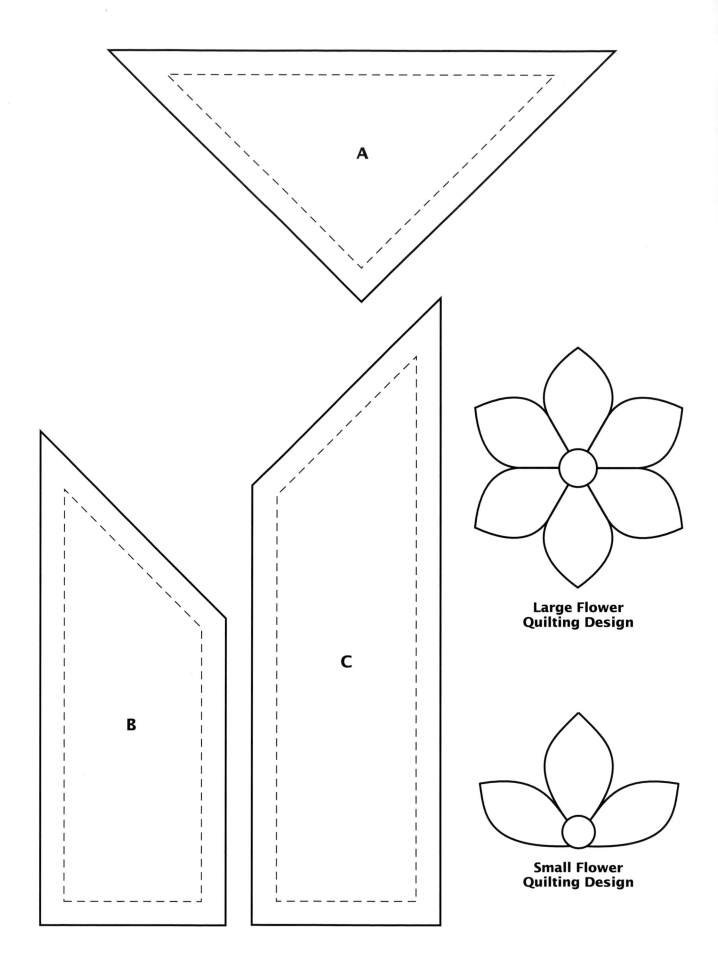

Large Flower Quilting Design

Small Flower Quilting Design

Trace twice or make two photocopies. Using the dashed line for placement, tape the halves together to make the complete design.

One-Half Block Quilting Design

Hospitality TABLE RUNNER

Sherry Sunday

Skill Level: Easy to Intermediate

Size: Finished table runner is 20½ × 53½ inches

Finished block is 14½ inches square

The pineapple is the symbol of hospitality, and the charming motifs in this centerpiece will make guests feel welcome in your home the whole year through. Sherry's center appliqué design is smaller than those in the outer blocks, so that the focus stays on decorative objects placed there, such as a pair of elegant candlesticks or a fruit compote.

TECHNIQUES YOU'LL NEED:

Starting and stopping, page 34
Outline quilting, page 45
Free-motion curves and points, page 70
Vermicelli stipple quilting, page 91

FABRICS AND SUPPLIES

FABRIC

- 2 yards of white tone-on-tone print fabric for the background and quilt back
- One 18 × 22½-inch piece ("fat quarter") of gold print fabric for the pineapple blocks
- One 18 × 22½-inch piece ("fat quarter") of dark green print fabric for the pineapple blocks and the center appliqué shape
- ⅓ yard of dark green multicolored print for the pineapple blocks
- ⅝ yard of dark red print for the pineapple blocks and the binding

MATERIALS

- One crib-size, lightweight cotton or cotton-polyester blend batting (45 × 60 inches)
- Rotary cutter, ruler, and mat
- Template plastic
- Threads to match appliqués
- Quilting thread to match the background fabric
- Rust-proof quilter's safety pins

CUTTING

The instructions are for quick cutting the background pieces and the binding. All of the measurements include ¼-inch seam allowances, unless otherwise noted. Cut the strips for the binding across the width of the fabric. **Note:** For appliqué shapes, no seam allowances are given. Trace these shapes onto template plastic and mark on the right side of the fabric, leaving ½ inch of space between pieces for seam allowances. Add a 3⁄16-inch seam allowance to these pieces when cutting them out of fabric.

From the white tone-on-tone print, cut:

Two 15-inch background squares

Two 11-inch squares. Cut each of these squares in half diagonally to make four background triangles.

One 21 × 13-inch background rectangle

One 24 × 58-inch piece for the quilt back. Trim to 2 inches beyond the edges of the quilt top after layering.

From the gold print, cut:

Eight D shapes

Two 3-inch A squares

From the dark green print, cut:

Eight E shapes

One B shape

From the dark green multicolored print, cut:

Two B shapes

From the dark red print, cut:

Eight 1½ × 4½-inch C rectangles

Eight F shapes

Four 3 × 45-inch binding strips

From the crib-size batting, cut:

One 24 × 58-inch piece. Trim to 2 inches beyond the quilt top after layering.

APPLIQUÉING THE PINEAPPLE AND CENTER BLOCKS

The following instructions are for cutting and placing the appliqué shapes on the background fabric and appliquéing them by hand. These blocks can also be appliquéd by machine or by using fusible webbing to fuse the shapes onto background fabrics.

PINEAPPLE BLOCKS

STEP 1. Trace appliqué patterns B, D, E, and F from page 217 onto template plastic or freezer paper and cut them out. Note that the pattern for piece B is one-fourth of the complete design. If you are tracing this piece onto template plastic, simply rotate it 90 degrees until all four quarters are traced. If you are using freezer paper, fold a 10-inch square in half vertically and horizontally to divide it into quarters. Open up the freezer paper and trace the one-fourth pattern from page 217 onto one section. Then fold the paper up again and place a few staples inside the design lines to stabilize it while you cut it out on the traced lines. Open it up, and you will have a complete B shape.

STEP 2. Fold a 15-inch white background square in half diagonally in both directions, and then horizontally and vertically. Open up the background square and position the small gold A square at the center. Then place a multicolored B shape over the A square, aligning the B shape with the horizontal and vertical folds, as shown in **Diagram 1.** Use straight pins to hold both shapes securely in position.

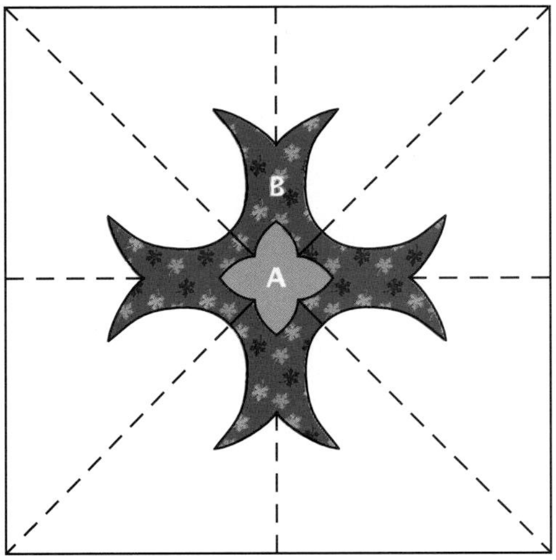

Diagram 1

STEP 3. Appliqué the inner edges of the B shape over the gold print center square using the blind stitch, as shown in **Diagram 2.** On the inner curves of the B shape, make small clips into the seam allowance, approximately ¼ inch apart, to make it easier to turn under. Also make a clip at each point, almost to the turning line to help make the points sharp and crisp.

Diagram 2

STEP 4. Appliqué the outer edges of the multicolored B shape, making clips along the inner curves and at inner points where necessary to make it easy to turn under the seam allowances.

STEP 5. Position the four gold print D shapes next to the inner edges of the B shape, so that when appliquéd in place, they will touch the B shape, as shown in

Diagram 3. Place red print C rectangles underneath the D shapes and dark green print E shapes underneath the outer edges of the D pieces. Place red print F shapes between the outer points of the B shape, as shown. Pin all of these pieces securely in place with straight pins. Appliqué the inner edges of the gold D shapes over the red C rectangles, making clips in the seam allowances where necessary. Appliqué the outer edges of the gold D shapes, making clips at inner points to keep them sharp. Appliqué the dark green E shapes in place at the outer edges of the D shapes, so that they meet, as shown. Appliqué the red print F shapes in place, as shown.

Diagram 3

STEP 6. Repeat Steps 1 through 5 to make another pineapple block.

THE CENTER BLOCK

STEP 1. Fold the 21 × 13-inch background rectangle horizontally and vertically to find the center point and pin the dark green print B shape at the center, as shown in **Diagram 4.** Appliqué the inner and outer edges in place, making clips into the seam allowances where necessary.

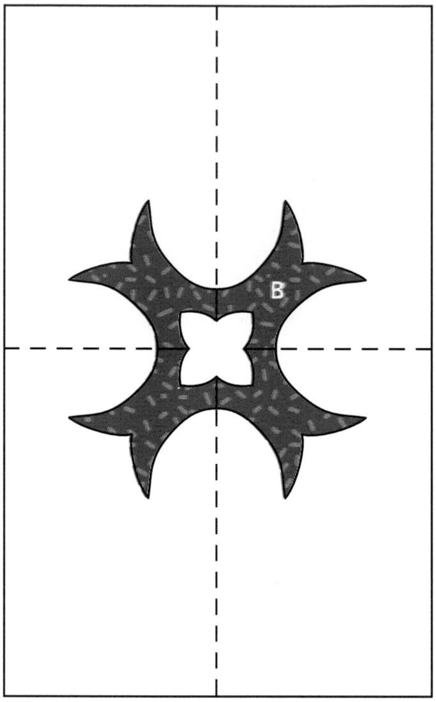

Diagram 4

ASSEMBLING THE TABLE RUNNER

STEP 1. Using ¼-inch seam allowances, sew a white background triangle to two sides of each pineapple block, as shown in **Diagram 5.** Press the seam allowances toward the pineapple blocks. Sew the completed 21 × 13-inch center block between the two outer pineapple blocks, as shown. Press the seam allowances toward the center block.

LAYERING AND BASTING

STEP 1. Place the backing fabric wrong side up on a flat surface and place the batting over it.

STEP 2. Place the quilt top over the batting and use quilter's rust-proof safety pins to baste the three layers together at 3-inch intervals. For more information on layering and basting, see page 19.

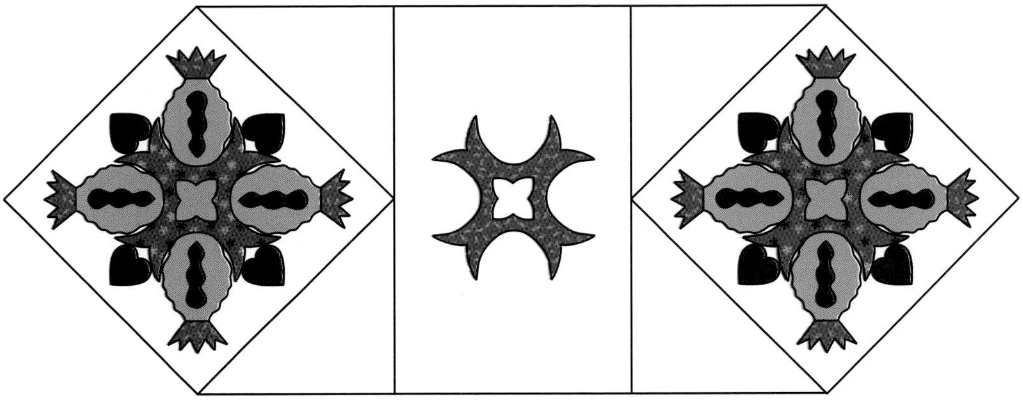

Diagram 5

MACHINE QUILTING

The quilting designs in this table runner can be quilted without marking any of the lines. If you wish to make sure that the lines of echo quilting are spaced at exact intervals, however, it can be helpful to use a quilting guide. If you wish to use this attachment and your machine does not have one, contact a local sewing machine dealer for one that will fit your machine.

STEP 1. Outline quilt ½ inch outside all of the appliqué shapes in the pineapple blocks and the center block, as shown in the **Quilting Diagram.**

STEP 2. Do two lines of free-motion echo quilting spaced at 1-inch intervals around the outside of each block, as shown in the **Quilting Diagram.** Note that the last line of outline quilting around the pineapple blocks is connected to the last line of outline quilting around the center block.

STEP 3. Fill in the remainder of the background with stipple quilting, as shown in the **Quilting Diagram.**

APPLYING THE BINDING

For diagrams and more information on applying binding to a quilt, see page 240.

STEP 1. Trim the quilt back and batting even with the edges of the quilt top.

STEP 2. Sew the binding strips together with diagonal seams. Trim these seams to ¼ inch and press them open.

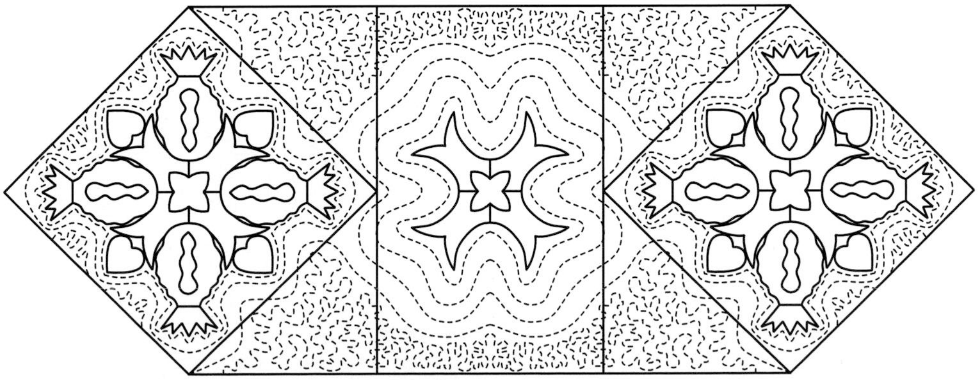

Quilting Diagram

STEP 3. At the beginning of the binding, turn under ½ inch and press the fabric in place. Then fold the entire binding strip in half, wrong sides together and press.

STEP 4. Position the raw edges of the binding at the edge of one of the long sides of the quilt, with 1 inch folded over at the beginning. Starting about 5 inches away from a corner, stitch the binding to the quilt with a ½-inch seam.

STEP 5. Stop ½ inch from the corner and backstitch to secure the threads. Clip the threads and remove the quilt from the machine. Fold the binding up to miter the corner and finger press the fold lightly.

STEP 6. Fold the binding down, matching the raw edges with the edge of the quilt and finger press it in place. Begin sewing at the top edge, taking a few backstitches to secure the threads, and continue stitching to the next corner. Repeat this process on all sides of the quilt.

STEP 7. As you approach the point where you began stitching, lay the end of the binding strip over the folded part at the beginning of the binding. End the binding seam by stitching across the fold.

STEP 8. Turn the binding to the wrong side and stitch it in place by hand with a blind stitch, mitering the corners.

Great Ideas!

TRY TAILOR TACKS FOR BASTING

If your sewing machine has a built-in basting stitch or tailor tack stitch, try using it for basting a small machine-quilting project. This will save you time in opening and closing lots of safety pins.

THRIFT SHOP SPECIALS

Browsing through thrift shops or secondhand stores can yield unexpected benefits for machine quilting. If you can find an old wool blanket that is in a state of disrepair, try recycling it by rolling it up to make a small, tightly rolled pillow for storing safety pins. Keep the safety pins open and stick them into the blanket; the lanolin in the wool will help keep the pins' points sharp and smooth. And whenever you remove safety pins from a project, you can immediately stick them into the pillow, which will keep them ready for future use at a moment's notice.

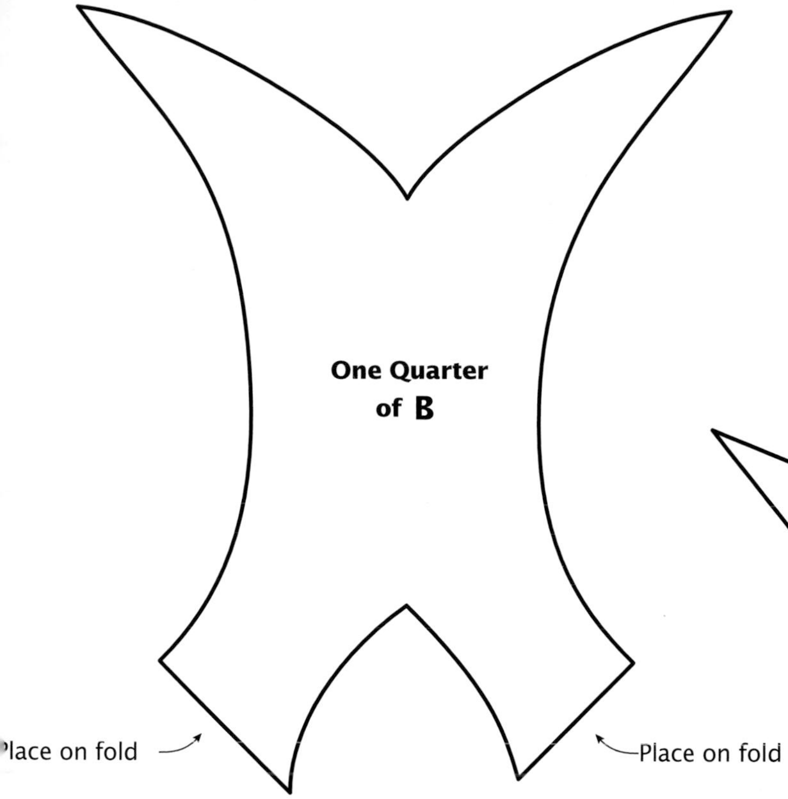
One Quarter
of B
Place on fold
Place on fold

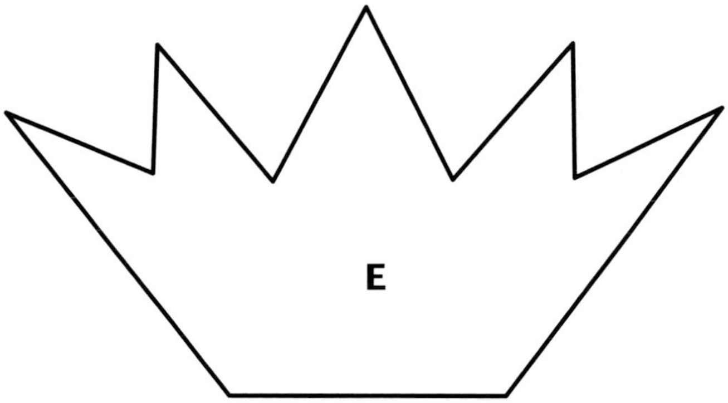
E

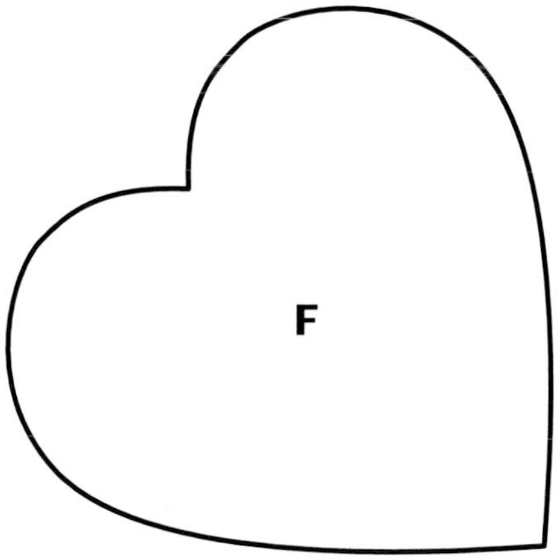
F

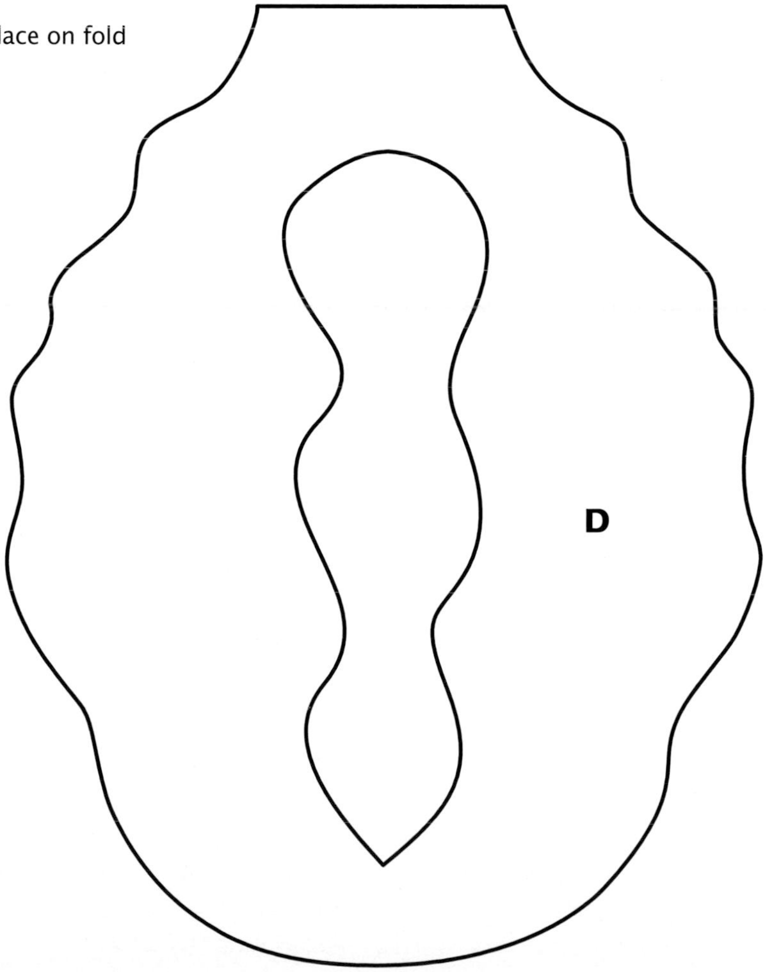
D

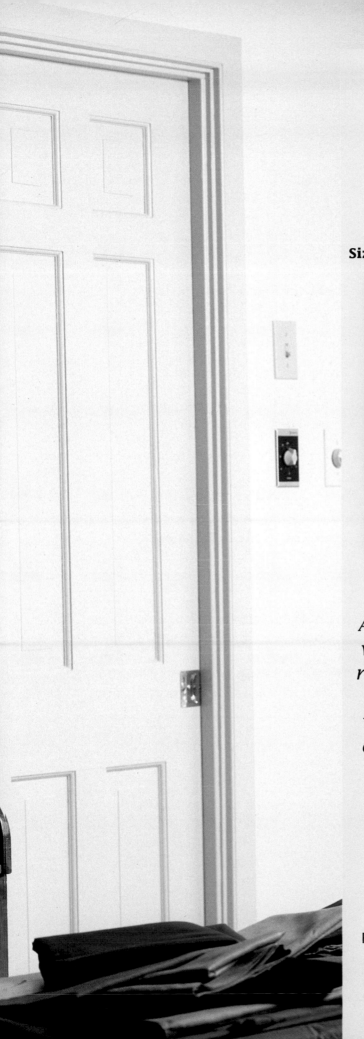

Amish WALL QUILT

Sherry Sunday

Skill Level: Easy

Size: Finished quilt size is 46 × 46 inches

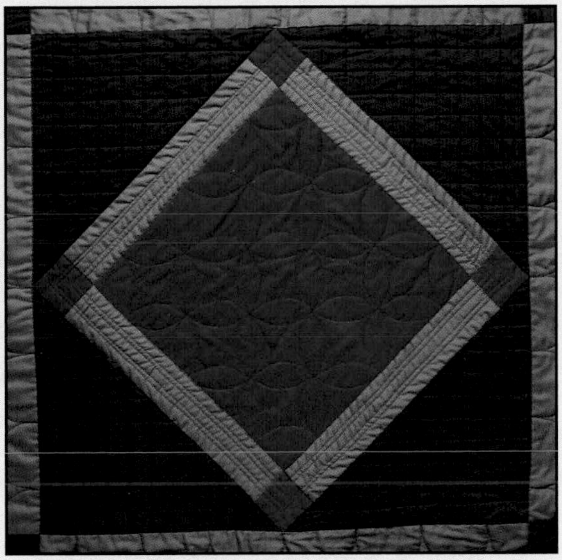

The bold geometric shapes and brilliant colors in this Amish-style quilt almost pulsate with energy. Take advantage of rotary cutting and quick-piecing techniques to make an easy wall quilt that will allow you to enjoy machine quilting designs like the pumpkin seed and clamshell patterns in large expanses of space.

TECHNIQUES YOU'LL NEED:

Starting and stopping, page 34
Channel quilting, page 53
Free-motion curves and points, page 70
Vermicelli stipple quilting, page 91

FABRICS AND SUPPLIES

FABRIC

- One 18 × $22\frac{1}{2}$-inch piece ("fat quarter") of red solid fabric for the center diamond and corner squares
- $1\frac{1}{4}$ yards of royal blue solid fabric for the large center triangles, small and large corner squares, and binding
- $\frac{3}{4}$ yard of green solid fabric for the inner borders and the sashing strips around the center diamond
- 1 yard of magenta solid fabric for the outer border
- $2\frac{7}{8}$ yards of black solid for the quilt back

MATERIALS

- One twin-size batting (72 × 90 inches)
- Rotary cutter, ruler, and mat
- 100 percent cotton threads for piecing
- Royal blue quilting thread for quilting
- Removable fabric marker or quilter's silver pencil

CUTTING

The following instructions are for quick cutting the pieces with a rotary cutter and ruler. All cutting measurements include $\frac{1}{4}$-inch seam allowances. Cut the strips for the binding across the width of the fabric.

From the red solid, cut:

One $12\frac{1}{2}$-inch A square

Four $2\frac{1}{2}$-inch B squares

From the blue solid, cut:

Two $11\frac{3}{4}$-inch squares. Cut each of these squares in half diagonally, for a total of four D triangles.

Four $4\frac{1}{2}$-inch F squares

Four $8\frac{1}{2}$-inch G squares

Five 3 × 44-inch binding strips

From the green solid, cut:

Four $2\frac{1}{2}$ inch × $12\frac{1}{2}$-inch C strips

Four $4\frac{1}{2}$ × $22\frac{1}{2}$-inch E strips

From the magenta solid, cut:

Four $8\frac{1}{2}$ × $30\frac{1}{2}$-inch H strips

From the black solid, cut:

Two $25\frac{1}{4}$ × $25\frac{1}{4}$-inch pieces for the quilt back

From the twin-size batting, cut:

One 50-inch square

PIECING THE QUILT TOP

STEP 1. To form the center unit, refer to **Diagram 1** and sew a green C strip to two opposite sides of the red A square. Sew a red B square to each end of the two remaining green C strips and sew these units to the two remaining sides of the A square. Sew the long side of a blue D triangle to each side of the center unit.

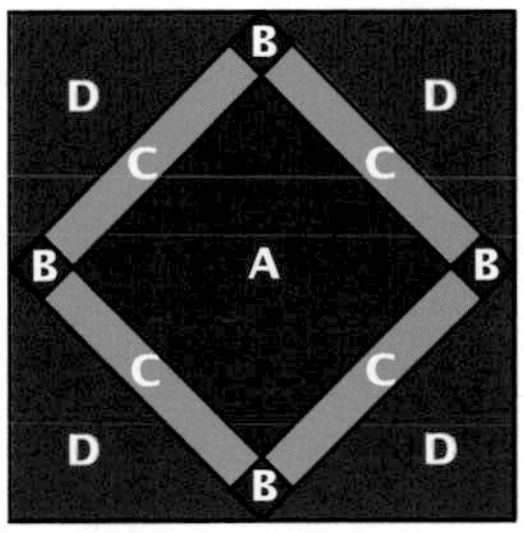

Diagram 1

STEP 2. Sew a green E strip to two opposite sides of the center unit. Sew a blue F square to each end of the two remaining green E strips and sew these pieced units to the two remaining sides of the center unit, as shown in **Diagram 2.**

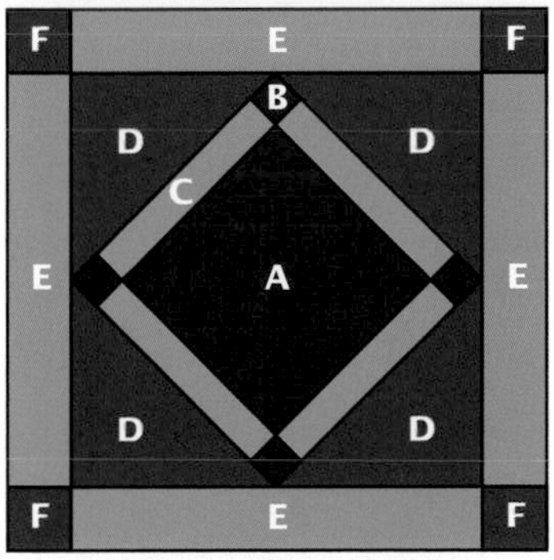

Diagram 2

STEP 3. Sew magenta H strips to two opposite sides of the center unit. Sew a blue G square to each end of the two remaining magenta H strips and sew these pieced units to the remaining two sides of the center unit, as shown in **Diagram 3.**

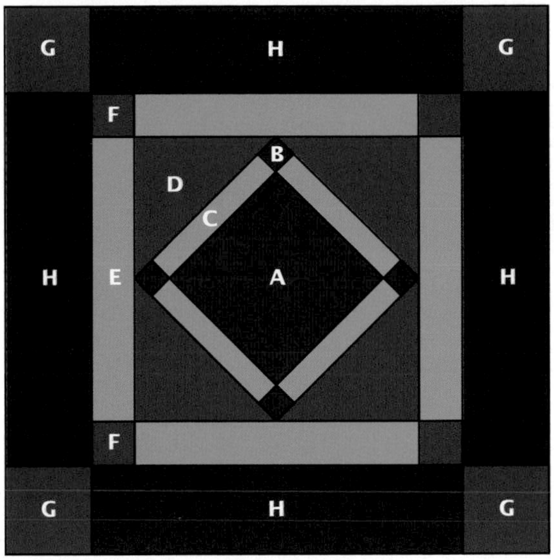

Diagram 3

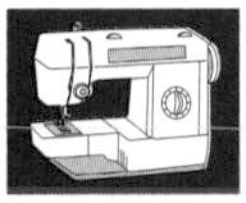

MACHINE QUILTING

STEP 1. With a removable fabric marker or quilter's silver pencil, mark the Pumpkin Seed Quilting Pattern from page 224 in the center red A square, as shown in the **Quilting Diagram** on page 222. When you are ready to quilt, note that this design is easiest to quilt by stitching machine-guided, curved "rows" that go diagonally. To do this, begin at the red starting dot, as shown, and quilt from one side of the center A square to the other, following the arrows. Then pivot the quilt and quilt to the same starting dot, following the arrows, as before. Repeat this process for all diagonal rows that are parallel to this one. Then, in the same manner, stitch all of the diagonal rows that go in the opposite direction, indicated by the blue starting dot and arrows. Note that near the corners of the A square, there are only short curved lines.

STEP 2. Mark the Clamshell Quilting Pattern from page 225 in the green E strips, as shown in the **Quilting Diagram.** When

Quilting Diagram

you are ready to quilt, note the starting dot and the directional stitching arrows on the pattern.

STEP 3. In the green C strips and red B squares, mark two double channels, as shown in the **Quilting Diagram.** The outer lines of each channel should be placed ½ inch in from the edges of the green C strips.

STEP 4. In the blue D triangles, mark a grid of vertical and horizontal crosshatched lines, spaced 1 inch apart, as shown in the **Quilting Diagram.**

STEP 5. In the blue F squares, mark the Circle Quilting Pattern on page 225.

STEP 6. In the magenta H strips, mark a diagonal grid of crosshatched lines, spaced at 1-inch intervals, as shown in the **Quilting Diagram.**

STEP 7. In the blue G squares, mark the Floral Quilting Pattern and continue the diagonal crosshatched lines in the background, as shown in the **Quilting Diagram.**

STEP 8. Sew the two 25¼ × 50-inch pieces of backing fabric together with a ¼-inch seam. Press the seam allowance open.

STEP 9. Layer and baste the quilt back, batting, and quilt top. For more information on layering and basting, see page 19.

STEP 10. Starting at the center of the quilt and working outward, quilt all marked designs. Use machine-guided techniques to quilt all straight lines as well as the pumpkin seed and clamshell patterns. Free-motion quilt the circles and floral quilting patterns.

APPLYING THE BINDING

For diagrams and more information on applying binding to a quilt, see page 240.

STEP 1. Trim the edges of the backing and batting even with the edges of the quilt top.

STEP 2. Sew the binding strips together with diagonal seams. Trim the seams to ¼ inch and press them open.

STEP 3. Fold the binding strip in half lengthwise, wrong sides together and press.

STEP 4. Position the raw edges of the folded binding strip at the edge of quilt sandwich, with 1 inch folded over at the beginning. Starting ½ inch from this fold, backstitch to secure the threads, and stitch the binding to the quilt with a ¼-inch seam allowance.

STEP 5. Stop stitching ¼ inch from the corner, backstitch to secure the threads, and stop. Remove the quilt from the machine and clip the threads. Fold the binding straight up and finger press the fold.

STEP 6. Fold the binding down again, aligning the raw edges with the edge of the quilt, and finger press it in place. Beginning at the top edge, stitch to ¼ inch from the next corner. Repeat this process on all four sides of the quilt.

STEP 7. As you approach the point where you began stitching, lay the end of the binding strip over the folded part at the beginning of the binding. End the binding seam by stitching across the fold.

STEP 8. Turn the binding to the wrong side of the quilt and stitch it in place by hand with a blind stitch, mitering the corners and taking a few stitches to secure the fold.

Floral Quilting Pattern

Pumpkin Seed Quilting Pattern

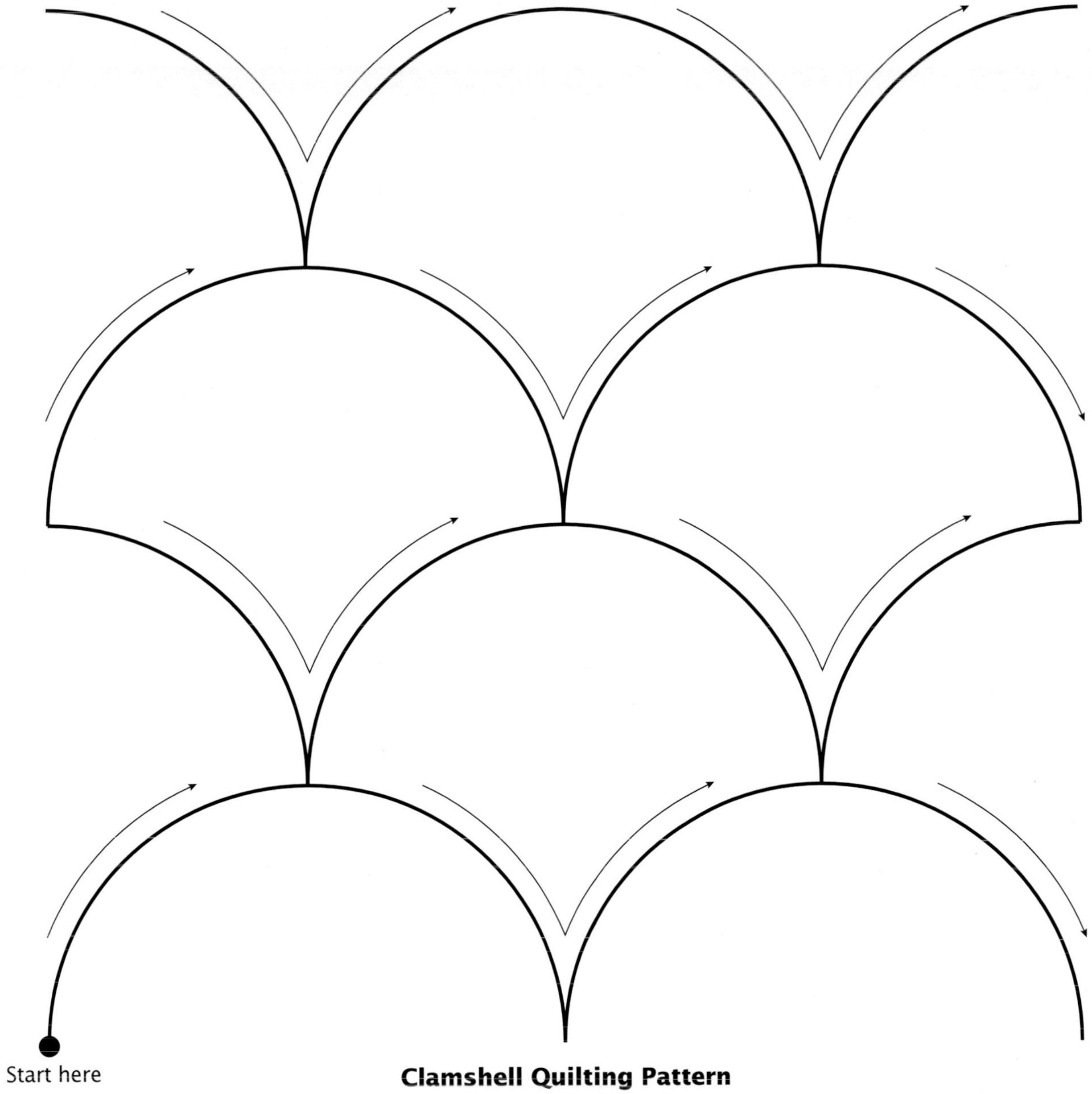

Clamshell Quilting Pattern

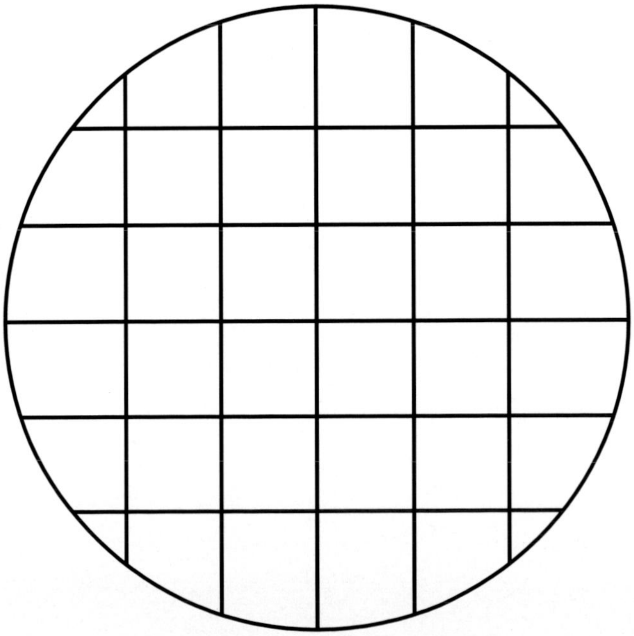

Circle Quilting Pattern

September
ROSE AND BUD

Sue Nickels

Skill Level: Intermediate

Size: Finished quilt is 47 inches square

Finished block is 15 inches square

This small quilt is much like the popular antique Rose of Sharon quilts made in the late 1800s. It is a favorite of both hand and machine quilters. Sue's use of dusty reds, greens, and golds makes this a charming autumn color scheme, and striking black blanket stitching accentuates the curves in the appliqué shapes.

TECHNIQUES YOU'LL NEED:

Starting and stopping, page 34
Stitch-in-the-ditch quilting, page 47
Free-motion curves and points, page 70
Vermicelli stipple quilting, page 91

FABRICS AND SUPPLIES

FABRIC

2 yards of tone-on-tone tan print for the background of the blocks and the outer border
1¼ yards of tan plaid fabric for the sashing strips, the corner squares in the outer border, and the binding
¾ yard of gold solid fabric for the inner border and the bud and flower appliqués
¼ yard of small red print for the corner squares in the inner border and the bud appliqués
¼ yard of large red print for the flower appliqués
1 yard of dark green solid for the stems, leaves, and center circles
10-inch scrap of dark green plaid fabric for the center circles
2½ yards of tan print for the quilt back

MATERIALS

Twin-size cotton batting (72 × 90 inches)
Rotary cutter, ruler, and mat
Heat-resistant template plastic
Spray-n-Starch brand liquid starch
Cotton swabs
Hand sewing needle
Transparent nylon (monofilament) thread (0.004) for quilting around the appliqué shapes
100 percent cotton 50-weight thread in black, gold, and tan
Rust-proof quilter's safety pins
Permanent marker
Removable fabric marker or quilter's pencil
Paper for pattern
Removable fabric marker or pencil

CUTTING

The following instructions are for cutting the pieces for patchwork with a rotary cutter and the appliqué pieces with scissors. The rotary cut pieces include ¼-inch seam allowances. The appliqué pieces are shown in the One-Quarter Block Pattern on page 238; trace these patterns onto heat-resistant template plastic and mark them on the wrong sides of the fabrics, leaving approximately ½ inch between pieces for seam allowances. Add the 3⁄16-inch seam allowances to each piece and mark grain line arrows on pieces A, B, C, and D and cut the pieces out on the marked lines. Clip inside points just barely to the seam line and clip inside curves halfway to the seam line.

From the tone-on-tone tan fabric, cut:

Four 16-inch background squares. These are slightly larger than needed to allow for shrinkage; when the blocks are completed, measure and cut each block to 15½ inches square.

Four 6 × 36½-inch outer border strips

One 2-inch center square

From the tan plaid fabric, cut:

Four 2½ × 15½-inch sashing strips

Four 6-inch corner squares for the outer borders

Five 2¼ × 44-inch binding strips

From the gold solid fabric, cut:

Four 2½ × 36½-inch inner border strips

Four H pieces

16 F pieces

From the small red print fabric, cut:

Four 2½-inch corner squares for the inner borders

16 E pieces

From the large red print, cut:

Four I pieces

From the dark green solid fabric, cut:

16 C pieces

16 D pieces

32 A pieces

32 B pieces

From the dark green plaid fabric, cut:

Four G pieces

From the tan print backing fabric, cut:

One 44 × 51-inch piece

Two 10½ × 44-inch pieces

From the twin-size batting, cut:

One 51-inch square

PREPARING PIECES FOR MACHINE APPLIQUÉ

STEP 1. With a permanent marker, make a full-size drawing of the One-Quarter Block Pattern on page 238. Rotate the design three times to create the full appliqué block pattern, as shown in **Diagram 1.** Label each piece with the correct letter. Place a 16-inch tan background square over the drawing and trace the full-size appliqué design onto the fabric with a removable fabric marker.

STEP 2. Position your ironing board at a height that will allow you to sit while preparing the appliqué pieces. Pour approximately 1 tablespoon of liquid starch into a cup. Set a dry iron on the cotton setting. Place one of the templates on the wrong side of the appropriate appliqué piece and finger-press the seam allowances all the way around the template. To make the turning lines sharper and more crisp, dip a cotton swab into the liquid starch and moisten a small area of the seam allowance thoroughly. Use the edge of your iron *near* the tip to press the dampened seam allowance onto the template, smoothing out folds or tucks as you press. Continue pressing until the starch is completely dry and continue this process around the entire template. Use your fingernail to release the seam allowances and gently remove the template from the fabric. Repeat this process for all appliqué pieces to make them perfectly shaped, with smooth edges that are ready to appliqué. **Note:** For pieces C, D, and F, this step is not necessary on areas that will be overlapped by another appliqué piece.

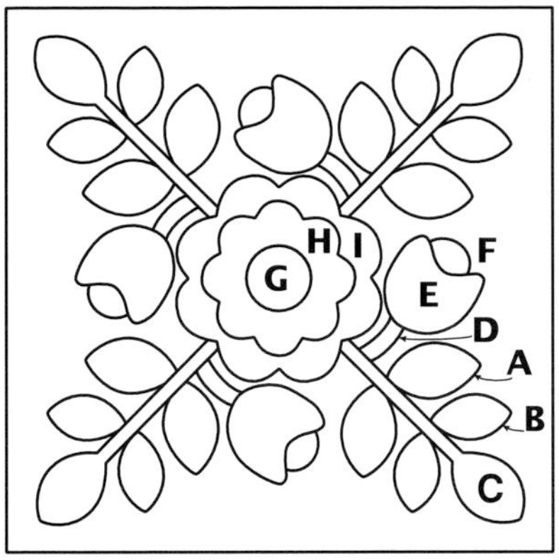

Diagram 1

APPLIQUÉING THE ROSE OF SHARON BLOCKS

STEP 1. Thread the top and bobbin of your machine with black thread and insert an open-toe appliqué foot. Set your sewing machine for a blanket stitch. If your machine does not have a blanket stitch, experiment with other zigzag or decorative stitches until you get an effect that pleases you. It is helpful to practice stitching on scrap fabric so you can adjust the stitch width and length for the look you like.

STEP 2. Place the dark green plaid center G circle on top of the gold H piece. Center the circle and baste it in place by hand, using a neutral thread. Press the pieces lightly. Leave 4-inch tails of thread and stitch the G circle onto the gold H piece with a blanket stitch, referring to **Diagram 2.** Turn the pieces slowly as you stitch around the circle, making sure that the needle is down in the fabric on the outside edge of the G circle when you pivot or turn the pieces, so that there are no breaks in the stitching line. When you have finished stitching, remove the pieces from the machine, leaving 4 inch tails of thread, and pull the top thread to the back side. Knot the threads and clip them close to the fabric. Next, place this unit on a red I piece, baste them together, and press. Machine appliqué this unit in the same manner, referring to **Diagram 2.** Repeat this process to make three more flower units for the remaining blocks.

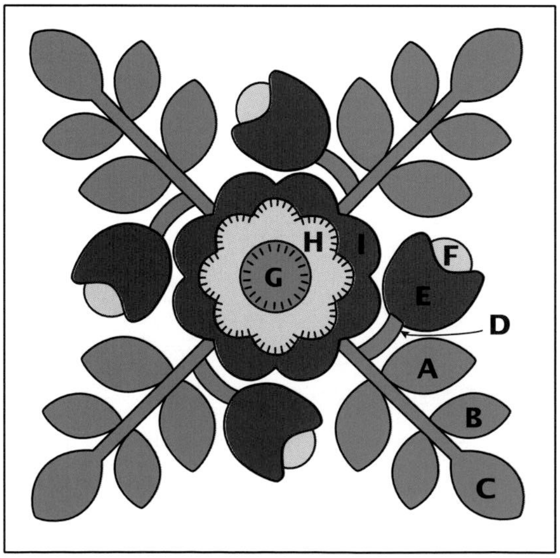

Diagram 2

STEP 3. Position the center units and all of the remaining appliqué pieces on the tan background squares. Pin them in place, and press each block lightly. Starting with piece D, machine appliqué the pieces on each background square with a blanket stitch or another decorative stitch. Take care to clip thread tails that will lie underneath another appliqué piece very close to the surface of the fabric. In all other cases, leave 4-inch thread tails. After you finish stitching the D pieces, appliqué the C stems and F bud tips, followed by the A and B leaves, the red E bud, and the central flower unit last. Pull the thread tails to the wrong side of the block, knot, and clip them close to the fabric.

STEP 4. If desired, carefully cut away the background fabric behind each central flower unit and E bud, leaving at least ¼ inch seam allowances. This will help the block lie flat. Remove basting threads and press. Measure your finished blocks and trim them to 15½ inches square.

ASSEMBLING THE QUILT TOP

STEP 1. Sew an appliqué block to both sides of a tan plaid sashing strip, referring to the **Quilt Assembly Diagram.** Press the seam allowances toward the sashing strips. Repeat for the remaining two appliqué blocks.

STEP 2. Sew a tan plaid sashing strip on both sides of the 2½-inch tan center square, referring to the **Quilt Assembly Diagram.** Press the seams toward the sashing strips.

STEP 3. Sew the three units of the quilt top together, as shown in the **Quilt Assembly Diagram.**

STEP 4. Measure across the center portion of the quilt top and make adjustments

Quilt Assembly Diagram

in the length of the border strips, if necessary. Sew two gold inner border strips to both sides of the quilt top, referring to the **Quilt Assembly Diagram.** Press the seam allowances toward the gold borders.

STEP 5. Sew a red 2½-inch corner block to both ends of the top and bottom gold inner border strips. Press the seams toward the gold borders. Sew the top and bottom gold borders to the quilt top, referring to the **Quilt Assembly Diagram,** and press the seam allowances toward the gold borders.

STEP 6. Sew two tan border strips to the sides of the quilt top, referring to the **Quilt Assembly Diagram.** Press the seam allowances toward the tan border. Sew a 6-inch tan corner square to each end of the top and bottom tan plaid border strips, as shown, and press the seam allowances toward the tan borders. Sew the top and bottom borders to the quilt top, as shown, and press the seam allowances toward the tan borders.

PREPARING THE QUILT BACK

STEP 1. With ¼-inch seam allowances, sew the short ends of the two narrow pieces of backing fabric together and press this seam open.

STEP 2. With right sides together, center this seam at the midpoint of the 51-inch edge of the other piece of the quilt back, as shown in **Diagram 3.** Sew this seam with a ¼-inch seam allowance and press the seam open. Trim the ends of the narrow strip even with the sides of the large piece of backing fabric, as shown by the dashed lines, creating a 51-inch square.

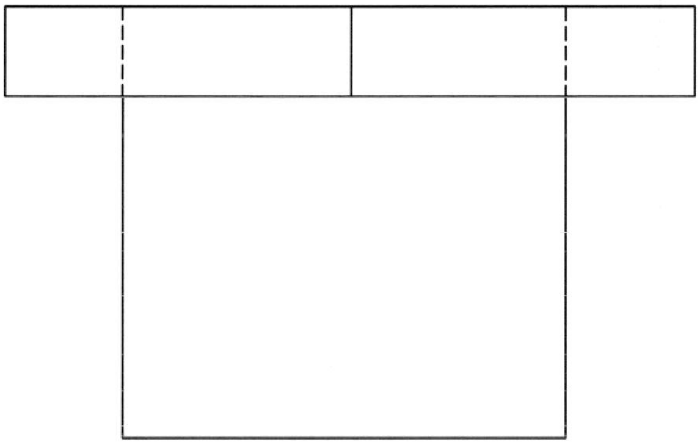

Diagram 3

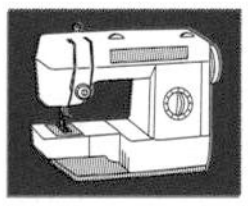

MACHINE QUILTING

STEP 1. Using a removable fabric marker or quilter's pencil, mark the Center Quilting Design from page 236 over the 2-inch square at the center of the quilt top, as shown in the **Quilting Diagram** on page 232.

STEP 2. Mark the Sashing Quilting Design on page 235 in the center part of the quilt, as shown in the **Quilting Diagram,** so that it is centered over each of the tan plaid sashing strips.

Quilting Diagram

STEP 3. Mark the Inner Border Quilting Design on page 235 in each of the gold inner borders, as shown in the **Quilting Diagram,** using the Corner Quilting Design on page 236 at each of the corners.

STEP 4. Mark the Corner Border Quilting Design and the Outer Border Quilting Design on page 237 in each of the tan outer borders, as shown in the **Quilting Diagram,** following the marking directions.

STEP 5. Layer the quilt back, batting and quilt top and baste them together with safety pins at 3- to 4-inch intervals. For more information on layering and basting, see page 19.

STEP 6. Starting at the center of the quilt and working outward, free-motion quilt around all of the marked designs, as shown in the **Quilting Diagram,** using monofilament thread in the top of your machine and cotton thread to match the backing in the bobbin.

STEP 7. Change to cotton thread in both top and bobbin of your sewing machine and do stipple quilting in the background of each appliqué block.

STEP 8. With cotton thread to match the tan background fabric in both top and bobbin, free-motion quilt the marked center quilting design, following the numbered steps in **Directional Stitching Diagram 1.**

STEP 9. Free-motion quilt the marked sashing quilting design, following the numbered steps in **Directional Stitching Diagram 2.** Do stipple quilting inside each of the feathered motifs, as shown.

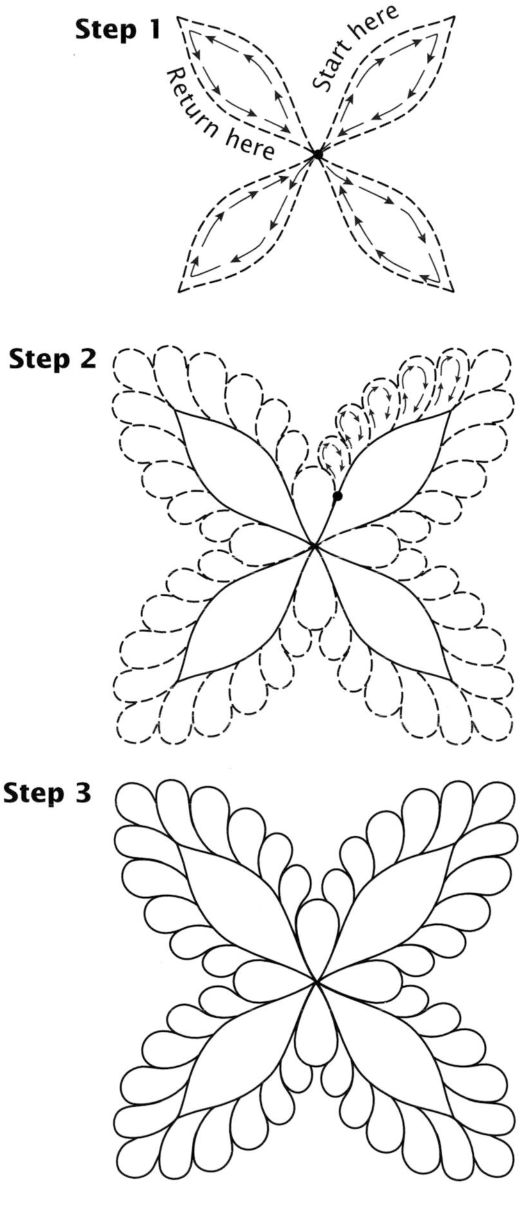

Directional Stitching Diagram 1

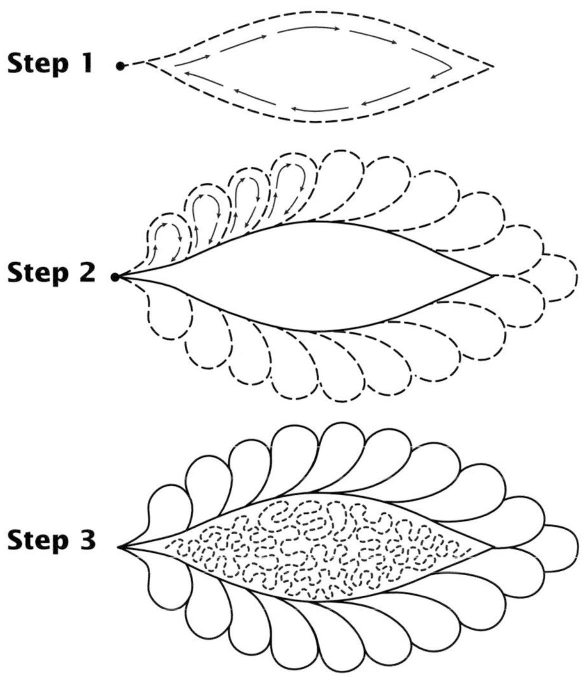

Directional Stitching Diagram 2

STEP 10. Stitch-in-the-ditch on either side of the gold inner borders and free-motion quilt the inner border quilting design, following the numbers in **Directional Stitching Diagram 3.**

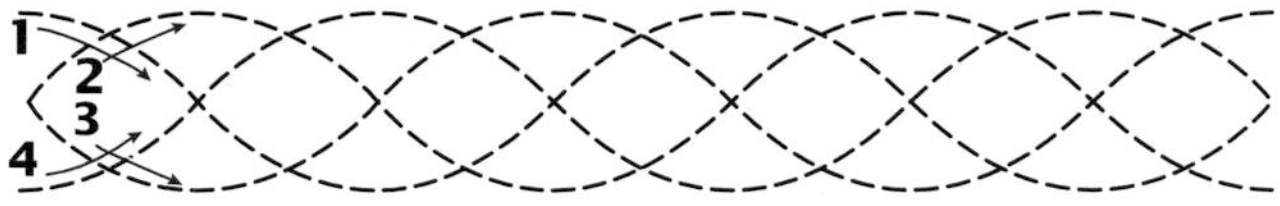

Directional Stitching Diagram 3

STEP 11. Free-motion quilt the outer border quilting design, following the numbers and arrows in **Directional Stitching Diagram 4.** Do stipple quilting inside each motif, as shown.

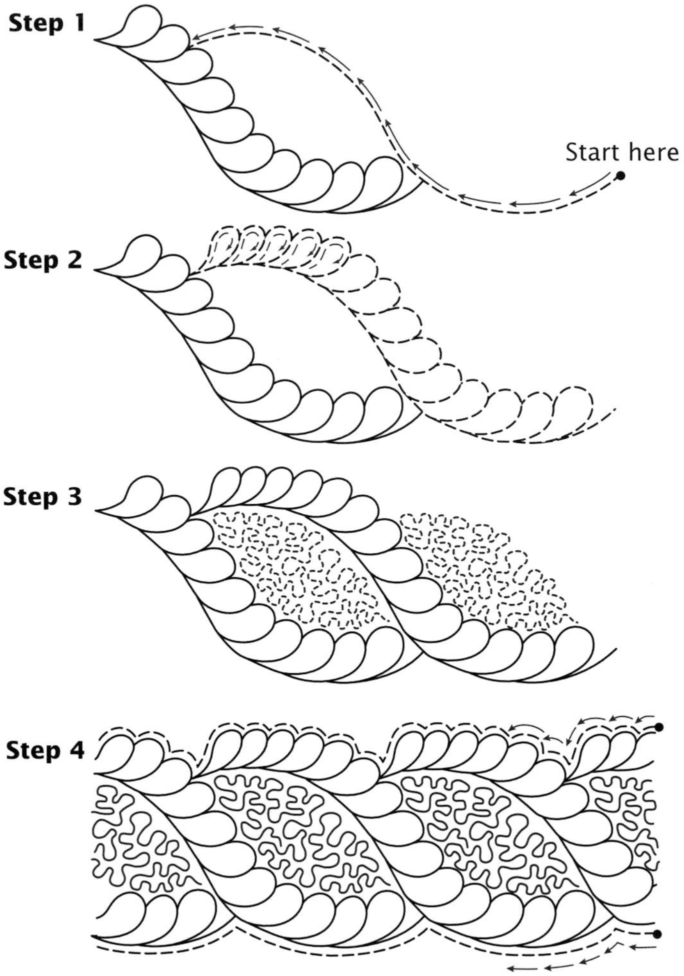

Directional Stitching Diagram 4

APPLYING THE BINDING

For diagrams and more information on applying binding to a quilt, see page 240.

STEP 1. Trim the edges of the backing and batting even with the edges of the quilt top.

STEP 2. Sew the binding strips together with diagonal seams. Trim the seams to ¼ inch and press these seam allowances open.

STEP 3. Fold the binding strip in half lengthwise, wrong sides together, and press.

STEP 4. Position the raw edges of the folded binding strip at the edge of quilt sandwich, with approximately 1 inch folded over at the beginning. Starting ½ inch from this fold, do three or four backstitches to secure the threads and start stitching the binding to the quilt through all layers with a ¼-inch seam allowance.

STEP 5. Stop stitching ¼ inch from the corner, backstitch to secure the threads, and stop. Remove the quilt from the machine and clip the threads. Fold the binding straight up and finger press the fold.

STEP 6. Fold the binding down again, aligning the raw edges with the edge of the quilt, and finger press it in place. Beginning at the top edge, stitch to ¼ inch from the next corner. Repeat this process on all four sides of the quilt.

STEP 7. As you approach the point where you began stitching, lay the end of the binding strip over the folded part at the beginning of the binding. End the binding seam by stitching across the fold.

STEP 8. Turn the binding to the wrong side of the quilt and stitch it in place by hand with a blind stitch.

STEP 9. Miter the corners by folding them out and back again, taking a few stitches to secure the fold.

Sashing Quilting Design

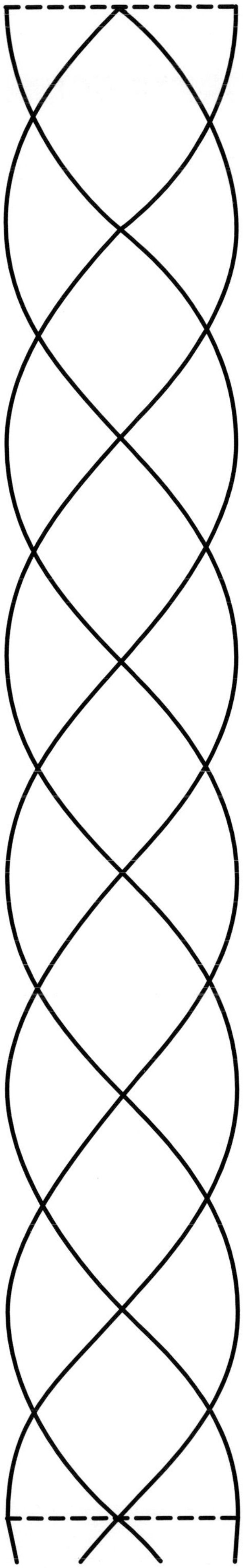

Inner Border Quilting Design

Center Quilting Design

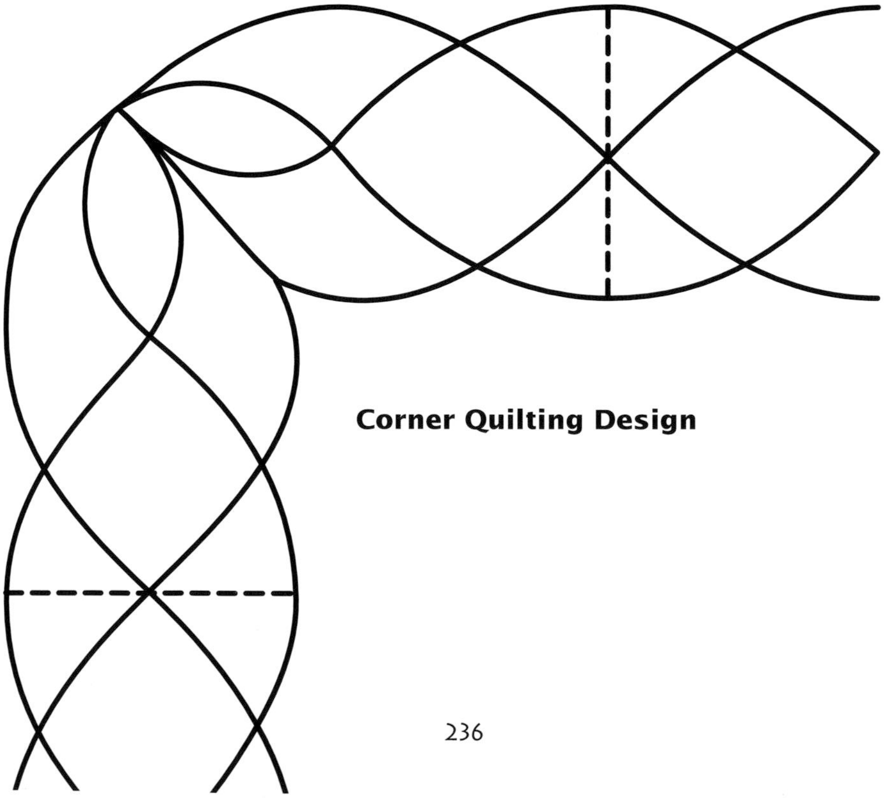

Corner Quilting Design

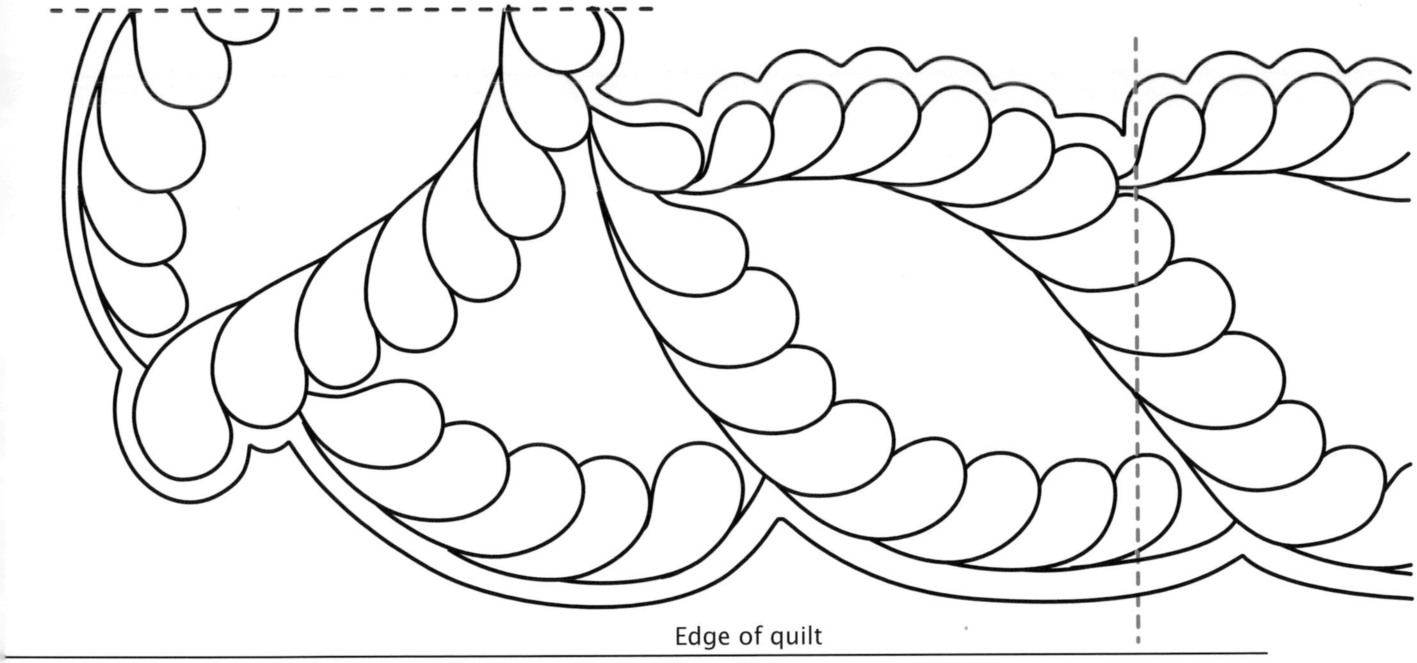

Corner Border Quilting Design

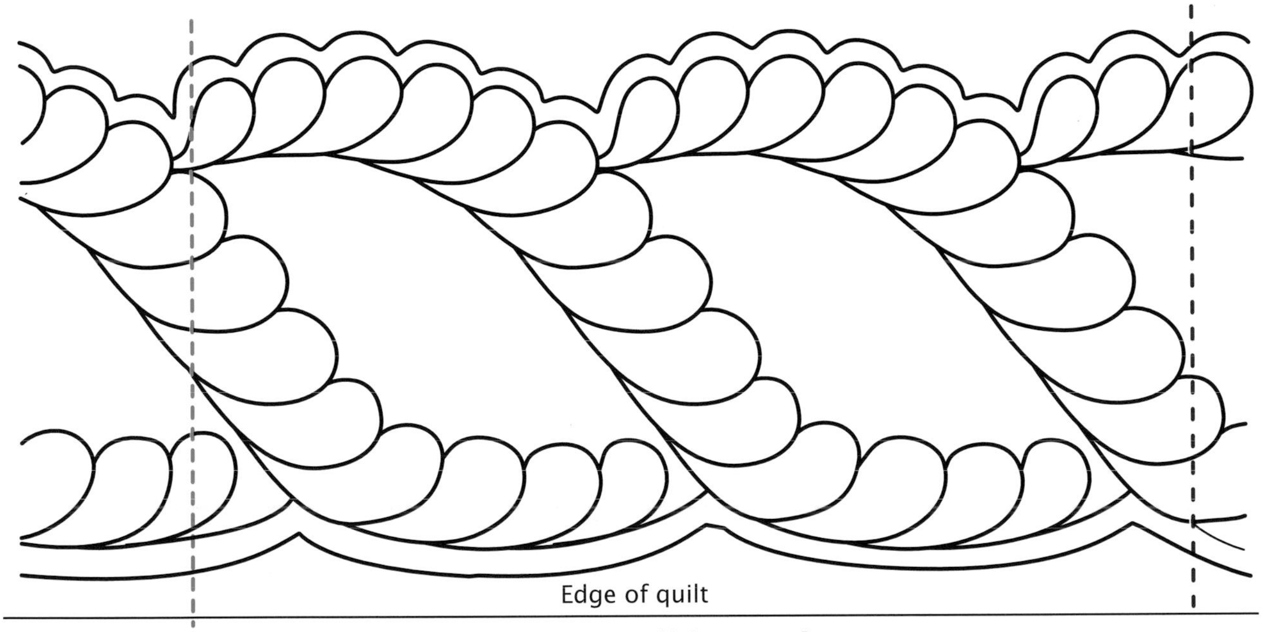

Outer Border Quilting Design

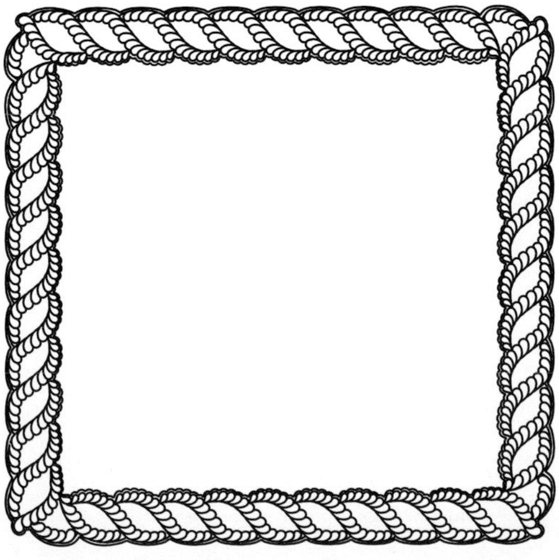

Entire Border Quilting Design

Marking Directions

1. Enlarge designs 200 percent.

2. Using the Corner Border Quilting Design, mark corners first inside the dashed lines, allowing for the seam allowance along the outside edge of the quilt.

3. Using the Outer Border Quilting Design, match the colored lines to mark ten full feathers to complete each side.

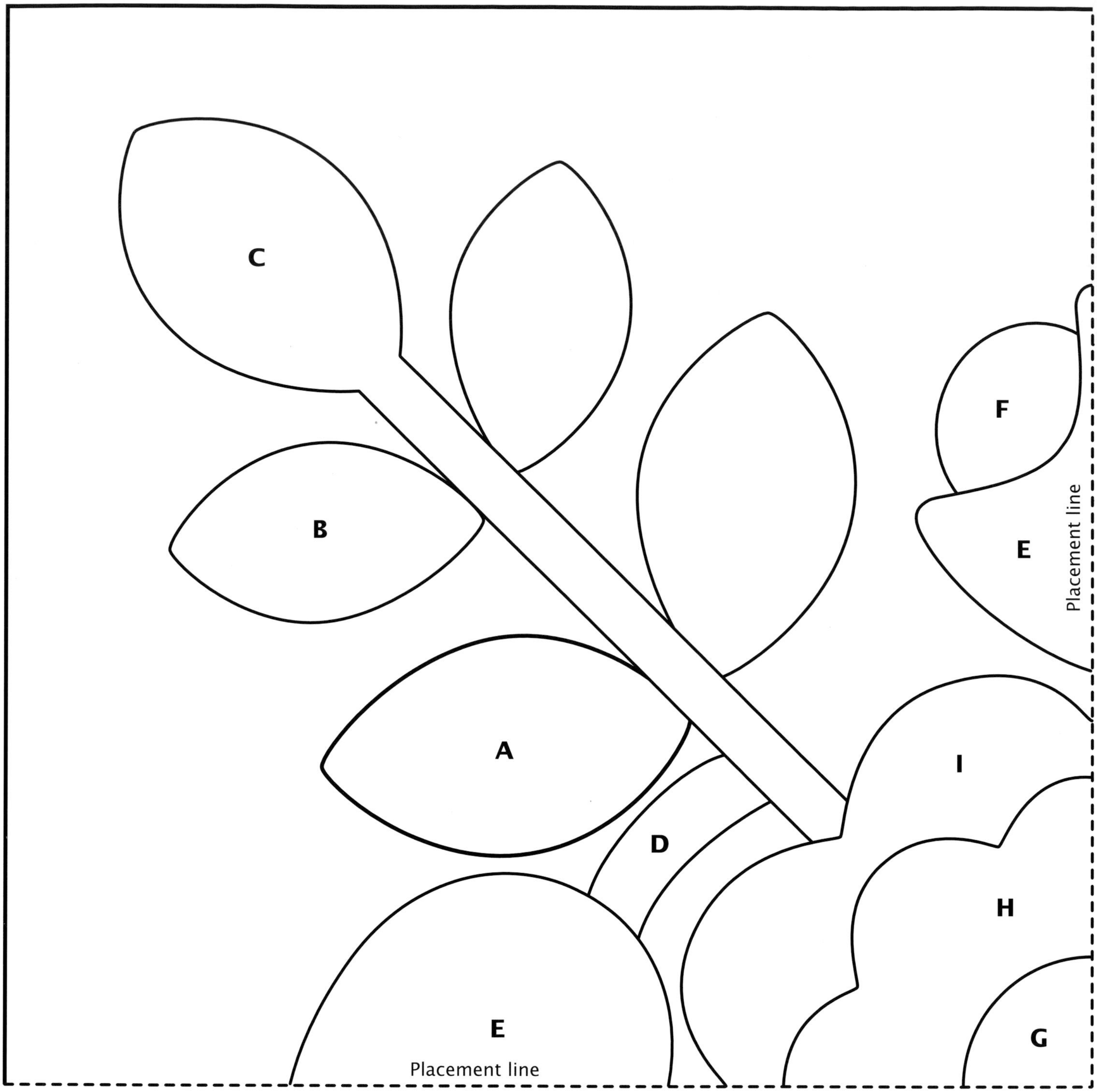

Join the two placement lines
of piece E to create the template.

One-Quarter Block Pattern

The Basics

Two things that are common to all of the projects in this book are how to transfer quilting designs onto the fabric and how to apply binding to the edges of a quilt or garment. You may use the following information for marking and binding any project, unless a particular technique is specified in the instructions. You'll also find helpful tips for how to manage large quilts at the sewing machine.

MARKING QUILTING DESIGNS ON FABRIC

Designs that are easily visible while you are stitching allow you to maintain a smooth flow in your stitching lines, and they make machine quilting fun, relaxing, and a joy to do. Read through the following marking methods and use the one or ones that are most appropriate for the fabrics in your projects.

TRACING DIRECTLY ONTO FABRIC

Fabrics that are light in color and easy to see through are perfect for this method of marking. All you need is a full-size quilting design consisting of dark, solid lines and a marking pen or pencil that will be easy to see on the fabrics in your quilt top. Simply place the quilt top over the quilting design you have selected, and use a removable fabric marker or pencil to trace the lines of the design directly onto the fabric. There are several types of marking tools appropriate for marking quilting designs. Each offers different benefits, and they are easy to find at quilt shops, fabric stores, or art supply stores. Use the following guidelines to choose the marking tools that will work best for you.

- **REMOVABLE FABRIC MARKERS:** These markers are available in a blue and, in some brands, a red color. They are easy to see on light fabrics, and they make nice, strong lines. The markings can be removed with water, by following the manufacturer's instructions found on the packaging. Before you use any marking device on a quilt top, remember that it is very important to test it on your own fabrics and in your own water for visibility and removability.
- **SILVER PENCILS:** Silver pencils, like the ones from Quilter's Choice or Berol, are suitable for marking light or dark fabrics, and the markings may not need to be removed after the quilting process is completed. These pencils may be less suitable, however, for very busy prints.
- **WHITE PENCILS:** The Nonce pencil by Collins works well for dark fabrics, and it may also be a good choice for print fabrics. It marks easily and has a soft lead, which will stay hard if you store it in a freezer when it is not in use.
- **GOLD PENCILS:** The gold pencil made by Caran D'ache is especially appropriate for dark fabrics because it is easy to use and does not require much pressure to create clean, highly visible markings.

USING A LIGHT BOX

A light box is helpful for marking dark fabrics, busy prints, or any fabric that is difficult to see through. Light boxes are widely available in quilt shops or art supply stores, or you can make a light box of your own by placing a piece of plexiglass over two cabinets, tables, or chairs, and putting a light source underneath it. When you are ready to use your light box for marking a quilt top, trace the quilting design you wish to use on a piece of tracing paper or bond paper and lay it on top of the light box. Tape it securely in place with pieces of masking tape and place your quilt top over the quilting design. Use a removable fabric marker or a quilter's pencil to trace the design onto your quilt top.

MARKING BLOCK DESIGNS WITH TRACING PAPER

This method allows you to make all of your markings on pieces of tracing paper rather than on the quilt top itself. For example, if you wish to mark an individual quilting design in multiple quilt blocks, simply cut eight or ten pieces of tracing paper the same size as your blocks. Mark the quilting design on one piece of paper and stack the other pieces underneath it. Hold the layers of paper together with straight pins or paper clips. Remove the thread from the top and bobbin of your sewing machine, and free-motion quilt the design through all the pieces of paper at once. This will perforate each piece of paper along the exact lines of the quilting design. Pin the marked pieces of paper on the blocks in your quilt top and stitch the designs, following the perforated lines. The paper is easy to remove after you have finished quilting, since it has been stitched through twice.

MARKING BORDERS WITH TRACING PAPER

Tracing paper can also be used to mark and stitch symmetrical designs in the borders of a quilt by following these steps. Asymmetrical designs must be marked individually to avoid creating mirror images.

STEP 1. Cut and tape together pieces of tracing paper the same width and length as the borders in your quilt top. Mark the quilting design on the top fold, as shown in **Diagram 1.**

Diagram 1

STEP 2. Remove the thread from the top and from the bobbin of your sewing machine, and stitch on the marked lines, perforating the paper on the exact lines of the design, as shown in **Diagram 2.**

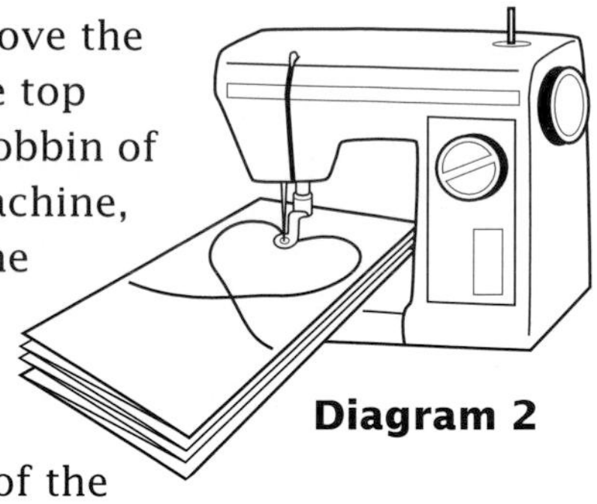

Diagram 2

STEP 3. Unfold the tracing paper, as shown in **Diagram 3,** and use safety pins to pin it in position on the border of a layered quilt sandwich. Thread your sewing machine with the threads you plan to use, and quilt the marked designs through the tracing paper. It will be easy to remove the paper after you have finished quilting.

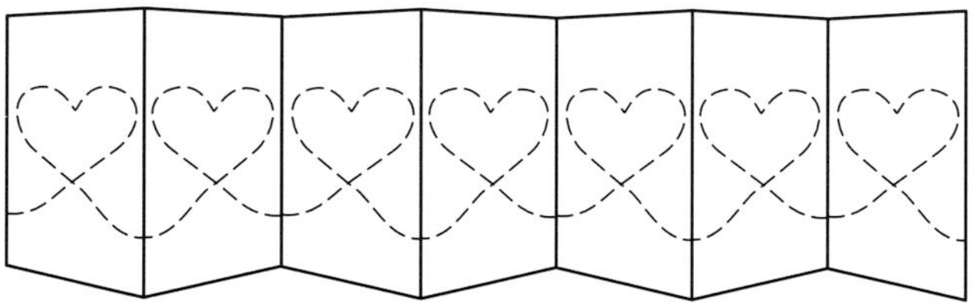

Diagram 3

APPLYING BINDING TO A QUILT

For most of the quilts in this book, the binding is applied with double-fold binding strips cut on the crosswise grain of 44-inch-wide fabric. Although the width of the cut strips or the size of the seam allowances may vary from project to project, the process of applying the binding is essentially the same, unless otherwise specified.

STEP 1. Trim the edges of the quilt back and the batting even with the edges of the quilt top.

STEP 2. Sew the binding strips together with diagonal seams, as shown in **Diagram 4.** Trim these seams to ¼ inch and press them open.

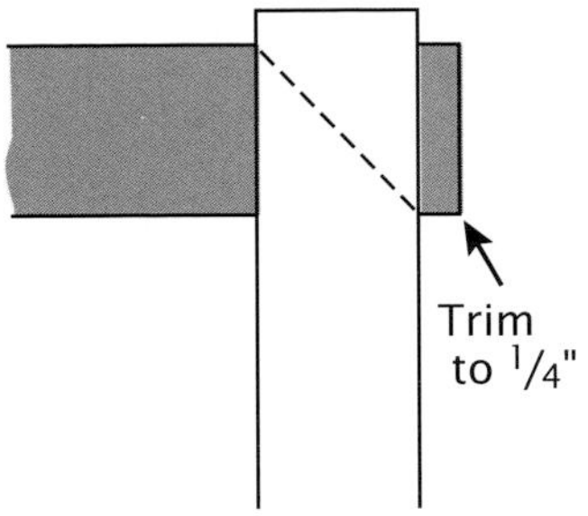

Diagram 4

STEP 3. Fold the binding strip in half lengthwise, wrong sides together, and press.

STEP 4. Position the raw edges of the folded binding strip at the edge of the quilt sandwich, with approximately 1 inch folded over at the beginning, as shown in **Diagram 5.** Starting ½ inch from this fold, do three or four backstitches to secure the threads and start stitching the binding to the quilt through all layers with a ¼-inch seam allowance.

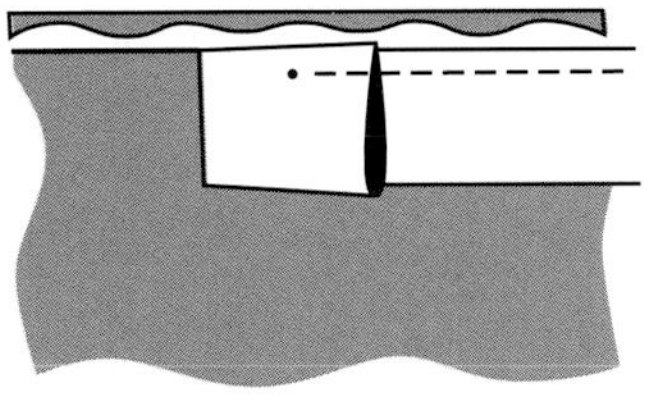

Diagram 5

STEP 5. Stop stitching ¼ inch from the corner, backstitch to secure the threads, and stop. Remove the quilt from the machine and clip the threads. Fold the binding straight up, as shown in **Diagram 6** and finger press the fold.

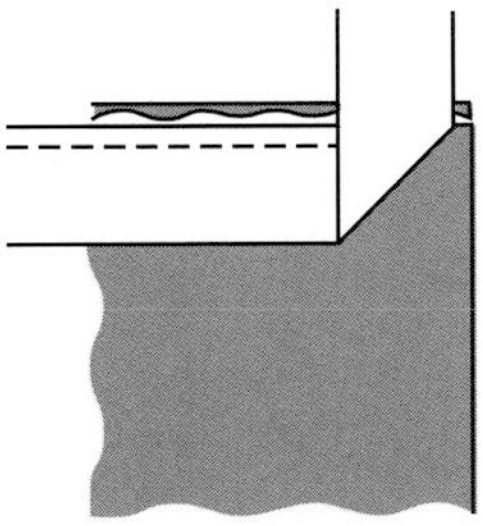

Diagram 6

STEP 6. Fold the binding down again, aligning the raw edges with the edge of the quilt, as shown in **Diagram 7,** finger press it in place. Beginning at the top edge, stitch to ¼ inch from the next corner. Repeat this process on all four sides of the quilt.

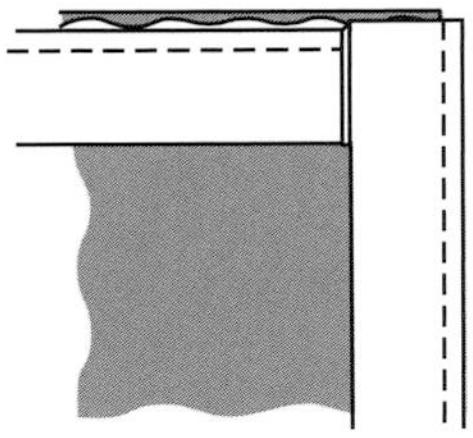

Diagram 7

STEP 7. As you approach the point where you began stitching, lay the end of the binding strip over the folded part at the beginning of the binding, as shown in **Diagram 8.** End the binding seam by stitching across the fold, as shown.

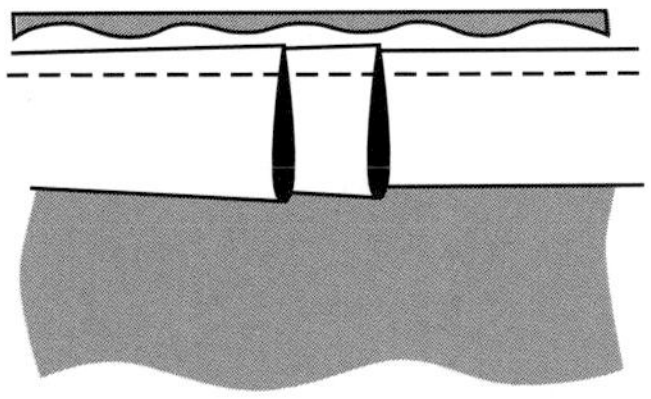

Diagram 8

STEP 8. Turn the binding to the wrong side of the quilt and stitch it in place by hand with a blind stitch, as shown in **Diagram 9.**

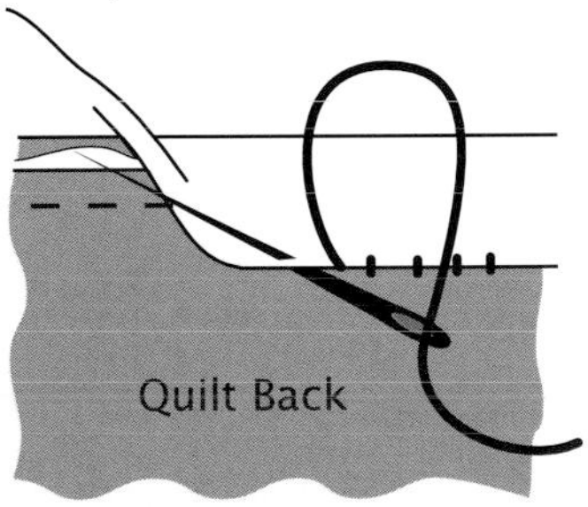

Diagram 9

STEP 9. Miter the corners by folding them out and back again, as shown in **Diagram 10,** taking a few stitches to secure the fold, as shown.

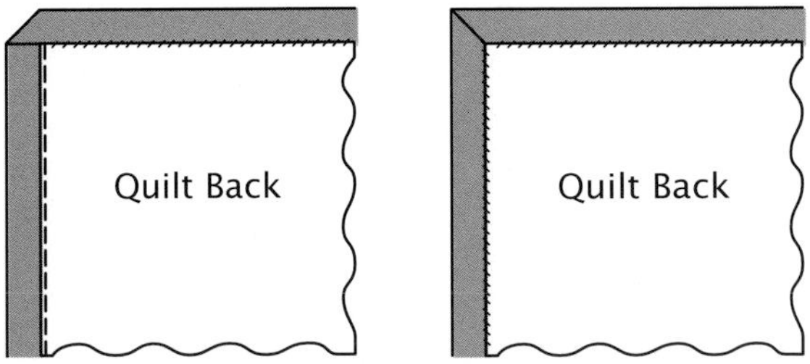

Diagram 10

HANDLING A LARGE QUILT

A common rule of thumb in machine quilting is that up to 30 inches of a quilt can be guided through a sewing machine easily. This means that it is possible to stitch at the center of a 60-inch quilt without much difficulty because half of it, or 30 inches, will fit comfortably between the needle and the head of the machine at the right. In order to stitch on a quilt that is larger than 60 inches, however, it is necessary to deal both with the bulk of the quilt that lies between the needle and the arm of the machine and with the part of the quilt that lies to the left of the needle. The following tips and strategies from the pros will help you learn to manipulate a large quilt through your sewing machine and make it easier to win the "battle of the bulk."

MULTIPLE TABLES FOR MORE SUPPORT

My philosophy for working with a large quilt is to focus only on the 6 inches of fabric that my hands are working on and to try to make every stitch as beautiful as I can. This allows me to find pleasure in every moment, without thinking about the mountain of fabric that is left to quilt. To help make the quilting process as effortless as possible, I like to push together several tables and desks, so that the entire weight of my quilt is supported while I stitch. It is much easier to move a quilt through the sewing machine when none of the weight pulls down over the edge of a table.

–Caryl Bryer Fallert

MAKE AN EASY EXTENSION TABLE

A simple, low-cost way to create a large extension for a sewing table is to purchase a 4 × 8-foot sheet of Celotex, which is a dense Styrofoam-like board that is used for insulation. This type of product is available at hardware stores and building supply centers. Celotex can be cut easily to any size you like with a craft knife. You can place it over the tops of two kitchen chairs next to your sewing table to provide more surface area for supporting a large quilt. Celotex has a slippery surface, which allows a quilt to glide over it smoothly. It's also lightweight, which makes it easy to set up when you want to quilt. To store, simply slide the sheet underneath a bed or stand it in a closet.

–Sherry Sunday

SLIPPERY SURFACES ARE BEST

If the surface of your sewing machine or extension table is rough, it can be difficult to slide a quilt easily over it. I recommend spraying some spray furniture polish on a soft cotton cloth and wiping it along the bed of your sewing machine and the surface of whatever table you are working on. If the furniture polish is completely dry, it will not hurt your sewing machine or damage the fabric in your quilt. The idea is to keep all surfaces smooth and slippery, so that your quilt will not drag on rough spots.

–Debra Wagner

EASY ACCORDION PLEATS

For a large quilt that has cotton batting in it, I put accordion pleats in the part that goes through the arm of the sewing machine to the right of the needle and the rest of the quilt lies spread out on a table. This allows the quilt to stay flat during the quilting process, rather than being tightly rolled up for long periods of time. To make accordion pleats in a quilt, just use your fingers to form pleats that are approximately 6 inches apart and 3 or 4 inches high to the right of your stitching area, as shown in **Diagram 1.** This will draw up the bulk of the quilt and make it go through your machine fairly easily. When you have finished stitching in one area, move the quilt to the next quilting area and make new accordion pleats where they are needed.

–Debra Wagner

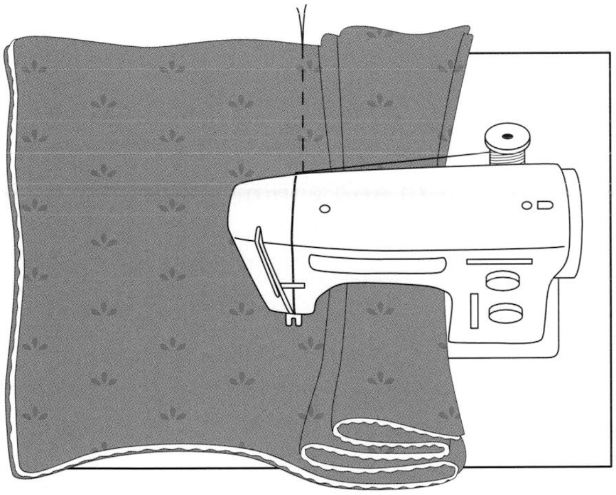

Diagram 1

BINDER CLIPS FOR PLEATS

I like to make accordion pleats in the part of a large quilt that lies on the right side of the sewing machine needle. Big black plastic binder clips are great for keeping the tops of these pleats from sliding near the stitching area. I do not use binder clips to the left of the needle because the quilt can lie on the sewing table as I stitch. Binder clips are easy to remove, sturdy, inexpensive, and readily available at any office supply store.

–Hari Walner

NEEDLE DOWN FOR GREATER STABILITY

If you find that you need to stop during the quilting process to refold or reroll a large quilt, make sure that you leave the needle in the down position while folding. This will stabilize the quilt and keep you from getting gaps in your stitching line. And after you have finished rerolling the quilt, check to make sure that the needle is still straight and unbent, so that the stitching line will remain smooth.

–Anne Colvin

STITCH FROM THE OUTSIDE IN

When I baste the layers of a large quilt together, I place safety pins at 2½- to 3-inch intervals over the entire surface, sometimes using as many as 1,000 safety pins for a double-size quilt. Because the safety pins are so close to each other, the quilt is completely stabilized. Then I quilt around the outer edges of the borders and stitch toward the center, rather than working from the center of the quilt outward. This allows me to remove as many pins as possible before reaching the center area, which is the most difficult area to quilt. Removing the pins makes the quilt lighter and much easier to manipulate between the needle and the arm of the sewing machine.

–Jeannette Muir

QUILTING IN THIRDS

Here is a method I recommend for quilting on large polyester batts that have a lot of loft and are hard to manipulate through a sewing machine. Cut the batting for your quilt vertically into three equal sections. Place one piece of batting between the backing and top fabric at the center of your quilt, and baste the three layers together. Quilt this section of the quilt, rolling up the backing and top fabric to the right of the needle as you stitch. With no batting between them, the top and backing fabrics will be very easy to guide through your sewing machine. When you have finished quilting the entire center portion of the quilt, open it up and insert another section of batting on either side. Hand sew this second piece of batting to the first one, using a neutral color thread and doing whip stitches that are perpendicular to the edges of the batting. Smooth the quilt top and backing fabric over this piece of batting, baste the layers together, and quilt this part of the quilt. Because you will be working at the side of the quilt, there will not be a great deal of fabric to roll up, and the quilting process will be easy. To complete the quilting process, repeat these steps on the other side of your quilt.

–Debra Wagner

STABILIZING GRIDS

For a large quilt that is made up of blocks, I like to baste the layers together with safety pins, taking care not to place any of them directly over the seam lines between the blocks. Then I quilt in the ditch of each of these seams across the width and down the length of the quilt, removing pins as I go. This creates a grid of stitches that keeps the layers of the quilt from shifting. Without the added weight of 300 or 400 safety pins, a large quilt is lighter and much easier to manipulate through the sewing machine. When you are ready to quilt in the individual blocks, they will be stabilized, and you can place safety pins in any stitching area you like, removing them when you are ready to quilt in another block.

–Hari Walner

ROLLED EDGES FOR SMOOTHER STITCHING

When machine quilting any large project, the most important thing is to be in control of the quilt at all times. I've found that the bigger the quilt, the more quickly and easily it can become twisted, which makes it harder to quilt smoothly. It helps me to keep the edges neatly rolled up because this prevents the quilt from twisting. I often like to unroll a quilt during the quilting process and reroll the edges again to keep the rolls straight. To do this, I remove the quilt from the machine after finishing an area of stitching. Then I lay it out on the floor and reroll the edges from both sides toward the center. If you do this with a quilt that has cotton batting in it, the quilt will tend to stay rolled up naturally. If you use polyester batting, bicycle clips (available at quilt shops or sewing stores) are good for holding the roll of fabric to the left of the needle, which has a tendency to spread out. For the part of the quilt that lies to the right of the needle, you will not need bicycle clips because the small space between the needle and the arm of the sewing machine will hold the rolled fabric in place while you stitch.

–Sue Nickels

Quilt Supplies by Mail

Beautiful Publications, LLC
Continuous-Line Quilting Patterns by Hari Walner
13340 Harrison Street
Thornton, CO 80241-1403
(303) 452-3337

Caryl Bryer Fallert
Instructional brochures for Caryl Bryer Fallert's techniques
P.O. Box 945
Oswego, IL 60543

Crazy Ladies and Friends
Rust-proof safety pins
Dept. R, 1604 Santa Monica Boulevard
Santa Monica, CA 90404
(310) 828-3122

Dreamworld Enterprises, Inc.
Sewing table extensions
P.O. Box 192
6625 Stephens
Bonners Ferry, ID 83805
(800) 837-3261

English's Sewing Machines
Sewing/craft tables
7001 Benton Road
Paducah, KY 42003
(502) 898-7301

E-Z International
E-Z Washout marking pencils
95 Mayhill Street
Saddle Brook, NJ 07663
(201) 712-1234

Paula Jean Creations
Kwik Klip tools
1601 Fulton Avenue
Sacramento, CA 95825
(916) 488-3480

Little Foot, Ltd.
Little Foot and Big Foot presser feet
605 Bledsoe NW
Albuquerque, NM 87107
(505) 345-7647

A Quilter's Wardrobe
Patterns for quilted clothing by Anne Colvin
612 Huntington Court
Grapevine, TX 76051
(817) 488-1167

Web of Thread
Threads and spray fabric adhesive
1410 Broadway
Paducah, KY 42001
(502) 575-9700

Acknowledgments

Anne Thiessen Colvin creates at least one show garment for competition each year and is a three-time designer for the Fairfield Fashion Show. Anne's company, A Quilter's Wardrobe, features classic designs for jackets, sweat jackets, shirts, and vests, and her pattern line also includes appliqué collections, travel accessories, handbags, and quilting designs.

Caryl Bryer Fallert is internationally recognized for her award-winning art quilts, which are distinguished by scintillating colors and multilevel illusions of light and motion. She is best known for her three-dimensional "High-Tech Tucks" quilts and for her string-pieced quilts, including "Corona II: Solar Eclipse." In addition to her commission work, Caryl reserves time to create a body of personal, experimental quilts. She has lectured and conducted workshops for quilt and textile arts groups throughout the United States as well as in Japan, Switzerland, Germany, New Zealand, Australia, Ireland, and the People's Republic of China.

Jeannette Tousley Muir enjoys teaching, judging, designing and making quilts, entering competitions, collecting and restoring antique quilt tops, and writing. Her areas of specialization include machine quilting, precision hand piecing, precision machine piecing, and working with scrap fabrics. She is the author of *Precision Patchwork for Scrap Quilts . . . Anytime, Anywhere,* published by the American Quilter's Society, Paducah, Kentucky.

Many of **Sue Nickels's** quilts have been exhibited in local and national shows. In 1993 "Alberta Rose" won an Honorable Mention in the Full-Size Professional Appliqué category at the American Quilter's Society Show in Paducah, Kentucky, where she was also a faculty member. In 1994, she and her sister, Pat Holly, co-authored *60 Machine Quilting Patterns,* published by Dover Publications. Her quilts have been featured in many publications, including *America's Best Quilting Projects, Volumes I* and *II* by Rodale Press.

Caroline Reardon is Managing Editor of *Quiltmaker* magazine. She enjoys designing and using traditional patterns or pictorial appliqués to make quilts with a new look. Her work has appeared in both *Quilter's Newsletter Magazine* and *Quiltmaker* magazine, and in shows at the Botanic Gardens and the state capitol in Denver, Colorado, the American Quilter's Society show in Paducah, Kentucky, the American International Quilt Association show in Houston, Texas, and the Quilts '93 show in Louisville, Kentucky.

Sharee Dawn Roberts has received both national and international recognition for her high-fashion quilted clothing and special machine art techniques. Her clothing has been shown in galleries and exhibitions in the United States, Japan, and Europe. She has been a contributing editor for *The American Quilter, Creative Needle, Sew News,* and *Threads* magazines and has designed a line of appliqué patterns. Her first book, *Creative Machine Art,* was published by the American Quilter's Society in 1992. She owns "Web of Threads," a mail order and retail business specializing in decorative threads for the needle artist.

Sherry Sunday's quilts reflect the diversity of her varied interests as well as the rich influence of her Irish-Japanese heritage. Her new series of art quilts, "Imaginings," has its roots in landscape imagery. Each quilt invites the viewer to bring his or her own experience of nature into a personal interpretation of each piece. Her approach to "Perfectly Painless Appliqué" and unique machine-quilting techniques have made it possible for her to create large quilts in a fraction of the time she once spent. This enables her to spend more time sharing her joy in quiltmaking with others. She finds the use of accurate instructions and clear examples to be the key to winning top prizes and teaching opportunities at quilt shows nationwide.

Debra Wagner is a three-time first place winner at the American Quilter's Society show in Paducah, Kentucky, winning the Viewer's Choice Award in 1990. She contributed to and her work appears on the cover of the Singer Reference Library book *Machine Quilting.* She does commissioned work worldwide for both corporations and individuals. Her work has been displayed in the United States, Europe, and Japan. She is the author of *Teach Yourself Machine Piecing and Quilting, Striplate Piecing,* and *All Quilt Blocks Are Not Square.* She has taught machine techniques in both the United States and Japan.

Hari Walner owns Beautiful Publications, which publishes her continuous-line quilting designs. Hari's Autumn Trellis quilt was pieced by Shirley Wegert of Englewood, Colorado. Hari credits Barbara Johannah's work in the area of continuous-curve quilting and Harriet Hargrave's work in the area of free-motion quilting for opening up the world of machine quilting to her.

Bernina of America, Inc., provided the Bernina 1630 sewing machine used in the photographs. For more information about the products, write to Bernina of America, Inc., 3500 Thayer Court, Aurora, IL 60504.

Dreamworld Enterprises, Inc., contributed the extension table shown in the photograph on page 4. For more information about this product, write to Dreamworld Enterprises, Inc., P.O. Box 192, 6625 Stephens, Bonners Ferry, ID 83805.

Robert Kaufman Co., Inc., contributed Kona 100 percent cotton fabrics used for the quilt sandwiches in the photographs. For more information about these fabrics, write to Robert Kaufman Co., Inc., 129 West 132 Street, Los Angeles, CA 90061.

Index